D1597605

# ENCYCLOPEDIA

## of

# ACCOUNTING SYSTEMS

## CONTRIBUTORS TO VOLUME II

CURTIS D. EPLER, Certified Public Accountant, New York, N. Y.

V. L. FISHER, Certified Public Accountant; Controller, Merck Sharp & Dohme, Division of Merck & Co., Inc.

EUGENE F. FORAN, Business Counsellor, Eugene F. Foran and Associates, Decatur, Illinois

THOMAS J. GAFFNEY, ESQ., Member of the Philadelphia Bar

PAUL M. GERMAN, Vice President and Comptroller, Standard Milling Company, Kansas City, Missouri

A. J. HOEFER, Vice President, Libby, McNeill & Libby, Chicago

EARL W. KEHRBERG, Assistant Professor, Department of Agricultural Economics, Purdue University

KENNETH P. MAGES, Certified Public Accountant; Partner, Touche, Niven, Bailey & Smart, New York

EDWIN McINNIS, Vice President, Bank of America National Trust and Savings Association, San Francisco

NICHOLAS J. MERTENS, Certified Public Accountant; Partner, S. D. Leidesdorf & Co., New York

GEORGE OLSEN, Manager, New York Office, Schutte & Williams, Certified Public Accountants

F. D. SCOTT, Certified Public Accountant; Controller, Red Owl Stores, Inc., Minneapolis, Minnesota

W. W. STEGMAN, Controller, Kroehler Mfg. Co., Naperville, Illinois

LEWIS L. TANGUY, Certified Public Accountant; Member of Staff of Lybrand, Ross Bros. & Montgomery, Philadelphia

DR. IRVIN TULKIN, Co-author: J. Lewis Blass and Irvin Tulkin, "Dentist's Efficiency Book" and "Successful Dental Practice"

FORD C. WIGGINS, Controller, Lockwood, Kessler & Bartlett, Inc., Civil Engineers, New York

# ENCYCLOPEDIA
## of
# ACCOUNTING SYSTEMS

Edited by

## ROBERT I. WILLIAMS

CERTIFIED PUBLIC ACCOUNTANT; PARTNER, SCHUTTE & WILLIAMS,
NEW YORK AND MOBILE, ALABAMA; ADJUNCT ASSOCIATE PROFESSOR
OF ACCOUNTING, GRADUATE SCHOOL OF BUSINESS ADMINISTRATION,
NEW YORK UNIVERSITY

and

## LILLIAN DORIS

AUTHOR: MODERN CORPORATE REPORTS TO STOCKHOLDERS, EMPLOYEES,
AND THE PUBLIC; EDITOR: CORPORATE TREASURER'S AND CONTROLLER'S
HANDBOOK

## VOLUME II

Englewood Cliffs, N. J.

## PRENTICE-HALL, INC.

Twelfth Printing.....April, 1970

PRINTED IN THE UNITED STATES OF AMERICA

27506—X

# Preface

This *Encyclopedia of Accounting Systems,* comprising five volumes, describes and illustrates accounting systems for diversified industries, businesses, and professions. Each system has been presented by a specialist in the particular field.

The selection of the industries was made with a view to meeting the greatest need of practicing accountants. The number of firms in the industry, the existence of peculiar accounting problems, and the opportunity to present varied types of cost systems and to explain unusual procedures for the reduction of clerical expenses were factors in the selection. Industries that are dominated by a few giant corporations or regulated by a public body which prescribes an accounting system were not selected. Nor were industries chosen in which there is a widespread use of a uniform system of accounts sponsored by, and available through, a trade association in the field.

To assure equal coverage and comprehensiveness in all sections, each author was asked to follow, as far as possible, the uniform outline prepared by the Editors. Thus, with changes to fit special situations, each section treats the following subjects in the order indicated:

1. Characteristics of the industry that affect the accounting system.
2. Functional organization of the business.
3. Principles and objectives of the accounting system.
4. Classification of accounts and books of account.
5. Peculiarities of procedures for: sales-receivables cycle; purchases-payables cycle; cash receipts and disbursements.
6. Cost system.
7. Time and payroll system.
8. Plant and equipment records—depreciation.
9. Reports to management.
10. Special time-saving devices.
11. Modification of the system for small businesses in the field.

In addition to achieving comprehensive coverage, the established arrangement permits the accountant quickly to pick up ideas from numerous industries that might be used in making improvements in existing systems, in solving troublesome problems, and in answering clients' questions.

Attention is given in each industry to the practices peculiar to the particular business. The problem areas, accounting-wise, are fully covered.

The text assumes that accountant-readers know the fundamentals of accounting methods, the manual and machine methods commonly used in an accounting office, and the ordinary procedures for handling cash, accounts receivable, accounts payable, payroll, and the like, and for maintaining internal check and control. If there is nothing worthy of mention under a particular topic in the uniform outline, the author has either omitted the topic or indicated that conventional methods and procedures are used.

Explanations of general accounting problems, which arise in all businesses and which are fully covered in accounting texts, have been deliberately avoided. Similarly, discussions of techniques for budgeting, developing standard costs and standard burden rates, and the like, which are explained at length in specialized accounting texts, have been omitted. An exception has been made in the case of the P/V technique of analysis for profit-planning. Because of its comparative newness as a management tool, the explanation of this technique, given in the accounting system for the carbonated beverages industry, is welcomed by the Editors.

The Editors considered it advisable not to prescribe any accounting terminology but to permit each author to use the terminology common to the industry or to follow his accustomed practice.

More than 500 diagrams and forms, specially designed for the particular industries, have been reproduced with great care to assure complete legibility. Standard forms and simple forms that may be purchased from form stationers have not been reproduced. Filled-in forms have been presented whenever the author felt that such specimens were needed to clarify the explanation.

The Editors are grateful to the trade associations, groups, and informed individuals whose recommendations resulted in bringing together the authors who have made this *Encyclopedia of Accounting Systems* an authoritative master reference of modern accounting practice. The Editors are deeply grateful to the authors for their whole-hearted co-operation and their generosity in making their knowledge and talents available to the industries covered and to the accounting profession.

On behalf of the authors, grateful appreciation is expressed to the numerous associations and business organizations that co-operated with the authors by making material available to them. Appropriate credit lines have been included in the particular sections, except where anonymity was desired.

ROBERT I. WILLIAMS
LILLIAN DORIS

# Contents

# CONTENTS

# 14

# Cotton and Synthetic Weaving Mills

by

NICHOLAS J. MERTENS

Certified Public Accountant; Partner, S. D. Leidesdorf & Co.,
New York

## Industry characteristics that affect the accounting system

**Nature of the business.** Cotton and synthetic (rayon, nylon, and the like) woven goods manufacturers buy raw cotton, cotton yarn, and synthetic fibers in staple or continuous-filament form, which they make into fabrics that are sold to converters, manufacturers of household and apparel items, industrial users, and retailers. From the original bale of cotton or staple fiber to the finished product, the raw material undergoes numerous operations. A basic knowledge of these processes is helpful in understanding the accounting control procedures that must be applied.

Cotton and synthetic woven goods manufacturing comprises three basic functions: (1) spinning yarn, (2) weaving, and (3) finishing.

*Spinning yarn.* Yarn produced by textile manufacturers is made from raw cotton in the bale, or from synthetic fiber materials, generally called "staple," which is cut to uniform short lengths. The latter is purchased from manufacturers of synthetic staple and yarns.

The processes of converting both of these raw materials into yarn are essentially the same. The basic objective involved in both cotton and spun synthetic yarn manufacturing is to take a mass of non-oriented fibers (as from the bale), parallel them, reduce them in cross section to the desired fineness, and impart a twist that binds the fibers together.

The first stage consists of opening the bale and feeding the raw material into a series of machines that loosen and mix the material and remove foreign matter. The material emerges as a loose, blanket-like sheet known as "lap," which is about 40 inches wide and wound into a 50-pound roll.

The lap is fed into the carding operation, which further opens and cleans the material and tends to parallel the fibers. It also reduces the lap to a rope-like strand known as "sliver" (rhymes with "diver") and winds the sliver into a cylindrical can.

For extra-strong or fine yarns, sliver is combed, an operation that further parallels the fibers and removes the shorter ones.

Cans of card sliver are then taken to the next operation, known as "drawing." Drawing consists of doubling several strands of card sliver between sets of rolls and drafting them to a reduced diameter in successive operations so as to obtain greater uniformity of the sliver. The drawn sliver is wound into cylindrical cans for further processing.

Cans of drawn sliver are placed at the roving frame, where the slivers are further doubled and drawn, then given a slight twist and wound on a bobbin. Roving may be performed in one or more operations, according to the type of equipment used. This process produces a strand that is now much firmer and smaller than sliver and is called "roving."

In the spinning operation, the roving bobbins are placed on a spinning frame, the roving is passed between rolls for a final drawing, and a twist is applied by means of a ring or traveller in winding the roving on the spinner bobbin. The amount of twist can be varied by changing the speed at which the roving is delivered to the spinner bobbin.

The spinning operation completes the process of yarn manufacture; the high twist given to the yarn prevents further reduction in diameter by means of the processes previously described. Single yarns, however, are unsuitable for sewing threads and for fabrics requiring high strength. In these cases, ply yarns serve best. Accordingly, two (sometimes more) ends of spun yarn are combined and twisted together on a twisting frame. Such machines are more or less similar to spinning frames.

Yarn sizes are designated by a number which expresses the length in a given weight of yarn. Spun yarn sizes are stated in "counts," a count being the number of 840-yard "hanks" in a pound. Thus, spun yarn 20's contain 16,800 yards per pound. Filament yarn sizes are stated in deniers, that is, the weight, in grams, of 9,000 meters of yarn. The twist is designated in turns per inch.

*Weaving.* Yarn used by a mill in the weaving of cloth may be spun cotton or spun synthetic, either of the firm's own manufacture or purchased from a spinner. It may also be continuous-filament synthetic (rayon, nylon, dacron, and the like), which is yarn produced by chemical processes and purchased from the manufacturer in continuous lengths wound on bobbins, cones, beams, and so on.

The yarns that constitute a woven textile fabric are known as "warp" and "filling"; the former runs lengthwise and the latter crosswise.

The filling yarn may be delivered to the weaver directly on spinning bobbins which fit the loom shuttles, or it may be rewound onto such bobbins from larger packages, such as cones or cheeses. The filling bobbins are inserted in the loom shuttle by hand in some cases, but more often are placed in a battery on the loom, from which they are automatically fed to the shuttle as needed.

The first operation in preparing a warp from bobbins, cones, or cheeses consists of placing a large number of yarns parallel to each other on a warp or section beam. This beam resembles a large spool. In some cases, spun or continuous-filament yarn may be purchased on section beams.

On a slasher, the yarn from several warp or section beams is drawn off, passed through a vat of sizing liquid (which makes the yarn easier to weave), dried on a succession of cylinders, and rewound upon a loom beam.

In the weaving operation, the warp threads are drawn from the back of the loom and through the loom, where the filling is interlaced with the warp, and the woven cloth is wound on a roll at the front of the loom. Interlacing is effected by raising a portion of the warp yarns, thus forming an opening called the "shed," and passing the filling yarn through the shed by means of a shuttle. Many different types of weaves can be achieved by varying the number and sequence of warp yarns that are raised.

After a suitable length of cloth is woven, the roll of cloth is removed from the loom, inspected for defects, folded or rolled, and packed for shipment or stocked for finishing.

For certain types of fabrics, the yarns are dyed before weaving, and simple or very complex patterns can be produced in weaving. However, the great majority of cotton and synthetic goods are made from undyed yarns, and the cloth is later subjected to finishing operations.

*Finishing.* As just indicated, most cotton and synthetic goods are woven in the grey (natural color) and are then bleached (in the case of cotton), dyed or printed, and finished. Finishing operations bring the fabric to the required width and impart desired physical characteristics, such as smoothness, suppleness, stiffness, and the like.

These operations are sometimes performed by the weaving mill and sometimes by commercial finishers for the mill. In other instances, the fabric is sold in the grey to converters, who have the dyeing, printing, and finishing operations performed. Inasmuch as finishing usually changes the length of the woven fabric, consideration has to be given to this factor in the determination of costs. Furthermore, the cost calculation should allow for the expected amount of seconds that issue from the finishing processes.

**General features.** The cotton and synthetic weaving industry is highly competitive, in part because many staple fabrics are made by many different mills. In addition to domestic competition, manufacturers are confronted with severe competition from foreign countries, especially Japan. Profits are therefore dependent on efficient operations and timely and economical buying of raw cotton or yarns. Some manufacturers protect themselves against cotton price fluctuations by hedging transactions on the cotton exchanges.

By producing a large volume of staple fabrics for stock rather than against specific orders, the cotton and synthetic goods manufacturer is able to reduce substantially the impact of seasonal variations in demand, except in the apparel trades. The industry has done an outstanding job in promotion, so that today cottons and synthetics are an important factor in the fashion field. As the result of tremendous strides in the development of novelty weaves, mixtures, and finishes, staples have lost some of their relative importance.

**Functional peculiarities.** *Buying.* Since cotton is a natural fiber and its production is more or less unpredictably affected by weather, insects, fungus growths, politics, and the like, cotton prices are subject to daily fluctuations. To keep their mills at a fairly uniform level of operations, manufacturers must buy cotton and put it into work in advance of sales orders. Thus, they run the risk that a future price drop in cotton will reduce the selling price of woven goods. To minimize this risk, manufacturers frequently hedge by selling cotton futures on one of the exchanges. Frequently the reverse may be true in that the manufacturer, without having raw cotton on hand, accepts orders at firm prices calling for deliveries of woven goods in the future. In this case he might buy cotton futures to minimize market risks. The accounts involved in these transactions are discussed later.

Synthetic fiber and continuous-filament prices are free from frequent fluctuations. The principal purchasing problem is that of obtaining desired quantities under producers' allocations in times of tight supply. Sometimes purchases are made from secondary sources at price premiums.

*Production.* A sizable portion of goods is made for stock, that is, material is put into process on the basis of sales estimates rather than of actual orders. Production control and scheduling therefore require accurate, up-to-date records that reflect sales trends and permit prompt adjustment of production schedules.

Production planning is often complicated, particularly with respect to fancy goods, which are usually produced in fairly short runs. On the other hand, planning may be relatively simple in mills producing a limited number of staples, where loom setups run for months without change.

In undergoing a large number of operations, cotton is usually subject to losses in material length or weight, and it is essential to establish control points in order to measure such losses or gains. The findings at these control points are then used for adjustment of inventories, and corrective steps can be taken to reduce variances in material usage. Further details on this problem are given at pages 415 et seq.

In many cases, important cost differentials arise from the type of material and pattern being run and the length of time between pattern changes.

*Selling.* Sales of cotton and synthetic woven goods are made either directly by the manufacturing company or through selling agents and brokers. Selling agents play an important role in the industry, and many manufacturers depend on their judgment as to the type of goods to be manufactured. Often the selling agent relieves the manufacturer of the need for a styling department and, if sales are factored through the agent, of the need for a credit and accounts receivable department.

*Financing of customers' accounts.* Some manufacturers sell and bill direct to customers without the services of a factor, while others, although they do the selling, assign their accounts to a factor, in which case they may draw funds against their accounts receivables. As just mentioned, still other manufacturers make use of selling agents, in which case sales usually are factored, sometimes by the selling agent.

**Asset peculiarities.** Characteristically, a large investment in fixed assets is required. Over the past many years, the return on investment for many cotton and synthetic goods manufacturers has been less than for manufacturing industry as a whole.

**Ownership peculiarities.** In the early years of the industry, mills were generally owned by partnerships, but because of rapid growth and the need for additional capital, most mills today are in corporate form. Through merger and other forms of acquisition, many mills have become fully integrated concerns, thereby obtaining full control of their products from raw material to finished fabrics and, in some instances, to consumer goods, such as sheets, pillow cases, towels, and so on.

**Principal accounting problems.** The principal accounting problems arise from the need for accurate control of materials and inventories and for complete information as to cotton and synthetic prices.

## Functional organization

**Division into departments or activities.** The organization chart for cotton and synthetic goods manufacturers does not differ greatly from organization charts for manufacturing corporations in general. Inasmuch as cotton purchases and hedging transactions are of the utmost importance, this function usually is handled by a special department independent of the general purchasing department. Quite frequently the responsibility for cotton transactions is assumed by the president; in very large corporations, a special officer is appointed. The person responsible for purchasing raw cotton in the open market and for transactions on the cotton exchanges must keep informed of cotton requirements to be able to cover sales as well as to liquidate hedging positions on the cotton exchanges. He informs the financial department of his transactions so that it can arrange to meet his cash requirements, and he maintains a list of outstanding commitments.

The organization chart shown in Figure 1 represents a completely integrated company which manufactures cotton piece goods and does its own selling and finances its customers.

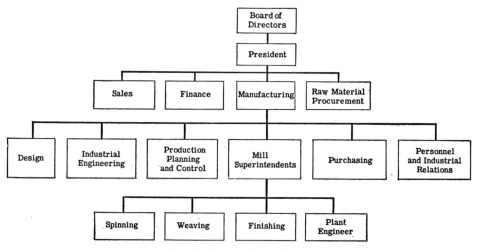

**Fig. 1. Organization Chart.**

## Classification of accounts and books of account

**Comment on classification of accounts.** A typical woven goods mill, if its operations begin with raw cotton or synthetic fiber and culminate in finished fabrics, would have most, though not necessarily all, of the accounts that appear in the accompanying chart of accounts. A mill purchasing its yarns would, of course, have somewhat different accounts. The account numbers shown are only illustrative and would vary from one company to another.

### Balance sheet accounts.

| | Debits from | Credits from |
|---|---|---|
| *CURRENT ASSETS* | | |
| *Cash* | | |
| 1010  Cash in Banks ............... | Cash Receipts Journal | Cash Disbursements Journal |
| 1020  Petty Cash ................... | Cash Disbursements Journal | Cash Receipts Journal |
| *Securities* | | |
| 1110  U. S. Gov't Securities .......... | Cash Disbursements Journal | Cash Receipts Journal |
| 1120  Investments—Stocks ........... | Do | Do |

| | | Debits from | Credits from |
|---|---|---|---|
| 1130 | Investments—Bonds .......... | Cash Disbursements Journal | Cash Receipts Journal |
| 1180 | Rsve. for Fluctuations in Mkt. Value .................... | General Journal | General Journal |

*Accounts and Notes Receivable*

| | | Debits from | Credits from |
|---|---|---|---|
| 1210 | Due from Factors ............. | Sales Journal or General Journal | Cash Receipts or General Journal |
| 1220 | Accounts Receivable—Trade, Unfactored ................... | Sales Journal | Do |
| 1230 | Notes Receivable—Unfactored .. | General Journal | Cash Receipts Journal |
| 1280 | Rsve. for Discounts and Allowances .................... | Do | General Journal |
| 1281 | Rsve. for Doubtful Accounts.... | Do | General Journal or Cash Receipts Journal (For recoveries) |
| 1290 | Deposits on Open Cotton Contracts .................... | Cash Disbursements Journal or General Journal | Cash Receipts Journal or General Journal |

*Merchandise Inventories*

| | | Debits from | Credits from |
|---|---|---|---|
| 1410 | Provisionally Priced Cotton .... | Purchase Journal | General Journal |
| 1411 | Raw Cotton, Opening Inven. Plus Purchases, Fixed ........ | General Journal, Purchase Journal | Do |
| 1412 | Raw Cotton—Used ............ | General Journal | Standard Journal |
| 1413 | Other Fibers, Opening Inven. Plus Purchases ............. | General Journal, Purchase Journal | General Journal |
| 1414 | Other Fibers—Used .......... | General Journal | Standard Journal |
| 1415 | Cotton Yarn, Opening Inven. Plus Purchases ............. | General Journal, Purchase Journal | General Journal |
| 1416 | Cotton Yarn—Used .......... | General Journal | Standard Journal |
| 1417 | Other Yarn, Opening Inven. Plus Purchases ................. | General Journal, Purchase Journal | General Journal |
| 1418 | Other Yarn, Used ............ | General Journal | Standard Journal |
| 1419 | Goods in Transit ............. | General Journal, Purchase Journal | General Journal |
| 1431 | Work-In-Process, Material ..... | Standard Journal | General Journal, Standard Journal |
| 1432 | Work-In-Process, Direct Labor.. | Do | Do |
| 1433 | Work-In-Process, Burden ...... | Do | Do |
| 1449 | Grey Goods ................. | Do | Do |
| 1451 | Finished Goods, Firsts ......... | General Journal, Standard Journal | Do |
| 1452 | Finished Goods, Seconds ...... | Do | Do |
| 1471 | Inventory of Waste .......... | General Journal | Do |
| 1472 | Inventory of Supplies, Direct .. | General Journal, Purchase Journal | Do |

|  |  | *Debits from* | *Credits from* |
|---|---|---|---|
| 1473 | Inventory of Supplies, Indirect . | General Journal, Purchase Journal | General Journal, Standard Journal |
| 1474 | Inventory of Rags and Remnants | General Journal | Do |
| 1491 | Rsve. for Mkt. Value Adjustments ..................... | Do | General Journal |
| 1492 | Rsve. for Other Inven. Adjustments ..................... | Do | Do |
| 1493 | Rsve. for Variances in Inventory | Do | Do |

*Other Current Assets*

|  |  |  |  |
|---|---|---|---|
| 1510 | Due from or to Subsidiary ..... | Cash Disbursements or Sales Journal | Cash Receipts or Purchase Journal |
| 1610 | Sundry Current Assets ......... | Various | Various |

*Other Assets*

|  |  |  |  |
|---|---|---|---|
| 1710 | Investment in Subsidiaries ..... | Cash Disbursements Journal | Cash Receipts Journal |
| 1750 | Cash Surrender Value of Life Ins. | General Journal | General Journal |

*Fixed Assets*

|  |  |  |  |
|---|---|---|---|
| 1810 | Land ....................... | Purchase Journal | General Journal or Cash Receipts Journal |
| 1820 | Buildings .................... | Do | Do |
| 1825 | Rsve. for Depreciation, Buildings | General Journal | General Journal or Standard Journal |
| 1830 | Leasehold Improvements ....... | Purchase Journal | Do |
| 1835 | Rsve. for Amortization—Leasehold Improvements .......... | General Journal | Do |
| 1840 | Machinery .................. | Purchase Journal | General Journal or Cash Receipts Journal |
| 1845 | Rsve. for Depreciation, Machinery ................... | General Journal | General Journal or Standard Journal |
| 1850 | Office Equipment .............. | Purchase Journal | General Journal or Cash Receipts Journal |
| 1855 | Rsve. for Depreciation, Office Equip. ..................... | General Journal | General Journal or Standard Journal |
| 1860 | Autos and Trucks ............. | Purchase Journal | General Journal or Cash Receipts Journal |
| 1865 | Rsve. for Depreciation, Autos and Trucks ................ | General Journal | General Journal or Standard Journal |

*Deferred Charges*

|  |  |  |  |
|---|---|---|---|
| 1910 | Prepaid General Insurance ..... | Purchase Journal | Insurance Register |
| 1920 | Prepaid Pension Insurance ..... | Do | General Journal or Standard Journal |
| 1930 | Prepaid Group Insurance ...... | Do | Do |

|  |  | Debits from | Credits from |
|---|---|---|---|
| 1940 | Prepaid Rent ................ | Purchase Journal | Standard Journal |
| 1950 | Prepaid and Deferred Taxes ... | Purchase or General Journal | Do |
| 1960 | Prepaid Interest .............. | Cash Receipts Journal | Do |
| 1970 | Deferred Advertising .......... | Purchase Journal | Do |
| 1990 | Misc. Prepaid and Deferred Items | Do | General Journal or Standard Journal |

*Current Liabilities*

|  |  | Debits from | Credits from |
|---|---|---|---|
| 2010 | Accounts Payable, Trade ...... | Cash Disbursements Journal | Purchase Journal |
| 2020 | Notes Payable, Banks ......... | Do | Cash Receipts Journal |
| 2030 | Notes Payable, Factor ........ | Do | General Journal |
| 2040 | Loans Payable ............... | Do | Cash Receipts Journal |
| 2100 | Accrued Payroll .............. | Do | Payroll Journal |
| 2101 | Accrued Commissions ......... | Do | General Journal or Standard Journal |
| 2102 | Accrued Bonuses ............. | Do | Do |
| 2103 | Accrued Vacation and Holiday Pay ..................... | Do | Do |
| 2201 | Employee State Unemploy. Ins. Withheld .................. | Do | Payroll Journal |
| 2202 | Employee Fed. Income Tax Withheld .................. | Do | Do |
| 2203 | Employee Savings Bond Deductions ..................... | Do | Do |
| 2210 | Accrued F.I.C.A. .............. | Do | Standard Journal |
| 2211 | Accrued State Unemploy. Ins... | Do | Do |
| 2250 | Accrued Interest Payable ...... | Do | Do |
| 2259 | Accrued Misc. Items .......... | Do | Various |
| 2300 | Accrued Real Estate Taxes .... | Do | General Journal |
| 2309 | Accrued Misc. Taxes .......... | Do | Do |
| 2350 | Rsve. for Fed. Taxes on Income. | Do | Do |
| 2355 | Rsve. for State Taxes on Income. | Do | Do |
| 2390 | Dividends Payable ............ | Do | Do |

*Long-Term Liabilities*

|  |  | Debits from | Credits from |
|---|---|---|---|
| 2400 | Notes Payable, Banks (Long-Term) .................... | Do | Cash Receipts Journal |
| 2410 | Other Long-Term Liabilities .... | Do | Do |

*Capital Stock and Surplus*

|  |  | Debits from | Credits from |
|---|---|---|---|
| 2500 | Preferred Stock, Authorized .... | General Journal | General Journal |
| 2501 | Preferred Stock, Unissued ...... | Do | Cash Receipts Journal |
| 2510 | Common Stock, Authorized .... | Do | General Journal |
| 2511 | Common Stock, Unissued ...... | Do | Cash Receipts Journal |

|  |  | *Debits from* | *Credits from* |
|---|---|---|---|
| 2520 | Capital Surplus ............... | General Journal | General Journal |
| 2530 | Earned Surplus ............... | Do | Do |
| 2540 | Profits and Loss—Current Year. | Do | Do |
| 2550 | Dividends Paid .............. | Do | Do |

## Income and expense accounts.

|  |  | *Debits from* | *Credits from* |
|---|---|---|---|
| 3010 | Gross Sales—Yarns ............ | General Journal | Sales Journal |
| 3011 | Gross Sales—Grey Goods ...... | Do | Do |
| 3012 | Gross Sales—Finished Goods ... | Do | Do |
| 3110 | Returns—Allowances—Yarns ... | Sales Returns Journal | General Journal |
| 3111 | Returns—Allowances—Grey Goods ..................... | Do | Do |
| 3112 | Returns—Allowances—Finished Goods ..................... | Do | Do |
| 3120 | Customers' Discounts .......... | Cash Receipts Journal | Standard Journal |
| 3210 | Cost of Sales at Standard—Yarns | Standard Journal | Do |
| 3211 | Cost of Sales at Standard—Grey Goods ..................... | Do | Do |
| 3212 | Cost of Sales at Standard—Finished Goods ................. | Do | Do |
| 3350 | Material Price Variance ....... | Do | Do |
| 3351 | Capacity Variance ............. | Do | Do |
| 3352 | Material Usage Variance ....... | Do | Do |
| 3353 | Direct Labor Variance ........ | Do | Do |
| 3354 | Burden Variance .............. | Do | Do |
| 3355 | Profit or Loss on Cotton Manipulation ..................... | Do | Do |
| 3356 | Waste Recoveries ............. | General Journal | Cash Receipts Journal, General Journal |
| 3360 | Mill Ledger Control Account ... | Various | Various |
| 3400 | General and Administrative Expenses | | |
| 3401 | Officers' Salaries .............. | Do | General Journal |
| 3402 | Office Payroll ................. | Do | Do |
| 3403 | Payroll Taxes ................ | Standard Journal | Do |
| 3404 | General Taxes ................ | Do | Do |
| 3405 | Travel and Entertainment ...... | Purchase Journal | Do |
| 3406 | Dues and Subscriptions ........ | Do | Do |
| 3407 | Office Maintenance ............ | Do | Do |
| 3408 | Depreciation ................. | Standard Journal | Do |
| 3409 | Repair and Maintenance ....... | Do | Do |
| 3410 | Insurance ................... | Insurance Register | Do |
| 3411 | Professional Services .......... | Purchase Journal | Do |
| 3412 | Postage ..................... | Do | Do |
| 3413 | Rent ........................ | Do | Do |
| 3414 | Stationery and Printing ........ | Do | Do |
| 3415 | Office Supplies ............... | Do | Do |
| 3416 | Telephone and Telegraph ...... | Do | Do |

| | | *Debits from* | *Credits from* |
|---|---|---|---|
| 3417 | Directors' Fees ................ | Cash Disbursements Journal | General Journal |
| 3418 | Donations .................... | Purchase Journal | Do |
| 3419 | Employees' Retirement Fund ... | General Journal | Do |
| 3420 | Credit and Collections ......... | General Journal, Purchase Journal | Do |
| 3421 | Transfer Agents' Fees .......... | Purchase Journal | Do |
| 3500 | Selling Expenses .............. | | |
| 3501 | Salesmen's Salaries and Commissions ...................... | General Journal | Do |
| 3502 | Brokers' Commissions .......... | Purchase Journal | Do |
| 3503 | Sales Office Payroll ............ | General Journal | Do |
| 3504 | Payroll Taxes ................. | Standard Journal | Do |
| 3505 | General Taxes ................ | Do | Do |
| 3506 | Travel and Entertainment ...... | Purchase Journal | Do |
| 3507 | Dues and Subscriptions ........ | Do | Do |
| 3508 | Sales Office Maintenance ....... | Do | Do |
| 3509 | Branch Office Expenses ........ | General Journal, Purchase Journal | Do |
| 3510 | Insurance .................... | Insurance Register | Do |
| 3511 | Postage ...................... | Purchase Journal | Do |
| 3512 | Sales Office Rent .............. | Do | Do |
| 3513 | Stationery and Printing ........ | Do | Do |
| 3514 | Office Supplies ............... | Do | Do |
| 3515 | Telephone and Telegraph ....... | Do | Do |
| 3516 | Sample Expense .............. | General Journal, Purchase Journal | Do |
| 3530 | Advertising—Space—Magazines . | Purchase Journal | Do |
| 3531 | Advertising—Space—Newspapers | Do | Do |
| 3532 | Advertising—Space—Trade Journals .................. | Do | Do |
| 3533 | Advertising—Space—Miscellaneous | Do | Do |
| 3540 | Booklets and Folders .......... | Do | Do |
| 3541 | Display and Display Materials.. | Do | Do |
| 3542 | Direct Mail .................. | Do | Do |
| 3543 | Shows and Trade Conventions .. | Do | Do |
| 3544 | Co-operative Advertising ....... | Do | Do |
| 3545 | Art Work and Production ...... | Do | Do |
| 3546 | Advertising Agency Fees ....... | Do | Do |
| 3560 | Shipping Department Payroll ... | Payroll Journal | Do |
| 3561 | Shipping Department Expenses . | Purchase Journal | Do |
| 3562 | Shipping Supplies and Expenses. | Do | Do |
| 3563 | Outgoing Freight and Cartage .. | Do | Do |
| 3564 | Outside Warehousing .......... | Do | Do |
| 3610 | Interest Income—Investments .. | General Journal | Cash Receipts Journal |
| 3611 | Interest Income—Other ........ | Do | Do |
| 3612 | Dividends Received ........... | Do | Do |
| 3620 | Profit or Loss on Sales of Capital Assets ..................... | Do | General Journal |
| 3630 | Other Income ................ | Do | Cash Receipts Journal |

|  |  | *Debits from* | *Credits from* |
|---|---|---|---|
| 3650 | Interest Expense—Banks ....... | Standard Journal | General Journal |
| 3651 | Interest Expense—Cotton Brokers | Purchase Journal | Do |
| 3652 | Interest Expense—Factors ...... | Standard Journal | Do |
| 3653 | Interest Expense—Sundry ...... | Purchase Journal | Do |
| 3654 | Factoring Expense ............ | Standard Journal | Do |
| 3655 | Provision for Doubtful Accounts. | General Journal | Do |
| 3656 | Sundry Other Charges ........ | Various | Do |

## Mill ledger accounts.

### *Productive Departments*

|  |  |  |  |
|---|---|---|---|
| 0101 | Direct Labor ................. | Payroll Journal | General Journal |
| 0211 | Supervision ................... | Do | Do |
| 0215 | Depreciation—Machy. and Equip. | Standard Journal | Do |
| 0331 | Indirect Labor ................ | Payroll Journal | Do |
|  | Direct Labor Expenses |  |  |
| 0332 | Overtime Premium .......... | Do | Do |
| 0333 | Make-up Pay ............... | Do | Do |
| 0334 | Idle Time .................. | Do | Do |
| 0360 | Payroll Taxes ................ | Standard Journal | Do |
| 0361 | Compensation Insurance ....... | Insurance Register | Do |
| 0370 | Repair and Maintenance M. and E. ....................... | Purchase Journal | Do |
| 0375 | Sizing Materials .............. | Do | Do |
| 0376 | Dyes and Chemicals .......... | Do | Do |
| 0377 | Supplies—Sundry ............ | Do | Do |
| 0378 | Outside Finishing ............ | Do | Do |

### *Distributive Departments*

*General Manufacturing Expenses*

|  |  |  |  |
|---|---|---|---|
| 0210 | Factory Administration Salaries. | Payroll Journal | General Journal |
| 0213 | Factory Office Salaries ......... | Do | Do |
| 0217 | Depreciation—Furniture and Fixtures ..................... | Standard Journal | Do |
| 0220 | Insurance—General ........... | Insurance Register | Do |
| 0226 | Ad valorem Taxes—Other than Real Est. .................. | Standard Journal | Do |
| 0227 | Rental of Equipment .......... | Purchase Journal | Do |
| 0360 | Payroll Taxes ................ | Standard Journal | Do |
| 0361 | Compensation Insurance ....... | Insurance Register | Do |
| 0362 | Group Insurance ............. | Various | Do |
| 0363 | Holiday and Vacation Expenses.. | Standard Journal | Do |
| 0364 | Welfare .................... | Payroll Journal, Purchase Journal | Do |
| 0375 | Supplies—Other than Operating. | Purchase Journal | Do |
| 0374 | Mill Village Expense—Net of Rents .................... | Payroll Journal, Purchase Journal | Payroll Journal, General Journal |
| 0380 | Stationery and Supplies ........ | Purchase Journal | General Journal |
| 0381 | Postage ..................... | Do | Do |
| 0382 | Telephone and Telegraph ...... | Do | Do |
| 0383 | Traveling Expense ........... | Do | Do |
| 0384 | Automobile Expense .......... | Do | Do |

|  |  | Debits from | Credits from |
|---|---|---|---|
| 0385 | Subscription and Dues ......... | Purchase Journal | General Journal |
| 0386 | Misc. Factory Expenses ........ | Do | Do |

*Building Department*

|  |  | Debits from | Credits from |
|---|---|---|---|
| 0216 | Depreciation—Buildings ....... | Standard Journal | General Journal |
| 0218 | Amortization—Leasehold Improvements ................ | Do | Do |
| 0225 | Real Estate Taxes ............. | Do | Do |
| 0221 | Insurance—Buildings .......... | Insurance Register | Do |
| 0230 | Guards' Wages ............... | Payroll Journal | Do |
| 0360 | Payroll Taxes ................ | Standard Journal | Do |
| 0361 | Compensation Insurance ....... | Insurance Register | Do |
| 0371 | Repair and Maintenance—Labor | Payroll Journal | Do |
| 0372 | Repair and Maintenance—Contract ...................... | Purchase Journal | Do |
| 0373 | Materials and Supplies ........ | Do | Do |
| 0390 | Water ..................... | Do | Do |

*Power Department*

|  |  | Debits from | Credits from |
|---|---|---|---|
| 0101 | Labor ...................... |  |  |
| 0211 | Supervision .................. | Payroll Journal | General Journal |
| 0215 | Depreciation—Machy. and Equip. | Standard Journal | Do |
| 0222 | Boiler Insurance ............. | Insurance Register | Do |
| 0360 | Payroll Taxes ................ | Standard Journal | Do |
| 0361 | Compensation Insurance ....... | Insurance Register | Do |
| 0370 | Repair and Maintenance ....... | Purchase Journal | Do |
| 0377 | Supplies ..................... | Do | Do |
| 0388 | Outside Services ............. | Do | Do |
| 0389 | Purchased Power ............. | Do | Do |
| 0395 | General Ledger Control Account. | Various | Various |

**Books peculiar to the business.** A "standard journal" is referred to in the charts of accounts presented above. This is a multicolumnar form of general journal by months that is particularly useful for entries made fairly frequently, yet not often enough to merit an individual journal. Figure 2 is an illustration of a page from a standard journal and of typical entries thereon.

The following records, not mentioned in the accompanying chart of accounts, are essential in the operations of a woven fabric mill, especially a mill using raw cotton.

1. *Cotton contract record.* Raw cotton may be purchased spot, that is, at a specified price for prompt delivery. But more frequently, the major portion of a mill's supply is purchased on extended contracts. Such a contract specifies the quantity and the period of delivery, which may be months ahead and extend over a period of months. The quality of the cotton is specified as to staple length, fiber diameter, and grade—the latter with reference to standards established by the government or to special

STANDARD JOURNAL

YEAR 19___  Page ___

| ACCOUNT | NO. | January Dr. | January Cr. | February Dr. | February Cr. | November Dr. | November Cr. | December Dr. | December Cr. |
|---|---|---|---|---|---|---|---|---|---|
| Depreciation | | | | | | | | | |
| Mill Ledger Control | 3408 | $4,000.00 | | $4,000.00 | | $4,200.00 | | $4,700.00 | |
| Reserve for Depreciation | 3360 | 258,000.00 | | 261,100.00 | | 266,175.00 | | 266,550.00 | |
| Buildings | 1825 | | $40,000.00 | | $41,000.00 | | $42,500.00 | | $42,500.00 |
| Amortization—Leasehold Improvement | 1835 | | 2,000.00 | | 2,000.00 | | 2,000.00 | | 2,000.00 |
| Machinery | 1845 | | 200,000.00 | | 201,500.00 | | 204,700.00 | | 205,100.00 |
| Office Equipment | 1855 | | 5,000.00 | | 5,100.00 | | 4,975.00 | | 5,450.00 |
| Autos and Trucks | 1865 | | 15,000.00 | | 15,500.00 | | 16,200.00 | | 16,200.00 |
| Depreciation | | | | | | | | | |
| Buildings – Lease Bldg. Dept. | 0216 | $40,000.00 | | $41,000.00 | | $42,500.00 | | $42,500.00 | |
| Amortization–Leasehold Improvement | 0218 | 2,000.00 | | 2,000.00 | | 2,000.00 | | 2,000.00 | |
| Machinery and Equipment (Production Dept.) | 0215 | 175,000.00 | | 176,500.00 | | 179,650.00 | | 179,800.00 | |
| Machinery and Equipment – Power Dept. | 0215 | 25,000.00 | | 25,000.00 | | 25,200.00 | | 25,300.00 | |
| Office Equipment – Distributive Dept. | 0217 | 1,000.00 | | 1,100.00 | | 775.00 | | 750.00 | |
| Mill or Village Expense – " | 0374 | 10,000.00 | | 10,000.00 | | 10,700.00 | | 10,700.00 | |
| Automobile Expense – " | 0384 | 5,000.00 | | 5,500.00 | | 5,500.00 | | 5,500.00 | |
| General Ledger Control | 0395 | | $258,000.00 | | $261,100.00 | | $266,175.00 | | $266,550.00 |
| To distribute depreciation and amortization expenses for the month. | | | | | | | | | |

Fig. 2. Standard Journal.

Date_____

Contract No._____

No. Bales_____

Grade_____

Staple_____

Purchase Price_____

Shipment_____

Destination_____

Fixing Instructions:_____

_____ BUYER

_____ SELLER

_____ BROKER

**FIXATIONS**

| DATE FIXED | BALES OF COTTON | BASIS | MONTH | FUTURES | FIXED PRICE |
|---|---|---|---|---|---|
| | | | | | |
| | | | | | |

**SHIPMENTS**

| INV. NO. | DATE INV. | DATE PAID | BALES | MARK | WEIGHT | RE-WEIGHT | PROV. PRICE | FIXED PRICE | AMOUNT |
|---|---|---|---|---|---|---|---|---|---|
| | | | | | | | | | |
| | | | | | | | | | |

**LOSS IN WEIGHT CLAIMS**

| INV. NO. | LOSS | PRICE | AMOUNT |
|---|---|---|---|
| | | | |
| | | | |

**Fig. 3. Cotton Contract Record.**

**REJECTIONS**

| DATE | BALES | MARK | WEIGHT | PROV. PRICE | FIXED PRICE | AMOUNT |
|---|---|---|---|---|---|---|
| | | | | | | |
| | | | | | | |

**REPLACEMENTS**

| DATE | BALES | MARK | WEIGHT | RE-WEIGHT | PROV. PRICE | FIXED PRICE | AMOUNT |
|---|---|---|---|---|---|---|---|
| | | | | | | | |
| | | | | | | | |

**Fig. 3a. Cotton Contract Record (Reverse Side of Fig. 3).**

types used by the mill. Under the terms of the standard cotton contract, if the cotton received is unsuitable, as determined by the mill's cotton classer, subject to the findings of a regularly constituted arbitration board, the purchaser can reject and return such cotton for replacement. The price may be (a) a single price fixed at the time of contract, or (b) a stated amount (which is called "basis") above or below the price of cotton for future delivery in a specified month, on a cotton exchange such as New York or New Orleans. Under this method, the mill buyer has the option, from date of contract to a date dependent upon the futures month, of deciding when to notify the seller to "fix the price," that is, apply the "basis" to the futures market price to obtain the actual price for the cotton purchase contract. The period allowed for fixing price may be many months, and the mill may fix portions of the contract at various prices. Actual delivery of cotton on the contract may begin prior to the time of price fixing, and any cotton delivered before its price is fixed is billed at basis applied to futures market price at time of shipment. Retroactive price adjustment is made when the price is fixed.

The cotton contract  record should contain details as to quantities, quality, delivery dates specified, price, qualities actually billed, prices charged, rejections, claims for weight differences, price adjustments, and so on, so that proper fulfillment of the contract and the financial transactions relating thereto may be verified. (See Figures 3 and 3a.)

2. *Cotton position records.* If a mill organization is large, or if a mill uses several grades or staples, it may, for financial purposes, desire to look at its cotton position (Figure 4). An over-all position record may serve this purpose if all cotton used is quite similar in price. Other circumstances may dictate cotton position records by types of cotton. In either event, the elements of position are the same, all reduced for this purpose to equivalent cotton at 500 pounds to the bale.

At any time, the debit items are:

a. Inventories of raw cotton and the raw cotton content of stock in process (inclusion optional, often not used), grey goods, and finished goods. Quantities of raw cotton held at provisional prices are excluded.

b. Undelivered raw cotton on contract at fixed prices.

c. Open cotton futures contracts (hedges) bought.

The credit elements are:

a. Raw cotton sales contracts at fixed prices.

b. Raw cotton equivalent of undelivered goods on sales contracts at fixed prices.

c. Open cotton futures contracts (hedges) sold.

When a position has been obtained at a given date, it can readily be kept

COTTON POSITION

Date

| | BALES | | |
|---|---|---|---|
| | Class A | Class B | Class C |

Cotton inventory .....................................
Cotton contracts—fixed price ......................
Stock in process inventory—raw cotton equivalent...
Manufactured goods inventory—raw cotton equivalent
Cotton futures (hedging) contracts outstanding—long

Deduct:
   Cloth sales contracts—cotton required .............
   Cotton futures (hedging) contracts outstanding—
   short .........................................
   Cotton received at provisional price ..............

NET COTTON POSITION: Long (short) .........

**Fig. 4. Cotton Position Record.**

current—daily if desired—by adding (1) new cotton purchases at fixed price, (2) previous cotton purchases on which the price has just been fixed, and (3) cotton futures purchased; and by deducting (1) cotton sales, if any, at fixed price, (2) cotton required for firm sales contracts, (3) cotton futures sold. A running position record should be checked and adjusted at desired intervals by taking inventory of all elements.

In addition to maintaining position records for hedging purposes, for purposes of efficient operation a mill needs to keep similar records with respect to raw material, stock in process, and finished goods inventories, scheduled deliveries of raw materials, and scheduled deliveries for sales contracts. Raw material records would include long staple cotton and foreign cottons, which are excluded from the cotton position records because there is no futures market available for hedging.

3. *Cotton hedging record.* If the mill engages in hedging operations by means of buying and selling cotton futures contracts on one of the exchanges through brokers, an adequate record is necessary at all times of the contract quantities, months, and prices of all open hedges, and of cash deposited or received under "margin calls." (See Figure 5.) Separate records must be kept for each broker if several are involved.

Hedging can be accomplished, to some extent at least, by purchasing cotton on a "basis," as previously described, and by proper timing of price-fixing orders.

4. *Bale record.* Under this heading may be found several raw material

BROKER

ADDRESS

| BOUGHT | | | | | | | | SOLD | | | | | | |
|---|---|---|---|---|---|---|---|---|---|---|---|---|---|---|
| Date | #B/C | Applied | # √ | Delivery | Price | Dr. | | Date | #B/C | Applied | # √ | Delivery | Price | Cr. |
| | | | | | | | | | | | | | | |
| | | | | | | | | | | | | | | |
| | | | | | | | | | | | | | | |
| | | | | | | | | | | | | | | |
| | | | | | | | | | | | | | | |

Fig. 5. Cotton Hedging Record.

410

perpetual inventory records. For each type and size of staple fiber, cotton yarn, or continuous-filament synthetic yarn, it may be desirable to keep an individual record of each bale or case by number, weight, price, warehouse location, and date put into production or otherwise removed from inventory. (See Figure 6.)

| RAW MATERIAL BALE RECORD | | | | | | | |
|---|---|---|---|---|---|---|---|
| Material _____ Vendor _____ | | | | | | | |
| Description _____ | | | | | | | |
| Date Received _____ Price _____ | | | | | | | |
| Warehouse Location | | Bale or Cotton Number | | Weight | | Date Used | Remarks |
| Sect. | Aisle | Shipper | Mill | Shipper | Mill | | |
| | | | | | | | |
| | | | | | | | |

Fig. 6. Raw Material Bale Record.

In the case of raw cotton, a mill generally assigns a number to each bale and tags the bale with its number; the bale record is kept consecutively by these numbers. The cotton bale record should include the shipper's bale number and the grade, staple, billing weight, receiving weight, and price. The listing is usually by lots, so that the broker or merchant, invoice number, and contract number are readily ascertained. If the record is kept mechanically, all of the above information should be coded on the individual cards.

5. *Woven stock record.* This is basically a perpetual inventory of goods on which finishing operations remain to be performed. Sometimes it includes finished consumer goods, such as sheets, pillow cases, towels, and other items. The record is ordinarily kept by style and woven width and

| WOVEN STOCK RECORD | | | | | | | |
|---|---|---|---|---|---|---|---|
| Style No. _____ | | | | | | | |
| Description _____ | | | | | | | |
| Date Packed | Bale, Roll or Carton Number | Quality | Yards | Sales Order or Process Lot Number | Invoice or Assignment Date | Shipment or Removal Date | Remarks |
| | | | | | | | |
| | | | | | | | |
| | | | | | | | |

Fig. 7. Woven Stock Record.

reflects goods received from production, goods transferred to the mill's own finishing department or shipped to outside finishers, goods allocated to be so transferred or shipped, and the unallocated balance on hand. (See Figure 7.) Mills that produce goods only on order do not require this record.

6. *Payroll analysis.* Because of the extreme importance of labor efficiency, it is customary in many mills to analyze the payroll for purposes of showing overtime premiums, idle and waiting time, and make-up pay, which is money paid to pieceworkers whose earnings at a piece rate fall short of their minimum guarantee. Payroll reconciliation with standard costs and with actual production costs, where applicable, is essential for costing purposes and valuable for internal control.

**Accounts peculiar to the business.** The following accounts listed in the chart of accounts merit comment.

1. *Deposits on Open Cotton Contracts.* Amounts paid to or received from cotton brokers or merchants as margin upon open futures contracts (hedges), against provisional-price cotton, or for undelivered fixed-price cotton are charged or credited to this account. Application of these amounts to completed transactions is by charging or crediting, as the case may require.

2. *Provisionally Priced Cotton.* Raw cotton may be delivered prior to the fixing of its price, in which case it is billed at a "provisional" price, representing the contract "basis" applied to the futures market at the date of shipment. Billings for such cotton should be charged to this account, and amounts of price adjustments should be debited or credited as the case may require. When the fixed price (or actual cost) of a lot of cotton has been reflected in this account, such amount should be transferred to the raw cotton purchase account, so that at any time the balance in the provisionally priced account shall include only cotton for which price adjustments have not been made.

2. *Due from Factors.* Mills that use factors usually operate under an agreement permitting the mill to draw up to 80 or 90 per cent of the accounts receivable assigned. The difference is to protect the factor against losses due to returns and allowances for defective merchandise. For details on the handling of this account, including the specific entries, see Section 13, "Cotton Goods Converters," Volume I, page 353.

3. *Reserve for Market Value Adjustments.* Cotton mills have found that they can interpret their own cost figures better and plan their prices more realistically if they take into account the most likely trend in raw material prices. Accordingly, many mills estimate in advance a percentage of cost of sales which in their opinion will equal the probable decrease in inventory values. Based on this percentage, an account called Profit or Loss on Cotton Manipulation is charged monthly with the estimated per-

centage of cost of sales, and an account entitled Reserve for Market Value Adjustments is credited. If the market does drop as anticipated, the inventory account is credited with sufficient dollars to bring its raw material content into line with market prices, and the Reserve for Market Value Adjustments account is debited. This procedure, through realistic pricing of ending inventory, minimizes the effect of year-end inventory valuation on profit and loss in the last month of the year.

For monthly statement purposes, and sometimes at the end of the fiscal year, many mills prefer to reflect in their accounts: (a) the difference on provisional cotton between the amounts billed and the cost, if the price had been fixed at the close of the period; (b) gain or loss on open futures contracts, if they had been closed on the futures market at the end of the period. These entries are alternatives to the reserve for market value adjustments described in the preceding paragraph and would require different book accounts.

## Peculiarities of procedures: sales-receivables cycle; purchases

**Accounting for sales.** The determination of total monthly sales is a comparatively simple operation for most cotton mills. Usually the sales journal is totalled for each day's invoices (for management's use), showing the total sales value of the invoices and the totals of the various types of add-on charges, such as freight and express, parcel post, and so on. The invoice copies are generally filed in an alphabetical customer file. Month-end totals are posted from the sales journal to the general ledger, crediting sales and the various expense accounts for add-on charges, and debiting accounts receivable.

**Billing and accounts receivable procedures.** Customer invoices are prepared from shipping tickets. Either the extensions and footings are precalculated and checked and the invoices prepared on a typewriter, or the invoices are prepared on a billing machine which automatically extends and adds the items on the invoice. Where accounts receivable are sold to a factor, the original invoice is sent to the customer, while two copies are prepared for the factor along with a copy of the bill of lading as evidence that the shipment has been made. Sometimes the factor prepares the invoices. The mill has no further interest in the sale unless subsequent returns are made by the customer or other adjustments are required.

In many instances, although customers place their orders months in advance, when the time comes for shipment they are frequently not ready to accept the merchandise. It is the custom of the trade in these instances to bill the customer for the merchandise, and it becomes his property although it is physically retained by the mill. The invoice is usually placed in a "bill and hold" file until the customer advises the mill as to shipping instructions.

**Credit and collection peculiarities.** Except where a mill uses a selling agent or factor, credit and collection procedures are the same as for manufacturers in general. Where the mill uses a selling agent, credit and collection are frequently handled by the latter. Where a mill finances through a factor, the customer's credit must be approved by the factor prior to acceptance of the order; the factor otherwise will charge the mill for bad debt losses.

**Cotton receiving and adjustment procedure.** It is very important that raw cotton be properly checked and examined upon arrival at the mill. The first step is to weigh each bale and compare the result with the weight billed, because cotton is generally purchased at receiving weight, and each party is entitled to adjustment on this basis. The "classer" for the mill determines whether or not the cotton is of specified staple length and grade, or else equal to previously submitted samples, if the cotton has been purchased in the latter manner. In the case of substandard quality, the parties may agree to a price adjustment, or, by agreement with the shipper or upon finding of an arbitration board, the mill may reject the unsuitable bales and require the replacement of them. Claims may also be made for excess tare (wrapping) and false packing (foreign materials) discovered when the cotton is opened.

**Supply purchases.** Supply purchases in a mill are a very substantial item. They include not only the usual items of stationery, building maintenance, utilities, and the like, but also many textile machinery parts that have an extremely short life, such as the shuttles for looms. Supplies, therefore, are ordinarily controlled very closely, and current records are kept as to the amounts purchased and prices paid. At least one or two machinery manufacturers supply standard lots of replacement parts, each part packaged with a re-order blank. When the part is used, the re-order blank is promptly sent to the manufacturer.

## Production and cost system

**Use of standard costs.** Many weaving mills employ a standard cost system, which is vital as a control over manufacturing efficiency and as a guide to price determination. However, inasmuch as cotton woven goods are manufactured from raw materials that are subject to daily price fluctuations, it is customary, in submitting prices to the selling organization, to use the current price of cotton or a price at which it is believed the cotton may be acquired at a future date. Where the mill has an opportunity to get a very large order but at a reduced price, standard cost data enable it to determine whether the selling price will bring in something above direct costs.

Direct labor cost and fixed and variable overhead expenses are budgeted by department, and unit rates per machine hour or labor hour, based on normal capacity in machine or labor hours, are established. Operating statements are periodically prepared by department, showing actual labor costs, actual machine or labor hours, and actual overhead expenses. These figures are respectively compared with standard labor cost, normal capacity, and standard overhead allowance, permitting computation of labor, capacity, and overhead variances. Whereas capacity and overhead variances are usually computed monthly, labor variance is often computed weekly or even daily. A summary of the departmental statements is the basis for transferring labor and overhead to work-in-process inventory as follows:

|  | Debit | Credit |
|---|---|---|
| Work-in-process inventory—Labor and Overhead .......... | xxxx | |
| Labor accounts ......................................... | | xxxx |
| Expense accounts ....................................... | | xxxx |
| Capacity variance ...................................... | xxxx or | xxxx |
| Labor variance ......................................... | xxxx or | xxxx |
| Overhead variance ...................................... | xxxx or | xxxx |

**Cost centers.** The number of departments or cost centers established varies from mill to mill, but a rule often followed is to consider groups of similar operations as centers. Mill Ledger accounts Nos. 0211–0378 are maintained by each mill at the established cost centers, as, for example, spinning and twisting operations. Copies of the departmental operating statements are distributed to the respective department managers for comments, explanations of variances, and plans for correcting unfavorable variances.

**Price and yield standards for material.** Price and yield standards are established for each direct material or group of materials. Supply materials are charged to expense at actual cost. A mill manufacturing a limited number of similar products can make its material clearance at each control point by comparing the quantity of material issued to the first operation with the quantity of material produced in the last operation for a given period of time. The difference is material-usage gain or loss, assuming that work in process remains constant or that its variation is small compared with the volume of production. In some mills it is necessary to establish material yields by lots instead of by time periods.

In determining standards for calculating cotton yield variances, it is customary to make an allowance for reusable cotton waste. For example, the original mix may contain 3 pounds of reusable waste in addition to 100 pounds of first-run raw cotton, from which 99 pounds of yarn, 3 pounds of reusable waste, and 1 pound of non-reusable waste are obtained.

The usual minimum number of points at which yields are checked are: (1) raw cotton to yarn, (2) yarn to woven yards, and (3) woven yards to finished goods.

*Raw cotton to yarn.* To determine whether or not the proper yield of spun cotton yarn has been obtained, the following steps are required. First, it is necessary to accumulate the pounds of yarn spun, by count, and the raw pounds of cotton opened and reusable waste added. Then, for each yarn count, the appropriate yield factor is applied to the amount spun in order to determine the standard pounds of raw and waste cotton needed. For example:

| Yarn Count | Yarn Production | | Yield Factor | | Standard Pounds of Raw & Waste Cotton Required | Actual Pounds of Raw & Waste Cotton Picked | Variance |
|---|---|---|---|---|---|---|---|
| 1/18 | 10,186 lbs. | × | 106.5 | = | 10,848 | | |
| 1/20 | 18,413 lbs. | × | 104.3 | = | 19,205 | 46,400 | (362) |
| 1/22 | 15,195 lbs. | × | 105.2 | = | 15,985 | | |

The above example indicates that 362 pounds more cotton was used than required at standard. Assuming that the standard material price of cotton is 30 cents per pound and that standard labor and overhead is 28 cents per pound, the loss is determined and the appropriate entries are made as follows:

362 lbs. @ .30/lb. for material          = $108.60
362 lbs. @ .28/lb. for labor and overhead = 101.36

| Account | Debit | Credit |
|---|---|---|
| Work-in-Process—Material ...................................... | | $108.60 |
| Work-in-Process—Labor and Overhead ......................... | | 101.36 |
| Material Usage Variance ....................................... | $209.96 | |
| | $209.96 | $209.96 |

*Cotton yarn to woven yards.* The checks made at this point are:

1. Calculated (standard) weight per woven linear yard.

2. Weight of yarn consumed compared with calculated (standard) weight of yards woven.

3. Take-up length of the original warp compared with woven linear yards. This reflects the decrease in the length of the warp caused by interlacing of warp and filling.

After the gains or losses are determined, the appropriate entries are made.

*Woven yards to finished yards of cotton.* In those instances where the cotton mill finishes its own cloth, it is necessary to determine whether the cloth has undergone more or less than the standard amount of shrinkage. For example, if cloth is expected to shrink 2 per cent, it is obvious that for every 100 yards of finished goods slightly more than 102 yards of grey cloth must be put into process. To determine the yield, it is necessary to accumulate yards finished. After the gains or losses are determined, the appropriate entries are made.

When goods are transferred to finished stock, the entries made are as follows:

|  | Debit | Credit |
|---|---|---|
| a. Finished Goods Inventory .......................... | xxxx |  |
| b. Work-in-Process—Material ......................... |  | xxxx |
| c. Work-in-Process—Labor and Overhead ............. |  | xxxx |
| d. Material Usage Variance .......................... | xxxx  or | xxxx |
| e. Labor and Overhead Variance ..................... | xxxx  or | xxxx |

a = Standard value of goods transferred to finished stock.

b and c = Total value of goods put in process at standard cost (Material, Labor, and Overhead).

d and e = Standard cost of goods lost or gained in process (Material, Labor, and Overhead).

**Pricing of raw materials.** Raw materials are priced throughout process at standard cost. In some instances, raw material inventories are priced at actual cost. Where raw materials are costed at standard, the difference between standard and actual cost is shown by the following entries:

|  | Debit | Credit |
|---|---|---|
| a. Raw Material Inventory .......................... | xxxx |  |
| b. Accounts Payable ................................ |  | xxxx |
| c. Material Price Variance ......................... | xxxx  or | xxxx |

a = Standard material price.

b = Actual invoice amount.

c = Difference between a and b.

If the raw material inventories are carried at actual price, the material price variance is calculated when the materials are transferred to work in process. The entries are then as follows:

|  | Debit | Credit |
|---|---|---|
| a. Work-in-Process—Material ....................... | xxxx |  |
| b. Raw Material Inventory .......................... |  | xxxx |
| c. Material Price Variance ......................... | xxxx  or | xxxx |

a = Standard material price.

b = Actual price.

c = Difference between a and b.

**Cost of goods sold.** When standard costs are used, the cost of goods sold during a given period is arrived at by multiplying unit sales of a given product by the standard cost for this product—for example, 1,200 yds. sold @ $1.25 standard cost=$1,500.00. In preparing the profit and loss statement, cost of goods sold is stated at standard cost and the resulting gross profit is then adjusted on the basis of manufacturing variances for the month.

**Arrival at cost without standard cost system.** In the absence of a standard cost system, many cotton mills use average actual costs as a guide to price determination, as illustrated on the following page.

|                                    | *Units*     | *Dollars*  |
|------------------------------------|-------------|------------|
| Opening inventory .................................. | 50,000 lbs. | $125,000   |
| Material consumed ............................. | 48,000      | 18,000     |
| Direct labor ....................................... |             | 54,000     |
| Overhead expenses ............................... |             | 60,000     |
| Less: Units spoiled or wasted ..................... | (1,000)     |            |
| Total Production ............................ | 97,000      | $257,000   |
| Average cost per unit ......................... |             | $2.65      |
| Less: Units completed @ $2.65 .................... | 46,000      | 121,900    |
| Closing inventory .............................. | 51,000      | $135,100   |

It must be realized that average costs are not always accurate for specific yarns or fabrics. In the case of yarn, costs vary according to the count or denier and twist. The finer counts and higher twists are more costly to make because of the longer manufacturing cycle involved. Similarly, in the case of woven goods, such factors as loom speed and loom efficiency may considerably vary the cost of different fabrics. To overcome the disadvantages of using average actual costs, without going into an excessive amount of expensive clerical detail in order to accurately determine unit product costs, managements use a standard cost system.

**Production reports.** In order to have goods available in the varieties and at the time required by customers or by various departments of the mill, it is necessary to have records on a current basis showing: (1) the position of production orders against customer orders or against orders by other mill departments, (2) the position of work-in-process against production orders issued, (3) the position and physical location of inventories of raw material, cloth, and finished goods.

**Reports on goods to be processed.** These reports, one for each department, supply information as to the amount of materials to be put into process in a given department, such as the number of pounds of cotton to be opened and picked, or the number of pounds of cotton to be carded, or the number of pounds of yarn to be woven, and so on. Data for each type of yarn or cloth are grouped together.

An example of such a report is that pertaining to orders for weaving yarn into cloth. Figures for pounds (or yards) put into process and pounds (or yards) of the department's product ordered by a subsequent department—or by customers, in the case of woven or finished goods—are entered weekly and are cumulated for the season to date. The balance of "free goods" (available for transfer to another department or for sale to the customer) or goods required to be processed can then be obtained. Pounds or yards representing future orders indicate the extent to which orders for putting goods into process are not required at the current moment.

In entering pounds or yards of materials to be put into production, allowances should be made for working losses or seconds, so that enough materials are put into process to cover the amount of production required from a given department.

**Finishing order.** In the case of a mill that operates a finishing department, the finishing order for putting goods into this department is similar to that employed by converters who use independent finishers. For details on transmitting and following up finishing orders, see Section 13, "Cotton Goods Converters," Volume I, page 362.

**Grey goods control in finishing department.** The form used by the mill to control grey goods in the finishing department is similar to that used by a converter who employs an independent finisher (see Section 13, "Cotton Goods Converters," Volume I, page 363). When the grey (often spelled "greige") goods department is instructed to transfer goods to the finishing department, the latter is charged on the form for yardage ordered transferred. As finishing orders are issued, the number of yards ordered into process, the date, and the number of the finishing orders are entered. As each lot is finished, the date of completion, number of yards of first- and second-quality goods, and the percentage of working loss and seconds are entered. The cumulative total of yardages transferred to the finishing department minus the cumulative total of yards put into process represents inventory of grey goods on hand at the finishing department. This amount is entered on the form.

**Case goods and open stock control at the finishing department.** As finishing orders are issued, the finishing department is instructed to ship goods to specific customers or to place goods in stock for future shipping instructions. These subsequent instructions may require finished goods to be shipped by the case, or they may necessitate shipping part of a case; in the latter event, the remainder of the case is transferred from a case goods control record to an open stock control record. For details on the latter two controls, see Section 13, "Cotton Goods Converters," Volume I, pages 363 et seq.

## Plant and equipment records—depreciation

**Need for fixed asset records.** Because of the large investment in machinery and equipment, many mills maintain a property record. This book lists every machine and major piece of equipment by number and location. The numbers are painted or stamped on the machine itself. The record contains complete identification, including original cost and date and source of purchase. It also shows major repairs and parts replacements.

**Depreciation.** The industry practice has been quite generally to depreciate equipment over the expected useful life allowed for Federal income tax purposes. Because most of the wearing parts of textile machinery are replaceable individually and are too small in cost to be capitalized, the actual physical life of equipment generally has exceeded the original estimates. In recent years there has been an acceleration in cost-saving improvements, and consequently large sums have been spent on replacement equipment.

## Reports to management

**Financial reports.** A daily report for management showing cash balances in its various banks is usually required.

Weekly reports should show the following:

1. Cash requirements
2. Bank loans
3. Sales for week and month to date
4. Sales commitments
5. Raw material commitments
6. Open cotton futures (hedging) contracts

At the end of each month, reports conforming more or less to the following suggested types should be prepared for submission not later than the tenth of the next month. The availability of some of these reports will depend upon the nature of the cost system.

1. Operating statements showing monthly and year-to-date figures compared with the prior year and including:

   a. Statement of income.

   b. Statement of cost of goods manufactured, showing amount and cost per pound or yard produced for each item of cost, by plants. However, in the case of a mill producing a large variety of items, it may be impractical to show cost of goods per pound or yard for each item.

   c. Statement of cost variances from standard.

   d. Sales by fabric, style, or construction and average sales price for each.

   e. Income by style or construction (if such information is available).

   f. Income per loom per week by style or construction, based on either standard or actual costs.

   g. Payroll cost analysis compared with standard, by department and job classification.

2. Month-end balance sheet.
3. Fixed asset commitments.
4. Budget report showing budgeted and actual figures for the month and year to date.

Quarterly budget reports, instead of the monthly reports suggested, may be adequate in many companies. In addition, it is frequently desirable to prepare a quarterly statement of application of funds to supplement the regular monthly reports.

**Operating reports.** Among the many operating reports that are often required, the following are usually deemed essential:

1. Weekly and monthly production reports showing:
   a. Actual production by product, style, or construction.
   b. Standard production by product, style, or construction.
   c. Per cent of actual to standard for each item.
   d. Percentage distribution of actual production according to first quality, seconds, and short lengths.
2. Monthly material consumption report by classes of raw materials.
3. Weekly waste reports, by classes of raw materials.
4. Monthly report of cotton position (see Figure 4, page 409.)
5. Monthly safety report.

# 15

# Dentists

by

## DR. IRVIN TULKIN

Co-author: J. Lewis Blass and Irvin Tulkin, "Dentist's Efficiency
Book" and "Successful Dental Practice"

**Functions of dental practice.** The average dental office is a two-person organization, made up of the dentist and his secretary-assistant. The functions performed by each are shown in the organization chart (Figure 1).

**Essentials of the system.** The system described here furnishes all of the accounting and office records required to (1) schedule services for each patient and compute the costs and fees for the service; (2) determine income and expenditures for tax purposes; and (3) keep track of outstanding accounts. The system does not involve the usual books of account, nor does it entail the making of double entries. The operation of the system is described in four sections: (1) the patient's service record; (2) records of income and expenditure; (3) accounts receivable procedure; (4) office procedure records.

## The patient's service record

**The schedule of services.** The schedule of services is a predetermined plan of the order and time sequence in which the services are to be rendered to the patient. It constitutes the patient's record (see Figure 2), and is an indispensable aid in arranging appointments and satisfactory payment terms. Each of the 30-minute units can be used for separate appointments, or several units may be combined into 60-minute or 90-minute periods. By means of accurate scheduling, the dentist can predict the approximate completion date and can see at a glance the progress of his work with each case.

Acknowledgment is made to J. Lewis Blass and Irvin Tulkin, *Successful Dental Practice*, J. B. Lippincott Company, 1947, pp. 71–73, 99, 108–119; also to the Professional Fee Association, New York, for forms reproduced in Figures 6, 7, 8, and 9.

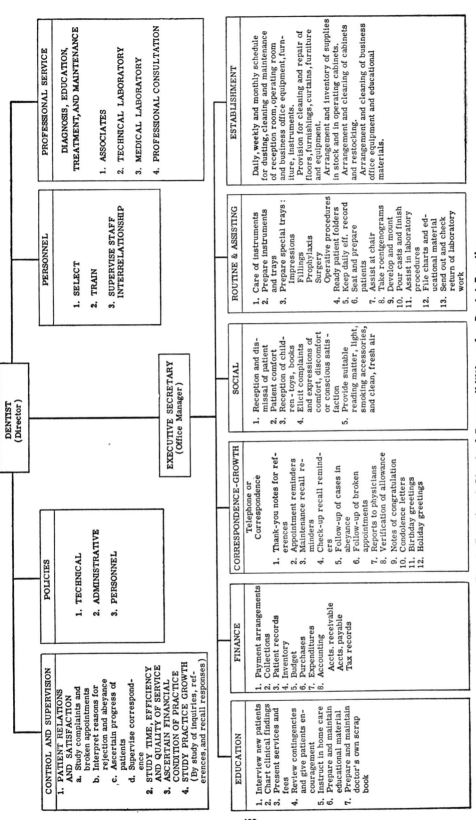

**DENTIST** (Director)

**POLICIES**
1. TECHNICAL
2. ADMINISTRATIVE
3. PERSONNEL

**PROFESSIONAL SERVICE**
DIAGNOSIS, EDUCATION, TREATMENT, AND MAINTENANCE
1. ASSOCIATES
2. TECHNICAL LABORATORY
3. MEDICAL LABORATORY
4. PROFESSIONAL CONSULTATION

**PERSONNEL**
1. SELECT
2. TRAIN
3. SUPERVISE STAFF INTERRELATIONSHIP

**CONTROL AND SUPERVISION**
1. PATIENT RELATIONS AND SATISFACTION
   a. Study complaints and broken appointments
   b. Interpret reasons for rejection and abeyance
   c. Ascertain progress of patients
   d. Supervise correspondence
2. STUDY TIME, EFFICIENCY AND QUALITY OF SERVICE
3. ASCERTAIN FINANCIAL CONDITION OF PRACTICE
4. STUDY PRACTICE GROWTH (By study of inquiries, references, and recall responses)

**EXECUTIVE SECRETARY** (Office Manager)

**ESTABLISHMENT**
Daily, weekly and monthly schedule for dusting, cleaning and maintenance of reception room, operating room and business office equipment, furniture, instruments.
Provision for cleaning and repair of floors, furnishings, curtains, furniture and equipment.
Arrangement and inventory of supplies in stock and in operating cabinets.
Arrangement and cleaning of cabinets and restocking.
Arrangement and cleaning of business office equipment and educational materials.

**ROUTINE & ASSISTING**
1. Care of instruments
2. Prepare instruments and trays
3. Prepare special trays :
   Impressions
   Fillings
   Prophylaxis
   Surgery
   Operative procedures
4. Ready patient folders
5. Keep daily eff. record
6. Seat and prepare patients
7. Assist at chair
8. Take roentgenograms
9. Develop and mount
10. Pour casts and finish
11. Assist in laboratory procedures
12. File charts and educational material
13. Send out and check return of laboratory work

**SOCIAL**
1. Reception and dismissal of patient
2. Patient comfort
3. Reception of children - toys, books
4. Elicit complaints and expressions of comfort, discomfort or conscious satisfaction
5. Provide suitable reading matter, light, smoking accessories, and clean, fresh air

**CORRESPONDENCE-GROWTH**
Telephone or Correspondence
1. Thank-you notes for references
2. Appointment reminders
3. Maintenance recall reminders
4. Check-up recall reminders
5. Follow-up of cases in abeyance
6. Follow-up of broken appointments
7. Reports to physicians
8. Verification of allowance
9. Notes of congratulation
10. Condolence letters
11. Birthday greetings
12. Holiday greetings

**FINANCE**
1. Payment arrangements
2. Collections
3. Patient records
4. Inventory
5. Budget
6. Purchases
7. Expenditures
8. Accounting
   Accts. receivable
   Accts. payable
   Tax records

**EDUCATION**
1. Interview new patients
2. Chart clinical findings
3. Present services and fees
4. Review contingencies and give patients encouragement
5. Instruct in home care
6. Prepare and maintain educational material
7. Prepare and maintain doctor's own scrap book

**Fig. 1. Functional Chart of Responsibilities of a Dental Practice.**

423

The patient's record shows at the bottom what the total fee will be and how it is computed. The fee is made up of (1) fixed hourly costs; (2) variable costs, including supplies and technician's fees; (3) contingency fees; and (4) professional service fees.

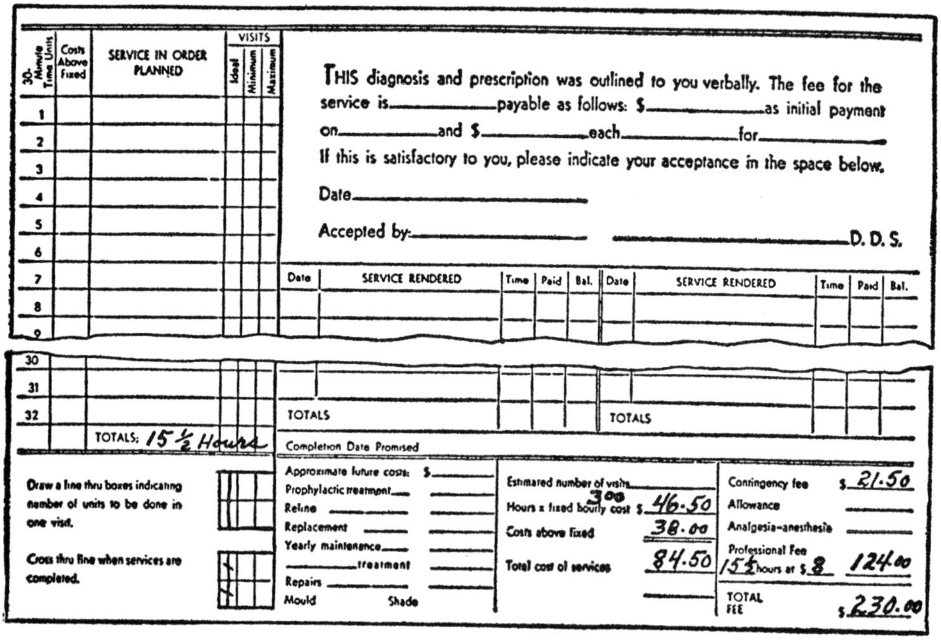

**Fig. 2. Patient's Record—Service Schedule.**

The form also allows for estimating the approximate future costs to the patient for prophylactic treatment, relining, replacement, and yearly maintenance and repairs. The dentist makes this computation at the time of scheduling, and tells the patient what future costs are likely to be. This practice helps to maintain patient confidence, understanding, and appreciation of the benefits and limitations of dentistry.

**Fixed hourly costs.** The fixed hourly cost is determined by finding the total cost of all items of fixed overhead for the previous two or three years and dividing this sum by the number of hours spent in the office during that period. Thus, if the average of three years' overhead costs is $4,500 a year, with a total of 1,500 hours per year spent in the office, the hourly fixed overhead is $3. The fixed cost to be applied to each case is found by multiplying the hours of service shown on the patient's schedule of service by the fixed hourly rate.

The annual fixed-overhead items include the following:

1. Rent
2. Telephone
3. Electricity
4. Gas

5. Janitor service
6. Salaries of paid employees
7. Gifts and tips
8. Laundry service
9. Stationery, postage, printing, and other office supplies
10. Dentist's uniforms and shoes
11. Dental society dues
12. Convention expenses
13. Postgraduate course expenses
14. Dental magazines and periodicals for reception room
15. Accountant's fees
16. Dry cleaning for office draperies, and so forth
17. Collection and legal fees
18. Uncollectible accounts
19. Upkeep and replacement of equipment (10-year basis)
20. Depreciation of office equipment (10-year basis)
21. Insurance: fire, theft, liability, malpractice
22. Interest on business indebtedness
23. Business and office property taxes
24. Losses from fire and theft

**Supplies and technician's fees.** Supplies and technician's fees are variable in amount and are computed separately for each case. They are shown on the patient's record as "costs above fixed."

**Contingency fees.** To the sum of the professional fee, fixed cost, and variable costs for the particular case, 10 or 20 per cent must be added to cover special or unknown difficulties or complications that often arise during treatment, such as patient illness, broken or canceled appointments, undiscovered defects, changes in treatment, and many other unpredictable conditions.

**Fees for professional services.** The fee for professional services may be determined on a *unit fee* or on an *hourly* basis.

*Unit fee basis.* This method sets a fixed charge for each operation; for example, $3 for an extraction, $100 for a full denture, and so forth. In establishing the unit fee, the determinants of the fee are fixed costs, variable costs, the dentist's compensation, and profit. Despite its general use, this method does not insure an equitable fee to the patient or the dentist because it tends to set a small charge for operative and treatment services, to be compensated for by the larger fees for prosthetic replacements. The customary unit charge becomes the amount the patients expect to pay, regardless of varying difficulties in different operations.

The custom of setting a unit fee leads also to the itemization of operations, and very often patient and dentist become involved in the discussion of a price list of fillings and bridges. As a result, the relationship is shaken. However, owing to community custom, it is often difficult to change fees abruptly from a unit basis to an hourly basis. Nevertheless, the aim should be to establish an hourly basis for fees.

*Hourly basis.* This method requires the dentist to set a goal for his yearly income. The amount is influenced by the limits of his average patient's means, the location of the practice, and the dentist's skill, aptitude, and connections. For example, if a dentist spends 1,500 hours yearly in his office, only 80 per cent at best, or 1,200 hours, can be productive. If he sets his income goal at $9,600 net yearly, he must charge $8 per hour for professional services to meet this goal. Figure 1 is designed for the use of the hourly basis in computing fees for professional services.

## Records of income and expenditures

**Basic income and expenditures records.** Three separate records, kept in an 8½ x 11-inch loose-leaf book, constitute the complete record of income and expenditures. These records are (1) the daily efficiency record, (2) the monthly expense and tax record, and (3) the annual summary sheet.

**The daily efficiency record.** This record, illustrated in Figure 3, shows the number of patients treated and whether they are in progress of treatment, prior patients returning for additional treatment, emergency patients, or new patients. Space is provided to record broken and canceled

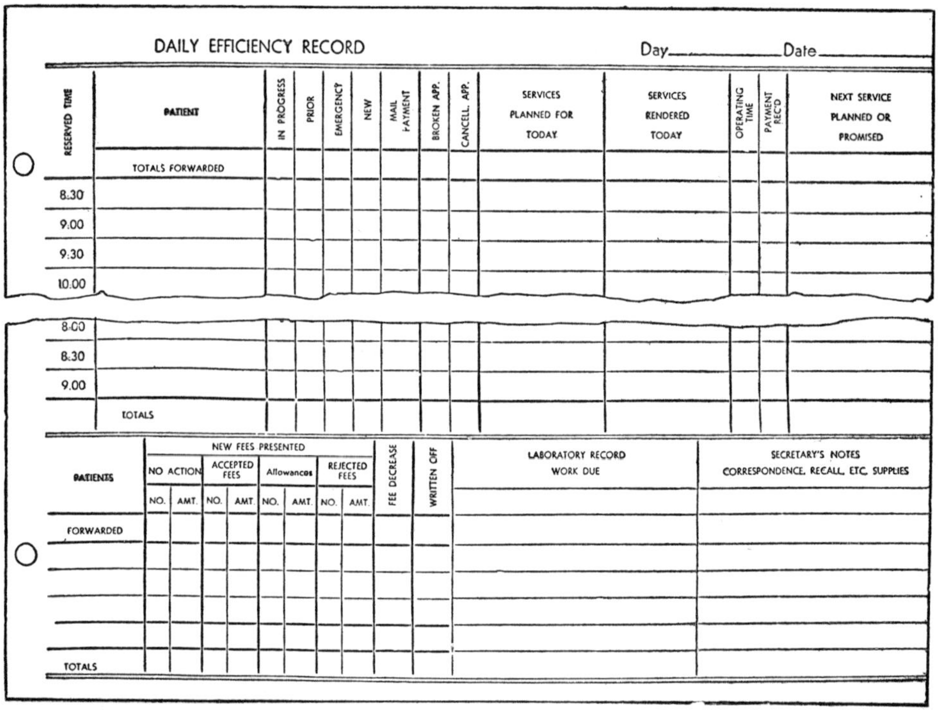

Fig. 3. Daily Efficiency Record.

appointments and to enter the services planned for the day, the services rendered, and the services planned for the next visit. Space is also provided for the time spent in operating and for a record of payments received.

The record of services rendered, time spent, and work planned for the next session is entered by the doctor during the appointment period. The secretary transcribes the record of work done to the patient's record card and enters on the proper day sheet the service planned for the patient's next appointment. The secretary can enter the payment received on the daily record at any time that she is in the operating room.

The record of new fees, kept on the day sheet, includes those accepted or rejected and the amount of allowances granted. The total of each column is carried forward daily to the next day sheet until the end of the month. At that time, the total for the month is transferred to the annual summary.

Fees decreased or written off are entered on the day sheet to maintain a correct list of outstanding contracts. The record of new fees presented is a guide in determining the reasons for abeyance, allowances, or rejection of services.

By entering on the day sheet the laboratory record of work due, disappointments in delivery and oversights can be avoided.

The space for secretary's notes may be used for recording the reasons for the rejection or postponement of services. It also serves to list necessary supplies, emergency treatment, or other reminders for the dentist or his secretary.

Each day's sheet is removed from the book to the doctor's office. The next day's sheet appears and furnishes the doctor with a plan of the next day's work. This sheet saves time, eliminates the need for scanning each patient's individual record to know the services to be rendered, and permits preparation of necessary instruments and materials before each patient's arrival.

**Expense and tax record.** An expense record, illustrated in Figure 4, is kept for each month. All expenses entered under Columns 1, 2, and 3 are for items that are to be deducted from gross income in preparing the income tax report. Items in Column 4 may not be deducted. At the end of each month, totals from the monthly expense sheet are carried forward to the appropriate disbursement columns on the annual summary.

The employee tax record at the bottom of the monthly expense sheet provides an easy means of recording necessary payroll information.

Purchases of gold and other precious metals are entered in Column 2 of the form. Dentists try many new products in small quantities; hence, no completely satisfactory inventory procedure has been developed. The more commonly used items, such as gold and laboratory supplies, are best purchased in large quantities. The dentist can use the previous year's supply bills as a guide in determining the quantities that are to be purchased.

EXPENSES FOR THE MONTH OF........................................19.........

| 1. | | | 2. | | | 3. | | | 4. | | |
|---|---|---|---|---|---|---|---|---|---|---|---|
| DEPRECIATION<br>INTEREST<br>SALARIES<br>DUES<br>MISCELLANEOUS | | | LABORATORY<br>SUPPLIES<br>PRINTING<br>OFFICE RENT<br>STATIONERY | | | REPAIR CLEANING<br>TELEPHONE LIGHTS<br>LAUNDRY DRUGS<br>SOCIAL SECURITY<br>TAXES PETTY CASH<br>GIFTS | | | NON-DEDUCTIBLE<br>EQUIPMENT AND FURNISHINGS<br>PERSONAL<br>BOOKS COURSES<br>INVESTMENT INCOME TAX | | |
| DATE | ITEM | AMOUNT | DATE | ITEM | AMOUNT | DATE | ITEM | AMOUNT | DATE | ITEM | AMOUNT |
| 1 | | | 1 | | | 1 | | | 1 | | |
| 2 | | | 2 | | | 2 | | | 2 | | |
| 3 | | | 3 | | | 3 | | | 3 | | |
| 4 | | | 4 | | | 4 | | | 4 | | |
| 30 | | | 30 | | | 30 | | | 30 | | |
| 31 | | | 31 | | | 31 | | | 31 | | |
| | TOTAL | | | TOTAL | | | TOTAL | | | TOTAL | |

EMPLOYEE TAX RECORD

| NO. | NAME | WEEK | SALARY | WITHHELD | SOC. SEC. | MISC. | NET |
|---|---|---|---|---|---|---|---|
| | | | | | | | |
| | | | | | | | |
| | | | | | | | |
| | | | | | | | |
| | | | | | | | |
| | | | | | | | |
| | | | | | | | |
| | | | | | | | |
| | | | | | | | |
| | | | | | | | |

**Figure 4. Monthly Expense Sheet.**

**Annual summary.** This one-page report (Figure 5), which allows space for month-to-month entries, offers a composite picture of the practice for one year. The total income and disbursements are always available for tax reports, for comparison, and for budget planning. The form furnishes a cumulative record of the number and types of patients treated or interviewed each month, and the number and amount of accepted, rejected, and allowance fees. It also records the fees that have been written off or decreased, the number of broken and canceled appointments, and the time spent at the chair.

To compute the outstanding contracts at the end of a month, the new contracts are added to the amount of the last known monthly outstanding contracts, and from the total are subtracted the current month's income and fee deductions.

The number and amount of accepted contracts are an important index of the growth of the practice, and, when compared with receipts, can be a guide to the efficiency of arranging terms, granting credit, and collecting fees. Rejected fees can also serve as an index of the administrative efficiency of diagnosis, education, and presentation. Allowances, fee decreases,

# ANNUAL SUMMARY

Year: _____

## BUDGET

| MONTH | CASH BALANCE | RECEIPTS | | | 1. | | | 2. | | | | 3. | | | | | | | DISBURSEMENTS | | | | 4. (NON-DEDUCTIBLE) | | | | TOTAL |
|---|---|---|---|---|---|---|---|---|---|---|---|---|---|---|---|---|---|---|---|---|---|---|---|---|---|---|---|
| | | PRACTICE INCOME | OTHER REVENUE | TOTAL | DUES.—MISC. INTEREST DEPREC. | SALARIES | LABORA-TORY | MDSE. STATION-ERY | RENT | PHONE | LIGHT CLEAN | GAS REPAIR | PETTY CASH | DRUGS LAUN-DRY | TAXES SOCIAL SEC'TY | GIFTS | P. G. STUDY BOOKS | PER-SONAL | FURNIT. EQUIP'T | INCOME TAX. | | | | | | |

TOTAL

## PATIENTS

| MONTH | IN PROG. | PRIOR | EMER. | NEW | BROKEN APP. | CANCELLED APP. | PRODUCTIVE TIME |
|---|---|---|---|---|---|---|---|

TOTAL

## FEES PRESENTED

| OUTSTANDING CONTRACTS | | NO ACT'N | | ACCEPTED | | REJECTED | | DECREASE | CANCELLATION WRITTEN OFF | ALLOWANCE | |
|---|---|---|---|---|---|---|---|---|---|---|---|
| NO. | AMOUNT | NO. | AMOUNT | NO. | AMOUNT | NO. | AMOUNT | | | NO. | AMOUNT |

TOTAL

**Fig. 5. Annual Summary**

429

and those written off for discontinuance, moving, death, or other causes are essential records in keeping the amount of outstanding contracts current.

The amounts budgeted for the various classes of expenditures are entered at the beginning of the year in the budget space at the top of each of the four columns.

## Accounts receivable procedures

**Fee-payment methods.** Three methods of payment may be offered to patients:

1. During the course of treatment. Cash payment is made in full before the completion of treatment.

2. After completion of treatment. A monthly charge or bill is contemplated.

3. On time over an extended period. This credit budget account provides that services will be completed before full payment is made. Arrangements are made for the payment of unpaid balances after the completion of the work. Although a bank or finance company may be used, the greatest scope for practice expansion and the best way to maintain good doctor-patient relationships is to have a credit plan under which payments are made directly to the doctor. The services of a professional fee association may prove helpful, since it brings in a third party.

**Assuring collection of fees.** To assure full collection of fees, the following practices are recommended: (1) The doctor should always feel certain that the patient has accepted without reservation the full need of the diagnosis and treatment plan before quoting a fee. (2) The patient should accept the fairness of the fee before terms of payment are discussed. He should not be encouraged to arrange payments that will conflict with his other essential personal needs. (3) After accepting the fee, the patient should be asked how he would like to pay for the services. If the patient's suggestion is not satisfactory, the doctor should be prepared to offer an alternative cash or credit plan to fit the needs of the patient and the doctor's practice. (4) Patients should be asked for a retainer of from 20 to 30 per cent. Less should be required, of course, where it imposes a strain on deserving patients. The patient should be asked, "What is the most you can conveniently give us as a down payment?" If the balance on the account is to be paid before services are completed, the balance should be divided into equal payments during the course of treatment. On a budget account, terms up to one year may be made.

**Signed contracts.** A signed contract is advisable in all cases. In credit accounts, it is essential. A form of budget plan agreement is shown in Figure 6. On the back of the budget plan agreement is a record of the patient's account, which is the same as that shown in Figure 8.

## P. F. A. BUDGET PLAN AGREEMENT

1. The doctor whose signature appears on this agreement has rendered or agrees to render professional services to _____. A complete description of services are described on the patients office record which is hereby made a part of this Plan by incorporation as fully and completely as though the same were set forth in full herein. Upkeep services as agreed to expires_____

2. Now, in consideration of the professional service rendered or to be rendered the Patient whose signature appears hereafter, on or before the date mentioned below, promises to pay to the order of said Doctor at the office of said Doctor or such other place as the Doctor may in writing designate, the total sum of_____ _____ Dollars_____to be paid in accordance with the following Schedule:

3. Payment agreement... A Total Sum of_____Dollars is agreed to. $_____to be paid on date_____ leaving a balance of $_____to be paid in_____installments;_____installments of $_____each, and_____installments of $_____each, the first installment to be due and payable_____and one each of the remaining installments to be due and payable each and every successive_____thereafter until the entire balance is paid in full.

4. It is understood and agreed that the payment of either the "Total Sum" or any of the successive installments hereof on the due date or dates is of the essence of this contract and that upon failure to pay either the "Total Sum" or any of the installments thereof as hereinbefore set forth on their due dates the Doctor may declare the unpaid balance on the entire "Total Sum" and each and all of the installments thereof immediately due and payable without notice together with all reasonable collection costs.

5. The Doctor shall not be liable for damages in the event of delays due to no fault or neglect on his or her part; or by other delays caused by circumstances beyond control.

6. In the event of death of either the Doctor or the patient prior to the completion of the services contracted for, the amount due and owing to the Doctor shall be computed on the basis of the services rendered as shown on the Patients office record.

7. Any provision of this Plan prohibited by law of any state shall, as to said state be ineffective, without invalidating the remaining provisions of the Plan.

DOCTOR_____      PATIENT_____

DATE_____

WITNESS_____      GUARANTOR_____

*Courtesy, Professional Fee Association, New York.*

**Fig. 6. Budget Plan Agreement.**

**Patient's payment memo.** Whether or not the doctor uses the services of a professional fee association, the patient is given a payment memo similar to that in Figure 7. The *exact amount* and *date* for *each payment*

PAYMENT MEMO

PAYMENT BOOKLET

☐ Cash Arrangement    ☐ Credit Budget Contract

PROFESSIONAL FEE ASSOCIATION

☐ Prepayment Contract    ☐ Special Arrangement

SUBSCRIBER DOCTOR

Total Fee:      Date:

Allowance:      Weekly Promise:

Net Fee:      Monthly Promise:      Patient: ................

Down Payment:      Balance Due:      Address: ................

Payment to be completed by................

All payments, unless otherwise agreed upon, are made *directly* to the Doctor. Maintain a Good Credit Reputation by making all payments on date promised. Consult the Doctor if a change becomes necessary. You will be notified if payments fall behind.

Services may or may not be completed at date set for final fee payment. If arrangement proves unsatisfactory, it can be changed to another, if mutually agreed upon.

The Doctor subscribes to the Professional Fee Association to free more of his time for treating patients.

© P.F.A. 1953

*Courtesy, Professional Fee Association, New York.*

**Fig. 7. Patient's Payment Memo.**

should be clearly filled in on the reverse side (Figure 8). As payments are made, they are recorded on the payment memo, with the date, the amount paid, and the balance owed.

| NAME | | | | | | RESIDENCE PHONE | | BUSINESS PHONE | | MAILING ADDRESS | | |
|---|---|---|---|---|---|---|---|---|---|---|---|---|
| Inst. No. | Date Due | Amount of Installment | Date Paid | Amount Paid | Balance Owed | Inst. No. | Date Due | Amount of Installment | Date Paid | Amount Paid | Balance Owed | |
| | | Total Amount | | | | | | Brought Forward | | | | |
| D. P. | | | | | | 17 | | | | | | |
| 1 | | | | | | 18 | | | | | | |
| 2 | | | | | | 19 | | | | | | |
| 3 | | | | | | 20 | | | | | | |
| 4 | | | | | | 21 | | | | | | |
| 5 | | | | | | | | | | | | |
| 14 | | | | | | 31 | | | | | | |
| 15 | | | | | | 32 | | | | | | |
| 16 | | | | | | 33 | | | | | | |

*Courtesy, Professional Fee Association, New York.*

**Fig. 8. Patient's Payment Record (Reverse side of Fig. 7).**

The same entries that are made in the patient's payment memo are made on the reverse side of his budget plan agreement. There is thus a duplicate office record of the patient's payment memo. This record can be used for all three types of accounts—cash, charge, and budget.

**Prepayment plan.** Doctors who wish to contract for maintenance or other services, such as children's dentistry, on a private prepayment basis, may use the form illustrated in Figure 9.

## PROFESSIONAL FEE ASSOCIATION

### PREPAYMENT PLAN

Date Started                                    Expiration Date

For the sum of $............................per month or $............................quarterly the following services *only* will be rendered:

Cancellation must be mutually agreed upon. If the patient cancels the contract before the expiration date, and has received more services than total paid in, he shall pay the balance due to the doctor at his regular fees.

All payments are made to Dr. ........................................................................................
No other services are included with this contract.
The patient promises to call for appointments as instructed.
Failure to appear for treatment does not cancel any payment obligation.

Patient Signature............................................Doctor Signature........................................

*Courtesy, Professional Fee Association, New York.*

**Fig. 9. Prepayment Plan Agreement.**

**Collection procedure.** There is nothing unusual about the billing and collection procedure. The Professional Fee Association makes available a number of forms of reminder notices and collection envelopes to aid in the collection of past-due accounts. The secretary keeps track of collections through the collection list described on page 434 and the patient's payment record (Figure 8).

## Office procedure records

**Non-accounting forms.** In the same loose-leaf book in which the three accounting records described on pages 426–430 are kept, four additional office records are maintained: (1) telephone and correspondence list, (2) abeyance list, (3) collection list, and (4) recall list. These are non-accounting records that are essential for good office practice.

**Telephone and correspondence list.** When an active patient breaks an appointment, or when a definite appointment cannot be arranged, the secretary enters the patient's name, address, telephone number, and other pertinent information on the correspondence list (see Figure 10). This form can also be used as a memorandum for future correspondence and

| | | Telephone and Correspondence List | | Month | |
|---|---|---|---|---|---|
| NAME | ADDRESS | TELEPHONE | PURPOSE | ACTION AND RESULT | |
| | | | | | |
| | | | | | |
| | | | | | |
| | | | | | |
| | | | | | |
| | | | | | |

Telephone Calls: Broken appointments, fill in appointments, verification of appointments. Physician consultation or reports. Supply house or laboratory.

Correspondence Memo: Notes of thanks for reference. Birthday or other greetings. Condolence letters. Congratulations.

Note position of patient's name in this book on his record. Cross out name when attended to. Transfer to next telephone and correspondence list if further action is planned. If no further immediate action is planned, transfer to Abeyance, Collection, or Recall list.

Patients who do not have an appointment must appear on one of these lists if they are an active member of the practice.

**Fig. 10. Telephone and Correspondence List.**

telephone calls to a laboratory, a physician, or a patient. The name is crossed off when an appointment is made or when the correspondence or telephone call is attended to. After writing or telephoning a patient with no results, the secretary transfers the name to the following month's reminder. When it is decided to take the name off the list, it should be transferred to the abeyance or collection list.

The name of every active patient must appear in the book. If the patient has no appointment, his name should be on one of the other lists.

**Abeyance list.** The name of a patient who discontinues treatment should be entered on the abeyance form (Figure 11) until it is decided to write off the balance of the contract and transfer his record to the inactive file.

| Abeyance List | | | | |
|---|---|---|---|---|
| Month | | | | |
| NAME | ADDRESS | TELEPHONE | ACTION | NOTE |
| | | | | |
| | | | | |
| | | | | |

Enter patients who discontinue treatment. Note last position of patient on this sheet on his records. When no further action is contemplated place records in inactive file. Write off on all records.

Fig. 11. Abeyance List.

**Collection list.** Fees due for completed work or from patients who discontinue treatment, whatever the payment arrangement may be, are recorded on the collection list (Figure 12). The name and amount are transferred to the following month's collection list if the bill is not paid in full. The fee is written off from the list of outstanding contracts when no further collection action is contemplated.

| COLLECTION LIST | | | Month | | | |
|---|---|---|---|---|---|---|
| NAME | ADDRESS | TELEPHONE | DUE | BILLED | PAID | NOTES |
| | | | | | | |
| | | | | | | |
| | | | | | | |

Note last position of patient's name in this book on his record.   Cross off if paid in full. Transfer balance due to next month's list. If no further action is planned, write off on all records.

Fig. 12. Collection List.

**Recall list.** At the patient's last visit, his name is entered on the recall list (Figure 13) for the month when he is to be notified. To personalize

| | Recall List | | Month | |
|---|---|---|---|---|
| NAME | ADDRESS | TELEPHONE | PURPOSE | MISC. NOTES |
| | | | | |
| | | | | |
| | | | | |

| | | | | |
|---|---|---|---|---|
| | | | | |
| | | | | |

Enter patient's name at time of last visit. Write this month's date on patient's record. Cross off names of patients making recall. Transfer those who do not, to next recall list. Note number of notices. After 2 notices place six months ahead. MAKE all entries on patient's record - noting position in book.

**Fig. 13. Recall List.**

the recall correspondence, the remarks column may be used to note some special point for future observation. It is important to enter the date of recall on the patient's personal record, should he come in before his recall date. When the patient reports, his name is crossed from the recall list. If he does not respond after two notices are sent to him, his name is entered from four to six months ahead for another recall reminder.

# 16

# Department Stores

by

KENNETH P. MAGES

Certified Public Accountant; Partner, Touche, Niven, Bailey & Smart,
New York

## Industry characteristics that affect the accounting system

**Nature of the business.**  Although a department store is established essentially to sell merchandise, it has many of the characteristics of a personal service organization and, in some of its operations, the characteristics of a manufacturer.  For example, in the conduct of a beauty salon, optical department, or soda fountain and restaurant, it has the characteristics of a service establishment.  In the manufacture of draperies and other decorators' items, in the women's alteration rooms and the men's busheling rooms, and in the furniture finishing department and the appliance repair department, it encounters the problems of a manufacturer.

Merchandise seldom is sold by department stores without the accompaniment of certain services which, in most instances, the customer receives without charge.  Some stores make deliveries and offer the services of charge accounts, layaways, and other credit facilities, while others operate primarily on a cash-and-carry basis, offering no charge accounts or free delivery.  Even full-service stores, in recent years, have ventured into what is called open-selling, self-selection, or self-service, the terms representing different degrees of service.

Department stores operate as single units or as groups of units of approximately similar size with centralized accounting.  In recent years, many stores operating as a single unit have opened branch stores and thus have taken on most of the characteristics of multi-unit operation.

The sales volume of department stores is quite seasonal.  The month of December produces about 14 per cent of the business, the months of September, October, and November contribute another 27 per cent, and the remaining eight months produce 59 per cent.

Practically every department store leases some of its departments to outsiders (rarely to an extent above 10 per cent of its total sales) under contracts which grant a commission to the store of from 10 per cent to 20 per cent of sales. Such leased (or licensed) departments are not distinguishable by the customer from "owned" departments. The operator (lessee) owns the merchandise and, in addition to paying the commission, reimburses the store for direct advertising and salary costs and such other expenses as are specified in the agreement.

**Functional peculiarities.** Buying is decentralized among numerous buyers. In addition, the services of affiliated or resident buying offices are used. Each buyer, working under the supervision of a divisional merchandise manager, is responsible for the selling and operation of his department.

**Ownership peculiarities.** Most stores had their origin many years ago in the form of individual proprietorships. Today the ownership is generally in the form of a corporation, but partnerships and individual proprietorships are found among the smaller stores.

In recent years a considerable number of ownership groups have come into existence through parent companies' acquiring stores in different cities throughout the country by means of the exchange of stock. The various stores in the group do not constitute a chain, in the ordinary sense, since each newly acquired store generally continues to operate as a separate company with the same management and staff that existed prior to the change of ownership.

**Financing peculiarities.** Many stores, in recent years, have financed their growth by selling their installment receivables to banks. Some stores have sold their buildings to insurance companies and other financial institutions and have then leased them back on a long-term basis. On a seasonal basis, stores resort to short-term bank loans, particularly in the early fall, when inventories are mounting in anticipation of the Christmas season.

**Principal accounting problems.** The principal accounting problems relate to (1) inventory levels and valuation, (2) expense control, and (3) the evaluation of selling departments and branch stores.

## Functional organization

**Functional areas.** Department store organizations are divided into four general areas called "pyramids." These areas are merchandising, publicity, superintendency, and control. Personnel is considered a fifth pyramid in some stores. A number of stores use a two-pyramid setup, dividing the organization into departments performing the selling function and those performing the nonselling functions.

**Responsibility of the control division.** The control division is, of course, responsible for all accounting and closely related procedures. The typical controller's office is divided into three main parts: (1) the credit and collection department; (2) production departments, including cashier, sales auditing, accounts receivable, accounts payable, timekeeping and payroll, and sometimes receiving and marking; and (3) staff departments, including general accounting and statistical, insurance, internal audit, inventory work, taxes, and other recordkeeping.

The office departments that are the source of entries into the books of account are cashier, sales auditing, accounts payable, payroll, and general accounting and statistical. They function as follows:

The *cashier's* office accepts payments on account from customers in person or by mail, counts all cash receipts from the salespersons' receipt bags (or from the tube room, if that device is used), and prepares the daily bank deposit. Petty cash disbursements are made from a fund maintained in the cashier's office.

The *sales auditing department* processes all saleschecks written to cover charge sales, accounts for missing saleschecks, audits the register readings and tapes, processes other items such as cash refunds and charge credits, determines commissions on sales where applicable, accumulates sales by department and by salesperson, and performs other similar operations.

The *accounts payable department* makes the accounting distribution of merchandise purchase and expense invoices and prepares the checks for the payment of all invoices.

The *payroll department* prepares the payroll on the basis of recorded time, and from commission data supplied by the sales auditing department, prepares the paychecks or pay envelopes, and makes the accounting distribution of the payroll expense.

The *general accounting and statistical department* makes the entries and the related calculations in the retail inventory ledger and thus arrives at figures relating to cost of sales, ending inventories, and the like. It develops similar data for selling departments that do not use the retail inventory method, and computes workroom net costs, which are deductions from gross margin.

## Principles of the system

**Principles to be applied in accounting for income.** In most cases, sales are recorded at the time they are made rather than at the time the cash is received. At some stores, however, C.O.D. sales are not recognized as sales until the money is received from the delivery department or the delivery agency. "Will call" or "layaway" sales may be recognized (1) at the time of sale, (2) as payments are made on them, or (3) upon final payment, depending upon the policy of the store or department.

The accounting system should be designed to record income by selling departments in such a manner that reports of sales can be rendered by department on daily, weekly, monthly, and yearly bases. If sales are made at more than one store location, sales must be determined by store. In such instances, sales by department for each store should be accumulated as well as sales by department for all stores combined.

Sales by type—that is, cash, charge, C.O.D., and will call—are automatically developed in establishing controls over these classes of sales. Similarly, sales by salesperson within each department may be automatically figured, although at many stores the sales by salesperson are not balanced precisely to the aggregate of sales by department, even though the individual's sales figures are used for computing sales commissions.

**Principles to be applied in accounting for costs.** The accounting system relating to cost of sales should be designed to accommodate the retail inventory method. Purchases, discounts from vendors, sales, markdowns, inventory shrinkage, and so on, are recorded on a departmental basis. Purchases are accumulated at both cost and retail.

Under the retail method of inventory valuation, the cost of sales is not affected by any lag in the flow of invoices covering purchases. Thus, if there is a lag in the flow of invoices that is not picked up by an adjusting entry for merchandise in transit at the end of the month, the inventory figure in the balance sheet will be somewhat understated, as will the liability for accounts payable. However, the income statement will not be distorted. The retail inventory method automatically relieves the inventory account and charges cost of sales within the same accounting period. (See page 457 for further discussion of the retail inventory method.)

At the year-end, for balance sheet purposes, some stores have adopted the last-in, first-out method of inventory. This LIFO calculation is superimposed upon the value determined by the retail inventory method by establishing a valuation account for the difference between the cost or market as determined under the retail inventory method and the cost as determined from the LIFO application.

**Principles to be applied in accounting for expense.** Stores follow the accrual method of recording expenses. Since the control over expense is one of the most difficult and yet most important phases of the operation, the accumulation and proper classification of these expenses by expense center are very significant. This subject is discussed more fully at page 440.

**Accounting period.** Since the sales pattern in a department store varies from day to day, and since each day has its specific characteristics, the week forms a normal cycle. For the same reasons, many stores have abandoned the calendar month and have adopted a 12-month year consisting of four 5-week months and eight 4-week months established in such a way that each quarter consists of a period of four weeks, one of five weeks, and a third one of four weeks. This plan is frequently called the 4-5-4 plan. Other stores have divided their year into 13 months of 4 weeks each. Either of the above plans may be adopted with or without the 52- or 53-

week fiscal year. If the fiscal period follows the normal pattern, such as ending on January 31 each year, both the 13-month year and the 4-5-4 plan result in odd days which show up in the first and last periods.

## Classification of expense accounts

**Comment on chart of expense accounts.** For more than 25 years, department stores generally have subscribed to a rather uniform chart of expense accounts. This was the result of the need for gathering expense data nationally and followed the publication in 1920 of a standard chart of expense accounts by the Controllers' Congress of the National Retail Dry Goods Association. Data gathered on the basis of such recommended expense accounting have been published annually by Harvard University since 1920. Although stores have introduced many variations of the standard expense accounting recommended by the N.R.D.G.A., the recommended classification of accounts has influenced considerably the accounts used by stores.

**Chart of expense accounts.** The classification of expenses recommended by the Controllers' Congress of the N.R.D.G.A. was completely revised in its *Expense Center Accounting Manual,* which was made available in January, 1955. In this new manual, the Controllers' Congress provides for 71 expense centers for the largest stores, with suggestions for fewer centers in medium- and smaller-sized stores. The centers for the B, C, and D levels are shown at pages 441–443.

If a store feels that it is too small to use even the B group above, it is urged to limit its classification of expenses to the natural divisions outlined below.

The natural divisions are found in varying degrees within the expense centers listed above. However, all natural divisions are not found in each center. The natural divisions are as follows:

| | | | |
|---|---|---|---|
| 01 | Payroll | 10 | Communication |
| 02 | Rentals | 11 | Pensions |
| 03 | Advertising | 12 | Insurance |
| 04 | Taxes | 13 | Depreciation |
| 05 | Imputed interest | 14 | Professional services |
| 06 | Supplies | 15 | Donations |
| 07 | Services purchased | 16 | Losses from bad debts |
| 08 | Unclassified | 17 | Equipment rentals |
| 09 | Traveling | 18 | Contra credit |

For 35 expense centers at the D level, the *Expense Center Accounting Manual* recommends a work measurement unit to be used by stores in computing production per man-hour for internal use, for comparisons with other stores, and for submitting data to Harvard for its annual study of department store operating results.

## Controllers' Congress Expense Center Accounting Manual

## Chart of Expense Centers

### Group B—14 expense centers

| E.C. Number | Name |
|---|---|
| 110 | General Management |
| 120 | Real Estate Costs |
| 130 | Furniture, Fixture and Equipment Costs |
| 140 | Other Fixed and Policy Expenses |
| 200 | Control and Accounting |
| 210 | Control and Office Management |
| 220 | Accounting and Payroll |
| 230 | Accounts Payable |
| 240 | Cash Office |
| 250 | Sales Audit |
| 300 | Accounts Receivable and Credit |

### Group C—36 expense centers

| E.C. Number | Name |
|---|---|
| 110 | General Management |
| 120 | Real Estate Costs |
| 130 | Furniture, Fixture and Equipment Costs |
| 140 | Other Fixed and Policy Expenses |
| 210 | Control and Office Management |
| 220 | Accounting and Payroll |
| 230 | Accounts Payable |
| 240 | Cash Office |
| 250 | Sales Audit |
| 300 | Accounts Receivable and Credit |

### Group D—71 expense centers

| E.C. Number | Name |
|---|---|
| 110 | General Management |
| 121 | Real Estate Costs—Excl. Service and Whse. Bldg. |
| 128 | Real Estate Costs—Service and Whse. Bldg. |
| 131 | Fur. Fix. and Equip. Ccsts—Excl. Service and Whse. Bldg. |
| 138 | Fur. Fix. and Equip. Costs—Service and Whse. Bldg. |
| 140 | Other Fixed and Policy Expenses |
| 211 | Control and Office Management |
| 215 | Mail and Messenger Service |
| 221 | General Accounting and Statistical |
| 225 | Timekeeping and Payroll |
| 230 | Accounts Payable |
| 240 | Cash Office |
| 250 | Sales Audit |
| 310 | Credit |
| 321 | Pre-billing |
| 325 | Billing |
| 330 | Bill Adjustments |
| 340 | Layaway |

# Controllers' Congress Expense Center Accounting Manual

## Chart of Expense Centers (Continued)

### Group B—14 expense centers

| | |
|---|---|
| 400 | Sales Promotion |
| 500 | Superintendency and Building Operations |
| 610 | Personnel |
| 620 | Employee Welfare |
| 630 | Supplementary Benefits |
| 700 | Material Handling |

### Group C—36 expense centers

| | |
|---|---|
| 410 | Publicity and Display Management |
| 420 | Advertising |
| 430 | Shows and Exhibits |
| 440 | Display |
| 510 | Service and Operations Management |
| 520 | General Telephone Service |
| 530 | Protection |
| 540 | Miscellaneous Customer Services |
| 560 | Escalators and Elevators |
| 570 | Cleaning |
| 580 | Maintenance of Properties and Utilities |
| 610 | Personnel |
| 620 | Employee Welfare |
| 630 | Supplementary Benefits |
| 720 | Receiving and Returns to Vendors |
| 730 | Checking and Marking |
| 750 | Transfer Hauling |
| 760 | Delivery |

### Group D—71 expense centers

| | |
|---|---|
| 410 | Publicity and Display Management |
| 421 | Art Work and Photography |
| 422 | Copy Production |
| 423 | Newspaper and Shopping News |
| 425 | Direct Mail |
| 427 | Radio and Television |
| 429 | Other Advertising and Publicity |
| 430 | Shows and Exhibits |
| 441 | Display Production |
| 445 | Sign Shop |
| 511 | Service and Operations Management |
| 515 | Supply Purchasing |
| 520 | General Telephone Service |
| 530 | Protection |
| 540 | Miscellaneous Customer Services |
| 560 | Escalators and Elevators |
| 570 | Cleaning |
| 581 | Maintenance of Properties |
| 585 | Utilities |
| 611 | Personnel |
| 613 | Employment |
| 615 | Training |
| 617 | Training Squad |
| 621 | Hospital and Medical Service |
| 625 | Other Employee Welfare |
| 630 | Supplementary Benefits |
| 721 | Receiving |
| 725 | Returns to Vendors |
| 730 | Checking and Marking |
| 750 | Transfer Hauling |
| 761 | Delivery—General |
| 763 | Freight, Express and Parcel Post |
| 765 | Package Delivery |
| 767 | Furniture Delivery |
| 769 | Garage |

821 Direct Selling—Owned Retail Departments
825 Direct Selling—Owned Cost Departments
831 Other Direct and General Selling
834 Mail and Telephone Orders
837 Personal Shopping Service
840 Maintenance of Stock
851 Retail Selling Supervision
855 Cost Selling Supervision
861 Merchandise Adjustment
863 Service Desks
865 Customers Returned Goods Room
867 Cashiering, Inspecting, Wrapping and Light Packing
869 Crating and Heavy Packing
910 Merchandise Management
921 Buying
924 Comparison Shopping
927 Testing
930 Domestic and Foreign Buying Offices

800 Direct and General Selling
820 Direct Selling—Owned Departments
830 Other Direct and General Selling
840 Maintenance of Stock
850 Selling Supervision
860 Selling Service
900 Merchandising
910 Merchandise Management
920 Buying
930 Domestic and Foreign Buying Offices

## Peculiarities of procedures: sales-cash receipts cycle; purchases-payments cycle

**Accounting for sales.** The typical department store revolves around its selling departments. The number of such departments varies from 40 to 200 or more, depending upon the degree of detail required by the merchandising philosophy of the store. The names of the selling departments and the merchandise coverage of each have been fairly standardized over the years. The Controllers' Congress of the National Retail Dry Goods Association established standard departmental classifications (numbers and names) for its annual study of merchandising results, and the Federal Reserve Banks adopted these departments for their monthly reports on sales, stocks, and inventories. The Bureau of Labor Statistics recognizes the same departmental breakdown in its price indexes for department stores.

Until 1953, the standard grouping consisted of 68 departments (plus some subdivisions of departments), 13 of which were "basement" departments. The merchandise content of each of these departments has been defined by the Federal Reserve Banks. In 1953, the Controllers' Congress published a revision of its standard department list, together with revised descriptions of the merchandise content of each. The main feature of the revision was a scheme for expanding or subdividing the departments so that all stores requiring more than the smallest or basic number would "fan out" along the same general lines.

Since each selling department in a department store has its own buyer (in some instances, especially where there are more than 200 selling departments, a buyer may handle from two to five or more departments), and since a group of buyers often reports to a divisional merchandise manager, there is need for a considerable amount of sales data for each department. Not only are sales determined for each department, but sometimes they are determined by classification of merchandise within a department. Furthermore, sales may be determined by location, if the store operates branches, and by salesperson within the department. The determination of sales by department, location, and salesperson results in a tremendous volume of paper in the form of saleschecks (plus a considerably smaller number of cash or sales register totals) which must be processed by the sales-auditing department of the store. Since saleschecks are written by the individual salespeople on the selling floor, their preparation frequently is not perfect. The procedures for handling saleschecks must take this shortcoming into consideration.

**Salescheck procedures.** The typical department store salescheck is approximately 4¼ inches by 7¾ inches and consists of two copies plus a tissue, or three full copies. The original usually is divided into two main parts and a stub. The top 40 per cent of the space is used for the name and address of the person to whom the article is to be sent. After it is detached, it becomes a record of deliveries. The middle 50 per cent of the space is devoted to the name and address of the purchaser and an enumeration of the merchandise. The bottom 10 per cent is the stub, which is used for a variety of purposes. The duplicate usually can be separated at the same points as the original. The top 40 per cent is a delivery label to be attached to the package. The next 50 per cent is a packing slip. The bottom 10 per cent is a multi-purpose stub. The third copy, or the tissue, which is not perforated, is used for reference purposes, such as to duplicate the salescheck if the original does not reach the office, to settle complaints, and the like.

Variations are necessary both in the detail to be written on the salescheck and in the movements of the various parts of the salescheck for each of the following major kinds of transactions:

> Cash takes
> Cash sends
> Charge takes
> Charge sends
> C. O. D.'s
> Will calls
> Employees' discounts on any of the above
> "By cash" on any of the above

Charge sales are of various types, the most common being (1) 30-day charge accounts, (2) installment sales, and (3) revolving credit, which essentially is a cross between the 30-day and the installment type. The amount of each type of charge sales is determined in the aggregate and not necessarily by department or salesperson.

In most cases, the salesgirl works from a single book of saleschecks which are prenumbered and bound 50 to a book. This single sales book is used for all types of sales that require a salescheck. In a few instances, however, stores have designated special C.O.D. saleschecks to call the delivery department's attention to the required collection. The special C.O.D. salescheck is most widely used in New York City, where the C.O.D. problem is quite acute. Also, a special sales book is sometimes used for cash sales. This usage occurs usually where the tube system rather than the cash register is used for cash sales. Generally speaking, a cash salescheck is simpler in design and less expensive than a charge or combination salescheck.

The salesperson enters each salescheck on a daily tally, which may be a simple card form or an envelope, with spaces for the amount of each sale opposite a printed number that corresponds to the last two digits of the salescheck number. The tally provides a means of determining which saleschecks were written each day, and thus simplifies accounting for all numbers. It is also used for accumulating sales by salesperson where the store does not insist that the figures be taken from the saleschecks themselves.

With the use of a tally envelope instead of a tally card, the tissue copy of the salescheck is placed in the envelope. If the store operates under a system known as *tally audit* (explained below), the original salescheck also is placed in the envelope.

Returned sales are recorded by the writing of a cash refund or a charge credit, or by the preparation of a similar document in the form of a call tag issued to the delivery department. A well-designed call tag will provide, as a by-product, the cash refund or charge credit form, so that, when the call tag is removed from the incoming merchandise, it can be matched to this form, which is held pending receipt of the merchandise.

Cash sales commonly are recorded on a cash register on the selling floor, in which case a salescheck is written only if a delivery to the customer is involved or if there are other special circumstances, such as an employee discount or Federal excise taxes. Where cash registers are not used in this way, all cash sales are recorded on saleschecks and processed through a cashier on the selling floor or a central cashier reached by pneumatic tubes.

C.O.D. and will-call sales are recorded on saleschecks whether or not a cash payment is made. Where a cash payment, commonly called "by cash," is made, the salescheck is routed through the selling-floor cashier or the central cashier. Where no cash payment is made, the routing is determined by the method of audit.

Charge sales are recorded on a salescheck and the routing is determined by the method of audit.

Three audit systems are described below: (1) register audit or floor audit, (2) tally audit, and (3) post audit.

**Register audit or floor audit.** Within the past few years, a new method of handling sales has arisen, called "register audit" or "floor audit." Under this system, all sales (cash, charge, C.O.D., and will call) are recorded on the register and, where cash is not involved, the salescheck is placed in the cash drawer. (See Figure 1.) Thus, at the end of the day there should be enough cash and saleschecks in the register drawer to balance with the totals of the register. In the audit department, the register totals are analyzed and recapped, by hand or by machine, to produce sales figures by department and by salesperson. The obvious economy under the floor audit system is that there is less combining of sales figures to get the over-all figure by department than is required if the totals of cash, charge, C.O.D., and will-call sales have to be combined after they have been accumulated separately. On the other hand, register audit requires a rather complete coverage of the store by registers in order to provide adequate customer service. However, it *is* possible to adopt register audit for less than all of the departments.

**Tally audit.** Under the tally audit system, the salesperson places the saleschecks for charge, C.O.D., and will-call sales in numerical order and

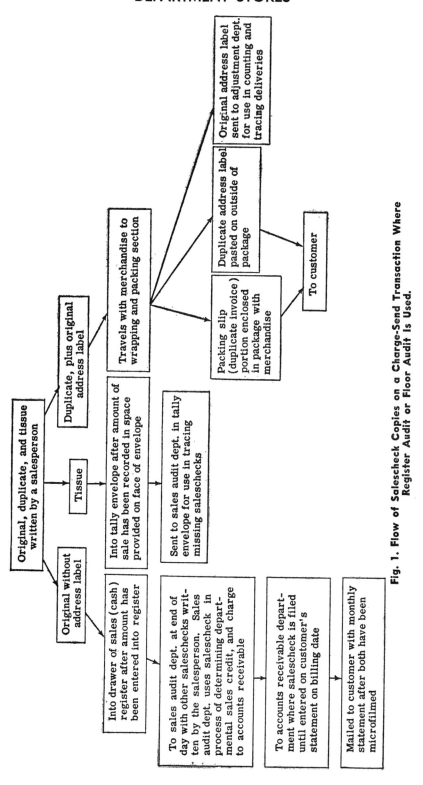

**Fig. 1. Flow of Salescheck Copies on a Charge-Send Transaction Where Register Audit or Floor Audit Is Used.**

sends all of them in an envelope which contains the tissue copy to the office at the close of the day. This simplifies the accounting for salescheck numbers, since no sorting operation is necessary. It also speeds up the duplication of missing saleschecks, since the tissue copy is available at the time it becomes known that the salescheck is missing. Under this system, cash sales are determined from cash register readings or from cash sales-checks processed by floor cashiers or tube-room cashiers.

**Post audit system.** Under the post audit system, which is occasionally encountered, the original salescheck for charge sales, C.O.D., and will-call sales is sent directly to the accounts receivable department (or to the de-livery department or will-call department). Only a stub of the salescheck, showing the department number, salesperson number, and amount (which have been compared with related information in the body of the sales-check), is sent to the sales audit department. The departmental figures determined from these stubs are balanced in total with the figures supplied by the departments that receive the full original copy.

**Billing.** The "billing" operation is accomplished when the salescheck is written, since the salescheck is, in the final analysis, an invoice. Depart-ment store customers, however, customarily do not pay from the invoice but wait until the monthly statement is received.

The methods of preparing statements in department stores fall into two broad classes: (1) cycle billing and (2) end-of-month billing. The older method, end-of-month billing, consists of mailing the customer a statement covering the purchases for a full calendar month, with a cut-off date some-where between the 25th and the last day of each month. Cycle billing is explained at page 449.

*Techniques of end-of-month billing.* One of three plans may be used for end-of-month billing:

1. Continuous ledger plan. The statement is the original, and the ledger page, continuous one month after the other, is the duplicate.

2. Fold-over statement. The original statement is mailed to the cus-tomer, and the carbon copy, showing only the beginning-of-the-month balance and the current month's transactions, is bound at the end of the month to form a ledger. The disadvantage of this method, in comparison with the continuous-ledger plan, is that it is necessary to go to several dif-ferent binders if reference to several months' history of a particular cus-tomer's account is required.

3. Recordak plan. Only an original customer's statement with a stub on the right-hand side is prepared. The posting on this statement shows the month's transactions in the same manner as the continuous and fold-over plans. The stub is removed before the statement is photographed and is used to set up the beginning balance on the statement at the start of the next month. This system is very economical as far as posting and

space requirements for storage of ledgers are concerned. It usually is supplemented, however, by a customer history record which offsets some of the savings.

*Cycle billing.* Under cycle billing, each customer receives a statement covering a full month's purchases, but the period covered does not coincide with the calendar month. Different segments of the alphabet cover different periods. Thus, one cycle may terminate on the 5th of the month and another on the 6th; others, on the 8th, 10th, 11th; and so on. Most of the cycle plans provide for about 20 cycles.

Practically all cycle billing systems utilize a single-sheet statement on which only the amounts of the transactions (charges, credits, and payments) are machine-posted on the closing or billing date. The statement and posting media are microfilmed to provide a detailed record for the store and then are mailed to the customer. As a by-product of the billing operation, the bookkeeping machine clears the totals of charges, credits, and payments on a separate ledger card for each customer, which then shows the total activity for that cycle. These customer ledger cards generally provide space for from three to four or more years' history.

Since the media under cycle billing are posted to the records only once a month for each customer, the problem of physical and accounting control over loose media in the files is very important. Physical control is achieved by using well-designed filing equipment that can be locked when necessary and by limiting the number of people who have access to the files during the month. Accounting control, at the outset, was provided by having a separate control account for each tray or section of a cycle. Later installations have but a single control for each cycle. Obviously, the fewer the controls, the less the necessity for transfers between controls to correct sorting errors, but the greater the difficulty in locating posting errors.

A later trend has been to eliminate individual cycle controls and to set up separate proofs of billing. Among retail accountants, however, there are many who are firmly opposed to the elimination of individual cycle controls. In setting up proofs of billing, separate records are made of the media released for billing during the calendar or fiscal month. A single total, or two or three separate totals of such media, are then proved against the amounts billed during the period. In building up this separate record, the cut-off date of each cycle must be observed in order that only the media billed during the month shall be registered in such record. For example, a salescheck written on March 10 for a cycle that closes on March 15 will have been billed at the end of March, and accordingly will be registered on a separate record of March billings. However, a salescheck written on March 18 for the same cycle would appear in the register for April billings because it will not be billed until April 15.

**Credit and collection procedures.** Collection procedures vary on the basis of the type of account, different techniques being used for charge or open accounts, revolving-credit accounts, and installment accounts.

**Authorization methods.** The authorization problem in department stores is a troublesome one because of the necessity for speed. The authorization of charge sales can be made prior to the release of the merchandise to the customer by a telephone system from the sales floor to the credit office or by use of pneumatic tubes. In many instances, however, the customer's identification plate (Charga-Plate, credit plate, and the like) is accepted as authorization for all purchases up to a set amount, such as $25, $50, or even higher. Likewise, in many cases charge purchases below some set amount, such as $10 or $5, are given to the customer without any authorization. The soundness of this liberal floor release policy has been demonstrated by the low bad debt losses experienced by department stores.

In those instances where the store wishes to prevent further charges to an account because of "over limits," the matter is handled by personal request to the customer over the telephone or by mail. Where this step does not curtail charges to the account, the larger charges are intercepted under the drawback system involving deliveries, described below, or by the system of routine authorization of sales above the floor release limit through the use of the telephone or the tube system. In very rare cases, a notice to watch for attempted use of certain charge accounts might be sent to the selling floor.

**Drawback system.** If merchandise is to be delivered, many stores use the drawback system. Under this plan, the original copy of the charge salescheck is reviewed by someone from the credit department after the customer has left the store and after the merchandise has been released for delivery. The checking is completed prior to actual delivery of the merchandise to the customer. If the sale is disapproved, the delivery department is notified by the preparation of the drawback form, and the merchandise is held at that point for a limited time pending ultimate disposition of the sale.

**Cash receipts.** There is no peculiarity about the cash receipts operation. The sheer volume of transactions makes division of cash-handling duties practical, and this distribution results in a good system of internal control. Cash is taken in at the floor registers, in the tube room, and directly by the cashier's office. The cash registers receive the major part of the cash sales and provide control totals by department and frequently by salesperson. The cash, together with a report of the register reading, is sent directly to the cashier's office in the change bags of individual salespeople or cashiers. The register tapes are sent to the sales audit department. The total cash turned in is verified by the cashier's office against the reports, and the verified reports are then turned over to the sales audit department for comparison with the register-tape totals.

A number of department stores throughout the country have made arrangements with banks to process all collections on accounts receivable. The bank credits the store's bank account immediately for all receipts and sends to the store either the bill head, if the customer has enclosed it, or the envelope itself on which the customer's name and address and the amount of the payment are indicated. The use of a bank for processing cash receipts is especially advantageous, since the deposit is credited to the store's bank account from 24 to 72 hours sooner than it otherwise would be. Where this arrangement is made, the return envelopes included with the statement when it is mailed to the customer are marked for a special post office box to which the bank has access. Different post office boxes can be used for different types of accounts or for sections of the accounts.

Customers are urged to return the bill head when making payments whether in person or by mail. The bill head is sent from the cashier's office directly to the accounts receivable department to be used as a posting medium (or to that department from the sales audit department, which received it from the cashier's office). If the bill head is not returned, a remittance slip is prepared or the information is placed on the customer's envelope.

The cash receipts book of a department store usually is not a book as such, but might consist of a peg strip form with all of the sources of the daily receipts printed on successive lines. Examples of the printed descriptions are: gross cash sales, accounts receivable collections, collections of vendors' debit balances, demonstrator allowances, mail order cash, waste paper sales, vending machine collections, advertising allowances, and others. At the end of the month, a summary of the peg strips becomes the cash receipts entry for the month.

**Purchase orders.** Purchase orders are written by the buyers at the store or in the market. (See Figure 2.) A minimum of four copies of the purchase order, used as follows, is typical:

| | |
|---|---|
| Original | —to the vendor |
| Duplicate | —to Accounts Payable Department |
| Triplicate | —to Receiving and Marking Department |
| Quadruplicate | —to unit control section and then returned to buyer |

The distinguishing feature of a department store order is a space (blocked out on the original copy) for inserting the expected selling price. Since stores commonly follow extensive budgeting procedures relating to inventory and purchasing, frequently called an "open-to-buy" system, it is usually necessary that the retail value be known when the order is placed. This retail value is used for (1) determining the amount of orders placed and open orders (some stores make this determination by using cost figures

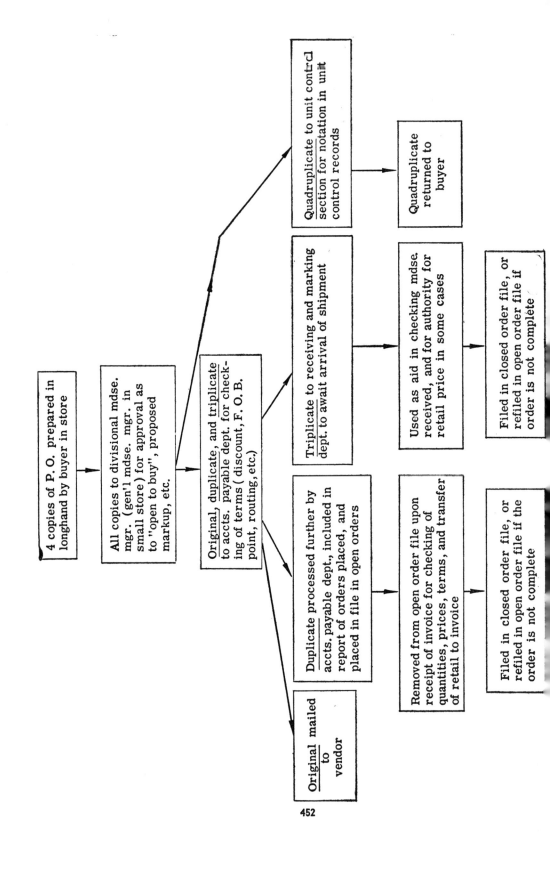

- 4 copies of P. O. prepared in longhand by buyer in store

- All copies to divisional mdse. mgr. (gen'l mdse. mgr. in small store) for approval as to "open to buy", proposed markup, etc.

- Original, duplicate, and triplicate to accts. payable dept. for checking of terms (discount, F. O. B. point, routing, etc.)

- Quadruplicate to unit control section for notation in unit control records
  - Quadruplicate returned to buyer

- Triplicate to receiving and marking dept. to await arrival of shipment
  - Used as aid in checking mdse. received, and for authority for retail price in some cases
  - Filed in closed order file, or refiled in open order file if order is not complete

- Duplicate processed further by accts. payable dept., included in report of orders placed, and placed in file in open orders
  - Removed from open order file upon receipt of invoice for checking of quantities, prices, terms, and transfer of retail to invoice
  - Filed in closed order file, or refiled in open order file if the order is not complete

- Original mailed to vendor

452

and then raising them to estimated retail by use of percentages), and (2) "retailing" incoming shipments under a pre-retailing system.

Since, under the retail inventory method, it is necessary to know the retail value of all items going into inventory, the retail price is inserted next to each item listed on the invoice and these prices are accumulated. In many stores the retail price for each item is indicated by the buyer after the merchandise has been received and checked, but just prior to the time it is marked. In other stores, the retail price of each item appearing on the purchase order is transferred to the invoice by a clerk in the order-checking office and is indicated on the price tickets appearing on the merchandise *without further approval* by the buyer. This latter system is known as "pre-retailing."

In some stores the pre-retailing system applies only to certain classes of merchandise or to certain departments, such as those dealing largely in staples, where the retail price is likely not to change between the time the order is placed and the time the merchandise is marked; in other departments, such as ready-to-wear, a buyer's approval is necessary before the merchandise is marked even though the retail price may have been transferred to the invoice.

**Receiving.** Department stores receive merchandise in one or more central locations, but almost never on the selling floor. There may be some exceptions, as in the case of food departments, where perishable items are delivered directly to the selling floor.

Shipments are checked in the receiving department, generally against the invoice (see Figure 3). If an invoice is not available, checking slips are prepared. Blind checking, that is, checking a shipment without the use of a purchase order or an invoice, is seldom used. Since a chronological record of receipts (receiving record) is necessary, and since some of the information on the receiving record should appear on the invoice before it can be recorded and paid, the use of unit receivers for this purpose has become popular in recent years. Under this system, several copies of a receiving record are headed simultaneously by using a mechanical device, such as a writing register or a peg board. Several of the copies are ejected from the machine or are lifted from the peg board, but one or two copies remain in the machine or on the peg board. These latter copies are not complete in themselves but are part of a continuous form on which only one line of information from the full receiving slip appears; they serve as a control. The ejected copies are attached to the cartons, which are then transferred to the checking and marking areas. The ultimate disposition of a typical three-part unit receiver is as follows:

Original —attached to the invoice as an invoice apron.
Duplicate —used at time of checking and marking to show the size

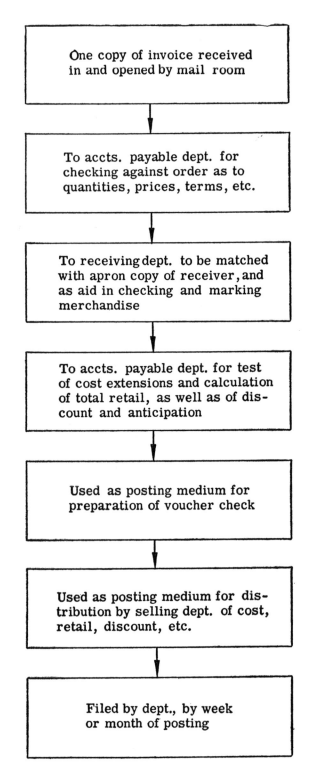

**Fig. 3. Flow of Vendor's Invoice for Merchandise Where Invoice Is Received by Mail.**

and color distribution of the shipment, and then sent to buyer and to unit control.

Triplicate —follows merchandise into stock or to selling floor.

The forms are prenumbered and the numbers correspond with the numbered lines of the key sheet that remains in the register or on the writing board. After the invoices have been processed for buyers' signatures (if the store requires a buyer's signature), and by the accounts payable department, they may be checked against the key sheet, so that all shipments are accounted for and some protection afforded against the payment of duplicate invoices.

**Purchase and expense payments.** In practically all department stores, the volume of purchases is great enough to warrant the use of mechanical equipment to provide for the accumulation of purchases and the preparation of checks. Purchases are recorded by department and sometimes by classification of merchandise within a department. The typical information appearing on the purchase distribution sheet for each department would be date of invoice, vendor, invoice cost, invoice retail, and cash discount available. Where the voucher check is prepared simultaneously with the original of certain sections of the distribution sheet, the vendor's name would not appear on the voucher portion of the check.

The accounts payable department generally makes the distribution of the purchase and prepares the voucher check; in many instances, it even mechanically signs the checks. Two basic systems are used in preparing the purchase distribution sheet and voucher checks: (1) the dual system, and (2) the unit system.

*Dual system.* A batch of invoices is sorted by department, posted to the departmental purchase distribution sheets, and then re-sorted by vendor and posted to the voucher check. Some of the voucher checks may have been in the open-voucher file, having been prepared for prior invoices. The two runs, that is, the distribution run and the voucher run, must balance.

*Unit system.* Under the unit system, the purchase distribution sheet and the voucher check are prepared simultaneously. This method becomes complicated if a built-up voucher is used, that is, if a store attempts to accumulate all the invoices from one vendor on one voucher. In such cases, particularly if the vendor sells to more than one department, a single voucher might have to be extracted from the file several times during a "run" covering all departments. However, many department stores have abandoned the use of a built-up voucher and now put each invoice on a separate voucher even though a number of invoices from the same vendor may be processed on the same day. This change has made the use of the unit system more practical than in the past.

Accounts payable ledgers are seldom, if ever, used in department stores. However, some stores use what is loosely called a ledger system. Actually, the ledger consists of an extra copy of the voucher portion of the check, which provides for an accumulation of the purchases by vendor. Without this record, the accumulated purchases from any one vendor would have to be determined by an analysis of the invoices or copies of the voucher checks.

Two copies are made of the purchase distribution sheets: one remains as the official office copy and is the basis for posting amounts to the retail inventory ledger; the other is the buyer's copy.

Voucher checks generally are limited to two or three copies. The distribution of a three-copy voucher check is as follows:

Original        —to the vendor
Duplicate       —filed alphabetically by vendor
Triplicate      —filed numerically by check number (as the check register)

It will be noted that no copy of the voucher check is attached to the invoice, which in the above illustration would be filed by department. Obviously, if it were felt that a copy of the voucher check should be attached to the invoice, a fourth copy would have to be prepared, unless the invoices were filed alphabetically, in which case the duplicate could be attached to the invoice. Some of the newer bookkeeping machines automatically provide a check register as a by-product of the unit posting operation described above. In such instances, no copy of the voucher check is necessary for filing by check number.

Under some accounts payable systems, the upper portion of the voucher check is prepared by the same bookkeeping machine on which the bottom portion is prepared, but as a separate run; in other instances, the upper portion is prepared on a special check-writing machine which prepares the check register and may or may not sign the check at the same time. Where checks are signed in the accounts payable department under this method, appropriate features are provided on the machine to permit the establishment of a proper system of internal control. A machine signature, properly controlled, is the preferred method because of the great volume of checks issued.

If a machine signature is used, the number of checks signed should be reconciled with the machine controls by someone independent of the signing process, and then the checks should be released immediately to the mailing department. Similarly, if a manual signature system is used, the checks should be released immediately to the mailing department and should not be returned to the accounts payable department.

The totals from the purchase and expense distribution sheets give rise to the entries charging Cost Purchases and expense and crediting Accounts Payable. A summary of the net amount of checks issued serves as the basis of the entry crediting Cash and charging Accounts Payable. Discount earned is set up as a part of the Accounts Payable entry, by showing the latter figure net of discounts, or as a part of the Cash Disbursements entry.

**Discount and anticipation.** A prime requirement of the department store accounts payable department is to process invoices quickly enough to be able to take advantage of the regular cash discount (which ranges from 1 per cent to 8 per cent, depending upon the type of merchandise) and the additional cash discount (anticipation) which is permitted by certain vendors if an invoice is paid *before* the regular discount date. Anticipation is computed at an annual rate of 6 per cent for the exact number of days prior to the discount date that the payment is made.

It is common practice for stores to charge invoices to Purchases at the gross amount net of trade discounts and to consider the actual cash discount and anticipation taken as an addition to gross margin, department by department. At the end of the year, under the retail inventory method, this results in an overstatement of the inventory value, which is corrected by setting up an allowance for discounts in inventory, computed on the basis of the relationship of the average discount for each department to that department's year-end inventory. No adjustment to this reserve is made on a month-to-month basis.

## Cost of sales and inventory

**Inventory practices peculiar to the business.** With very few exceptions, which occur primarily in the food departments, departmental inventories are valued at lower of cost or market, as determined by the retail inventory method. The retail inventory method formula for arriving at the value of inventory at cost and retail (see below) is applied separately for each department. This method at the same time provides departmental percentages of initial markups, markdowns, discounts, stock shortages, and gross margin. The necessary statistics are maintained for each department and in total; subtotals for groups of departments may be introduced where desired.

The formula under the retail inventory method is as follows:

1. Beginning inventory at retail plus purchases at retail, plus additional markups (if any), minus sales, minus markdowns, minus estimated shrinkage at retail, equals ending inventory at retail.

2. Ending inventory at retail multiplied by the applicable cost percentage equals ending inventory at cost or market, whichever is lower. The applicable cost percentage is obtained by dividing the total of the beginning inventory and purchases at cost by the total of the beginning inven-

tory, purchases, and additional markups at retail. The applicable cost percentage is the complement of the "markon percentage." Thus, if the applicable cost percentage is 60 per cent, the markon percentage is 40 per cent.

3. Beginning inventory at cost plus purchases at cost (including freight in) minus ending inventory at cost equals cost of sales.

The retail inventory computations are usually made monthly. The applicable cost percentage is arrived at by taking the inventory at the beginning of the fiscal period plus the cumulative purchases and markups to date. The prevailing practice among department stores is to use a six months' cumulative percentage—that is, cumulative through the first six months and starting over again at the beginning of the fall season, or second six months. Only in unusual cases would a single month's markup percentage be acceptable for pricing the ending inventory.

The information necessary to compile the departmental figures is derived from the following sources:

*Opening inventory.* Retail and cost are the same as the closing inventory for the previous accounting period (see "Closing inventory" below).

*Purchases.* When an invoice for merchandise is received, it is extended at retail and entered in the departmental purchase record at both cost and retail. At the close of each month, the total purchases at cost and retail are carried to the departmental inventory record.

*Price revisions.* When the selling price of any article is to be changed, the buyer prepares a price revision form that shows description, quantity, old price per unit, revised price per unit, and the reason for the price revision. The marker prepares new price tags *only from the price revision form* and affixes them to the merchandise. The form is extended and the amount of the revision determined. The price revision forms are summarized for each department by types, such as markups, markdowns, and markdown cancellations, and at the end of the accounting period the amounts are carried forward to the departmental inventory record.

*Sales.* The departmental net sales are obtained from the audited sales report; likewise, discounts allowed employees and others are obtained from the sales audit department.

*Stock shortages.* In the departmental inventory record a column is provided for estimated stock shortages, expressed as a percentage of sales. If interim physical inventories reveal shortages in excess of the estimate, the estimate is increased. At the close of the accounting period, a physical inventory is taken by departments at retail and compared with the book inventory of the department before the estimated shortages as determined above is deducted. The difference between the two figures represents the actual amount of the shortage or overage at retail, and the estimated shortages are adjusted to the actual amounts determined at the inventory date.

*Closing inventory.* Retail is determined from the book inventory which has been adjusted to the actual physical inventory.

Cost or market, whichever is lower, is determined by applying to the retail the applicable cost percentage as set forth in the formula above.

In applying the retail inventory method, distinction must be made between markdown cancellations and markups. Markups enter into the applicable cost percentage, but markdown cancellations offset markdowns, which do not enter into the applicable cost percentage. A markdown cancellation occurs when goods are marked down for a sale and the original retail price is subsequently restored on the unsold merchandise.

**Control of inventory levels through open-to-buy's.** The control of inventory levels is achieved through "open-to-buy" plans for each department. These plans are discussed in connection with reports at page 463.

## Payroll procedures peculiar to the business

**Timekeeping and payroll.** Although time clocks are being used in an increasing number of stores, most stores still have their employees sign an attendance sheet. Because of the considerable shifting of salespeople from one department to another, these sheets are usually kept within the department. After review by the department manager, they are forwarded to the timekeeping and payroll department for the preparation of the payroll.

The executive payroll is made up separately for whatever pay period applies—monthly, semi-monthly, or weekly. The non-executive payroll is usually made up weekly. Preparation of this payroll is complicated by the variations in the basis of earnings of both full-time and part-time employees. In addition to the usual straight-time and overtime elements, there are commissions on sales (straight commissions or quota bonus plan), added commissions on selected items, PM's ("push money" or "premium money") on special items, allowances for new charge accounts, and the like.

Payroll payments are usually made in cash, although some stores pay by check and at less frequent periods than once a week. Facilities are usually provided for cashing paychecks in the store.

**Allocation of payroll expense.** The charging of earnings to the various expense accounts is made on the basis of the selling or non-selling departments in which the employees work. Usually this is determined by reference to the employee's number, which incorporates the number of the selling or non-selling department.

The salaries of employees who perform more than one function should be apportioned on the basis of the time devoted to each function. For employees who permanently divide their time among different duties, the split may be fixed; for example, 50 per cent to assistant buying and 50 per cent to selling. For employees who are temporarily shifted from one function to another, transfers of payroll should be made to the appropriate accounts, provided that a significant amount of time is involved, say, 20 per cent of an employee's time for a payroll period.

## Plant and equipment records—depreciation

**Depreciation methods.** Stores generally do not maintain a plant ledger in which the individual fixed assets are shown separately and on which depreciation is computed individually. Instead, assets are grouped into the broad categories of land and buildings, improvements to leased property, store fixtures and equipment, and rolling equipment (automobiles and trucks). Within these categories there might be further refinements reflecting differences in depreciation rates.

In the case of rolling equipment, and sometimes office machines, the record of acquisition dates is kept by individual items, and upon disposition or trade-in the accumulated depreciation applicable to that item is precisely determined.

In most cases, the depreciation of property and equipment is computed on a straight-line basis. In the case of fixtures on the selling floor, the rate should take into account the short life occasioned by the display aspects of the fixtures.

## Reports to management

**Financial reports.** The major financial reports, issued on a monthly basis, are:

1. Balance sheet
2. Income statement
3. Detailed statement of operating expenses

Although there are no peculiarities in the balance sheet and income statement, the detailed statement of operating expenses in a department store is peculiar in the following respects: The percentage which each expense is of net sales is shown, as well as a comparison both with the budget and with the last year. In many areas of expense where records of production are kept in terms of some common denominator, the standard production per hour and the actual production per hour may also be shown. (See Figure 4.)

**Departmental merchandising and operating reports.** Departmental merchandising reports are prepared monthly for each selling department. They show the following information for each month and cumulatively: dollar net sales, percentage of sales returns, initial markup percentage, dollar markdowns and markdown percentage, stock shortage percentage, percentage of workroom costs, cash discounts percentage, dollar gross margin, and percentage of gross margin. Such reports also show the corresponding figures for the preceding year, as well as other data, such as

Expense Center _____ No. _____

Period _____

| Week Ending | Paid Hours | Dollars | | | | Employees (40 hr. units) | | | | Production | | | | |
|---|---|---|---|---|---|---|---|---|---|---|---|---|---|---|
| | This Year | This Year | Budget | Last Year | | This Year | Budget | Last Year | | Hours Worked | Units of Work | Per Hour | | |
| | | | | | | | | | | | | Actual | Standard | % |

Fig. 4. Payroll and Production Analysis.

average gross sale, turnover, required markup, expected markdown percentage, required gross margin percentage, and other items. The departmental merchandising report may show direct operating expenses and contribution to occupancy and overhead. It may also show an allocation of occupancy and overhead leading to a departmental net profit figure.

In some cases the departmental operating statement is divided into two reports. The first statement, which is issued early each month, shows only the elements leading to gross margin, while the second statement, issued several working days later, starts with gross margin and ends with contribution to occupancy and overhead, or ends with net profit if occupancy and overhead are allocated to the selling departments.

The contribution type of statement probably is the most widely used,

OPERATING EXPENSE REPORT

Month _____     Department _____

|  | Month | | Year to Date | |
|---|---|---|---|---|
|  | This Year | Last Year | This Year | Last Year |
|  | Amount % | Amount % | Amount % | Amount % |
| Net sales ...................... | $ | $ | $ | $ |
| Gross margin and cash discount .. |  |  |  |  |
| Direct expenses ................ |  |  |  |  |
| Contribution ................... |  |  |  |  |
| DETAIL OF EXPENSE: |  |  |  |  |
| Publicity: |  |  |  |  |
| Newspaper advertising ........ |  |  |  |  |
| Other advertising ............ |  |  |  |  |
| Window display .............. |  |  |  |  |
| Buying: |  |  |  |  |
| Salaries and commissions ...... |  |  |  |  |
| Traveling expense ............ |  |  |  |  |
| Merchandise clericals .......... |  |  |  |  |
| Selling: |  |  |  |  |
| Salespeople ................ |  |  |  |  |
| Other personnel .............. |  |  |  |  |
| Total direct expense .......... | $ | $ | $ | $ |
| Distributed charges: |  |  |  |  |
| Administrative ................ |  |  |  |  |
| Occupancy .................... |  |  |  |  |
| Publicity .................... |  |  |  |  |
| Buying ...................... |  |  |  |  |
| Selling ...................... |  |  |  |  |
| Delivery .................... |  |  |  |  |
| Indirect expense ................ |  |  |  |  |
| Total expenses ................ | $ | $ | $ | $ |
| Operating profit ................ |  |  |  |  |

Fig. 5. Departmental Operating Expense Report.

although many stores arrive at both a contribution figure and a net profit figure for each department. Generally speaking, the contribution is the amount remaining after deducting direct expenses from departmental gross margin. (See Figure 5.) The items considered to be direct expenses for selling departments may vary from store to store, depending upon the philosophy of management, but, as a general rule, they should cover those easily identified expenses that would be eliminated if the department were eliminated. Such expenses are buyers' and assistant buyers' salaries, salespeople's salaries, stock help, advertising costs (including space charge), travel, and delivery. In some cases, stores will include as direct expenses interest on investment in inventory as well as salaries of unit control clerks. The inclusion of delivery as a direct expense is proper only if package delivery costs and furniture delivery costs are separately allocated on the basis of package pieces (or units) and furniture pieces (or units) delivered for each department.

In recent years there has been an increasing trend toward the preparation of departmental reports depicting data as to classifications of merchandise within selling departments. Rarely are such reports tied in to the general accounting system. In most cases, the classification data relate to sales and inventory; in other cases, markdown information is supplied. Only in rare instances will classification reports provide information as to gross margin. In some cases "open to buy" is computed by classification.

**Departmental merchandise plans and open-to-buy reports.** Merchandise plans are prepared at six-month intervals to establish planned sales, inventory, and markdown levels for the coming season. Using these planned figures, the monthly "purchase power" or "open to buy" is computed as follows:

> Ending inventory
> + Planned sales for month
> + Expected or normal markdowns
> — Beginning inventory

Using the merchandise plans as a starting point, open-to-buy reports are prepared at weekly or ten-day intervals to reflect the current status of the plan. On this report, orders placed are deducted from the open to buy; sales are deducted from inventory; and receipts (closed orders) are added to inventory. Once a month, the open-to-buy reports are corrected or brought into line with the official inventory as computed by the retail inventory method.

**Unit control reports.** Outside of the accounting department, all stores keep some records of the movement of goods in terms of physical quantities or units. In some instances—for example, furniture and appliances—this is a perpetual inventory system; in other cases, like ready-to-wear, it is primarily a sales analysis prepared from stubs of price tickets; and in still other cases—for example, notions, hardware, and cosmetics—it consists of taking periodic inventories to determine unit sales by a reverse calculation. (Under reverse calculation, previous unit inventory plus purchases minus present inventory gives units of sales.)  From this mass of detail, a wide variety of unit reports relating to sales and stock by color, size, price, style, material, and the like, are prepared, which permit buyers to place new orders intelligently.

## Suggested modification for a small business

If the services rendered to customers are the same as those offered by large stores, the accounting system for small department stores cannot be very different from that of large stores.  Simplification can result, however, from the use of fewer selling departments, fewer expense accounts, and fewer reports.

Because of the wide dissemination of information in the trade press and at conventions regarding elaborate selling department breakdowns, classification analyses within selling departments, and detailed expense accounting, many smaller stores fall into the error of adopting techniques that are applicable only to larger stores where close contact with operations is difficult.

# 17

# Drugs (Manufacturing)

## (Decentralized Distribution and Customer Receivable Accounting)

by

**V. L. FISHER**

Certified Public Accountant; Controller, Merck Sharp & Dohme,
Division of Merck & Co., Inc.

## Industry characteristics that affect the accounting system

**Nature of the business.** The drug manufacturing industry, by its nature, is dedicated to the preservation of human life. It is relied upon by the medical profession to provide ever-improved life-saving and distress-relieving remedies. It is engaged in an ever-expanding search for new chemicals and compounds to combat the major diseases not yet conquered by medical science.

The standards of manufacturing that must be maintained are of the highest in modern industry. Minimum requirements are established by various government agencies, but in many cases even more stringent standards are voluntarily set by the industry itself.

Research is a fundamental requirement in the industry. The success of the industry and the fulfillment of its social responsibilities require a large expenditure of effort and monies in this phase of the business. New discoveries and products must be thoroughly tested and proven safe and efficacious by clinical tests before they can be released for sale.

The threat of epidemics requiring large quantities of life-saving vaccines is ever present. To provide for any emergency, maintenance of proper inventories and the ability to produce the needed items quickly are important. On the other hand, many products of this type have a short, effective life and therefore cannot be produced and stockpiled indefinitely.

**Types of establishments.** A large proportion of the products manufactured by the drug industry are of such a nature that a doctor's prescription is required before they can be sold. A firm manufacturing principally products of this nature is known as an *ethical* drug manufacturer. As distinguished from the ethical manufacturer, firms producing drugs requiring no prescription and which are therefore sold "over-the-counter" are known as *proprietary* drug manufacturers. Although some of the products dispensed only by prescription involve more complicated manufacturing procedures, the principal difference between the ethical and the proprietary firms lies in the area of advertising, promotion, and distribution.

**Governmental and other control.** Because of the variation in strength, purity, and stability of crude drugs and raw materials, state and Federal agencies have passed food and drug laws. These laws set up certain standards with which the drug industry must comply.

The National Institutes of Health establish the standards for human biologicals. The Agriculture Research Service (formerly the Bureau of Animal Industry) sets standards for veterinary biologicals. The *U. S. Pharmacopoeia* and *National Formulary* set standards for drugs and certain pharmaceutical preparations.

The National Institutes of Health and the Agriculture Research Service are Federal Government agencies. The *U. S. Pharmacopoeia* and *National Formulary*, although prepared by private groups, including representatives from industry, medicine, and pharmacy, are recognized by law as the official standards for many drugs and pharmaceutical preparations. *New and Non-official Remedies*, published by the American Medical Association, includes still another group of drugs or preparations found acceptable by their Council on Pharmacy and Chemistry.

Narcotics and their preparations, of course, probably have the strictest governmental control of all pharmaceutical groups. Certain other materials, such as alcohol, have special control requirements. All of these regulations and government control measures affect the requirements of the accounting system to varying degrees.

**Taxes and licenses.** Large quantities of alcohol are used in the industry. Federal taxes paid on alcohol purchases are substantial and call for close control, not only to comply with government regulations, but to insure correct and complete claims for drawback of the tax on alcohol used in the production of approved medicinal products. Additional tax refund can be obtained if these products are exported.

**General features.** Several general features have an important bearing on the accounting system:

*Seasonal nature.* Depending upon the products of the particular firm, the seasonal factor may vary in degree of fluctuation. However, there are many drug preparations for infections and ailments more prevalent during the winter months. Inventory build-up of such products must be controlled not only from the standpoint of effective dating but also from the standpoint of financial control.

*Research.* In recent years, the industry has undertaken a major role in medical research which was originally covered largely by medical centers and institutions of higher learning. Year by year, the efforts and expenditures have increased. The results have been highly productive and the therapeutic agents discovered have greatly affected the practice of medicine and the progress of the industry. These discoveries continue to bring about rapid obsolescence of older products.

*Medical services.* New products developed by research may consist of combinations of well-known drugs or of entirely new compounds. After gaining all possible information from test tubes and animal experimentation, it is often necessary to make clinical trials of the new drug. This is accomplished by the company medical staff in institutions with which they may be connected or by outside clinical investigations.

The clinical evidence of both safety and efficacy of the drug must be compiled and submitted to the various agencies that have been set up to safeguard the welfare of the public. Only after those agencies have evaluated the tests and have given official approval can the drug be removed from quarantine and marketed.

Research efforts are providing new drugs for which no medical literature exists. Technical publications and informative brochures must be provided for the information and guidance of physicians using the new drugs.

*Quality control.* Safety, identity, and uniform quality of products are a basic requirement in the industry. Although Federal, state, and local regulations assure the minimum compliance with acceptable pharmaceutical practice, the industry itself usually sets standards far above the actual legal requirements.

There are myriad controls and control records that must be made throughout the production procedures. Every container of each raw material must be tested and identified upon receipt and before use. Dangerous drugs, as well as pathogenic material, must be handled with extreme care and every precaution observed to prevent contamination of or with other materials or products. Constant testing and inspection must be carried on for the sake of safety, standardization, and compliance with the multitude of regulations as well as with individual company standards. Rejections and discards, particularly with respect to new products, may be sizeable and usually represent a complete loss.

**Functional peculiarities of the business.** Materials for the production of drugs and medicines are gathered from all parts of the world. The source of a material sometimes becomes inaccessible, or the material may be too costly for production. Synthesis of components necessary to form a compound has thus become one of the important functions of the industry. This ability to develop the necessary materials has provided many life-saving (so called "wonder") drugs not otherwise possible and at progressively lower cost. Inventory-valuation problems multiply as rapidly changing production techniques continue to improve the yields of such products.

The relationship of the manufacturer with the trade is unusual in the ethical drug industry. The manufacturer's products are not advertised to the lay public, but, through professional journals, to doctors, dentists, druggists, veterinarians, and the members of allied professions. Company sales representatives make regular calls on doctors and druggists. These men are usually graduates of pharmacy schools or men who have had pre-medical work in college. Their work is a service to the doctors by keeping them informed of new developments and uses of drugs. The sales effort is directed toward influencing the doctor to write prescriptions for the company's products. The products are purchased through the druggist.

Technical data for the doctors' use and technical publications play an important role in the promotion of products.

**Principal accounting problems.** The various characteristics peculiar to the industry present no particularly troublesome accounting problems. As in most processing industries, the accurate determination of manufacturing cost and the proper valuation of inventories comprise the principal area of concern.

Major manufacturers usually carry a large number of products of varying package sizes at many locations. Anywhere from 20,000 to 50,000 customers are usually serviced by hundreds of sales representatives. The nature of the business requires that orders be processed within 24 hours of receipt. These conditions result in a very large volume of transactions that require a complete integration of inventory control, warehousing, production planning, and sales statistics.

Continually changing processes, uncertainty of yields, production cycles, product obsolescence, and other factors introduce variables that must be constantly evaluated. The development and use of standard costs which will accurately reflect cost of goods and proper inventory valuations, while providing budgetary and administrative control, are therefore the area in which the most effort is required.

Nearly all prescription products and many of the "over-the-counter" items are packaged in a number of different strengths or dosage forms, and each of these in a number of different package sizes. In addition to this, a different finish or labeling is required for the various foreign markets. Since many firms have a large number of products in their line, it can readily be seen that comprehensive product statistics are very important and require careful development from the accounting records. Only if the records are designed to provide reliable data will they be of value to management in gauging the market, controlling the inventory, and directing promotional effort.

Selling in foreign markets, as all major firms in the industry do, creates many specialized financial and accounting problems. The scope of the problems varies, depending upon whether manufacturing operations are conducted in foreign locations, the type of corporate structure, and various other factors. In any case, the accounting treatment of exchange and conversion problems and the method of reflecting foreign operations in consolidated statements are always troublesome areas.

## Functional organization

**Functional divisions.** The major functional divisions or activities in most firms in the industry include:

| | |
|---|---|
| Production | Research |
| Sales and promotion (domestic) | Medical |
| Warehouse and distribution | Quality control |

Foreign operations

In addition to these, there are corollary functions, such as purchasing, engineering, package development, personnel, and various other administrative groups.

The grouping or arrangement of the various functional activities naturally varies among firms. Regardless of this, each will have its effect upon and be affected by accounting. The responsible accounting executive is dependent upon each of the functional areas for some part of the basic information that is eventually reflected in the accounting records. He, in turn, furnishes facts and figures to the functional areas and to management, both for advance planning and as a report of results obtained for information and necessary action.

**Chart of organization.** One form of organization is shown in Figure 1. The relationships of the various accounting departments with the other functional areas in this organization, as well as the interrelationships between various functional areas, can best be illustrated by relating them to some of the principal functions of the accounting group.

*Accounting for domestic sales and related functions:*

1. Sales forecasts and sales budgets are developed and furnished to the budget department through the joint efforts of the sales and the economic research divisions.

2. Copies of customer sales invoices and credits prepared by domestic branches are sent by branches direct to machine accounting for preparation of accounting entries and accumulation of various sales statistics which, in turn, are furnished to the sales division and the economic research division.

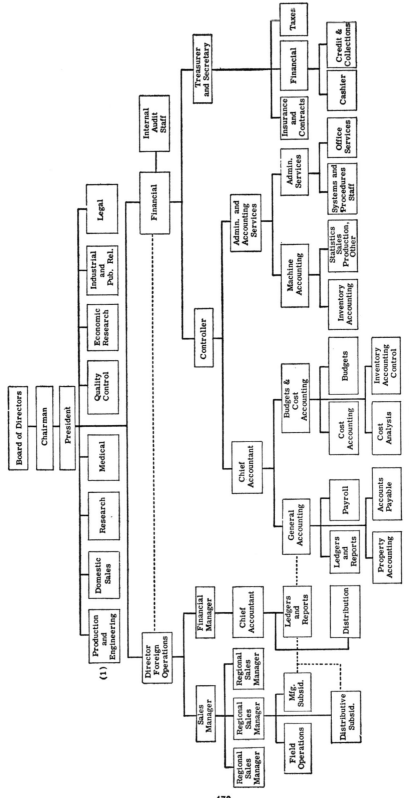

**Fig. 1. Organization Chart.**

(1) Includes purchasing, package development, receiving, warehousing, and production control.

470

3. Credit and collection policies are developed jointly by the sales and the financial departments. Branch credit managers supply the financial department with aging analyses for control purposes. The financial department arranges to have credit report services made available to branches.

4. Customer collections are deposited by branches in blocked bank accounts and reported to the financial department. This department accounts for and controls the transfer of such funds into operating accounts.

5. Branch disbursements are reported to an accounting department for audit and recording.

*Inventory accounting:*

1. Domestic warehouse and branch inventories are charged on the basis of production and finishing department reports and credited for reported sales and transfers between warehouse and branches.

2. Cycle inventories are taken by branch personnel and the physical counts are reported to accounting for reconciliation and control.

3. Inventory detail records for raw materials and supplies are maintained by the production control department. The one set of records serves two purposes, for example, inventory accounting and making information available for production.

*Accounting for production and related functions:*

1. Material standards are based on formulas provided by quality control or standard methods supplied by the biological production department.

2. Labor standards come from engineering.

3. Various data for the development of burden rates are supplied by production and engineering.

4. Material usage, labor utilization, material transfers, in-process inventories, production losses, and the various other normal production reporting are supplied by production to accounting.

5. Accounting departments furnish various periodic statistical reports to production departments and production management.

6. Cost estimates are supplied by the cost department to the sales division for setting selling prices.

*Accounting for foreign operations:*

1. In the form of organization illustrated, a separate financial and accounting group maintains the records for sales other than direct export sales. This group is functionally responsible to the company's over-all financial executive.

2. Sales statistics are prepared by export accounting for export sales personnel as well as for company management.

*Other relationships and interrelationships:*

1. Budgeting for production and production service departments brings the close relationship between those departments and accounting into full play. The budget figures are developed by the budget department from production forecasts. They are modified and resolved through the combined efforts of the budget analysts and production personnel. Engineering provides floor-space allocations, distribution of engineering services, including heat, light and power, and other vital information. Production service departments provide the distribution of their services to production departments and to other service departments.

2. The sales division provides the basic advertising, promotion, and distribution budget figures.

3. There are close interrelationships between the research, medical, and sales divisions in product development and marketing.

4. Personnel authorizations and employee benefit information are supplied to the payroll department by industrial and public relations, which includes the personnel department.

In addition to these examples, there is a close relationship between accounting and all basic functions of the business. Many of the relationships are informal and not charted as such, but their existence is essential to the accounting department not only in its performance of a proper accounting job but also in its making the best use of accounting figures for planning and control.

## Principles and objectives of the system

**Principles to be applied in reflecting income, costs, and expenses.** The analysis of sales is a very important function which provides vital information to management. A large number of sales invoices and a long line of products normally preclude keeping such information on the general books. With few exceptions, therefore, sales are recorded in one account and sales information is developed on a statistical basis and disseminated to the various members of management in a series of reports.

A listing of sales by individual products, showing quantity and dollars for each size package of each product, is required by the people directly responsible for sales. For general management purposes, however, sales of products can be combined into a limited number of groups or classifications with perhaps a few major products being reported separately.

Many ways of classifying sales are available, and the choice must necessarily depend upon the individual firm. As a general rule, domestic and foreign sales are separated. A commonly used classification is a division between pharmaceuticals and biologicals. Other product groups might include:

Antibiotics        Sulfas
Vitamins         Narcotics
Blood Products

Company specialties—products protected by patents and therefore not sold by others—as opposed to competitive products, warrant special analysis. Government contract sales and any special processing sales usually comprise separate groups. Analysis by branches or territories and perhaps by types of customers or trade channels is important.

In all of these reports, comparison with prior periods provides added value.

It is fundamental that costs must be analyzed product by product and by product group. Cost systems vary widely as to the amount and accuracy of product costs provided. The cost system outlined in a later section will provide standard manufacturing cost for each product for this purpose. In addition to variances from standard, there are other non-departmental, non-standard cost items which require separate analysis. These might include, among others, deletions and discards, book inventory adjustments, and idle-plant expenses. These costs require close consideration and control by both the accounting group and production management.

Accounting for selling, promotion, warehousing, distribution, research, medical, and administrative expenses is usually done on an over-all basis. Control is exercised in total by departments and reported by general classifications. In the preparation of statistical operating reports, however, many different methods of allocating expense to products may be used.

Administrative control requires the development of comparative statistics for relating the amount of expense in various departments or classifications to the volume of services performed or, as in the case of advertising, to the products to which it applies.

Other—non-operating—income and expenses require special analysis. The major concern with the important items is whether they are properly controlled and correctly accounted for.

**Specific objectives of the system.** The specific major objectives which the system is designed to accomplish are:

1. To provide not only accurate but sufficiently interpretive financial and operating figures for management use in basic planning for the business.

2. To provide a report of actual performance as compared with existing plans reflected in the budget for each department and for each area of the business.

3. To provide the information necessary for control and to indicate any needed corrective action in any of the various areas of the business.

Although these objectives are common to any well-run business, they incorporate those objectives which are more or less peculiar to drug manufacturing. If they are achieved, the accounting system will serve to provide the facts needed to evaluate and control any situation.

## Classification of accounts and books of account

### Balance sheet accounts.

| Control | | Debits from | Credits from |
|---|---|---|---|
| | *ASSETS* | | |
| 36 | *Cash* | | |
| 36–1 | Cash in Banks ........ | Voucher Distribution Journal, Cash Receipts Journal, Cash Disbursements Journal | Cash Disbursements Journal |
| 36–21 | Domestic Branch Bank Accounts .......... | Cash Receipts Journal | Cash Receipts Journal |
| 36–51 | Export Bank Accounts. | Do | Do |
| 36–61 | Plant Working Funds.. | Voucher Distribution Journal | Cash Disbursements Journal |
| 36–65 | Domestic Branch and (Blood) Donor Center Working Funds (an imprest fund) ...... | Do | Do |
| 37 | *Investments* (*Non-Affiliated*) | General Journal | General Journal |
| 38 | *Notes and Accounts Receivable* | | |
| 38–1 | Notes Receivable—Domestic ............ | Do | Cash Receipts Journal, Sales Journal |
| 38–35 | Notes Receivable—Export ............. | Do | Do |
| 38–45 | Accounts Receivable—Domestic .......... | Sales Journal, Cash Disbursements Journal | Cash Receipts Journal, Sales Journal |
| 38–75 | Accounts Receivable—Export ........... | Sales Journal, Voucher Distribution Journal | Cash Receipts Journal, General Journal |
| 38–80 | United States Alcohol Tax—Domestic ..... | Voucher Distribution Journal | Do |
| 38–81 | United States Alcohol Tax—Export ....... | General Journal | Cash Receipts Journal |
| 38–82 | Accounts Receivable—Export—Held for Exchange ............ | Do | Do |
| 38–85 | Accounts Receivable—Employees ........ | Voucher Distribution Journal, Cash Disbursements Journal | Do |
| 38–89 | Unissued Defense Bonds | Voucher Distribution Journal | Cash Receipts Journal, General Journal |

| Control | | Debits from | Credits from |
|---|---|---|---|
| 38–90 | Advances — Domestic— Travel, Etc. ........ | Voucher Distribution Journal, Cash Disbursements Journal | General Journal, Cash Receipts Journal |
| 38–92 | Advances for Construction .............. | Voucher Distribution Journal | General Journal |
| 38–93 | Advances — Export — Travel, Etc. ........ | Voucher Distribution Journal, General Journal, Cash Disbursements Journal | General Journal, Cash Receipts Journal |
| 38–95 | Accounts Receivable— Miscellaneous ....... | Voucher Distribution Journal, General Journal | Cash Receipts Journal |
| 38–96 | Accounts Receivable— Deposits on Containers | Voucher Distribution Journal | Voucher Distribution Journal, Cash Receipts Journal |
| 38–97 | Accounts Receivable— Leased Car Agreements | General Journal | Voucher Distribution Journal |
| 38–99 | Exchange for Cash .... | Cash Disbursements Journal | Cash Receipts Journal |
| 39 | *Accrued Income* | | |
| 39–1 | Accrued Interest—Domestic ............ | General Journal | Do |
| 39–2 | Accrued Interest—Export .............. | Do | General Journal |
| 39–11 | Accrued Royalties—Domestic ............ | Do | Cash Receipts Journal |
| 39–12 | Accrued Royalties—Export .............. | Do | Do |
| 39–13 | Accrued Dividends—Domestic ............ | Do | Do |
| 39–14 | Accrued Dividends—Export .............. | Do | Do |
| 40 | *Reserves for Doubtful Accounts* | | |
| 40–1 | Reserve for Doubtful Accounts—Domestic . | Do | General Journal |
| 40–50 | Reserve for Doubtful Accounts—Export | Do | Do |
| 41 | *Inventories* | | |
| 41–1 | Stores—Chemical Stock | Voucher Distribution Journal, General Journal | Do |
| 41–2 | Stores—Synthetic Chemicals .............. | Do | Do |
| 41–4 | Bleedings in Transit ... | General Journal | Do |
| 41–5 | Miscellaneous Manufacturing Materials .... | Voucher Distribution Journal, General Journal | Do |

| Control | | Debits from | Credits from |
|---|---|---|---|
| 41–8 | Stores—Production Animals .............. | Voucher Distribution Journal, General Journal | General Journal |
| 41–9 | Materials in Transit and Received Damaged .. | Voucher Distribution Journal | Do |
| 41–10 | Stores—Packaging Supplies .............. | Voucher Distribution Journal, General Journal | Do |
| 41–14 | Stores—Printing Stock | Voucher Distribution Journal | Do |
| 41–15 | Stores—General ....... | Voucher Distribution Journal, General Journal | Do |
| 41–16 | Stores—Fuel and Service Supplies ........ | Voucher Distribution Journal | Do |
| 41–22 | Supplies at Manufacturers .............. | Voucher Distribution Journal, General Journal | Do |
| 41–25 | Sample Materials and Supplies at Manufacturers ............ | Do | Do |
| 41–30 | Work in Process ...... | General Journal, Voucher Distribution Journal | Do |
| 41–36 | Work in Process at Manufacturers ...... | Voucher Distribution Journal, General Journal | General Journal, Voucher Distribution Journal |
| 41–37 | Work in Process at Outside Printers ........ | Do | General Journal |
| 41–39 | Work in Process—Export | General Journal | Do |
| 41–40 | Returned Goods ...... | Do | Do |
| 41–43 | Filled Stock .......... | Do | Do |
| 41–45 | Bulk Stock .......... | Voucher Distribution Journal, General Journal | Do |
| 41–50 | Finished Goods—Warehouse ............. | Do | Do |
| 41–51 | Bulk, Concentrates and Supplies—Warehouse | Do | Do |
| 41–55 | Finished Goods—Domestic Branches ..... | General Journal | Do |
| 41–60 | Finished Goods in Transit | Do | Do |
| 41–80 | Domestic Samples—Warehouse ......... | Voucher Distribution Journal, General Journal | Do |
| 41–81 | Export Samples—Warehouse .............. | Do | Do |
| 41–82 | Domestic Samples—Promotional Mailing Department .......... | Do | Do |
| 41–85 | Export Consignments | General Journal | Do |
| 41–86 | Finished Goods Packed for Shipment—Export | Do | Do |

| Control | | Debits from | Credits from |
|---|---|---|---|
| 41–87 | Bulk, Concentrates and Supplies Packed for Shipment—Export | General Journal | General Journal |
| 41–88 | Samples Packed for Shipment—Export .. | Do | Do |
| | Balance sheet classification: | | |
| | Sub Control Accounts 1–9 incl.—Raw Materials | | |
| | Sub Control Accounts 10–29 incl.—Supplies | | |
| | Sub Control Accounts 30–39 incl.—Work in Process | | |
| | Sub Control Accounts 40–89 incl.—Finished Merchandise | | |
| **46** | *Investments in and Due from Affiliated Companies and Branches* | | |
| 46–1 | Investments in Affiliated Companies ........ | Voucher Distribution Journal, General Journal | Cash Receipts Journal, General Journal |
| 46–11 | Investments in Affiliated Companies (Contra). | General Journal | General Journal |
| 46–16 | Due from Affiliated Companies and Branches .......... | Voucher Distribution Journal, Sales Journal, General Journal | Cash Receipts Journal, General Journal |
| **48** | *Fixed Property* | | |
| 48–1 | Land and Land Improvements ........ | General Journal | General Journal |
| 48–11 | Buildings ........... | Do | Do |
| 48–21 | Machinery and Equipment ............. | Do | Do |
| 48–31 | Automobile Equipment. | Do | Do |
| 48–41 | Furniture and Fixtures. | Do | Do |
| 48–51 | Library ............. | Do | Do |
| 48–61 | Emergency Facilities .. | Do | Do |
| 48–90 | Leasehold Improvements | Do | Do |
| 48–91 | Construction, Betterment, and Maintenance in Progress ........ | Voucher Distribution Journal, Cash Disbursements Journal, General Journal | Do |
| 48–99 | Retirements in Progress | General Journal | Cash Receipts Journal, General Journal |

| Control | | Debits from | Credits from |
|---|---|---|---|
| 49 | *Reserves for Depreciation* | | |
| 49–1 | Reserve for Depreciation of Land Improvements ............ | General Journal | General Journal |
| 49–11 | Reserve for Depreciation of Buildings .... | Do | Do |
| 49–21 | Reserve for Depreciation of Machinery and Equipment ......... | Do | Do |
| 49–31 | Reserve for Depreciation of Automobile Equipment ............. | Do | Do |
| 49–41 | Reserve for Depreciation of Furniture and Fixtures ............. | Do | Do |
| 49–61 | Amortization of Emergency Facilities ..... | Do | Do |
| 49–90 | Reserve for Depreciation of Leasehold Improvements ............ | Do | Do |
| 50 | *Trade Marks, Patents, Copyrights, Etc.* | Do | Do |
| 51 | *Prepaid Expenses* | | |
| 51–1 | Prepaid Taxes ........ | Voucher Distribution Journal | Do |
| 51–2 | Prepaid Insurance ..... | Voucher Distribution Journal, General Journal | Voucher Distribution Journal, General Journal |
| 52 | *Deferred Accounts* | | |
| 52–2 | Deferred Building Rentals ............... | Do | General Journal |
| 52–7 | Deferred Promotional Expenses—Domestic.. | Do | Do |
| 52–10 | Deferred Expense—In Transit and Received Damaged .......... | Do | Voucher Distribution Journal, General Journal |
| 52–14 | Postage and Narcotic Stamps ............ | Voucher Distribution Journal, Cash Disbursements Journal | General Journal |
| 52–15 | Miscellaneous Finished Goods Clearing Account .............. | General Journal | Do |
| 52–16 | Deferred Expense—Miscellaneous .......... | Voucher Distribution Journal, General Journal | Do |

| Control | | Debits from | Credits from |
|---|---|---|---|
| | *LIABILITIES* | | |
| 56 | *Notes and Accounts Payable* | | |
| 56–1 | Notes Payable—Banks . | Voucher Distribution Journal | Cash Receipts Journal |
| 56–11 | Audited Vouchers Payable .............. | Cash Disbursements Journal | Voucher Distribution Journal |
| 56–21 | Unaudited Vouchers Payable ............ | General Journal | General Journal |
| 56–31 | Accounts Payable—Domestic Salesmen's Expenses ............. | Do | Do |
| 56–81 | Accounts Payable—Sales and Use Taxes Invoiced | Voucher Distribution Journal | Sales Journal |
| 56–82 | Accounts Payable—City Wage Tax Withheld.. | Do | General Journal |
| 56–83 | Accounts Payable—Unemployment and Disability Insurance Taxes Withheld ........... | Do | Do |
| 56–84 | Accounts Payable—Federal Insurance Contributions Tax Withheld .............. | Do | Do |
| 56–86 | Accounts Payable—Federal Income Tax Withheld — Foreign Addresses and Non-resident Aliens ......... | Do | Do |
| 56–87 | Accounts Payable—Temporary Disability Benefit Contributions ... | Do | Do |
| 56–88 | Accounts Payable—Pension Payroll Deductions .............. | Do | Do |
| 56–89 | Accounts Payable—Union Dues ........... | Do | Do |
| 56–90 | Accounts Payable—Employees ............ | Do | Do |
| 56–91 | Accounts Payable—Defense Bonds ........ | Voucher Distribution Journal, General Journal | Do |
| 56–93 | Accounts Payable—Export Sales Commissions ............. | Voucher Distribution Journal | Do |
| 56–94 | Accounts Payable—State Income Tax Withheld | Do | Do |

| Control | | Debits from | Credits from |
|---|---|---|---|
| 56–95 | Accounts Payable—Federal Income Tax Withheld .............. | Voucher Distribution Journal | General Journal |
| 56–96 | Accounts Payable—Group Insurance .... | Do | Do |
| 56–97 | Accounts Payable—Voluntary Health Plan ... | Do | Do |
| 56–99 | Accounts Payable—Employees' Contributions | Do | Do |
| 57 | *Dividends Payable* | | |
| 57–1 | Dividends Payable—Preferred ............. | Do | Do |
| 57–2 | Dividends Payable—Common ............. | Do | Do |
| 58 | *Accrued Expenses* | | |
| 58–1 | Accrued Federal Income Taxes ............. | Do | Do |
| 58–2 | Accrued Other Taxes .. | Do | Do |
| 58–4 | Accrued Vacation and Holiday Pay ....... | General Journal | Do |
| 58–11 | Accrued Payroll ........ | Cash Disbursements Journal, General Journal | Do |
| 58–15 | Accrued Pension Cost.. | Voucher Distribution Journal | Do |
| 58–18 | Accrued Employee Bonuses ............. | General Journal | Do |
| 58–20 | Accrued Distributors' Expenses .......... | Cash Receipts Journal, General Journal | Do |
| 58–21 | Accrued Unemployment and Disability Insurance Taxes ........ | Voucher Distribution Journal | Do |
| 58–22 | Accrued Federal Insurance Contributions Tax .............. | Do | Do |
| 58–31 | Accrued Domestic Salesmen's Automobile Depreciation ......... | Do | Do |
| 58–32 | Accrued Export Salesmen's Automobile Depreciation ......... | Do | Do |
| 58–40 | Accrued Royalties ..... | Do | Do |
| 58–42 | Accrued Professional Fees and Expenses... | Do | Do |
| 58–43 | Accrued Patent and Trade Mark Expenses | General Journal | Do |
| 58–91 | Accrued Interest on Notes Payable ...... | Voucher Distribution Journal | Do |

| Control | | Debits from | Credits from |
|---|---|---|---|
| 58–92 | Accrued Interest—Other | Voucher Distribution Journal | General Journal |
| 58–93 | Accrued Expenses—Miscellaneous .......... | General Journal | Do |
| 58–99 | Accrued Water Rent .. | Voucher Distribution Journal | Do |
| 59 | *Reserves* | | |
| 59–54 | Reserve for Unrealized Profit on Sales to Subsidiaries ............ | General Journal | Sales Journal |
| 60 | *Long-Term Debts* ....... | Voucher Distribution Journal | Cash Receipts Journal |
| 61 | *Capital Stock—Preferred and Common* ....... | General Journal | Cash Receipts Journal, General Journal |
| 62 | *Surplus* | | |
| 62–1 | Surplus—Earned ...... | Do | General Journal |
| 62–11 | Profit and Loss ....... | Do | Do |
| 62–71 | Dividends—Preferred . | Do | Do |
| 62–72 | Dividends—Common .. | Do | Do |

## Income and expense accounts.

| | | | |
|---|---|---|---|
| 66 | *Gross Sales* | | |
| 66–1 | Gross Sales to Customers | General Journal | Sales Journal |
| 66–50 | Cash Sales to Employees | Do | Cash Receipts Journal |
| 66–51 | Process Sales (processing materials owned by others) .......... | Do | Sales Journal |
| 67 | *Net Sales to Subsidiary Companies and Branches* .......... | Do | Do |
| 70 | *Merchandise Returns* .... | Sales Journal | General Journal |
| 71 | *Allowances* ............ | Do | Do |
| 73 | *Cash Discounts Allowed* | | |
| 73–1 | Cash Discounts—Domestic Sales ........ | Cash Receipts Journal | Do |
| 73–2 | Cash Discounts—Export Sales ............. | Do | Do |
| 75 | *Cost of Goods Sold* | | |
| 75–1 | Gross Standard Cost of Goods Sold—Domestic | General Journal | Do |
| 75–2 | Gross Standard Cost of Goods Sold—Export . | Do | Do |
| 75–3 | Gross Standard Cost of Returns—Domestic .. | Do | Do |
| 75–4 | Gross Standard Cost of Returns—Export ... | Do | Do |
| 75–5 | Standard Cost of Extra Goods on Special Offers ............... | Do | Do |

| Control | | Debits from | Credits from |
|---|---|---|---|
| 75–6 | Net Standard Cost of Goods for Employees' Stores ............. | General Journal | General Journal |
| 75–8 | Net Standard Cost of Goods Sold to Subsidiaries ............ | Do | Do |
| 75–24 | Alcohol Drawback—Export ............... | Do | Do |
| 75–26 | Other Miscellaneous Costs .............. | Do | Do |
| 75–27 | Net Loss on Returns— Domestic ........... | Do | Do |
| 75–28 | Net Loss on Returns— Export ............ | Do | Do |
| 75–29 | Expenses Applicable to Returns ............ | Do | Do |
| 75–30 | Variances—Price—Raw Materials ......... | Do | Do |
| 75–31 | Variances—Price— Work-in-Process Labor ................ | Do | Do |
| 75–32 | Variances—Price—Supplies .............. | Do | Do |
| 75–34 | Variances—Materials .. | Do | Do |
| 75–35 | Variances—Direct Labor | Do | Do |
| 75–36 | Variances—Burden .... | Do | Do |
| 75–38 | Variances—Printing ... | Do | Do |
| 75–40 | Printing Additions and Revisions Expense— Domestic ......... | Do | Do |
| 75–41 | Printing Additions and Revisions Expense— Export ............ | Do | Do |
| 75–43 | Corrections of Standards .............. | Do | Do |
| 75–50 | Revisions of Standards —Raw Materials and Supplies ........... | Do | Do |
| 75–51 | Revisions of Standards —Work in Process .. | Do | Do |
| 75–52 | Revisions of Standards —Bulk and Filled Stock .............. | Do | Do |
| 75–53 | Revisions of Standards —Finished Goods— Warehouse ........ | Do | Do |
| 75–54 | Revisions of Standards —Finished Goods— Branches ........... | Do | Do |
| 75–55 | Revisions of Standards— Finished Goods—Export .............. | Do | Do |

| Control | | Debits from | Credits from |
|---|---|---|---|
| 75–57 | Standard Cost of Miscellaneous Goods Removed from Stock—Domestic and Export | General Journal | General Journal |
| 75 58 | Adjustment of Raw Materials and Supplies to Lower of Cost or Market ........... | Do | Do |
| 75–60 | Adjustment of Book to Physical—Raw Materials and Supplies.. | Do | Do |
| 75–62 | Adjustment of Book to Physical—Bulk and Filled Stock ........ | Do | Do |
| 75–63 | Adjustment of Book to Physical—Finished Goods—Warehouse .. | Do | Do |
| 75–64 | Adjustment of Book to Physical—Finished Goods—Branches ... | Do | Do |
| 75–65 | Adjustment of Book to Physical—Finished Goods—Export ..... | Do | Do |
| 75–75 | Idle Plant Facilities ... | Do | Do |
| 75–76 | Over or Under Absorbed —Service Expenses .. | Do | Do |
| 75–80 | Discards and Deletions —Raw Materials and Supplies ........... | Do | Do |
| 75–81 | Discards and Deletions —Work in Process .. | Do | Do |
| 75–82 | Discards and Deletions —Bulk and Filled Stock .............. | Do | Do |
| 75–83 | Discards and Deletions— Finished Goods—Domestic ............ | Do | Do |
| 75–84 | Discards and Deletions —Finished Goods— Export ............ | Do | Do |
| 75–87 | Manufacturing Losses and Defects and Finishing Bulk Loss Allowance ........... | Do | Do |
| 75–91 | Standard Cost of Quality Control Samples.. | Do | Do |
| 75–92 | Cost of Processing Materials for Outside Manufacturers ...... | Do | Do |
| 75–93 | Accelerated Amortization | Do | Do |
| 75–94 | Package Design Expenses | Do | Do |

| Control | | Debits from | Credits from |
|---|---|---|---|
| 75–95 | Substitution of Materials and Deviation from Standard Methods .............. | General Journal | General Journal |
| 75–97 | Stability Losses (a quality-testing expense) . | Do | Do |
| 75–98 | Quality Control Expenses—Export ..... | Do | Do |
| 75–99 | Salvage Adjustments .. | Do | Do |
| 75–100 | Illness Payroll ........ | Do | Do |
| 4 | Domestic General Selling Expenses .......... | Voucher Distribution Journal, Cash Disbursements Journal, and General Journal | Voucher Distribution Journal, Cash Receipts Journal, and General Journal |
| 5 | Domestic Promotional Expenses ............. | Do | Do |
| 6 | Domestic Warehouse Shipping Expenses ...... | Do | Do |
| 7 | Domestic Branch Shipping Expenses .......... | Do | Do |
| 8 | Export Selling and Administrative Expenses | Do | Do |
| 9 | Export Promotional Expenses ............. | Do | Do |
| 10 | Export Shipping Expenses | | |
| 11 | Research Expenses ...... | Do | Do |
| 12 | Administrative and General Expenses ....... | Do | Do |
| 13 | Medical Expenses ....... | Do | Do |
| 34 | Income Credits ......... | Do | Do |
| 35 | Income Charges ........ | Do | Do |

**Record books.** In addition to the standard general ledger and subsidiary ledgers, various other ledgers are maintained as necessary to accumulate the costs of the production, service, and other general expense controls not included in the above listing. Postings to these ledgers are from journals or tabulated data summarizing the transactions of the period. Not shown are detailed expense accounts for the expense controls 4 through 13, which are maintained by departments. Expense accounts common to more than one department carry the same number. A limited number of accounts, as required, are provided in controls 34 and 35 in subsidiary ledgers.

## Peculiarities of procedures: sales-receivables cycle; purchases-payables cycle; cash receipts

**General.** As previously indicated, a large number of transactions must be recorded. Under such conditions and the requirements for customer service, it is usually desirable to decentralize the sales and collection activities to the individual branches.

In addition to providing for sound accounting for sales and cash receipts, the procedures used should be designed to provide all the basic information required for development of vital statistics. The exceptional transactions are usually not sufficient to present any major difficulties in standardizing the procedure. Because of the large number of transactions, a heavy volume of individual pieces of paper must be handled. Once a procedure has been established, the need for simplification must be constantly emphasized or the cost may become excessive for the information provided.

**Accounting for sales.** The recording of domestic sales differs greatly from that of export sales, and the procedures will therefore be described separately.

*Domestic Sales.* Sales of products on the domestic market are made in various ways, depending on the type of sales organization. Sales organizations whose policies call for contracts with wholesalers to distribute their products differ substantially from organizations engaging a large sales force who sell direct to the drug stores, hospitals, and other institutions. The difference is in the creative detail selling and the size and volume of orders.

The system described here assumes a sales organization whose sales policies require salesmen to concentrate on creative selling among doctors, with subsequent sales contacts with outlets such as drug stores, hospitals, institutions, and so forth. A limited number of wholesalers are also part of the distribution system. The sales, therefore, can be classified as direct sales and sales to wholesalers.

In order better to service customers, the sales organization is divided into sales districts, and each district is serviced by a sales branch warehouse. Each branch is a complete operating entity in that service provided by the branch for customers in the sales district includes sales service, order processing, credit and collection, and customers' accounts receivable.

Sales service provided to wholesalers involves salesmen calling on outlets who order through wholesalers. Such orders written by the salesmen, called *transfer orders,* are sent directly to the wholesaler for filling. These orders are not accounted for on the books, but copies are sent to the machine accounting department for statistical tabulation. Such statistics are used as control features for analyzing sales to wholesalers. Sales service provided to direct customer outlets (including replenishment of wholesalers' inventories) results in orders prepared by salesmen or orders prepared by the customer.

*Foreign sales.* Sales in foreign countries may be made through the use of various types of sales organizations, such as the direct employment of sales representatives in foreign countries, sales through foreign distributors (outright sales or sales on a consignment basis), and the formation of forcign or domestic subsidiary companies. The type of organization selected is often influenced by economic or political factors existing at home or abroad.

When sales are made direct to a foreign customer, orders are sent direct to the home office by the salesman. When required, an import license and an exchange permit must accompany the order. Upon receipt of the order in the home office, the customer's credit is checked; if his credit is found to be satisfactory, the order is registered. The registration number serves as an identification for all forms and correspondence pertaining to the order. An export binder is then prepared in duplicate, one copy of which is forwarded to the warehouse, authorizing the packing of the merchandise for shipment; the other copy is filed pending shipment. When shipment is made, a hectograph invoice master is prepared from information shown on the export binder and multiple copies are reproduced. For accounting purposes, one copy of the invoice is used for accounts receivable posting and another is used in the machine accounting department in the preparation of inventory accounting and statistical sales data.

Sales to subsidiaries are initiated through the preparation of an order by the subsidiary company; such orders are handled similarly to, but separately from, foreign customer orders. Movement of merchandise between parent company and subsidiary company is recorded in an intercompany receivable account. Sales to subsidiaries are segregated on the parent company's books, and, if invoiced above cost, a reserve for such markup is created. The creation of this reserve serves to offset the income resulting from the markup until the subsidiary sells the merchandise to a customer. At that time the parent company will transfer the amount of the markup to income.

**Billing—Domestic.** Figure 2 depicts the order-processing routine in the branches. The order system described is a "one-time writing" method that has proved economical and flexible in that, through its use, peak-load volumes can be handled with a minimum of effort. The system of billing does not require an order register because it is a pre-billing system, and for control purposes a tally sheet suffices when invoices are being numbered.

When the salesman writes the order, he originates the hectograph master, filling in the pertinent information, such as (1) date of order, (2) territory number (for sales statistical purposes), (3) salesman, (4) sales order number, (5) customer—sold to, (6) customer—ship to.

When a customer orders direct, the branch originates the hectograph master and follows the above-mentioned routine. Credit memoranda written for returned goods or price adjustments follow the same procedure and are accounted for accordingly.

On receipt of orders, the branch refers them to an order amplifier, who is responsible for the following:

1. Passing for credit. (Orders not cleared are referred to the credit manager.)
2. Assignment of customer narcotic number (when necessary).
3. Assignment of classification number.
4. Invoice date.
5. Branch registration number.

The information in item 3 is for sales statistical purposes; item 5 is assigned as a control of all billings.

The order (hectograph master) is given to an order pricer, who determines the unit price and extension and the total invoice charge. The order is then sent to the duplicating machine for the required documents for billing, accounting, and shipping. These are:

1. Invoice—Customer
2. Invoice (Duplicate)—Statistical (Home office)
3. Packing List (Drop Shipments)
4. Labels

The order is then sent to the shipping department. The duplicate is held in the branch office until notice of shipment is received from the shipping department. This is done by returning the original order (hectograph master) stamped as having been shipped. All orders pre-billed in a day are shipped the same day. The original orders are totaled (in dollar amount) and a control is established. The statistical copy of the invoice is tied into the control totals. Disposition of the original order and copies is as follows:

*Original order.* Sorted by date and accounts receivable control. These controls are segregated by states, and the originals sorted alphabetically by town and then alphabetically by customer within the town. They are forwarded to Accounts Receivable.

*Duplicate (statistical).* Sorted numerically by branch registration number. They are forwarded to Machine Accounting (home office).

**Accounts Receivable.** Assuming that customers' accounts receivable are decentralized, each branch maintains the accounts receivable ledgers for customers serviced by it. Each accounts receivable operation is broken down by controls. A control (Figure 3) may be established for customers within each state serviced by the branch, primarily for tax purposes. A large number of accounts within a state control may necessitate a further breakdown for ease in balancing daily postings and monthly trial balances.

Although customer account ledgers are decentralized and controlled locally by each branch, the home office maintains a central control for each branch. This is made possible by each branch reporting daily on each type of transaction by sending the home office (1) a separate transmittal ticket (Figure 4) for invoices, returns, and allowances issued; (2) a copy of

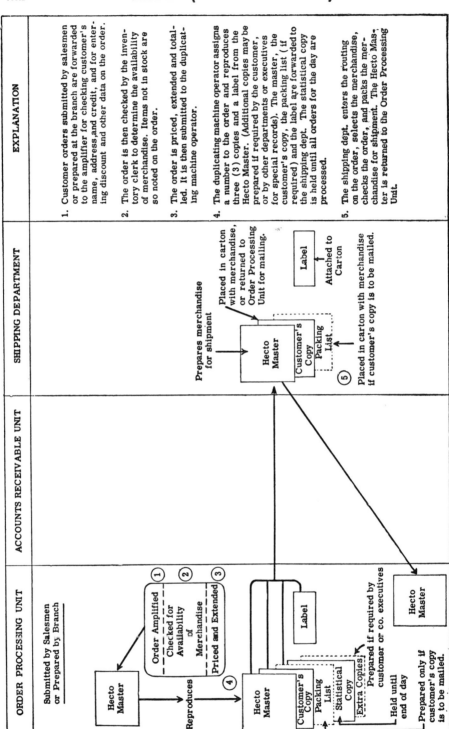

**Fig. 2. Order-processing Routine at Branches.** (*Continued on next page.*)

EXPLANATION

1. Customer orders submitted by salesmen or prepared at the branch are forwarded to the amplifier for checking customer's name, address, and credit, and for entering discount and other data on the order.

2. The order is then checked by the inventory clerk to determine the availability of merchandise. Items not in stock are so noted on the order.

3. The order is priced, extended and totalled. It is then submitted to the duplicating machine operator.

4. The duplicating machine operator assigns a number to the order and reproduces three (3) copies and a label from the Hecto Master. (Additional copies may be prepared if required by the customer, or by other departments or executives for special records). The master, the customer's copy, the packing list (if required) and the label are forwarded to the shipping dept. The statistical copy is held until all orders for the day are processed.

5. The shipping dept. enters the routing on the order, selects the merchandise, checks the order, and packs the merchandise for shipment. The Hecto Master is returned to the Order Processing Unit.

| ORDER PROCESSING UNIT | ACCOUNTS RECEIVABLE UNIT | SHIPPING DEPARTMENT | EXPLANATION |
|---|---|---|---|
| | | | 6. The dollar values shown on the Hecto Masters and on the statistical copies are totalled and compared for agreement, and the number of packages shipped is determined from the Hecto Masters. |
| | | | 7. The Hecto Masters are forwarded to the Accounts Receivable Unit for posting to the ledgers, and the bookkeeping machine tape is compared with the total dollar value of the Hecto Masters processed. |
| | | | 8. The Order Processing Unit attaches a transmittal form to the accumulated statistical copies and adding machine tapes (dollar value and number of packages shipped). The assembled data are forwarded to the Machine Accounting Department. |

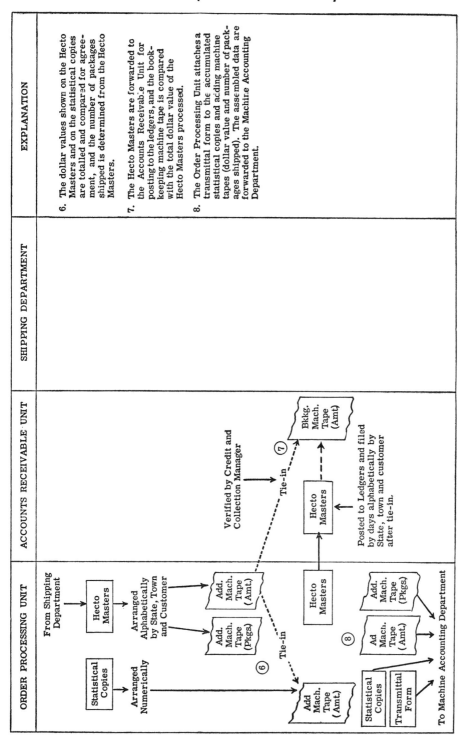

NAME OF COMPANY

ACCOUNTS RECEIVABLE MONTHLY CONTROL

BRANCH _____  STATE _____

MONTH _____ 195_

| 1 DATE | 2 Opening Balance | 3 Daily Invoice Totals | 4 Invoices Transferred | 5 Credit Memoranda Transferred | 6 Cash Disbursements | 7 DEBITS Branch Journal Vouchers | 8 Unpaid Notes | 9 Checks Returned By Bank | 10 Total Debits | 11 Daily Totals Misc. Returns |
|---|---|---|---|---|---|---|---|---|---|---|
| Opening Balance | | | | | | | | | | |
| 1 | | | | | | | | | | |
| 2 | | | | | | | | | | |
| 3 | | | | | | | | | | |
| 4 | | | | | | | | | | |
| 5 | | | | | | | | | | |
| 6 | | | | | | | | | | |
| 7 | | | | | | | | | | |
| 8 | | | | | | | | | | |
| 9 | | | | | | | | | | |
| 10 | | | | | | | | | | |
| 11 | | | | | | | | | | |
| 12 | | | | | | | | | | |

LEDGER TRIAL BALANCE

Continuation of Above

| 2 Daily Total Allowances | 13 Credit Memoranda Transferred | 14 Invoices Transferred | 15 CREDITS Cash Receipts and Discounts | 16 Branch Journal Vouchers | 17 Notes Receivable | 18 Bad Debts Charged Off | 19 | 20 Total Credits | 21 Closing Balance |
|---|---|---|---|---|---|---|---|---|---|
| | | | | | | | | | |

Fig. 3. Accounts Receivable Monthly Control.

490

accounts receivable transfer vouchers reflecting transfer of invoices to other branches for collection ( a transmittal letter and a copy of the invoice are sent to the receiving branches); and (3) a copy of accounts receivable journal vouchers reflecting miscellaneous transactions recorded on the customer accounts at the branch. In this manner of reporting, the home office controls are identical with branch controls.

At the end of each month, a trial balance is taken by transferring the balance shown on the customer ledger to the customer's statement for the

| DAILY REPORT OF INVOICES, CREDITS & MISCELLANEOUS INVOICES | | | | |
|---|---|---|---|---|
| CODE | TRANSACTIONS | | | Branch                     Date |
| .55 | Sales to Customers | | ☐ | Credit or |
| 66 | Returns from Customers | | ☐ | Invoice Nos.                 To |
| 76 | Allowances to Customers | † | ☐ | No. of Crs. or Inv. Attached |
| .63 | Shipments to Other Branches | * | ☐ | No. of Pkg. Units |
| 64 | Mdse. Destroyed at Branches | * | ☐ | $ Total of Sales or Credits |
| 74 | Mdse. Returned to Philadelphia | * | ☐ | Total State Taxes |
| 84 | Mdse. Issued as Samples | * | ☐ | Total City Taxes |
| 94 | Breakages | * | ☐ | |
| .54 | Miscellaneous | * | ☐ | Transportation or |
| 48 | | * | ☐ | Less Transportation |
| | † No Package Total — * No Dollar Total | | | Tel. & Tel. |
| | FOR HOME OFFICE USE ONLY. | | | Total |
| Terr. Code | | Card Punching | | |
| Card Selecting | | Balancing | | |
| Card Marking | | | | FA-277 |

(BRANCH CHECK PROPER SQUARE)

Fig. 4. Branch Transmittal Ticket for Invoices, Returns, and Allowances.

following month and totaling the amounts carried forward. If the totals of the customers' statements are in balance with the branch controls, the current month's statements are mailed to the customers and the accounts receivable monthly control report (Figure 5) is prepared and forwarded to the home office.

On receipt of the monthly reports, the home office checks them against the central controls. Differences are reconciled and a standard monthly journal entry is prepared. Accounting treatment is as follows:

Dr. 38–45 Accounts Receivable
Dr. 70 Returns
Dr. 71 Allowances

Cr.          56–81 Accounts Payable (Sales taxes invoiced)
Cr.          38–45 Accounts Receivable (Total of returns and allowances)
Cr.          66–1 Gross Sales to Customers

| ACCOUNTS RECEIVABLE MONTHLY CONTROL REPORT FOR HOME OFFICE _____ BRANCH | | | MONTH ENDED ____19– | | TOTAL BRANCH CONTROLS | FOR HOME OFFICE USE ONLY |
|---|---|---|---|---|---|---|
| | STATE OF | | STATE OF | STATE OF | | |
| Opening Balance | | | | | | |
| | | | | | | |
| DEBITS: | | | | | | |
| Daily Invoice Totals | | | | | | |
| Invoices Transferred | | | | | | |
| Credit Memoranda Transferred | | | | | | |
| Cash Disbursements | | | | | | |
| Branch Journal Vouchers | | | | | | |
| Unpaid Notes | | | | | | |
| Checks Returned by Bank | | | | | | |
| | | | | | | |
| | | | | | | |
| | | | | | | |
| TOTAL DEBITS | | | | | | |
| | | | | | | |
| Total Opening Balance and Debits | | | | | | |
| | | | | | | |
| CREDITS: | | | | | | |
| Daily Totals Mdse. Returns | | | | | | |
| Daily Totals Allowances | | | | | | |
| Credit Memoranda Transferred | | | | | | |
| Invoices Transferred | | | | | | |
| Cash Receipts and Discounts | | | | | | |
| Branch Journal Vouchers | | | | | | |
| Notes Receivable | | | | | | |
| Bad Debts Charged Off | | | | | | |
| | | | | | | |
| | | | | | | |
| | | | | | | |
| TOTAL CREDITS | | | | | | |
| | | | | | | |
| Closing Balance | | | | | | |
| | | | | | | |
| Ledger Trial Balances | | | | | | |

NOTE: Prepare this report as soon as accounts receivable monthly controls are completed and ledgers are balanced
Forward to general accounting dept. via air mail at or before closing time of third working day of following month.
Prepare duplicate copy for your files.

**Fig. 5. Accounts Receivable Monthly Control Report for Home Office.**

**Cash receipts.** Sources of cash receipts are generally as follows:

1. Sales of merchandise to customers
2. C.O.D. receipts from delivery companies and employees
3. Miscellaneous receipts

The cash receipts routine described outlines procedures where payments for merchandise are made to branch offices.

Receipts for sales of merchandise are processed by the branch cashier. All receipts for each day are deposited in the bank the same day. On receipt of cash or checks, a posting medium for accounts receivable is prepared. This medium may be the envelope, provided it bears the name of the customer. A rubber stamp is used to permit the sequential recording of the date of receipt, net amount, discount, and gross amount. If the envelope or posting medium does not contain the name of the customer, a collection report is prepared.

The checks and the posting media are sorted in accounts receivable-control order, and separate tapes are taken of each. When the tape of the posting media is in agreement with the tape of the cash receipts, the posting media are forwarded to the accounts receivable ledgers. The cashier prepares the bank deposit; the amount deposited in a depository bank account must be in agreement with the net cash shown on the posting media.

On receipt of the posting media, the discount clerk in Accounts Receivable determines the amount of cash discount to be applied in arriving at the gross amount to be credited to the customer's account. The total cash discount amount is given to the cashier, who prepares the weekly cash receipts report. This report is forwarded to the home office cashier.

On receipt of the weekly cash receipts reports from branches, the home office cashier verifies each for accuracy. The reports are used as a basis for determining the amounts to be transferred from the depository or collection bank accounts to the company's operating bank accounts. The information on each report is then posted to the cash book. A standard monthly journal entry is prepared, and the accounting treatment is:

Dr. 36–21 Domestic Branch Bank Accounts
Dr. 73–1 Cash Discounts—Domestic Sales

Cr.     38–5   Notes Receivable—Branches
Cr.     38–45 Accounts Receivable—Branches

**Purchase and payment procedure.** Purchasing and payment procedures in the industry are generally the same as any standard procedure. As in any organization, special features can be established to adapt a standard procedure to the type of accounting system employed. Figure 6 indicates: (1) purchase order and receiving procedure, (2) purchase and expense distribution, (3) accounts payable procedure, and (4) cash payment procedure.

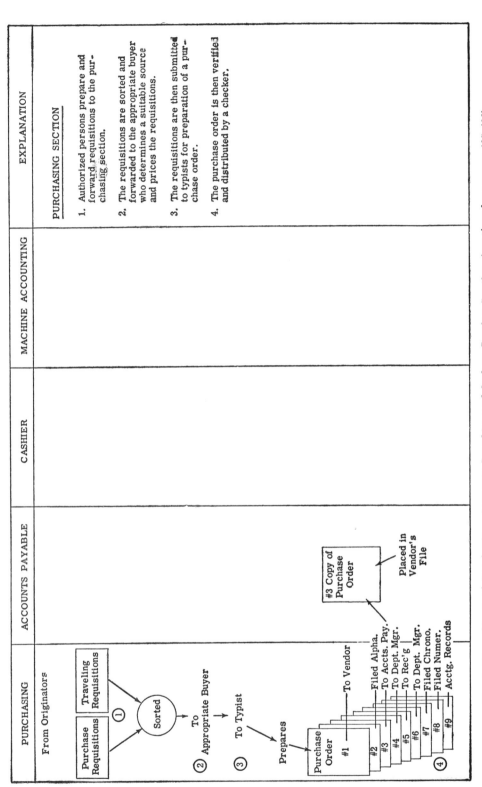

| PURCHASING | ACCOUNTS PAYABLE | CASHIER | MACHINE ACCOUNTING | EXPLANATION |
|---|---|---|---|---|
| From Originators | | | | PURCHASING SECTION |
| | | | | 1. Authorized persons prepare and forward requisitions to the purchasing section. |
| | | | | 2. The requisitions are sorted and forwarded to the appropriate buyer who determines a suitable source and prices the requisitions. |
| | | | | 3. The requisitions are then submitted to typists for preparation of a purchase order. |
| | | | | 4. The purchase order is then verified and distributed by a checker. |

**Fig. 6. Flow Chart of Purchasing, Accounts Payable, and Ledger Posting Routine** *(continued on pages 495–498)*.

494

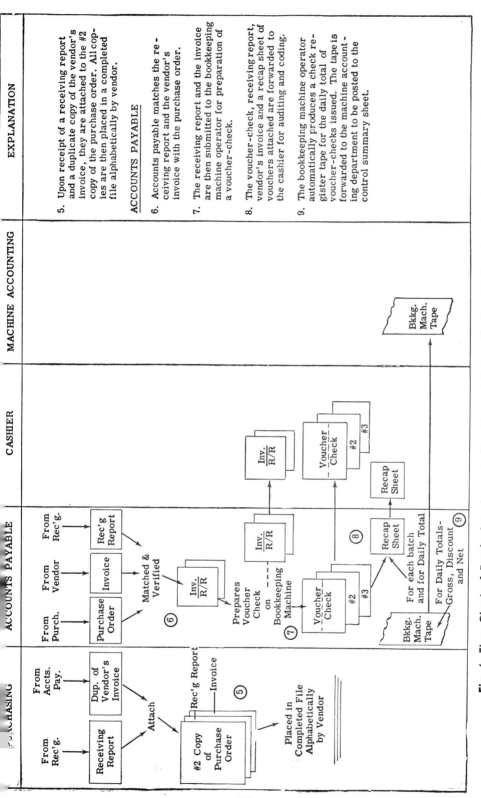

**EXPLANATION**

5. Upon receipt of a receiving report and a duplicate copy of the vendor's invoice, they are attached to the #2 copy of the purchase order. All copies are then placed in a completed file alphabetically by vendor.

ACCOUNTS PAYABLE

6. Accounts payable matches the receiving report and the vendor's invoice with the purchase order.

7. The receiving report and the invoice are then submitted to the bookkeeping machine operator for preparation of a voucher-check.

8. The voucher-check, receiving report, vendor's invoice and a recap sheet of vouchers attached are forwarded to the cashier for auditing and coding.

9. The bookkeeping machine operator automatically produces a check register tape for the daily total of voucher-checks issued. The tape is forwarded to the machine account-ing department to be posted to the control summary sheet.

**MACHINE ACCOUNTING**

Bkkg. Mach. Tape

**CASHIER**

Inv. R/R

Voucher Check #2 #3

Recap Sheet

**ACCOUNTS PAYABLE**

From Rec'g. — Rec'g Report

From Vendor — Invoice

From Purch. — Purchase Order

Matched & Verified ⑥

Inv. R/R

Prepares Voucher Check on Bookkeeping Machine ⑦

Inv. R/R

Voucher Check #2 #3

Recap Sheet ⑧

Bkkg. Mach. Tape

For each batch and for Daily Total

For Daily Totals- Gross, Discount and Net ⑨

**PURCHASING**

From Accts. Pay. — Dup. of Vendor's Invoice

From Rec'g. — Receiving Report

Attach

Rec'g Report — Invoice

#2 Copy of Purchase Order ⑤

Placed in Completed File Alphabetically by Vendor

**Fig. 6. Flow Chart of Purchasing, Accounts Payable, and Ledger Posting Routine** *(continuation of page 494).*

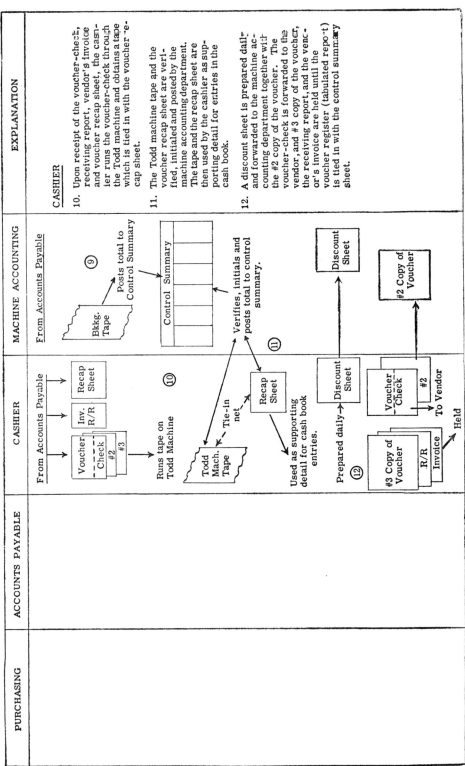

| PURCHASING | ACCOUNTS PAYABLE | CASHIER | MACHINE ACCOUNTING | EXPLANATION |
|---|---|---|---|---|
| | | From Accounts Payable<br>Voucher / Check #2 / #3 → Inv. R/R → Recap Sheet<br>⑩ Runs tape on Todd Machine<br>Tie-in net<br>Todd Mach. Tape ⟶ Recap Sheet<br>Used as supporting detail for cash book entries.<br>⑫ Prepared daily → Discount Sheet<br>#3 Copy of Voucher / R/R / Invoice — Voucher-Check #2 To Vendor — Held | From Accounts Payable<br>⑨ Bkg. Tape — Posts total to Control Summary<br>Control Summary<br>⑪ Verifies, initials and posts total to control summary.<br>Discount Sheet<br>#2 Copy of Voucher | **CASHIER**<br>10. Upon receipt of the voucher-check, receiving report, vendor's invoice and voucher recap sheet, the cashier runs the voucher-check through the Todd machine and obtains a tape which is tied in with the voucher recap sheet.<br>11. The Todd machine tape and the voucher recap sheet are verified, initialed and posted by the machine accounting department. The tape and the recap sheet are then used by the cashier as supporting detail for entries in the cash book.<br>12. A discount sheet is prepared daily and forwarded to the machine accounting department together with the #2 copy of the voucher. The voucher-check is forwarded to the vendor, and #3 copy of the voucher, the receiving report, and the vendor's invoice are held until the voucher register (tabulated report) is tied in with the control summary sheet. |

Fig. 6. Flow Chart of Purchasing, Accounts Payable, and Ledger Posting Routine *(continuation of page 495)*.

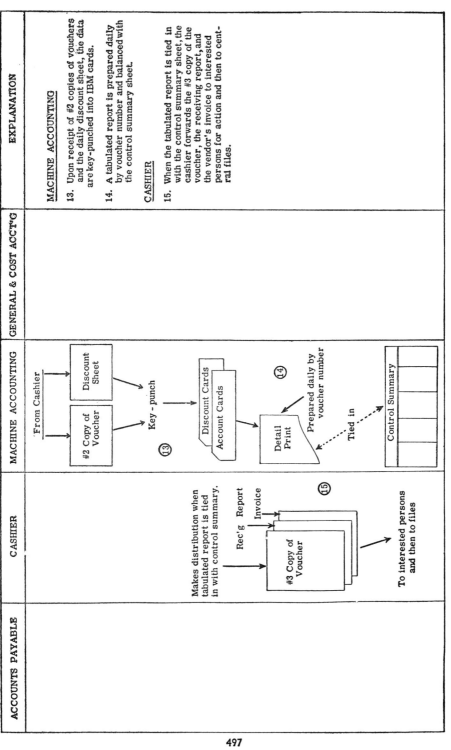

| ACCOUNTS PAYABLE | CASHIER | MACHINE ACCOUNTING | GENERAL & COST ACCT'G | EXPLANATION |
|---|---|---|---|---|
| | Makes distribution when tabulated report is tied in with control summary.<br><br>Rec'g Report<br>Invoice<br>(15)<br>#3 Copy of Voucher<br><br>To interested persons and then to files | From Cashier<br>Discount Sheet<br>#2 Copy of Voucher<br>Key - punch<br>(13)<br>Discount Cards<br>Account Cards<br>Detail Print<br>Prepared daily by voucher number<br>(14)<br>Tied in<br>Control Summary | | **MACHINE ACCOUNTING**<br><br>13. Upon receipt of #2 copies of vouchers and the daily discount sheet, the data are key-punched into IBM cards.<br><br>14. A tabulated report is prepared daily by voucher number and balanced with the control summary sheet.<br><br>**CASHIER**<br><br>15. When the tabulated report is tied in with the control summary sheet, the cashier forwards the #3 copy of the voucher, the receiving report, and the vendor's invoice to interested persons for action and then to central files. |

**Fig. 6. Flow Chart of Purchasing, Accounts Payable, and Ledger Posting Routine** (*continuation of page 496*).

497

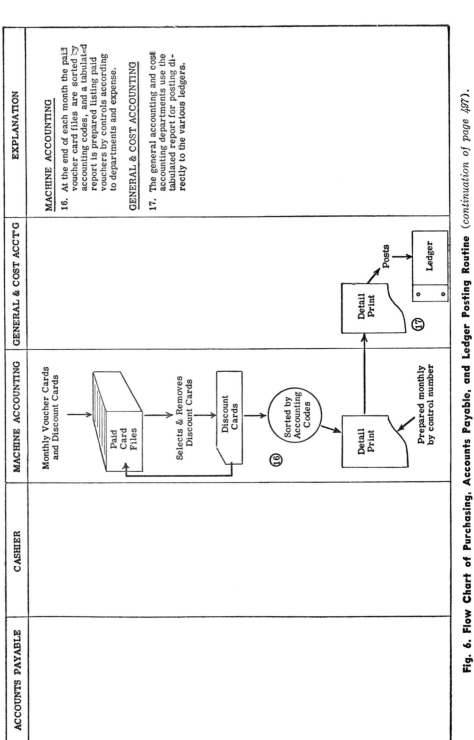

| ACCOUNTS PAYABLE | CASHIER | MACHINE ACCOUNTING | GENERAL & COST ACCT'G | EXPLANATION |
|---|---|---|---|---|

**MACHINE ACCOUNTING**

16. At the end of each month the paid voucher card files are sorted by accounting codes, and a tabulated report is prepared listing paid vouchers by controls according to departments and expense.

**GENERAL & COST ACCOUNTING**

17. The general accounting and cost accounting departments use the tabulated report for posting directly to the various ledgers.

Monthly Voucher Cards and Discount Cards

Paid Card Files

Selects & Removes Discount Cards

Discount Cards

Sorted by Accounting Codes

⑯

Detail Print

Prepared monthly by control number

Detail Print

Posts

Ledger

⑰

**Fig. 6. Flow Chart of Purchasing, Accounts Payable, and Ledger Posting Routine** *(continuation of page 497)*.

It will be noted that the application of machine accounting eliminates the manual preparation of a voucher register and expense distribution. In addition, the punched cards provide the potential for many other analyses. The elimination of manual operations, along with other features, results in both time and money savings while not detracting in any way from internal control.

## Distribution costs

**Allocation of distribution costs.** It is generally impractical in the industry to account for the cost of distribution by individual products.

Various methods of allocation to products may be used for the purpose of statistical analysis. The value of such allocations is dependent upon the method of distribution.

The over-all average for all branches, plus warehousing and other applicable costs, provides a working figure for planning and price setting.

## Cost system

**Selection of a cost system.** The need for accurate, detailed production costs has increased in the drug industry as its product lines have expanded through more and more research effort. The manufacturing complexities of some of the products of recent years have contributed to this need, as have general conditions and trends.

The system selected must provide for identification of each production lot of potent drugs, as well as the normal requirements for cost control, proper inventory valuation, planning, and price setting.

No one system is used uniformly throughout the industry. In most firms, the system varies, depending upon the nature of production of the various products. The system which will be discussed here is basically a specific-order system, accumulating costs by production formulas. There are a few exceptions where continuous-process costs must be used because of the nature of production.

Whether a specific-order or a process system is used, the selection remains between the use of the actual or the standard cost method of accounting. Here again, there is a wide variation of use throughout the industry. Very few firms use either actual or standard entirely. The combinations of the two methods vary widely. Standard costs, with but minor exceptions, are used in the system described here.

**Development of standard costs.** Standard costs are developed for each finished product marketed. Setting these standards naturally requires the establishment of standard costs for the basic raw materials, for supplies, for manufacturing labor and burden, and for packaging and finishing labor and burden. Loss allowances, where applicable, are built into the standard costs.

Current standards, which are intended to represent what the costs actually should be under prevailing circumstances, are used, as opposed to basic or ideal standards. The use of current standards requires rather frequent revision in order to reflect changes in prices and methods. Otherwise, such standards cease to be representative of what the costs actually should be under the existing circumstances.

The planned or budgeted volume of sales is in general the factor determining the level of operations at which standards are set. The standards thus represent the costs expected to be incurred if the anticipated prices are paid for materials and services, if the planned volume of goods are produced, and if the use of materials and services corresponds to that believed necessary for such production. Variances from these standards would represent deviations due to (1) efficiency of production, (2) prices of materials or services, (3) volume variation.

*Material standards.* The fact that drug formulas, once established, remain exactly the same in terms of materials used in each lot eases the problems in setting direct material standards. Forecasting material prices and determining normal material losses are the major considerations.

*Labor standards.* Standard direct labor time is established for each formula through time and motion studies or through averaging of past performance. Time may be applied to the formula in each of several departments.

Direct labor hour rates are established for each production department. To establish these rates, the total budgeted direct man-hours are related to the total dollar cost, using the maximum hourly rate for each of the various job classifications. The standard direct labor hours at this hourly rate in each of the departments where time is applied to a formula are the basis for establishing the standard direct labor cost.

*Burden standards.* Manufacturing burden rates are based on budgeted burden expenses. These expenses include the usual indirect wages, payroll taxes, supplies, testing expense, production expense, maintenance and repair, heat, light, power, and water, budgeted share of service, and so forth. The total departmental burden is related to budgeted direct man-hours for the department to provide the man-hour rate.

*Packaging or finishing labor and burden standards.* These standards are established in the same manner as manufacturing labor and burden. If these operations are paid for under an incentive pay plan, the departmental direct labor and departmental burden rates would be stated in terms of units rather than man-hours. In certain departments, machine-hours rather than man-hours must be used.

Packaging and finishing (finishing departments) as used here include all of the filling, labeling, and packaging operations involved in putting bulk products into the market containers ready for shipment to customers.

*Standards for intermediate mixtures.* In the drug industry, it is necessary to prepare intermediate mixtures, which are then used in the end product. These intermediates often go to the fifth and sixth step of processing before they are ready for use in the end product. Standard costs are developed for these intermediates in the same manner as for the finished products.

*Revisions of standards.* Revisions of standards are made whenever required by changing conditions. Under normal circumstances, changes in price of raw materials and supplies are small and are not adjusted until the cumulative effect is significant in terms of inventory valuation. Under certain circumstances, favorable material price variances may be deferred for a time and applied against the inventory write-down when the revision is effected. Standards are revised for changes in labor rates when significant enough to seriously affect inventory valuation. However, if an overall revision is being made, the labor rates will be brought into line at the same time.

Burden rates are reviewed each year after the annual budget is prepared. The significance of any change is also the governing factor here as to when standards are to be revised. Standards are revised currently for changes in specifications or for any substantial change in manufacturing procedure which would affect cost.

*Punched-card system for standard costs.* With a large number of products and many different package sizes and finishes, the task of maintaining standards manually becomes a heavy burden. This can be overcome by machine application with the standard cost file in the form of punched cards.

With the elements of cost on individual tabulating cards, electronic calculating equipment can be programmed in such a manner that extensions (quantities of material by unit costs and labor and burden rates by standard time) can be done accurately and automatically. The programming would include addition of all cost elements, division to reflect unit costs, and summary-card reproduction to complete the file. When completed, the file is printed on a tabulator in sheet form, which can be bound into book form. The listing will show each individual element of cost, the unit standard cost of material for each cost center which processes the product, and the total finished standard cost.

This system provides the advantages of an easy and simple method of maintaining and revising standards while at the same time reducing the incidence of error. It is possible, through use of the standard cards, to develop at any time an analysis of inventory by material, labor, and burden cost elements.

**Material control and costs.** The nature of the products of the drug industry is such that formulas and specifications are rigidly controlled by qualified technical personnel. Other than for formally approved changes in formulas, the identity and quantity of materials used each time are the same and are double-checked and approved by responsible personnel. The control of material from this standpoint is greater perhaps than in most other industries.

Receiving and handling of materials also receive special attention. Incoming materials are tested for identity, purity, and quality and are clearly marked to avoid improper use.

All charges to and credits from Work-in-Process are entered at standard cost. Raw material and supply inventories are carried at standard, with price variance charged to Cost of Goods at time of purchase. Recorded price variances are reviewed daily as well as cumulatively each month. Since the material standards are periodically revised to reflect prices being paid, the variances are not a good measure of purchasing efficiency. They do provide some basis for measurement of sudden changes or trends in prices, and they are supplied to the purchasing department for that purpose.

The accumulation of manufacturing cost begins with the issuance of a job order (formula). Materials are charged to the formula on the basis of material tickets issued. Additional materials issued in excess of the standard requirements because of spillage or other similar circumstances are charged to material variance when the formula is completed. This excess usage is uncommon.

Although the apothecary system and the metric system are used to describe quantities in formulas, for the purpose of accounting record-keeping these are converted to the decimal system.

Finished-product standards are based on a theoretical yield from each formula. Any quantity over or under the theoretical yield is accounted for as a material variance. If, for example, the yield realized is only 75 per cent of standard, 25 per cent of the material would be charged off as material variance.

Analysis of excess material usage and variation of yield (both reflected in the material variance account) for cost and production management control is developed through analysis of the various individual formulas closed out during the period.

Loss of a formula in process is charged to manufacturing losses rather than to a variance account.

**Labor control and costs.** Production employees account for full time on the job. This reporting is summarized by tabulating methods and tied in to total payroll paid on the basis of clock cards. Direct labor is recorded against each formula from the time reports for actual hours reported at the standard direct hour rate for the department. In practice, the composite labor and burden rate is applied as one.

The direct labor charged to each formula at standard rates is compared with the cost at actual rates, as provided by the tabulated report, and the difference is accounted for as a labor price variance. The difference between standard hours and actual hours reported is accounted for as direct labor variance.

Labor price variance is usually a minor factor. Direct labor time variance is brought to the attention of production supervisors through monthly budget comparison and other special reports. Overtime premium is charged to a separate account for control purposes.

**Burden control.** *Manufacturing departments.* Manufacturing operations are segregated into separate accounting controls for pharmaceutical, biological, and chemical production. Within each of these controls, there are many separate manufacturing, filling, and finishing departments.

Manufacturing departments, in general, are established for a group of similar or related operations. These operations usually pertain to more than one product and in many cases pertain to a substantial number of products. Any one product may therefore be partially processed in each of a number of manufacturing departments.[1] Most pharmaceutical products are packaged and finished in a common pharmaceutical packaging department. A common biological filling department fills and finishes most biological products.

The accumulation of variable direct costs by departments is accomplished through the payroll distribution journal and pre-coding of all requisitions for expense materials and supplies. Fixed costs such as depreciation of buildings, machinery, and equipment, office supplies, property taxes, and certain insurance costs are charged monthly on the basis of allocations determined at the beginning of the year.

*Production service departments.* Supervision, production control, stock, engineering, quality control, and the rest of the production service departments annually determine the percentage allocation of the services they render to production departments and to other service departments. These percentages of the approved budgeted expenses of the service departments are computed, and one-twelfth of the amount is journalized each month. The development of the total amount of expense to be distributed to each of the departments serviced, through the use of simultaneous equations, is accomplished on tabulating machines.

Such costs as light, heat, power, and water, accumulated in engineering departments, are in some instances metered to other departments in order

---

[1] The Idle Plant Facilities account (75–75) is charged with the fixed overhead of any department that is completely idle, that is, completely shut down for any reason. Some firms have developed a rated-capacity figure for each department and will prorate a percentage of a department's fixed overhead to idle plant when the department is operating at only a fraction of its rated capacity. However, where there are multiple-product departments, this practice is difficult to apply.

to provide accurate distribution. If not metered, the allocation is made on various bases, such as type of equipment and floor space.

The difference between the actual monthly expenses of service departments and the amount distributed on a predetermined basis is charged or credited, as the case may be, to Over- and Under-Absorbed Expenses under Cost of Goods Sold.

*Control of variable costs.* Control of variable costs is exercised through budgetary means, including the use of a flexible budget. The annual production department budgets start with the direct labor hour requirements to produce the quantity of products needed to fulfill sales forecasts adjusted for any desired changes in inventories. Experience provides the required ratio of indirect labor hours to direct labor.

Past experience is the principal tool used in setting the budget for other variable costs. This involves consideration of many factors and a determination of how much each cost will vary in relation to the level of activity. The level-of-activity measure may be standard direct labor hours, actual direct labor hours, machine hours, and so forth.

**Comparison of budgeted with actual expense.** The monthly budget comparison report prepared for each manufacturing department lists each expense account. An example is shown in Figure 7. Actual expenses for the month and for the year to date are compared with budgeted expenses. For this purpose, the budgeted variable expenses are shown at the amount applicable for the rate of operations. The Summary of Operating Data on the report shows the rate of operations for the month and for the year to date and the variances computed as follows:

1. Actual labor reported on production, plus or minus labor under or over reported on completed work, equals the standard labor on production.

2. Standard labor on production is related to budgeted labor at 100 per cent and the rate of operations is determined.

3. Actual expense is related to the budgeted expense at the rate of operations to determine the budget variance. As mentioned above, the budgeted expense at the rate of operations is the amount listed on the report.

4. The rate of operations is applied to the fixed expenses, and the difference between this amount and the budgeted amount at 100 per cent is the volume variance.

5. Variances resulting from deviations from standard methods are determined through analysis of completed formulas and shown on the report. Deviations result from various conditions, including recent changes in manufacturing processes which have not yet been reflected in revised standards.

The net total of budget and volume variance is reflected in the burden variance account on the Cost of Goods Sold schedule (Figure 8). Deviations from standard methods, along with substitution of materials, are

**MONTHLY COMPARISON OF ACTUAL TO BUDGETED EXPENSE**

Report 150-5

Dept. [        ]

FOR: _____ DEPT.

_____ MONTHS ENDED _____

LABOR MEASURE·
( ) Hours
( ) Units

| | SUMMARY OF OPERATING DATA | MONTH | TO DATE |
|---|---|---|---|
| 1 | ACTUAL LABOR REPORTED ON PRODUCTION | | |
| 2 | PLUS LABOR UNDER REPORTED ON COMPLETED WORK | | |
| 3 | LESS LABOR OVER REPORTED ON COMPLETED WORK | | |
| 4 | STANDARD LABOR ON PRODUCTION | | |
| 5 | BUDGETED LABOR AT 100% | | |
| 6 | RATE OF OPERATIONS (4 ÷ 5) | | |
| 7 | ACTUAL EXPENSE | | |
| 8 | BUDGETED EXPENSE AT RATE OF OPERATIONS (6) | | |
| 9 | BUDGET VARIANCE | | |
| 10 | VOLUME VARIANCE | | |
| 11 | MATERIAL VARIANCE | | |
| 12 | DEV. FROM STD. METHODS VARIANCE | | |
| 13 | TOTAL VARIANCE | | |

| BUDGET | | ACCOUNT | VARIANCE | | ACTUAL | |
|---|---|---|---|---|---|---|
| MONTH | YEAR TO DATE | | MONTH | YEAR – DATE | MONTH | YEAR TO DATE |
| | | 1–DIRECTORS' & MGRS. SALARIES * | | | | |
| | | 3–DIRECT WAGES | | | | |
| | | 4–INDIRECT WAGES | | | | |
| | | 5–OVERTIME PREMIUM | | | | |
| | | 12–TRAINING TIME | | | | |
| | | 13–CHANGE OVER AND CLEAN UP | | | | |
| | | 14–DELAY TIME | | | | |
| | | 15–MAKE UP TIME | | | | |
| | | 18–PROCESS ALLOWANCE | | | | |
| | | 22–NON UNIT MAKE UP PAY | | | | |
| | | NON UNIT NOT ON PRODUCTION | | | | |
| | | 30–ILLNESS AND TERMINATION PAY | | | | |
| | | 31–HOLIDAY AND VACATION PAY | | | | |
| | | TOTAL PAYROLL | | | | |
| | | | | | | |
| | | 23–24–UNEMPLOY. INS. – F.O.A.B. | | | | |
| | | 50–SUPPLIES | | | | |
| | | 66–TESTING EXPENSE | | | | |
| | | 67–PRODUCTION EXPENSE | | | | |
| | | 110–MAINTENANCE & REPAIRS | | | | |
| | | 111–MOVING & REARRANGING | | | | |
| | | 112–EQUIPMENT RENTALS | | | | |
| | | 120–TRAVEL, CON., & ENTER. | | | | |
| | | 126–STATIONERY | | | | |
| | | 129–DUES & SUBSCRIPTIONS | | | | |
| | | 159–MISCELLANEOUS | | | | |
| | | 189–MISCELLANEOUS CREDITS | | | | |
| | | 200–LOSSES & DEFECTS | | | | |
| | | 235–INVENTORY ADJUSTMENTS | | | | |
| | | 236–FINISHING BULK LOSSES | | | | |
| | | | | | | |
| | | TOTAL CONTROLLABLE EXPENSE | | | | |
| | | | | | | |
| | | 163–LIGHT, HEAT, POWER & WATER | | | | |
| | | 165–BUDGETED SHARE OF SERVICE | | | | |
| | | GENERAL OVERHEAD EXPENSES (LYO OPER) | | | | |
| | | OTHER FIXED CHARGES | | | | |
| | | | | | | |
| | | TOTAL NON–CONTROLLABLE EXPENSES | | | | |
| | | | | | | |
| | | TOTAL DEPARTMENTAL EXPENSE | | | | |

* Included in A/C 165

**Fig. 7. Monthly Comparison of Actual to Budgeted Expense.**

shown in a separate account in the same schedule. The total net variances reflected in the budget comparison reports ties into the books of account.

Setting standards of performance and analyzing variances from the standard after the fact is one method of control. More important and

| | Jan. 31 | Feb. 28 | May 31 | June 30 | YEAR TO DATE Current Year | Last Year |
|---|---|---|---|---|---|---|

**PARENT COMPANY**

COST OF GOODS SOLD

| | Jan. 31 | Feb. 28 | May 31 | June 30 | Current Year | Last Year |
|---|---|---|---|---|---|---|
| Gross standard cost of goods sold | | | | | | |
| Gross standard cost of returns | | | | | | |
| Net loss on returns | | | | | | |
| Expenses applicable to returns | | | | | | |
| Net standard cost of goods: | | | | | | |
| Sold to subsidiary companies | | | | | | |
| Total net standard cost of goods sold | | | | | | |
| Manufacturing costs: | | | | | | |
| Manufacturing and finishing losses | | | | | | |
| Variances - price | | | | | | |
| - materials | | | | | | |
| - labor | | | | | | |
| - burden | | | | | | |
| - printing | | | | | | |
| Printing additions and revisions exp. | | | | | | |
| Discards and deletions | | | | | | |
| Quality control samples | | | | | | |
| Over or under absorbed service exp. | | | | | | |
| Vacation and holiday pay | | | | | | |
| Substitution of materials and | | | | | | |
| deviation from standard methods | | | | | | |
| Total manufacturing costs | | | | | | |
| Other costs: | | | | | | |
| Changes in standard costs | | | | | | |
| Adjustment of book inventories: | | | | | | |
| To lower of cost or market | | | | | | |
| To physical counts | | | | | | |
| Idle plant facilities | | | | | | |
| Alcohol drawback - export | | | | | | |
| Quality control expense - export | | | | | | |
| Miscellaneous | | | | | | |
| Total other costs | | | | | | |
| Total cost of goods sold | | | | | | |
| Ratios to net sales: | | | | | | |
| Total net standard cost of goods sold | | | | | | |
| Total manufacturing costs | | | | | | |
| Total other costs | | | | | | |
| Total | | | | | | |
| Ratio total cost to sales | | | | | | |

**Fig. 8. Schedule of Cost of Goods Sold.**

more productive is the use of the preventative approach where it can be applied. One such application is reduction of the budget for estimated savings used in justifying the purchase of new capital equipment. Another is the requirement for budget committee approval of job orders for major maintenance. When the budget limit is reached, no further expenditures are permitted. Of course, there are instances when the expenditure must be made regardless of budgets, but an improvement in control is nevertheless obtained.

**Work-in-process.** Use of the specific-order cost system provides month-end work-in-process inventories without difficulty. The inventory detail consists of the formulas in process and uncompleted at any time. The value of the inventory includes actual material quantities requisitioned at standard cost, actual direct labor hours reported at the standard rate, and burden at the applicable departmental rate on direct labor.

**Inventory practices peculiar to the business.** Because of the nature and end use of the product, Government regulations and/or company quality policies require specific record-keeping of all raw material in-process and finished goods inventories, so that identity and distribution can be determined conclusively. Although inventory accounting need not be concerned with such records, it is directly affected through the necessity for recording finishing numbers, lot numbers, and so forth.

When raw material is purchased, it is tested and assayed, and only after quality control standards are met can it be used in production. Each lot received is identified by a lot number. Each issuance of the lot is identified by the Rx number into which the material is formulated. The raw material inventory record records this usage.

Inventory records of manufactured bulk material indicate the date of manufacture, and reports are prepared monthly showing those materials in bulk stock beyond control limitations. These reports are sent to Quality Control, who quarantine the material until new tests and assays have been made.

Finished goods inventories of sterile pharmaceuticals, biologicals, and antibiotics are identified by finishing numbers which must be recorded on the distribution to branch warehouses and then to the end-use customer.

Government regulations for distribution of narcotic products require the receipt of narcotic forms before the drugs can be issued. Monthly physical inventories must be taken and all distribution reported to the U.S. Treasury Department, Bureau of Narcotic Control. These regulations also demand complete accounting for the purchase and usage of all narcotic stamps.

Inventory control over loss and shrinkage in the drug industry differs from that in many other industries by the very nature of the products it manufactures and sells. Controls over the usual material storage and handling, and in-process and yield losses are those which are generally practiced in most manufacturing companies. However, owing to Government regulation and company quality standards, expiration dates must be imprinted on the labels of certain products. The expiration date represents the date after which the product cannot be sold. Those products with a short dating tolerance represent a high potential loss unless production and inventories are adequately controlled. Practical administration of this control must be considered in order to meet the sales demand.

Inventory control of all inventories is most successful when centralized in one department. However, this responsibility can be successfully administered only when an inventory investment policy exists. The policy is established by the sales, production, and financial divisions of the company after consideration has been given to several factors, such as sales requirements, seasonal demands, production facilities, material handling, and capital investment required. The machine accounting department provides information on finished goods inventories to the department responsible for control and distribution of inventories. With this information available, material is ordered for production, production is planned and scheduled, and distribution to all branch warehouses is made. Benefits gained are many; to name a few: minimum inventory investment, level production, and material handling in case, pallet, and carload lots, resulting in a better distribution with a minimum of out-of-stock items. The accounts payable department prepares a purchase commitment report which also provides controls of commitments for each type of inventory purchased.

## Plant and equipment records

**Peculiarities of fixed assets—depreciation.** Machinery and equipment used in the industry covers a wider than normal range. It includes machinery and equipment for:

| | |
|---|---|
| Production | Testing (Control) |
| Packaging | Research |

Occasionally it is highly specialized, not only as to drug manufacturing, but for the purpose of meeting the needs of a particular product. It may involve conversion of a standard machine or a complete internal engineering development to fill the peculiar requirements. Normally, this factor does not require special records or special depreciation methods. The possibility of rapid obsolescence of this type of equipment must be considered when depreciation rates are set.

Production equipment for chemical manufacturing usually consists of a number of individual pieces interconnected, with the combined unit having common use for a number of products. Each product may use varying percentages of the whole. Under these circumstances, problems of allocation of depreciation, repairs, and maintenance arise which in most cases can be resolved only by arbitrary allocations.

No special property records are required. Neither is there any accepted standard method in the industry for keeping the property records.

A composite depreciation rate for each of the normal general classifications of fixed assets is often used. These rates may vary from plant to plant. Machinery and equipment for chemical production, because of its nature, may warrant a substantially higher rate than other equipment.

## Reports to management

**Reports in general.** The drug manufacturing industry has no monopoly on problems in the area of providing management with effective internal reports. Its management is interested in the same areas of reports for information and for control purposes as are most other businesses. As is true in nearly any industry or in nearly any individual firm, there is a need from time to time for specially designed reports to cover new situations or conditions.

Simplicity and clarity, with the presentation of only the essential facts, should be the general rule. It is a rule not always easy to follow in the drug industry, with its multiple products and changing trends. To summarize and interpret the various data and to highlight the important facts in order to provide the motivation for executive action are the principal aims to be kept in mind in the preparation of all reports.

**Financial reports.** Reports for management executives consisting of financial data derived from the accounting records should include:

1. Statement of financial condition
2. Analysis of changes in financial condition
3. Report of cash position
4. Statement of inventories
5. Analysis of surplus
6. Statement of income and expenses
7. Report of reasons for changes in net profit
8. Financial and operating ratios, relationships, and trends
9. Comparison of actual operation with budget

These reports are usually presented to management along with comparisons with previous periods and explanatory comment. Financial ratios, as well as ratios of certain balance sheet items to applicable income or expense accounts, are extremely helpful to management in evaluating the information contained in the reports. Distribution within the management group will depend upon the desires of the individuals concerned. The reports may be varied as circumstances warrant and should be expanded or supplemented to meet the needs of the functional executives.

**General operating reports.** No firm line can or should be drawn between financial and operating reports. By adding ratios and comparative figures to indicate trends, various of the financial reports will also serve as basic general operating reports. Ratios are usually used to indicate the relationship of each of the cost and expense lines on the statement of income and expenses to net sales. The same ratios for a prior period or periods provide the trend picture. Many other ratios can be developed to indicate product mix, trend of major product lines, various important cost of goods factors, and trends of the various classes of selling, research, and administrative expenses. In order to preserve the clarity of the basic reports, it is usually desirable to present any lengthy comparisons as separate supplementary reports.

Other general operating reports should include:

Cost of goods schedule (see Figure 8)
Expense control statements (by classes or types of expense)
Schedule of other income
Schedule of other deductions
Monthly budget comparison reports
Quarterly inventory analysis
Personnel changes report

The monthly budget comparison reports should compare actual with budget by expense account by department for first-line supervision. For management review, these reports are usually summarized by controls, along with comparison of sales, cost of goods, and other income and deduction items.

**Reports for measuring sales efficiency.** Statistical sales report forms vary widely. In general, they should be designed to provide the sales organization with adequate information for the functions of sales forecasting, market research, product development, promotion, and sales control. Reports should provide detail such as gross sales, returns and allowances, net sales, and standard cost by product, by product line, and by product grouping such as specialty products, competitive products, and so forth. Sales reports should also be made by territories or other geographical grouping, as well as by class of customers.

**Reports for production.** Directly or indirectly, the production people are concerned with finished goods inventories, as well as with inventories of raw materials and supplies. Production planning must of necessity start with sales forecasts adjusted for inventory policy. Reporting for production therefore involves providing basic information from which production plans are laid, and then historical data for control and use in improving cost and efficiency. Reports for the production area would include:

1. Monthly finished goods inventory reports (for each location and in total—all locations).

2. Production plans reduced to terms of materials, supplies, manu-facturing man-hours, machine-hours, or units of production.

3. Monthly comparison of actual with projected sales, production, and inventories.

4. Daily and monthly historical reports on material losses, rejects, and discards. Daily and monthly operating reports on units produced, actual against standard, and proper examination of significant material and labor variances. Unusual variable costs are noted on the monthly budget com-parison of actual with budget.

**Reports for purchasing.** Reports prepared for purchasing are the pur-chase commitment report and the vendor purchases report. The purchase commitment report shows commitments at previous month-end, current-month purchases and payments, and end-of-month commitments for various inventory classes, construction in progress, and so forth. The vendor report lists dollar purchases by vendor.

**Research reports.** Research is one of the most difficult areas for which reports must be designed. Based on the establishment within the research group of various classifications and subclassifications of research effort, the following type of report of payroll expense has been found workable and of real value:

| Description | Previous Year | Current Year | | | To Date | % of Total |
|---|---|---|---|---|---|---|
| | | Jan. | Feb. | Mar. | | |
| 1. Class of Research | | | | | | |
| a. Sub-Class ............. | xxx | xx | xx | xx | xxx | 10% |
| b. Sub-Class ............. | xxx | xx | xx | xx | xxx | 10% |
| c. Sub-Class ............. | xxx | xx | xx | xx | xxx | 10% |
| Total .............. | xxxx | xxx | xxx | xxx | xxxx | 30% |
| 2. Class of Research | | | | | | |
| a. Sub-Class ............. | xxx | xx | xx | xx | xxx | 35% |
| b. Sub-Class ............. | xxx | xx | xx | xx | xxx | 35% |
| Total .............. | xxxxx | xxxx | xxxx | xxxx | xxxxx | 70% |
| Total Distributable ...... | xxxxx | xxxx | xxxx | xxxx | xxxx | 100% |
| Total Non-Distributable .. | xxxx | xxx | xxx | xxx | xxxx | — |
| Grand Total ............. | xxxxx | xxxx | xxxx | xxxx | xxxxx | |

Distributable payroll expense for a research activity is the counterpart of direct labor in production. Time is reported on punched cards, sum-marized, and reported as outlined. Non-distributable expense includes certain administrative and clerical costs.

# Hints about special devices to reduce record-keeping costs

**Utilization of office equipment.** Reduction of record-keeping costs in-volves approximately the same problem as in most other manufacturing industries. Standard equipment, including tabulating machines, is used. The source of savings lies in proper application of any of the various

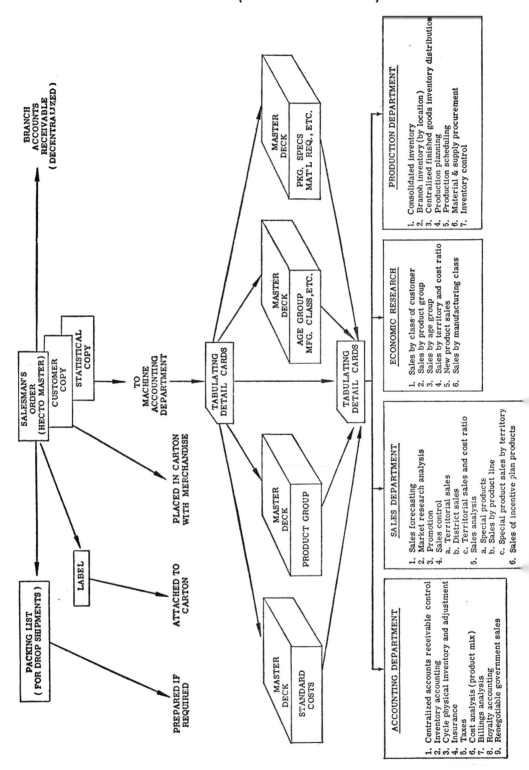

standard pieces of equipment that may be selected for use by the company. Not only substantial savings, but good accounting control can be realized from a completely integrated system which makes maximum use of a few basic source documents. The opportunity to take advantage of such a system is great in the drug industry, because of the large number of products, each in several different package sizes and with different finishes for export, as well as the large number of individual sales invoices that are written.

Figure 9 depicts the integration of two time-saving systems which provide simplicity, flexibility, promptness, and accuracy of information to interrelated departments of the drug industry. It shows the extensive use made of the information taken from the sales invoice. While the chart shows the flow of a copy of the invoice from the special customer order-invoice system described at pages 486–487, the method of preparing the invoice has no bearing on its further use for the purposes shown.

Once the invoice data are put on punched cards, the data are available for use as indicated, but such use is not at all automatic. Master card decks for standard costs, product groups, and so forth, must be maintained. Collation of these various files of information as part of an integrated system makes possible the information and controls shown.

Standard cost files maintained manually require many clerical hours to keep them on a current basis. A complete revision of standards is a major operation usually requiring the additional help of temporary employees for a period of from two to three months. With the file on punched cards, a complete revision can be made in from two to three weeks by one employee using standard tabulating equipment. The incidence of error, always high when doing such a job manually, is reduced to a minimum.

Distribution of service department expenses is another operation that can be readily adapted to machines. A distribution which required 500 man-hours was reduced to 4 hours by the use of standard tabulating equipment. If the new types of electronic equipment are used, the time can be reduced to substantially less than 1 hour.

These are but samples of savings which are possible through the development of an integrated system that makes full use of each piece of original information. Although the starting point may be different in individual companies, the same end results are usually possible.

## Modification of system for a small business

The system and chart of accounts described in this section can be readily contracted and applied to a small business. The same system can be expanded to accommodate, with little change, a very much larger business. Leaving aside the differences in other major functions in a small business

514 DRUGS (MANUFACTURING)

and their effect on the system, the modifications outlined below are suggested for a small business. Keep in mind that the degree to which the chart of accounts is contracted is almost entirely a question of how much information is required for management control and how much the firm wishes to spend for detailed reporting.

**Balance sheet accounts.** Many of the sub-accounts in accounts receivable, inventory, accounts payable, and accrued expense might be eliminated. If direct export sales or foreign operations are not a factor in the business, all applicable export accounts would be eliminated. Other than these, the rest of the accounts would normally be required in a small business.

**Income and expense accounts.** The standard and variance cost of goods sold sub-accounts, which make up nearly half of the total, can be eliminated if a standard cost system is not employed, as is likely to be the case in a small business. If standards are used, a number of sub-accounts might still be disposed of unless substantial detail is required. The need for various other sub-accounts will depend upon other phases of the system.

**Production and production service accounting.** This system provides for a large number of production and production service departments with their attendant accounting requirements. A small business would have only a small number of such departments. The principles involved would remain the same, however, so that the system could be applied, but on a smaller scale.

Use of the system with little modification can therefore be made by a small business by simply scaling it down through elimination of those parts which apply to functions or operations not existent in the small business.

# 18

# Engineers

by

GEORGE OLSEN

Manager, New York Office, Schutte & Williams,
Certified Public Accountants

and

FORD C. WIGGINS

Controller, Lockwood, Kessler & Bartlett, Inc.,
Civil Engineers, New York

## Characteristics that affect the accounting system

**Nature of the business.**[1]   Engineering is the combination of art and science by which materials and energy are made useful to mankind.   An engineer is one trained and experienced in developing the mechanisms and in directing the processes to effect the objectives of engineering.   Applied engineering involves the functions of research and invention, development and experimentation, design and planning, production and construction processing, operations, sales, and industrial management.

The principal branches of engineering include civil, mechanical, electrical, and chemical engineering, and their related fields.   *Civil engineering,* the oldest type of engineering, involves the design and supervision of dams, harbors, waterways, roads, airfields, railroads, and the like.   Related fields are mining engineering and metallurgical engineering, which involve the location and development of metallic and non-metallic minerals and the development of processes for extracting metals from ores, refining the products, and combining metals to form alloys for industry.   Also related is ceramic engineering, which performs similar functions with non-metallic minerals that enter into the making of glass, tile, enameled metals, and the

---

[1] Adapted, with permission, from *Engineering As a Career, a Message to Young Men, Teachers and Parents.*   New York: Engineers' Council for Professional Development, 1942.

like. *Mechanical engineering* deals with production machinery and equipment. It covers such subdivisions of engineering as aeronautical, automotive, marine, refrigeration and air-conditioning, and the like, many of which involve close collaboration with other fields of engineering. *Chemical engineering* involves the development of processes for changing materials in chemical content and form, usually for industrial uses.

An engineering firm may furnish more than one type of service or may confine its operations to one field. Where seasonal weather conditions curtail work, as in aerial surveying, which cannot be done when ground overgrowth conceals topographic evidences, year-round economic balance requires engaging in allied activities.

**Government control.** Most states require registration for the professional practice of engineering. The registration laws usually prohibit corporations from practicing engineering. However, the field of engineering is so far-reaching that many branches are outside the scope of the legislation and are conducted by corporations. Some old engineering firms, established before the registration laws were enacted, have continued as corporations.

**General features.** Pure research is seldom undertaken by private engineering enterprises, but organized research and exploration at the expense and in the interest of venture capital are within the scope of engineering endeavors. A large number of research and exploratory ventures have been undertaken in recent years by capital venturers seeking tax deductions against top-bracket income for expenses of exploration conducted by engineers.

**Functional peculiarities.** *Selling.* The end product of the work performed usually takes the form of a report, design, or drawing. If supervision services only are to be rendered, this becomes the end product. In any event, the selling technique requires an understanding of the client's desires and the method by which those desires can be satisfactorily met, as well as determination of the cost of performing the work. It is advisable to draw up a contract for each job. The contract should include: (a) description of the services to be performed, (b) an estimate of the time required for completion, (c) the fees to be charged—that is, lump sum, per diem, percentage of construction cost, or cost-plus-fixed fee—and (d) the time of payment of fees. A record of the contract is prepared for convenience in referring to its terms, for allocating the proportions of sales value of the contract, as estimated by the engineers, to the various departments, and for recording a cost summary of the job (see Figure 1).

*Financing.* Many engagements, such as designing and supervising construction of dams, canals, water systems, highways, and the like, are with public agencies, public utilities, and other companies capable of financing the projects. However, the terms of the engagement may require the engi-

JOB NO.    _____

REVISION   _____

DATE       _____

RECORD OF CONTRACT AND COST SUMMARY SHEET

Job Name and Location: _____

_____

Client and Billing Address: _____

_____

Description of Services Required: _____

_____

Form of Agreement: _____

Date of Agreement: _____

Payment and Billing Basis: _____

_____

_____

Insurance Requirements: _____

|                  | Sales Value | Per Cent | Estimated Cost | Actual Cost | P&L |
|------------------|-------------|----------|----------------|-------------|-----|
| Flying           |             |          |                |             |     |
| Photo Laboratory |             |          |                |             |     |
| Stereo-Plotting  |             |          |                |             |     |
| Aerial Drafting  |             |          |                |             |     |
| Field            |             |          |                |             |     |
| Ground Drafting  |             |          |                |             |     |
| Engineering      |             |          |                |             |     |
| Total            |             |          |                |             |     |

**Fig. 1. Record of Contract and Cost Summary Sheet.**

neer to expend large sums before any income is received. For example, the contract may call for payment only upon completion of work that may take several months. In other cases, the contract may call for the holding back of a portion of the fee—called a "contract retention"—until the completed job has been approved by the client. These conditions may create a need for outside financing by bank or other loans to supplement the engineer's own working capital.

**Asset peculiarities.** Inasmuch as engineering is service, the investment in plant is usually not large. However, civil engineers may have heavy investments in ground, aerial, photographic, and drafting equipment. The same is true of mining and metallurgical engineers and of engineers in other branches.

Among the assets may be Unbilled Accruals which arise in connection with accounting for jobs in progress. This account is explained at page 523.

**Ownership peculiarities.** The business is usually conducted as a sole proprietorship or partnership because of the state registration laws. As mentioned at page 516, the corporate form of organization is found where permissible.

**Principal accounting problems.** The principal accounting problem is that of relating costs of service—usually in terms of man-hours and dollars—and expenses to specific jobs. The solution is "pigeon-hole" accounting in the sense that a multitude of charges must be distributed to the proper slots, routinely, by manual or machine methods.

Where unbilled accruals for jobs in progress are carried on the books, the problem arises of obtaining the full co-operation of the engineers who must make the periodic estimates of the percentage of completion of the contract from which the entries are developed. The engineers must be able to comprehend the accounting requirements insofar as they relate to unbilled accruals.

## Functional organization

**Division into departments.** Each field of engineering covers sufficient subdivisions of special activities to require departmentalization of each kind of service. For example, a civil engineering firm might have the following operating departments:

1. Ground division
   Field
   Drafting
2. Aerial or photogrammetric division
   Flying
   Photo-laboratory
   Stereo-plotting
   Drafting
3. Design and supervision division
   Design
   Supervision of construction
4. Foreign division

The above organization is shown in chart form in Figure 2.

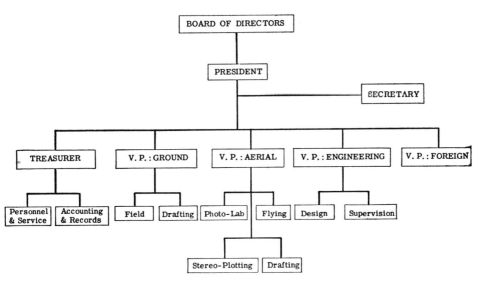

**Fig. 2. Organization Chart.**

## Principles of the system

**Principles to be applied in reflecting income, costs, and expenses.** Engineering practitioners of moderate size, whether individuals or firms, frequently adopt cash-basis accounting. When the scope of operations, in terms of volume and duration of contracts, requires information ordinarily obtainable from records kept on the accrual basis in order to match income with costs, jobs in progress must be accounted for, as explained at pages 523 et seq.

The type of contract and terms of billing govern the method of reflecting income. Established accounting practice permits the recognition of income on contracts: (1) when the work is completed, physically delivered, and accepted, (2) when each portion is delivered, and (3) progressively as work is completed.

There may be a waiting period between physical completion and acceptance of the work by the client. Ordinarily, income is reflected upon completion where the revenue can be substantially determined and acceptance of the work is not in doubt. Should a condition exist which casts doubt upon satisfactory performance, the engineer may not have the legal right to reflect income.

The practice of accruing earnings progressively with performance is sound where estimates of progress are comparable with partial deliveries and the method is consistently applied. (See page 523 for treatment of accruals.) Engineers generally apply this method of taking income into account where contracts are performed on a fee basis, or on any basis where income can be precisely determined during performance and where ultimate delivery is customarily devoid of hazards, as in the case of contracts with heavy-construction contractors.

Where a single contract involves more than one division of engineering activity, income is allocated to the divisions and, in turn, to the departments in which the work is performed. This allocation is made in accordance with the contract, where the contract price is segregated among various phases of work. If no segregation is made in the contract, income is allocated in proportion to the costs and expenses sustained by each department working on the contract.

The accounting principle of relating costs and expenses to income is applied on a departmental basis and then by jobs. The nature of the work and of the services rendered, and the feasibility of relating costs to contracts, permit a relatively high proportion of costs and expenses to be charged to departments and jobs. Indirect operating expenses are assigned to departments and then to jobs. Non-operating expenses may be similarly assigned where the engineer desires information as to the operational and non-operational costs and expenses of jobs.

## Classification of accounts and books of account

### Balance sheet accounts.

| Assets | Debits from | Credits from |
|---|---|---|
| Current Assets: | | |
| Cash in Banks | Cash Receipts | Cash Disbursements |
| Petty Cash | Cash Disbursements | Cash Receipts |
| | (Only when imprest amount of fund is changed) | |
| Receivables | | |
| Billed Accounts | Sales Journal | Cash Receipts |
| Retained Amounts | Do | Do |
| Unbilled Accruals | General Journal | General Journal |
| Reserve for Doubtful Accounts | Do | Do |
| Jobs in Progress | Do | Do |
| (Used in place of Unbilled Accruals if jobs are carried at cost) | | |
| Inventory—Supplies | Voucher Register | Do |
| Deposits on Bids, etc. | Do | Cash Receipts |
| Expense Advances | Do | General Journal |
| Property, Plant, and Equipment: | | |
| Land | Do | Cash Receipts or General Journal |
| Building | Do | Do |
| Engineering Equipment | Do | Do |
| Furniture and Fixtures | Do | Do |

|  | Debits from | Credits from |
|---|---|---|
| Automotive Equipment .............. | Voucher Register | Cash Receipts or General Journal |
| Leasehold Improvements ............. | Do | Do |
| Reserve for Depreciation .......... | General Journal | General Journal |
| (Separate reserve account for each classification and type of asset) | | |
| Prepaid and Deferred Expenses: | | |
| Prepaid Insurance ................... | Voucher Register | Do |
| Prepaid Interest ................... | Voucher Register, or Cash Disbursements, or Cash Receipts | Do |

*Liabilities*

| Current Liabilities: | | |
|---|---|---|
| Accounts Payable ................... | Cash Disbursements | Voucher Register |
| F.I.C.A. Taxes Withheld ............. | Do | Do |
| Federal Income Taxes Withheld ....... | Do | Do |
| Payroll Clearing ................... | Do | General Journal |
| Accrued F.I.C.A. Taxes .............. | Do | Do |
| Accrued State Unemployment Taxes... | Do | Do |
| Accrued Federal Unemployment Taxes. | Do | Do |
| Accrued Workmen's Compensation Insurance ......................... | Do | Do |
| Accrued State Franchise Taxes ........ | Do | Do |
| Federal Income Tax Payable ......... | Do | Do |
| Advances on Jobs .................. | General Journal | Cash Receipts |
| Deferred Income ..................... | Do | General Journal |

*Proprietorship*

| Proprietor's Capital ................... | General Journal or Cash Disbursements | General Journal or Cash Receipts |
|---|---|---|
| Proprietor's Drawings ................. | Do | Do |
| or | | |
| Partners' Capital .................... | Do | Do |
| Partners' Drawings ................... | Do | Do |

*Capital Stock and Surplus*

| Capital Stock ........................ | Do | Do |
|---|---|---|
| Earned Surplus ...................... | Do | Do |

## Income and expense accounts.

|  | Debits from | Credits from |
|---|---|---|
| Gross Income Billed—Ground .......... | | Sales Journal |
| Gross Income Billed—Aerial .......... | | Do |
| Gross Income Billed—Design .......... | | Do |
| Gross Income Billed—Foreign .......... | | Do |
| Gross Income Unbilled—Ground ....... | General Journal | General Journal |
| Gross Income Unbilled—Aerial ......... | Do | Do |
| Gross Income Unbilled—Design ........ | Do | Do |
| Gross Income Unbilled—Foreign ....... | Do | Do |
| Job Expense ......................... | Do | |
| Overhead Applied to Jobs .............. | Do | |

(Job Expense and Overhead Applied to Jobs are used in place of the job expense accounts listed below if job costs are carried in a Jobs in Progress account)

Direct Job Expense—Ground Field:

| | |
|---|---|
| Labor ........................... | General Journal |
| Professional Services ................ | Voucher Register |
| Supplies ......................... | Do |
| Postage, Freight, and Express ........ | Do |
| Room and Board .................. | Do |
| Travel Expense .................... | Do |
| Miscellaneous ..................... | Do |
| Direct Job Expense—Ground Drafting... | General Journal, |
| (Same detail as for Ground Field) | Voucher Register |
| Direct Job Expense—Aerial Flying ...... | Do |
| (Same detail as for Ground Field) | |
| Direct Job Expense—Aerial Photo-Laboratory ............................ | Do |
| (Same detail as for Ground Field) | |
| Direct Job Expense—Aerial Stereo-Plotting .............................. | Do |
| (Same detail as for Ground Field) | |
| Direct Job Expense—Aerial Drafting .... | Do |
| (Same detail as for Ground Field) | |
| Direct Job Expense—Design and Supervision ........................... | Do |
| (Same detail as for Ground Field) | |
| Direct Job Expense—Foreign ........... | Do |
| (Same detail as for Ground Field) | |

Indirect Expense—Ground Field:

| | |
|---|---|
| Salaries—Supervisory ................ | General Journal |
|     —Vacation, Holiday, and Sickness Pay ................. | Do |
|     —Trainees ................... | Do |
|     —Idle Time ................. | Do |
| Payroll Taxes ...................... | Do |
| Maintenance and Repairs ............ | Voucher Register |
| Insurance ........................ | General Journal |
| Depreciation ...................... | Do |
| Miscellaneous ..................... | Voucher Register |
| Indirect Expense—Ground Drafting ..... | General Journal, |
| Same detail as Ground Field. | Voucher Register |

| | |
|---|---|
| Indirect Expense—Aerial Flying ........ | |
| Same detail as Ground Field, with following additions: | |
| Salaries—Repairs and Maintenance .... | General Journal |
| Aircraft Gas and Oil ............... | Voucher Register |
| Indirect Expense—Aerial Photo-Laboratory ............................ | General Journal, |
| (Same detail as for Ground Field) | Voucher Register |

| | Debits from | Credits from |
|---|---|---|
| Indirect Expense—Aerial Stereo-Plotting. | General Journal, | |
|   (Same detail as for Ground Field) | Voucher Register | |
| Indirect Expense—Aerial Drafting ...... | Do | |
|   (Same detail as for Ground Field) | | |
| Indirect Expense—Design and Supervision | Do | |
|   (Same detail as for Ground Field) | | |
| Indirect Expense—Foreign ............. | Do | |
|   (Same detail as for Ground Field) | | |
| Administrative and General Expense: | | |
|   Salaries—Executive ................. | General Journal | |
|       —Office ..................... | Do | |
|       —Vacation, Holiday, and Sick- | | |
|         ness Pay ................ | Do | |
|       —Sales Promotion ............ | Do | |
|   Payroll Taxes ....................... | Do | |
|   Employee Welfare ................... | Voucher Register | |
|   Professional Services ................ | Do | |
|   Legal and Auditing ................. | Do | |
|   Supplies ........................... | Do | |
|   Postage, Express, and Freight ........ | Do | |
|   Telephone and Telegraph ............. | Do | |
|   Travel Expense ..................... | Do | |
|   Maintenance and Repairs ............ | Do | |
|   Cleaning Service and Supplies ........ | Do | |
|   Rent ............................. | Do | |
|   Heat, Light, and Water ............. | Do | |
|   Insurance ......................... | General Journal | |
|   Life Insurance ..................... | Do | |
|   Depreciation ....................... | Do | |
|   Franchise Taxes ................... | Do | |
|   Dues ............................. | Voucher Register | |
|   Publications and Subscriptions ........ | Do | |
|   Professional Registration Fees ........ | Do | |
|   Entertainment ..................... | Do | |
|   Advertising ....................... | Do | |
|   Contributions ...................... | Do | |
|   Interest Expense ................... | General Journal | |
|   Bad Debts ......................... | Do | |
|   Miscellaneous ...................... | Voucher Register | |
| Miscellaneous Income .................. | | Cash Receipts |
| Provision for Income Taxes ............ | General Journal | |

**Accounts and entries peculiar to the profession.** *Unbilled Accruals.*
Accounting for jobs in progress ordinarily extends from the date of the
contract to the date of completion and acceptance by the client. Where
preliminary expenses are incurred in accordance with pre-contract letters
of intent, accounting for jobs in progress may begin before the contract
date.

Two basic methods of accounting for jobs in progress are used: (1) *at
cost*, in which case costs are carried in a Jobs in Progress account as an

asset, similar to inventory; (2) *at contract or selling price,* in which case the proportionate part of the contract price represented by progress to date is carried in the Unbilled Accruals account as an asset, similar to accounts receivable. Under both methods, a subsidiary Job Cost Ledger is maintained for the purpose of accumulating costs and expenses by jobs (see Figure 5, page 527).

The pattern of entries to record jobs in progress is as follows: 1. Costs transferred to Jobs in Progress account:

```
Dr.  Jobs in Progress ...................  $
       (control and detail)
Cr.    Services (Salaries) ...............          $
Cr.    Material (Supplies) ..............
Cr.    Overhead (Expense allocations) ...
```

The costs thus accumulated on jobs in progress may remain in the Jobs in Progress account until delivery and acceptance of the work under contract, at which time the account is costed out to the Job Expense account in total as an offset to contract revenue. Should loss on the contract be anticipated or sustained prior to completion, an adequate reserve for loss should be established and charged against income. The reserve should be applied against the Jobs in Progress account, for the obvious reason that the accumulated costs in the latter account could otherwise exceed the related contract price.

Costs may be charged directly to Jobs in Progress, control and detail accounts, by jobs and by account classifications of salaries, supplies, and overhead expenses.

2. Jobs in progress carried as unbilled accruals:

```
Dr.  Unbilled Accruals ...................  $
       (control and detail)
Cr.    Gross Income—Unbilled ..........          $
```

This entry recognizes income earned on partial deliveries although actual physical delivery may not have taken place for any part of the work. It may represent estimates of completion priced at the contractual rate. Where parts of the work are actually delivered and accepted and billed at the partial billing price, the unbilled accruals are transferred to Receivables—Billed Accounts, inasmuch as there is an account stated between the engineer and the client, and Gross Income Unbilled is transferred to Gross Income Billed.

Job expenses are charged directly to cost and expense accounts, by jobs, for control purposes.

*Retained Amounts.* Contracts may provide for partial payments on account of the contract price for partial deliveries, determined in accordance with the terms, formula, or schedule provided in the contract, less retained amounts.  Usually about 10 per cent of the contract price is retained.  Entry for retained percentage is made at the time of billing for partial deliveries or completion of the work.  The account is usually carried until final acceptance of the work or a short period thereafter, unless the contract provides for release of retained amounts upon satisfactory completion of phases of the work.

1

Dr.  Receivables—Billed Accounts ........ $

Dr.  Retained Amount ...................

Cr.      Gross Income—Billed  ............          $

2

Dr.  Cash  .............................. $

Cr.      Retained Amount ................          $

## Peculiarities of procedures

**Accounting for revenue.**  Each operating department renders a monthly report (Figure 3) to the accounting department on each job in the department, showing the per cent of completion during the period. The form sets forth each section of the various operating departments. Each section inserts a per cent-of-completion figure opposite its name, under the date indicated.  Since this is a status report of a job, memo information as to the billing status is indicated on the form.

The data submitted on Figure 3 by the operating departments are summarized on another form (Figure 4) by the accounting department, which posts the current per cent of completion of each job by each phase of work —flying, photo-laboratory, stereo-plotting, drafting, and the like—to the record of per cent of completion reported at the end of the preceding period.  This posting enables the accounting department to calculate the per cent of progress and the amount of progress earnings, in terms of contract price, during the period.  The same result is derived by calculating and recording the amount of completion, based on the per cent reported on Figure 4 at the end of each period.  The progress earnings would be the difference between the calculated amounts of completion at the beginning and at the end of each period.

Where income is consistently recorded only at the conclusion of each contract, it is not necessary to determine progress earnings except for memorandum purposes.  Such memoranda are usually required by engineers who borrow to finance engagements in progress.

## Cost and expense factors

**Job cost ledger.**  The job cost ledger (Figure 5) is a subsidiary ledger in which direct departmental costs applicable to each job are assembled.  A

## PROGRESS STATUS

JOB. NO. _____

### PER CENT COMPLETED TO DATE

| Date | | | | | | | | | | |
|---|---|---|---|---|---|---|---|---|---|---|
| Flying | | | | | | | | | | |
| Photo Lab | | | | | | | | | | |
| Stereo | | | | | | | | | | |
| Aerial Drafting | | | | | | | | | | |
| Field | | | | | | | | | | |
| Ground Drafting | | | | | | | | | | |
| Engineering | | | | | | | | | | |

### BILLING STATUS

| BILLED | | | RECEIVED | | | BALANCE | | |
|---|---|---|---|---|---|---|---|---|
| Date | Amount | | Date | Amount | | Date | Amount | |
| | | | | | | | | |
| | | | | | | | | |
| | | | | | | | | |

| | | | | | | | | |
|---|---|---|---|---|---|---|---|---|
| | | | | | | | | |
| | | | | | | | | |

COMMENTS:

**Fig. 3. Job Progress Report.**

---

Per Cent Completed of Jobs in Progress for Period Ending _____

| Job# | Name | Fly. | Photo Lab | Ster. | Air Draft. | Eng. | Ground Surv. | Draft. | Bill Date |
|---|---|---|---|---|---|---|---|---|---|
| | | | | | | | | | |
| | | | | | | | | | |
| | | | | | | | | | |
| | | | | | | | | | |
| | | | | | | | | | |
| | | | | | | | | | |

**Fig. 4. Per Cent Completed of All Jobs in Progress.**

separate sheet is prepared for each department that does work on the job. The totals of the debits and credits are entered from the general journal and the voucher register and distributed to the appropriate expense classifications. At the end of each month the difference between the total of the debits and credits is entered in the Monthly Total column and added to the preceding accumulated total in the Total To Date column.

| | TOTAL | | | | DIRECT JOB EXPENSES | | | | | | |
|---|---|---|---|---|---|---|---|---|---|---|---|
| Date | Debit | Credit | Monthly Total | Total To Date | Labor | Prof. Services | Supplies | Postage Freight & Express | Rooms & Board | Travel Expense | Misc. |
| | | | | | | | | | | | |
| | | | | | | | | | | | |
| | | | | | | | | | | | |
| | | | | | | | | | | | |
| | | | | | | | | | | | |

JOB COST LEDGER Job No._____ Department_____

Fig. 5. Job Cost Ledger.

**Time records.** Time records of employees of the operating departments are essential in any system in which costing of jobs is an objective. Figure 6 sets forth the key data of the time record submitted by each employee to the accounting department: the name of the employee, his division or section, the time period, the identification of jobs, and the number of hours of each working day spent by the employee on each job.

The individual time records are used to prepare the payroll summary, which shows the gross salary, deductions, and net salary of all individuals by departments and in total. The accounting office calculates the compensation to be paid and also the amount to be distributed to jobs in the following manner: (1) by multiplying the number of hours charged by the employee to each job by the employee's hourly rate, and (2) summarizing such amounts by jobs and by departments. The total of this summary should agree with the total gross salaries of operating departments. The journal entry recording the payroll is as follows:

Dr. Direct Job Expense—(Each Operating Department)—Labor $
Dr. Indirect Expense—(Each Operating Department)—Salaries.
       Supervisory ............... $
       Vacation, etc. .............
       Trainees ..................
       Idle Time ................
Dr. Administrative and General Expense ......................
       Salaries—Executive ....... $
              —Office ..........
              —Vacation, etc. ....
              —Sales Promotion ..
Cr. Payroll Clearing (Net Payroll) ......................... $
Cr. F.I.C.A. Taxes Withheld ............................
Cr. Federal Income Taxes Withheld ........................

# WEEKLY TIME REPORT

NAME _____

DIVISION _____

WEEK ENDED _____

| JOB NO. or NAME | Mon. | Tues. | Wed. | Thurs. | Fri. | Sat. | Sun. | Total Hours | Reg. T. Overt. | Rate |
|---|---|---|---|---|---|---|---|---|---|---|
| | | | | | | | | | | |
| | | | | | | | | | | |
| | | | | | | | | | | |
| | | | | | | | | | | |
| TOTALS | | | | | | | | | | |

INDICATE • NEXT TO OVERTIME HOURS.
IF CHECK IS TO BE MAILED, GIVE ADDRESS.

_____

_____

## FOR OFFICE USE ONLY

| DIRECT | | | INDIRECT | | | |
|---|---|---|---|---|---|---|
| Hours | Amount | Job No. | Hours | Amount | Acct. No. |
| | | | | | |
| | | | | | |
| | | | | | |

| | | | |
|---|---|---|---|
| S. S. | | REG. | |
| W/H | | O. T. | |
| DIS. | | Total | |
| A. H. S. | | Ded. | |
| BONDS | | Total | |
| Total Ded. | | | |

APPROVED BY _____

REMARKS _____

**Fig. 6. Weekly Time Report.**

The usual entries are made to record the employer's share of payroll taxes and the payment of the payroll.

**Operating department overhead.** Indirect or overhead expenses of the operating departments are distributed to jobs by applying an estimated overhead rate, calculated for each department, to direct labor hours of that department on each job. The estimated rate is based on the formula of dividing budgeted overhead of the department by budgeted direct labor hours of the department. For example, if budgeted overhead of the photo-laboratory department for an annual period is $30,000, and expected direct labor hours are 6,000 hours, the estimated overhead rate would be $5 per direct labor hour. Each job would be charged $5 per actual direct labor hour.

If the cost method of accounting for jobs in progress is used, the estimated overhead would be recorded as follows:

        Dr.  Jobs in Progress .................... $
        Cr.      Overhead Applied to Jobs ........              $

If the selling-price method of accounting for jobs in progress is used, the development of a job account containing all indirect expenses, in addition to direct costs, applicable to each job is unnecessary. The indirect expenses are allocated to jobs, for job information purposes, by distributions to jobs on internal reports: the departmental profit and loss statement (see page 530) and related detail schedules. Comparison of budgeted and actual overhead expenses should be made monthly and any significant variances investigated.

Department overhead rates are used in order to charge jobs with a fair and reasonable apportionment of indirect expenses as jobs flow through the plant. It would not seem fair to charge a job with the overhead expenses of all departments on a blanket overall rate basis when only a few departments have served the job.

In calculating the overhead expenses chargeable to each department, the normal plant utilization should be taken into account. For example, overhead charges attributable to the flying department should be related to airplane utilization, which may not exceed 300 to 400 hours annually because of the seasonal factor.

**Administrative overhead.** Administrative expenses may also be allocated to jobs. Whether such allocations should be recorded on the books or carried on reports without bookkeeping entries is a matter of choice. For control purposes, it is preferable to allocate administration expenses on the books, following the same procedures described in the preceding paragraphs for applying overhead expenses of operating departments to jobs.

Upon completion of the job, income and costs are entered in total on the

Record of Contract and Cost Summary (Figure 1) by departments from the departmental profit and loss statement for the purpose of furnishing a complete history of the job.

## Reports to management

**Financial and operating reports.** Financial information is submitted to management in the customary form of a balance sheet and profit and loss statement, which may be prepared monthly. Accounts receivable details are furnished to management monthly.

The accounting system lends itself to the preparation of monthly reports showing essential job cost data.

Monthly job data reports include:

1. Departmental profit and loss statement—by jobs.
2. Expenses (operating and non-operating departments)—budgeted versus actual.

Monthly reports of job backlog (per record file of job data prepared when contracts are signed and uncompleted jobs in progress) include:

1. Backlog by departments and sections, by jobs.
2. Expected delivery dates.

**Statistical reports.** These reports include:

1. Production hours by departments and sections.
2. Non-production hours by departments and sections.

## Modifications of the system for small business

Where the owner has direct knowledge of the status and peculiarities of each contract, the details of job revenue and job cost control provided by the system described would not be necessary. A small business would, however, find it desirable to accumulate job costs and to identify expenses with jobs to the extent feasible. It would not ordinarily require progress earnings accruals, except from time to time for memo purposes to gauge progress efficiency.

# 19

# Estates and Trusts—Individual Fiduciary

by

**LEWIS L. TANGUY**

Certified Public Accountant; Member of staff of Lybrand,
Ross Bros. & Montgomery, Philadelphia

and

**THOMAS J. GAFFNEY, ESQ.**

Member of the Philadelphia Bar

## Characteristics that affect the accounting system

**Court jurisdiction.** Estates and trusts are generally under the jurisdiction of probate courts, and accountings are made direct to them. As a result, the accountings vary widely in form and content, for they must meet the statutory requirements and the court rules, decisions, and precedents of the particular state and of its local probate courts. These requirements differ in the various states and even in adjoining counties of the same state.

A formal accounting may not be required or may be waived by all the parties at interest in some situations, such as where the spouse or the children of the decedent are the sole beneficiaries, or where the estate is of nominal size.

There are three basic types of accounting systems for estates and trusts, all essentially on a cash basis. One system applies where the court requires or permits a classification of the transactions into a very few categories; the second applies where the practice is to present an extensive classification of the transactions; the third is substantially a statement of cash receipts and disbursements.

The following pages present (1) background information that should be helpful in setting up and operating an accounting system for an estate or trust and (2) three examples of an executor's account that show the basic methods of reporting. The system applies to estates and trusts administored by an individual fiduciary  An accounting system for estates and trusts administered by a corporate fiduciary is presented in Section 20.

**Nature and purposes of estates and trusts.** The estates and trusts considered in this section consist of the following:

1. Estates of decedents.
2. Estates of wards of the court, such as minors, and other persons judicially determined to be legally incompetent.
3. Trusts created under the wills of decedents (testamentary trusts).
4. Trusts created by an individual or individuals during life (*inter vivos* trusts).

Estates of bankrupts and of those whose assets are in the hands of a receiver are under the jurisdiction of other civil courts.

Estates and trusts have a common purpose in that the fiduciary (an individual or corporation, such as a trust company) ordinarily takes legal title to an asset or assets and at the same time assumes the duty of using them for the benefit of a designated person or institution.  For example, an executor under a will, or an administrator appointed by a probate court, assembles the assets of a decedent, pays his funeral expenses, his debts, the death taxes, and the expenses of administration, and then distributes the balance of principal and of income to the heirs in accordance with the will or the intestate laws.  As another example, the guardian of a minor may receive amounts payable to the minor under (1) a decedent's will, (2) workmen's compensation or social security laws, or (3) life or accident policies upon the death of the insured. The guardian invests these amounts and uses the income, if necessary, for the minor's support and education. If the income is not needed for these purposes, the guardian accumulates it until the minor (ward) becomes of age.  The assets of a legal incompetent, when placed in the possession of a guardian, are used for paying the incompetent's debts and for his support, if necessary.  The available income is used before principal.

In a trust created under a will, the trustee receives the assets (the principal or corpus) as a distribution from the executor or administrator after the estate has been administered; in a trust created under a deed, the trustee receives the assets from the grantor of the deed.  The trustee's duties are then (1) to invest and reinvest the principal, and (2) collect the income, pay from it the expenses of the trust, and make distribution in accordance with the terms of the will or deed.  A trust in which the beneficiaries are individuals may exist only for a limited time—in general, not more than 21 years after some life in being at creation of the trust.  A trust for charitable or similar purposes may be perpetual.

**Government control.** *Statutes and common law.*  The various states have enacted numerous statutes governing most phases of estates and trusts.  Where the statutes fail to apply to a given situation, recourse may be had to the common law.  As a result, estates and trusts can be closely controlled by the probate courts. In practice the control varies widely, and in those jurisdictions where only one judge handles probate court cases it can be expected that his personal characteristics will affect the degree of control exercised.

In view of the close control of the courts, the fiduciaries of well-managed estates and trusts usually keep in close touch with their counsel. Sales of real estate usually require court approval and a determination that the proposed sale is in the best interests of the estate; similarly, counsel may advise the fiduciary that the sale of an important asset and the consideration to be received should be approved by the court so that the fiduciary can avoid personal liability. Sales of securities through a stock exchange normally do not require court approval. In many cases, substantial fees to attorneys, C.P.A.'s, or others for services rendered should have court approval before payment by the fiduciary.

*Legal and nonlegal investments.* Legal investments are those meeting statutory specifications for investments of an estate or trust. The statute usually details the requirements, although not always. A state body, such as the State Corporation Commission in Virginia, may prepare an official list which shows some but not necessarily all of the eligible securities. In states that provide no lists, an organization, such as the state bankers association, may prepare an unofficial list of many of the securities which in the opinion of the organization's counsel meet the statutory requirements. Some states, such as Massachusetts, follow the "prudent man" doctrine which holds that fiduciaries must exercise the judgment and care which prudent men exercise in the management of their own investments.

Nonlegal investments are, of course, those that do not meet statutory requirements. Some wills specifically permit the fiduciary to invest in nonlegals as well as to retain nonlegals held by the decedent at death. The decedent's will may instruct the fiduciary to retain a specific investment. Even so, if a change in economic conditions causes a serious shrinkage in the investment, the beneficiaries may attempt to have the court surcharge the fiduciary with the shrinkage.

To minimize the possibility of a future surcharge (that is, personal liability for a loss), it would seem advisable for a fiduciary to discuss thoroughly his investment policy and plans with counsel.

*Incorporation of a business.* If the assets of an estate include a business, the court may permit the fiduciary to operate it until it can be sold as a going concern. If it seems to the fiduciary and the heirs that it is in the best interests of the estate to continue to operate it, they may, with court approval, have the business incorporated. Incorporation is desirable for at least three reasons:

1. It protects the other assets of the estate from the claims of creditors of the business.

2. It avoids personal liability of the fiduciary for the claims of creditors of the business.

3. It facilitates distribution of the estate, inasmuch as the shares, as assets of the estate, can be distributed in kind.

**Taxes, licenses, and fees.** Estates and trusts are subject to:

1. Death taxes, Federal and state.
2. Income taxes, Federal and frequently state.
3. Many of the taxes on property and on transactions, such as real estate, personal property, and sales taxes.
4. Fees for probating the will, filing accounts, and examinations by court-appointed examiners (attorneys).

**Financing.** A fiduciary seldom has occasion to do any financing of the operations of an estate or trust. Payment of the Federal estate tax is usually the largest item to be paid in an estate or in an *inter vivos* trust that is subject to the tax at the death of the grantor. This is usually met by the sale of assets, and, where there has been competent estate planning, the estate or trust will have assets available for the purpose.

Occasionally, a trustee holding improved real estate may require funds for extensive repairs or remodeling in order to produce more income. If, in the opinion of his counsel, the payments may be made from principal, the trustee can sell other assets, if available, to obtain the necessary cash, or he may obtain a mortgage on the property with court approval. If the payments are to be made from income, the project can be financed in the same way, but there should be a definite plan to repay the debt from income. Whether the payments are to be made from principal or from income seems to depend on the intent of the testator or the grantor. If the intent of the decedent appears to have been to provide for his widow and children, courts might permit the trustee to pay for the project from principal. If the intent appears to have been to keep the principal intact, the cost of the project might have to be paid from income. In the case of one large perpetual trust, the court decided (1) that the trustee could construct buildings on vacant ground received under the will and pay for them from principal, and (2) that improvements to existing buildings must be paid from income.

**Principal accounting problems.** Four factors in estate and trust accounting call for special discussion. These factors are:

1. Distinguishing between principal and income.
2. Distinguishing between real estate and personal estate.
3. Use of the cash basis.
4. Difference in value of assets for court and for tax accounting.

1. *Distinguishing between principal and income.* The distinction between principal and income in an estate or trust is necessary because in

many cases the persons designated in the will or deed of trust to receive the income for life (the life tenants) differ from those designated to receive the principal or corpus at the death of the life tenant (the remaindermen).

The distinctions between principal and income are shown in some detail below:

PRINCIPAL, IN GENERAL. *Principal* consists of the assets which a decedent owns at his death, or the assets which a donor transfers to a trustee either at the time of the initial grant or by subsequent *inter vivos* transfers. Gains on the sale or other disposition of assets represent the usual increases in principal. Losses on the sale or redemption of assets, payment of the debts of decedent, funeral expenses, death taxes, and taxes on capital gains decrease principal.

In some jurisdictions, advances and loans to an estate are treated as increases in principal when the cash is received and as decreases when they are paid. In other jurisdictions, they may be treated as items which neither increase nor decrease the total principal. The latter method seems preferable if a choice is permitted.

INCOME, IN GENERAL. *Income* is the return or the earnings on principal. It usually consists of interest on notes, mortgages and bonds, dividends on stocks, and rents.

INTEREST-BEARING OBLIGATIONS IN DEFAULT. Interest-bearing obligations usually cause little accounting difficulty unless the obligations go into default. In some states, when the defaulted obligation is later converted into cash and/or property which can be fairly apportioned, the proceeds are apportioned between principal and income in accordance with a statute or a local court decision.

PREMIUMS AND DISCOUNTS ON BONDS. If bonds are valued or purchased at other than par, the states are not always consistent as to the required method of treating the premium or the discount. The two methods usually followed are:

(1) Amortizing the premium against income over the period to earliest call date, or to maturity if the bond is not subject to call; but taking the discount, when realized, into income.

(2) Upon sale or redemption, taking into principal the gain or loss based on the original valuation, or on cost if the bond was purchased.

DIVIDENDS, GENERAL. Ordinary or regular dividends on stocks paid in cash are income. In some jurisdictions, stock dividends paid in shares of the issuing corporation of the same kind and rank as the shares on which such dividend is paid would be principal, and all other dividends paid in stock would be income. In other jurisdictions, some method of apportioning between principal and income may be used, such as intact value. (See the following subsection, "DIVIDENDS, INTACT VALUE.")

In complete or partial liquidations, disbursements of the corporate assets are usually considered principal. However, dividends, including cash dividends, paid from the assets of a corporation in liquidation, if declared before such liquidation began, or if representing payment of cumulative, preferred, or guaranteed dividends in arrears, would ordinarily be income.

In mergers, consolidations, and reorganizations, the corporation may designate the portion of the securities, cash, and other properties distributed to the stockholders that applies to arrearages in cumulative or guaranteed dividends. The portion so designated would ordinarily be income. If the corporation makes no designation, the fiduciary may have to make an apportionment in accordance with the local statutes or decisions.

DIVIDENDS, INTACT VALUE. Extraordinary (extra) dividends, whether paid in stock or cash, are apportioned in some states between principal and income on the basis of "intact value." This is the value required to be kept intact for the remaindermen and usually, in instances where the asset was received from the decedent, the value determined from the corporation's books is presumed to be its intact value; but its true value must always be shown. (The presumption may be rebutted by more compelling equitable factors.) If the fiduciary has purchased the asset, courts have frequently held that the purchase price is the intact value. If the extraordinary dividend reduces the corporation's book value of the stock below the intact value as above described, the portion of the dividend necessary to restore the intact value must be considered principal.

A simple illustration of the computation of the apportionment of an extraordinary dividend between principal and income based on intact value at date of death follows:

| | No. of Shares Outstanding | Per Corporation's Books | | Fiduciary's Ledger Value Per Share |
| | | Book Value * | | |
| | | Total | Per Share | |
|---|---|---|---|---|
| Value at date of death, 10/2/54.... | 1,000 | $105,270.00 | $105.27 | $92.00 |
| Value after extraordinary dividend of $15 per share paid 12/23/56... | 1,000 | 97,530.00 | 97.53 | |
| Intact value impaired ........ | | $7,740.00 | $7.74 | |
| Amount of dividend to be apportioned to principal in reduction of fiduciary's ledger value per share ........................ | | | | 7.74 |
| Remaining fiduciary's ledger value per share, 12/23/56... | | | | $84.26 |

* Book value consists of the capital, surplus, and reserves for contingencies (at date of valuation) after giving effect to any adjustments made in subsequent years applicable prior to the date of valuation. In surplus is included the income or loss for the period to the date of valuation determined by apportionment of the income or loss for the fiscal year in which the valuation date falls.

PROFITS AND LOSSES FROM OPERATING A BUSINESS. If the fiduciary is authorized to continue a business which the testator or grantor had been operating, the net income from the business becomes income to the estate or trust. Any increase in the value of the principal used in the business becomes principal, and all losses in any one calendar year, after the income from such business has been exhausted, shall fall upon principal.

RENTS AND ROYALTIES FROM NATURAL RESOURCES. Rents and royalties received from leasing lands containing commercial quantities of timber, minerals, oil, or other natural resources are apportioned differently in various states. Under common law all may be income; under the Uniform Principal and Income Act, all are principal because the lease represents a sale of the assets in place. Either method may work out unfairly and, as a result, some states make an apportionment. The Commonwealth of Pennsylvania, by a 1947 statute, established that two-thirds would be principal and one-third income.

ANIMALS FOR BREEDING. Animals held for breeding purposes, if owned by the decedent at death, are a part of principal. The offspring necessary to maintain the original number of animals ordinarily are principal, the remainder, income.

CLASSIFICATION OF EXPENSES AS PRINCIPAL OR INCOME. In a decedent's estate, the executor or administrator is primarily concerned with preparing the estate for distribution, and should pay the expenses from principal, except those directly related to the collection of income. The trustee, on the other hand, should pay the expenses of a trust from income, except those directly related to principal. In a ward's estate, the guardian should pay the expenses from income. He should also pay for the maintenance of the ward from income, but, if the income is not sufficient, he may use principal for this purpose. Permission of the court may be required.

PROVISIONS OF THE WILL. Even though the statutes, and so forth, may classify in much detail the items of principal and income, the will or deed of trust may provide for a different basis of determining principal and income. For example, the instrument may provide that all dividends paid in stock shall be principal.

2. *Distinguishing between real estate and personal estate.* In addition to classifying assets and transactions into principal and income, they usually are classified in the accounts between real estate and personal estate.

REAL ESTATE. Real estate normally passes direct to the heirs without coming into the possession of the executor or administrator, and as a result many probate court accounts of these fiduciaries contain no real estate account. If the real estate is left in trust, it ordinarily passes direct to the trustee.

If the will instructs or permits the executor to sell the real estate, or if the court orders the fiduciary to sell or mortgage it to pay debts and expenses, the books of account and the accounts filed with the probate court should include a real estate account, segregated between principal and income. If a trustee receives the real estate in trust, he should also provide for a Principal of Real Estate account and an Income of Real Estate account.

PERSONAL ESTATE. Personal estate consists of all assets owned by the decedent at death, except real estate. The fiduciary should provide a Principal of Personal Estate account for these assets and an Income of Personal Estate account for the recording of income produced by such personal property.

CLASSIFICATION AT THE DATE OF DEATH. The classification at the date of death governs thereafter as to whether an asset is real estate or personal estate. If the fiduciary sells real estate and invests the proceeds in bonds, the bonds are carried in the real estate account. If the decedent owned a mortgage at the date of his death, the mortgage is an asset of the decedent's personal estate. If later the fiduciary acquires the mortgaged real estate by foreclosure proceedings, the property becomes an asset of the personal estate. The proceeds of sale of such property are also an asset of the personal estate.

SEPARATE ACCOUNTS NOT ALWAYS REQUIRED. In some jurisdictions, where the parties have the same interests in the real estate and in the personal estate, the courts may not require the fiduciary to carry real estate and personal estate in separate accounts, or a court may require separate principal accounts for real estate and personal estate and permit the income from both to be shown in one income account. For his accounting records and for management purposes, a fiduciary may seek the advice of his counsel as to whether such classification is either necessary or desirable.

3. *Use of the cash basis.* Accounts or statements to be submitted to probate courts are prepared essentially on a cash basis. The following comments regarding the cash basis cover the usual problems.

APPRAISEMENT AS AT DATE OF DEATH. The assets which a decedent possesses at the time of his death are appraised by the fiduciary for both accounting and death tax purposes. Real estate may be an exception, as indicated at page 537.

INCREASES AND DECREASES IN PRINCIPAL. As a rule, recognized increases or decreases in principal arise from cash transactions. For example, the gain on the sale of a stock included in inventory at the date of death is the excess of the cash proceeds over the appraised value at such date. The gain on a sale of stock previously purchased for cash is the excess of the cash proceeds over the cost.

TRANSACTIONS NEITHER INCREASING NOR DECREASING PRINCIPAL. Transactions may result in no increase or decrease in principal; such transactions may be in cash or in kind. For example, a bond appraised at par at the date of death may mature or be redeemed at par. The purchase of an investment would result in no increase or decrease in principal, for cash would be decreased by the amount paid and investments would be increased by a like amount. Exchanges of securities in kind, as under a plan of reorganization, would be recorded without gain or loss being recognized. For example, $2,000 A.B.C. Manufacturing Co. 6's of 1960, having a book value of $1,880, are exchanged, under a plan, for $2,000 A.B.C. Manufacturing Co. 3's of 1975 and 6 shares of common stock, par $100 per share. The new securities would be entered in the accounts at $1,880, even though a gain or loss based on quoted market values may have to be reported for Federal income taxes.

REAPPRAISEMENT PRIOR TO DISTRIBUTION OF PRINCIPAL. When the estate is to be distributed in kind, the assets frequently are reappraised, so that the distribution will be equitable.

VALUATION UNDER A DEED OF TRUST. When a grantor transfers assets to a trustee under a deed of trust, the assets may be recorded at quoted market value as of the date of the transfer (which would be the basis for Federal gift tax), but it would be well to show also the "cost, or other basis," which may be required for Federal income tax returns.

RECOGNITION OF A SERIOUS LOSS. A departure from the cash basis occurs when an asset seriously shrinks in value with little chance of ultimate recovery. The trustee may reduce the cost or book value to a realistic amount and obtain approval of the court, either after presenting the facts in a petition to the court or by filing an account in which the loss has been claimed.

ALTERNATIVE METHODS FOR INSTITUTIONS. The purpose of many perpetual trusts is to found and operate hospitals, schools, museums, and similar nonprofit institutions. In some cases, the income from such trusts in recent years may not have been adequate to meet the operating expenses, with the result that the institutions may be in need of more meaningful operating statements. One of the following three alternative methods may provide a satisfactory solution:

(1) Incorporate the institution as a nonprofit organization. If incorporation seems advisable, the fiduciary should petition the court to grant permission to do so. If the court grants the trustee's petition to incorporate the institution, the accounts may then be placed on an accrual basis.

(2) Periodically adjust the results on a cash basis to substantially an accrual basis. Under this method, an auxiliary journal and general ledger are set up. A journal entry is prepared recording the balances of assets and liabilities shown on a cash basis in the institution's general ledger as of the beginning of the period. Additional entries should be made and posted to the auxiliary general ledger recording accounts receivable considered collectible, inventories, property and equipment, other assets, allowance for

depreciation and amortization, accounts payable, accrued expenses, and any other significant assets and liabilities as of the beginning of the period that are not recorded in the general books. The net credit (or debit) would be made to principal for such items as represent principal, and the remainder to undistributed income. Another entry should then be made setting up the increases and decreases in these assets and liabilities, with the contra entries to the respective income and expense accounts. The resulting assets, liabilities, principal, undistributed income, and income accounts for the period may then be presented in financial statements, set up in the form applicable to institutions which use the accrual basis.

(3) Use an accrual basis within the framework of a probate court account. In one case in Philadelphia, the trustee operates a school. To refine the results while continuing to use the cash basis, the trustee pays all invoices promptly so that at the end of a period the accounts payable are nominal, and sets up accounts, at the time of purchase, for the following types of assets:

(a) Buildings, automobiles, furniture, kitchen utensils, and the like (the cost of which is amortized in lieu of depreciation).

(b) Insurance and taxes (the cost of which is written off over appropriate periods).

Thus the results obtained are substantially on an accrual basis. The accounts so stated have been approved by the local court.

4. *Difference in value of assets for court and for tax accounting.* The basic difference between probate court and tax accounting is that the probate courts, in general, postpone taking a gain or loss until an asset has been converted into cash; the Internal Revenue Code in general requires the reporting of as high a value at death as can be sustained and subsequent profits as soon as they can be reasonably determined. Other differences also are frequent.

The values used for the more frequent transactions in probate court and Federal tax accounting are summarized below:

|  | *For a Probate Court* | *For Federal Taxes* |
|---|---|---|
| Inventory, decedent's estate | At quoted market values, if they can be obtained, or as appraised by appraisers selected by executor or administrator. | (a) As appraised by appraisers selected by executor or administrator, as of date of death, or <br> (b) As valued under optional valuation provisions (one year after date of death). <br> Both (a) and (b) are subject to Government examination. |
| Inventory, ward's estate.. | As appraised by guardian. | At cost, if it can be obtained. |

|  | *For a Probate Court* | *For Federal Taxes* |
|---|---|---|
| Assets, testamentary trust. | As to personalty received from executor or administrator, at values shown by schedule of distribution. | As to personalty received from executor or administrator, at values determined for Federal estate tax, or at cost to the executor or administrator, if purchased subsequent to death of decedent. |
|  | As to real estate received under will, at appraised value or not valued. | As to real estate received under will, at value determined for Federal estate tax. |
| Assets, *inter vivos trust*... | At quoted market values as of date of deed, or at cost. | At cost to donor or to last preceding purchaser (for Federal income tax); at quoted market values or cost to donor, depending on whether gain or loss is involved (for Federal gift tax). |
| Purchases of investments . | At cost. | At cost. |
| Stock dividends received.. | Not valued. | Under 1954 Code in general, are not valued. Under special provisions of 1954 Code, may be taxable. In effect, these dividends are valued. |
| Stock rights received ..... | Not valued. | Not valued. |
| Exchange of assets with no cash received ........ | No gain or loss recognized. | Gain or loss recognized in some cases. |
| Exchange of assets with cash received ........ | Book value reduced by cash received. | Gain recognized but not in excess of cash received. |
| Sale of an asset, in general | Gain or loss determined on book value or purchase price. | Gain or loss determined on cost basis. |
| Sale of stock rights....... | Proceeds applied in reduction of book value. | May be necessary to (a) Apportion the basis of the stock between the stock and the rights, or (b) Use zero as a basis. |

|  | *For a Probate Court* | *For Federal Taxes* |
|---|---|---|
| Sale of real estate owned by decedent at death... | If valued in the inventory, gain or loss based on the inventory value; if not valued, entire proceeds become an increase in principal of real estate. | Gain or loss is based on value determined for Federal estate tax. |
| Distributions in kind ..... | At reappraised values (usually quoted market values, if available). | At values determined for Federal estate tax or at subsequent cost. |

The differences in values relate primarily to investments, and it is ordinarily convenient to provide on the investment ledger sheets a memo column for recording the tax values of the respective investments.

## Functions of a fiduciary

**Activities of various fiduciaries.**  The activities of the fiduciary differ substantially if he is (a) executor or administrator of a decedent's estate, (b) trustee under a will or deed of trust, or (c) guardian of a ward's estate.

**Functions of executor or administrator.**  The executor or administrator of a decedent's estate has the following duties:

1. Probating the will, if any.
2. Taking out letters testamentary or of administration.
3. Advertising the letters.
4. Preparing the inventory.
5. Reviewing claims and paying the debts of the decedent.
6. Preparing and filing the last Federal income tax return of the decedent, the death tax and fiduciary income tax returns, and such returns as the State may require.
7. Preparing interim statements to parties at interest.
8. Preparing accounts for the probate court, when required.
9. Distributing the remaining assets, in accordance with the will or the intestate laws (and obtaining releases therefor).
10. Obtaining discharge as executor or administrator.

**Functions of a trustee.**  The duties of a trustee may be outlined as follows:

1. Accepting the trust.
2. Receiving assets of the trust, in distribution of a decedent's estate or under deed of trust from a grantor (an *inter vivos* trust).
3. Investing and reinvesting the principal and collecting the income.
4. Distributing the income.
5. Distributing the principal.
6. Preparing Federal fiduciary income tax returns and State tax returns.

7. Preparing accounts for the probate court.

8. Obtaining discharge as trustee.

**Functions of a guardian.**  The duties of the guardian of the estate of an adult who has become incompetent are in part those of an administrator of a decedent's estate and in part those of a trustee.  The principal duties are:

1. Obtaining appointment as guardian as the result of a petition of relatives, friends, or creditors.

2. Advertising the appointment (closely follows the procedure for advertising of letters testamentary).

3. Preparing an inventory (in much the same manner as for a decedent's estate).

4. Paying the debts, if any, of the ward.

5. Investigating the needs of the ward.

6. Applying the income and, if necessary, a part of the principal to the needs of the ward.

7. Investing and reinvesting the principal and collecting the income.

8. Preparing the individual income tax returns (Federal and State, if any) of the ward annually.

9. Preparing an account for the court upon the ward's recovery from his disability or at death, and, when the account has been adjudicated, turning over the assets to the ward or to the executor or administrator if the guardianship was terminated by death.  The guardian then obtains his discharge.

## Classification of accounts and the accounting records

**Statements affecting accounts.**  The statements which the fiduciary of an estate or trust prepares for filing with a probate court may consist of as many as four groups of statements: Principal of Personal Estate, Principal of Real Estate, Income of Personal Estate, and Income of Real Estate. Each group of statements consists basically of the following:

1. The inventory and appraisement or the beginning balance.

2. Increases (in the balance) during the period.

3. Decreases (in the balance) during the period.

4. Changes neither increasing nor decreasing the balance.

5. The closing balance.

The opening and closing balances each consist of the assets less any liabilities for which cash has been received (such as a mortgage) or has been withheld (such as payroll taxes).  These, in fact, are the balance sheets at the respective dates.  The changes during the period must be classified between (1) those relating to principal (corpus), such as gains and losses on investments, Federal income tax on gains, and, in a decedent's estate,

Federal estate taxes, debts of decedent, and administration expenses; and (2) those relating to the income account, such as interest, dividends, and rents received, and, in a trust, expenses paid.

As stated earlier, the original principal of personal estate consists of the personal property of the decedent at death or that conveyed by the grantor under a deed of trust. Principal of real estate consists of (1) real property which is owned by the decedent at his death and which comes into possession of a fiduciary by will or court order, or (2) real property conveyed to a trustee under a deed of trust. Subsequent sales of real estate may provide funds for investment in securities, with the result that the classification of accounts for both personal estate and real estate will be very similar. After a review of the will or the deed of trust, counsel may advise that, when the real estate has been sold, the income accounts and the principal accounts may be combined.

**Classification of accounts.** The classification of accounts for the Principal and Income of Personal Estate of an estate or trust would be as follows:

    Personal Estate:
      Assets of Principal:
        Cash
        Other assets:
          Bonds
          Stocks
          Mortgages
          Other
      Principal
      Assets of Income:
        Cash
        Other (usually, stock dividends)
      Income

In these classifications, the relationship of the accounts is as follows:

    Assets of Principal = Principal
    Assets of Income = Income

**Accounting records.** The accounting records ordinarily used in an estate or trust are as follows:

    1. Cashbook-journal
    2. Checkbook
    3. Asset ledger

*Cashbook-journal.* The cashbook-journal is shown in Figure 3 (pages 546–547). The entries appearing in the illustration represent a few typical transactions of a simple estate.

*Checkbook.* The checkbook need not be of special form or design, but if space is provided on the check for indicating the purpose of the payment, the record is more complete.

*Asset ledger.* The asset ledger provides a sheet for each asset owned, other than cash; for example, each issue of bonds and each issue of stock. A trial balance of the asset ledger should agree with the control column in the cashbook-journal shown in Figure 3. In a trust, this record would be referred to as the *investment ledger*. Figure 1 shows the suggested form of an asset ledger sheet and Figure 2 the reverse side thereof. In these exhibits are recorded an asset and the income therefrom appearing in Figure 3.

| City of Philadelphia, (Loan of June 1,1950) 3s, Jan. 1, 1966 SECURITY | | RATE AND MATURITY | | CLASS AND PAR | | | J & J 1 INT. OR DIV. PERIOD | |
|---|---|---|---|---|---|---|---|---|
| CERTIFICATE NOS. M23, 732, M23, 937-23960 ($1,000 ea.) | | | | | | | | |
| DATES 195- | PAR OR SHARES | DESCRIPTION | PRICE | AMOUNT Dr. | AMOUNT Cr. | | | TAX BASIS* |
| Apr 29 | 25,000 | Per inventory and appraisment filed May 15. | $105 40 | $26 350 00 | | | | |
| | | Interest accd. Jan.2 to Apr. 29, per invtry. & app. | | 245 83 | | | | |
| Jun 15 | (25,000) | Sale through Temple and Grove | 106 | | $26 500 00 | | | |
| | | Accd. interest collected | | | 245 83 | | | |
| | | Gain transferred to principal | | 150 00 | | | | |
| | | | | $26 745 83 | $26 745 83 | | | |

\* Fill in only when tax basis differs from accounting basis.

**Fig. 1. Asset (or Investment) Ledger.**
**(For assets other than cash—primarily investments.)**

| INCOME | | | | | | | | | MARKET QUOTATIONS | | | | |
|---|---|---|---|---|---|---|---|---|---|---|---|---|---|
| RECORD | DATES RECEIVABLE | COLLECTED | AMOUNTS | RECORD | DATES RECEIVABLE | COLLECTED | AMOUNTS | | DATE | SOURCE | TYPE | PRICE | AMOUNTS |
| | 195- 1m 16d | Jun 15 | 95 83 | | | | | | Apr 29 | Wall St.Jo. | Bid | $105 40 | $26,350 00 |

**Fig. 2. Asset (or Investment) Ledger—Reverse Side of Fig. 1.**

The form shown in Figure 2 provides date columns that may be used for either dividends or interest. For dividends, the published notice would be the source for the date of record and the date receivable. An entry in the Cashbook-Journal for the check when received would be the source of posting to the Date Collected and the Amount columns. Interest normally requires only the use of the Date Collected and Amount columns.

## ESTATE OF GEORGE S. BROWN, DECEASED

### CASHBOOK-JOURNAL

| Date | Received from or Paid to and Description | Account | Income Account Cash | | Principal Account Cash * | | Other Assets | | Principal | |
|---|---|---|---|---|---|---|---|---|---|---|
| | | | Dr. | Cr. | Dr. | Cr. | Dr. | Cr. | Dr. | Cr. |
| 1953 as of Apr. 29 | Per inventory and appraisement as of this date, filed May 15: | | | | | | | | | |
| | Bonds: | | | | | | | | | |
| | $25,000 City of Philadelphia, Penna. (Loan of 6/1/50) 3's, 1/1/66 @ 105.40.... | Investments | | | | | $26,350.00 | | | |
| | Interest accrued 1/2 to 4/29, 3 mos. 28 days... | Investments | | | | | 245.83 | | | |
| | On deposit in First Pennsylvania National Bank ............. | | | | $ 3,027.46 | | | | | |
| | Total inventory ......... | | | | $ 3,027.46 | | $26,595.83 | | | $29,623.29 |
| Jun. 15 | George C. Mark, funeral director.... | Funeral expenses | | | | $ 1,085.00 | | | $1,085.00 | |
| 15 | Nieder Bros., meats and groceries... | Debts of decedent | | | | 63.71 | | | 63.71 | |
| 15 | Temple & Grove, brokers, proceeds of sale of $25,000 City of Philadelphia, 3's 1/1/66 @ 106 ........... | Investments, gain or loss | | | 26,500.00 | | | $26,350.00 | | 150.00 |
| | Accrued interest 1/2 to 4/29, included in inventory........... | Investments | | | 245.83 | | | 245.83 | | |

| Date | Description | | Interest received | Administration | Taxes | | | |
|---|---|---|---|---|---|---|---|---|
| | Accrued interest 4/30 to 6/15, 1 mo. 16 days .......... | $95.83 | $95.83 | | | | | |
| Sep. 15 | A. M. Barr, Esq., legal services...... | | | 1,000.00 | | | | 1,000.00 |
| 15 | Register of Wills, state inheritance tax .......... | | | | 551.48 | | 551.48 | |
| Nov. 30 | A. M. Barr, Esq., probate costs, filing fees, etc., advanced .......... | | | | | 50.47 | 50.47 | |
| | | $95.83 | $29,773.29 | $ 2,750.66 | $26,595.83 | $26,595.83 | $2,750.66 | $29,773.29 |
| | | — | 2,750.66 | | | | | 2,750.66 |
| Nov. 30 | Balances per First Account (filed Dec. 2, 1953) .......... | $95.83 | $27,022.63 | $27,022.63 | | | | $27,022.63 |
| 1954 | | | | | | | | |
| Feb. 3 | Distribution to Hannah Brown Trate, daughter, remainder .......... | — | | $27,022.63 | | $27,022.63 | | |
| | | $95.83 | — | | | | | |
| | | $95.83 | $27,022.63 | $27,022.63 | | $27,022.63 | $27,022.63 | $27,022.63 |

**Fig. 3. Cashbook-Journal.**

* If there is a large number of investments, the fiduciary may desire two additional columns for other assets (debit and credit) as control columns for the par values and number of shares of investments.

## Reports to the court and to parties at interest in the estate or trust

**Reports to the court.**  The reports to the probate court having jurisdiction must follow the statutes, court rules, and local precedents; as a result, they vary widely in form.  Even the name varies.  For example, in Pennsylvania they are called "Accounts," in New York "Accounts of Proceedings," and in California "Accounts Current."

Three forms of reports to probate courts are illustrated in Figures 4 to 6 (pages 549–554).  They represent widely varying practices among three of the largest cities—Philadelphia, New York, and Chicago; also, three prevalent methods of presentation.  The transactions recorded in Figure 3 (cashbook-journal) are reported in the forms used in accounts filed in the respective localities.

The Philadelphia method presents the transactions in chronological order in each of the few classifications used.  New York uses an extensive classification with a summary.  The presentation for Chicago is essentially a statement of cash receipts and disbursements.

Detroit (Michigan), Camden County (New Jersey), Montgomery County (adjoining Philadelphia), and at least one county in Connecticut use classified forms of accounts closely resembling that of New York.

One county in Maine uses a classified form, but the required accounting is incomplete in that changes which do not increase or decrease total principal, such as the redemption of a bond at cost or the purchase of a bond, are not included in the account.

Further variances in practices are illustrated in the case of The Superior Court of California, which, at least for Los Angeles County, has some rules which the authors have not observed in other states.  These rules are as follows:

1. Investments owned by a decedent, except those which according to the will are to be distributed in kind, must be liquidated by the fiduciary; the proceeds of such liquidation may be reinvested only in United States and/or California obligations.

2. Claims against the estate must be approved by the court before payment by the fiduciary.

3. The account must be prepared on official court paper, which is prenumbered in the left-hand margin to correspond with double-spaced typing; the width of margins at the sides and at the top and bottom is also specified.

IN the ORPHANS' COURT of PHILADELPHIA COUNTY

ESTATE of GEORGE S. BROWN, DECEASED

FIRST ACCOUNT

of

HANNAH BROWN TRATE, EXECUTRIX

---

Decedent died April 29, 1953
Letters Testamentary granted May 10, 1953
First complete advertising May 11, 1953
Legal Intelligencer: May 11, May 18, and May 25, 1953
The Philadelphia Daily News: May 11, May 18, and May 25, 1953
Will No. 1485 of 1953

---

Account stated from May 10, 1953 to November 30, 1953

RECAPITULATION and INDEX

Principal—Personalty:

|  | Pages |  |  |  |
|---|---|---|---|---|
| Debits .......................... | 550 | .................... | $29,773.29 |  |
| Credits: |  |  |  |  |
| Funeral expenses, debts of decedent, and inheritance taxes.. | 550 | ...... | $1,700.19 |  |
| Administration expenses ....... | 550 | ...... | 1,050.47 | 2,750.66 |
| Balance ...................... | 550 | ........................................ |  | $27,022.63 |

Income—Personalty:

| Debits .......................... | 551 | ...................... | $95.83 |  |
| Credits ......................... | 551 | ...................... | — |  |
| Balance ...................... | 551 | ........................................ |  | $95.83 |

**Fig. 4. Report to Court (Page 1)—Philadelphia Method.***

(*Continued on page 550*)

* The rules effective January 1, 1955 have been used in preparing Fig. 4.

PRINCIPAL—PERSONALTY

Debits

The Accountant charges herself with Principal received as follows:

Goods, Chattels, and Credits of the decedent, as per inventory and appraisement filed May 15, 1953:

Bonds:

| | | | |
|---|---|---:|---:|
| $25,000 | City of Philadelphia, Penna. (Loan of June 1, 1950) 3's, due Jan. 1, 1966 @ $105.40 | $26,350.00 | |
| | Accrued interest from Jan. 2 to Apr. 29, 3 mos. 28 days... | 245.83 | |
| | | | $26,595.83 |
| | Cash, on deposit in First Pennsylvania National Bank | | 3,027.46 |
| | Total inventory | | $29,623.29 |

The Accountant further charges herself with the following increases in Principal:

1953

| | | | |
|---|---|---:|---:|
| Jun. 15 | Excess of amount received over book value on sale of $25,000 City of Philadelphia 3's, Jan. 1, 1966: | | |
| | Proceeds of sale @ 106 | $26,500.00 | |
| | Value included in inventory | 26,350.00 | |
| | | | 150.00 |

Changes in the corpus of the estate not increasing its book value:

1953

| | | | |
|---|---|---:|---:|
| Jun. 15 | Interest accrued from Jan. 2 to Apr. 29, 3 mos. 28 days on $25,000 City of Philadelphia 3's due Jan. 1, 1966, sold this day | $245.83 | |
| | Value included in inventory | 245.83 | |
| | Total debits | | $29,773.29 |

Credits

The Accountant claims credit for the following decreases in Principal:

1953

| | | |
|---|---|---:|
| Jun. 15 | George C. Mark, funeral director | $1,085.00 |
| Jun. 15 | Nieder Bros., meats and groceries, debts of decedent | 63.71 |
| Sep. 15 | Register of Wills, inheritance tax | 551.48 |
| | | $1,700.19 |

1953

Administration expenses:

| | | | |
|---|---|---:|---:|
| Sep. 15 | A. M. Barr, Esq., legal services | $1,000.00 | |
| Nov. 30 | A. M. Barr, Esq., probate fee, filing fee, etc., advanced.. | 50.47 | |
| | | | 1,050.47 |
| | Total credits | | $ 2,750.66 |
| | Balance in account, cash in bank | | 27,022.63 |
| | | | $29,773.29 |

**Fig. 4. Report to Court (Page 2)—Philadelphia Method.**

(*Continued on page 551*)

## INCOME—PERSONALTY

### Debits

The Accountant charges herself with income collected as follows:

1953

Jun. 15 Interest for 1 mo. 16 days from Apr. 30 to June 15 accrued on $25,000 City of Philadelphia 3's, Jan. 1, 1966, sold this day ......................... $95.83

Total debits ....................................................... $95.83

### Credits

The Accountant claims credit for disbursements of income, as follows:............. None

Balance of income, cash in bank ............................................... $95.83

$95.83

S/ HANNAH BROWN TRATE

Hannah Brown Trate, Executrix of the Estate of George S. Brown, Deceased.

(Followed by affidavit of Executrix)

(Subsequent to adjudication of the account by the Court, the Executrix would distribute the balance of principal and of income in accordance with the adjudication.)

**Fig. 4. Report to Court (Page 3)—Philadelphia Method.**

SURROGATE'S COURT
COUNTY OF NEW YORK

In the Matter of the Settlement of the Account of Proceedings of Hannah Brown Trate, as Executrix of the Last Will and Testament of George S. Brown Deceased

ACCOUNT of PROCEEDINGS
OF EXECUTRIX

File No. P    328    1953

The undersigned, Hannah Brown Trate, who resides at 11 West 111th Street, Borough of Manhattan, in the City, County & State of New York, does render the following account of her proceedings as Executrix of the Last Will and Testament of George S. Brown, deceased, from the 10th day of May, 1953, through the 30th day of November, 1953. On the 10th day of May, 1953, letters testamentary were issued to Hannah Brown Trate.

Deceased died a resident of the County and State of New York on the 29th day of April, 1953.

The New York estate tax was fixed by order dated the 10th day of September, 1953.

(The foregoing would be followed by a list of the schedules annexed, giving in detail the exact captions.)

**Fig. 5. Report to Court (Page 1)—New York Method.**

(Continued on page 552)

SUMMARY

THE FOLLOWING IS A SUMMARY STATEMENT OF
THE EXECUTRIX' ACCOUNT

PRINCIPAL ACCOUNT

CHARGES:

Amount shown by Schedule "A"
(Original capital of fund) ................................. $29,623.29
Amount shown by Schedule "A-1"
(Increases in capital) ..................................... 150.00
    Total principal charges ................................... $29,773.29

CREDITS:

Amount shown by Schedule "C"
(Administration expenses actually paid) .................... $ 1,601.95
Amount shown by Schedule "E"
(Creditors' claims actually paid) .......................... 1,148.71
Amount shown by Schedule "F"
(Legacies actually paid) ................................... 27,022.63
    Total principal credits ................................... $29,773.29

Principal balance on hand shown by Schedule "H" ............................ —

INCOME ACCOUNT

CHARGES:

Amount shown by Schedule "A-2"
(Total income received) ................................. $95.83
    Total income charges ................................... $95.83

CREDITS:

Amount shown by Schedule "F-1"
(Distribution of income to beneficiaries) .................... $95.83
    Total income credits .................................. 95.83

Undistributed income remaining on hand as shown by Schedule "H-1".......... —

COMBINED ACCOUNTS

Principal remaining on hand ........................................ None
Income remaining on hand ......................................... None
    Total on hand ................................................ None

The attached schedules,* which are severally signed by me, are part of this account.

S/ HANNAH BROWN TRATE
Executrix

**Fig. 5. Report to Court (Page 2)—New York Method.**

\* The schedules have been omitted for lack of space. They would have captions required by the Surrogate's Court and would supply the detail supporting the summary. Other schedules would contain additional information required by the Court. An affidavit by the fiduciary would follow the last schedule.

State of Illinois ⎱ ss:
County of Cook ⎰

In the Probate Court of Cook County

In the Matter of the Estate ⎱ File: 53 — P — 2127
of ⎬ Doc. 273
George S. Brown, Deceased ⎰ Page 40

First Current Account of Hannah Brown Trate,
   Executrix of the Last Will of George S. Brown, Deceased

To the Honorable Peter S. Doxdell,
   Judge of Said Court:

The undersigned Hannah Brown Trate, Executrix of the Last Will of George S. Brown, Deceased, respectfully submits her first current account covering the period of her appoint, ment, May 10, 1953, to December 15, 1953, the date of this account:

RECEIPTS

| Date | | Income | Principal |
|------|------|--------|-----------|
| 1953 | | | |
| May 10 | The First Pennsylvania National Bank, Inventory Item No. 2 ............................................... | | $3,027.46 |
| Jun. 15 | Net proceeds of sale of $25,000 City of Philadelphia 3's, Jan. 1, 1966, Inventory Item No. 1 ................... | | 26,500.00 |
| | Plus accrued interest ............................... | $341.66 | |
| | (a) Total income received ......................... | $341.66 | |
| | (b) Total principal received ..................... | | $29,527.46 |
| | (c) Total receipts .............................................. | | $29,869.12 |

(Income accrued at date of death is not included as principal.)

DISBURSEMENTS

| Voucher No. | Date | Description | Amount |
|-------------|------|-------------|--------|
| | 1953 | | |
| 2 | Jun. 15 | George C. Mark, Funeral Director ......................... | $1,085.00 |
| 3 | Jun. 15 | Nieder Bros., debt of decedent .............................. | 63.71 |
| 9 | Sep. 15 | A. M. Barr, Esq., attorney's fee on account .................. | 1,000.00 |
| | Nov. 30 | A. M. Barr, Esq., administrator's expenses advanced.......... | 50.47 |
| 11 | Sep. 15 | John B. Matthew, Cook County Collector, Illinois Inheritance Tax ....................................................... | 551.48 |
| | | Total disbursements ..................................... | $2,750.66 |

**Fig. 6. Report to Court (Page 1)—Chicago (Cook County) Method.**
(*Continued on page 554.*)

RECAPITULATION

RECEIPTS: Income ..................................... $  341.66
         Principal ................................... 29,527.46

         TOTAL RECEIPTS ...................................... $29,869.12

Disbursements ........................................ $ 2,750.66
Distributions ........................................    —

         TOTAL DISBURSEMENTS and DISTRIBUTIONS ...................... 2,750.66

Balance of cash in hands of Executrix ...................................... $27,118.46

ASSETS RECEIVED in KIND and DISTRIBUTED in KIND:

None

Respectfully submitted,
S/ Hannah Brown Trate

Hannah Brown Trate, Executrix
of the Last Will of George S.
Brown, Deceased

(Followed by affidavit of fiduciary )

**Fig. 6. Report to Court (Page 2)—Chicago (Cook County) Method.**

**Distributing the assets.** If the assets of an estate have been reduced to cash, distribution of an estate is comparatively simple. In some states, the fiduciary prepares an account and files it with the court; after the court adjudicates the account, the fiduciary prepares and files a schedule of distribution, showing the amount to be distributed to each beneficiary under the will or the intestate laws, as may be appropriate, the amounts which the fiduciary has distributed on account, and the balance that remains to be distributed. After the court approves the schedule of distribution, the fiduciary distributes the cash.

If the assets of an estate consist for the most part of securities and the trustee plans to distribute them in kind, he usually reappraises them at quoted market values as of the close of the account. Further, to avoid dissension among the heirs, the fiduciary may find it desirable to give each heir his pro rata share of each investment, insofar as is possible. If necessary, odd shares can be converted into cash.

At the time when the executor or administrator makes physical distribution of the assets, he must obtain a release from each distributee.

**Interim reports to the parties at interest.** The time required to settle a small estate frequently is at least six months; an estate on which the executor must pay a substantial amount of Federal estate tax is usually not ready for settlement for eighteen months, two years, or possibly a longer period.

In the meantime, parties at interest in an estate in the process of administration may be impatient to know how much they will receive and how soon they will receive it.

About the only statement that can be presented is a simple one in somewhat the following form, and, at that, many of the figures must be estimates:

ESTATE of GEORGE S. BROWN, DECEASED

(Date of death April 10, 195–)

SUMMARY of PRINCIPAL ACCOUNT

For the period from April 11 to Dec. 10, 195–

together with

Estimates of Amounts to become Available

for Distribution to the Legatees

| | | |
|---|---|---|
| Total value of assets of decedent at his death | | x x x |
| Gain or loss on liquidation of assets | | x x x |
| | | x x x |
| Less debts and expenses: | | |
| Paid: | | |
| Funeral expenses | x x x | |
| Debts of decedent | x x x | |
| Administration expenses | x x x | |
| Taxes | x x x | |
| | x x x | |
| Additional to be paid; estimated: | | |
| Debts of decedent | x x x | |
| Administration expenses, including legal and accounting fees and executor's commission | x x x | |
| Total debts and expenses, estimated | | x x x |
| Available for distribution, estimated | | x x x |
| Legacies (other than residuary legacies) | | x x x |
| Available for residuary legatees, estimated | | x x x |
| Share of residuary legatee No. 1 (say) one-half, estimated | | x x x |
| Share of residuary legatee No. 2 (say) one-third, estimated | | x x x |
| Share of residuary legatee No. 3 (say) one-sixth, estimated | | x x x |
| | | x x x |

When "accounts" are filed with the court, copies are usually submitted to all parties at interest.

In addition, fiduciaries of some trusts submit monthly statements of cash receipts and disbursements to the beneficiaries; others submit quarterly statements. Where no annual (or more frequent) accounting is made to the court, the fiduciary would give evidence of his good faith by submitting an annual account to the parties at interest, or a report which is perhaps more informative to them. This report might take the form shown in Figures 7 and 8.

ESTATE of GEORGE S. BROWN, DECEASED

SUMMARY of INVESTMENTS and of INCOME THEREFROM

For the Year Ended December 31, 195—

| | Balance, January 1, 195— | | Balance, December 31, 195— | | Quoted Market Values, December 31, 195— | | Income Received | Remarks |
|---|---|---|---|---|---|---|---|---|
| | No. of Shares or Par Value | Inventory Value or Cost | No. of Shares or Par Value | Inventory Value or Cost | Unit Value | Total | | |
| Bonds*: | | | | | | | | |
| Detail ............... | | | | | | | | |
| Stocks*: | | | | | | | | |
| Detail ............ | | | | | | | | |
| Mortgages*: | | | | | | | | |
| Detail ......... | | | | | | | | |
| Other investments*: | | | | | | | | |
| Detail ......... | | | | | | | | |
| Total investments and income ........... | | | | | | | | |

* At cost to fiduciary, except as noted (under Remarks).

**Fig. 7. Annual Report to Parties at Interest.**

ESTATE of GEORGE S. BROWN, DECEASED
SUMMARY of PRINCIPAL ACCOUNT
For the Year Ended December 31, 195—

|  | Cash | Assets of Principal as shown in Fig. 7 (page 556) | Principal |
|---|---|---|---|
| Balances, January 1, 195— .......... ............. | xxx | xxx | xxx |
| Sales of investments: | | | |
| Detail ......................................... | xxx | (xxx) | xxx |
|  | xxx | xxx | xxx |
| Purchases of investments: | | | |
| Detail ......................................... | (xxx) | xxx | |
| Other changes (such as exchanges): | | | |
| Detail ............................................ | | (xxx) | |
| Detail ............................................ | | xxx | |
| Balances, December 31, 195— ....................... | xxx | xxx | xxx |

( ) denotes red figures.

SUMMARY of INCOME ACCOUNT
For the Year Ended December 31, 195—

| | |
|---|---|
| Balance, January 1, 195— ............................................. | xxx |
| Income from investments, as detailed in Fig. 7 (page 556) .......................... | xxx |
| Expenses: | |
| Detail ................................................................ | xxx |
| Balance available for distribution ........................................... | xxx |
| Distributions: | |
| Detail ................................................................ | xxx |
| Balance, December 31, 195— ...................................... | xxx |

**Fig. 8. Annual Report to Parties at Interest. (Continued.)**

In the foregoing form of annual report, the order of statements shown emphasizes the investments and income in which many beneficiaries are primarily interested. The fiduciary may prefer to present Figure 8 ahead of Figure 7, and thus give more emphasis to the summaries of the principal and income accounts.

## Suggested modifications of system for large estates and trusts

The accounting records outlined under "Classification of Accounts" and the "Accounting Records" would apply to a very high percentage of estates and trusts. Where the volume is so great that the form shown in Figure 1 appears inadequate, the cashbook-journal can be expanded and a general ledger installed.

**Cashbook-journal.** The cashbook-journal can be expanded into a wider page to provide more columns for classifications and, if necessary, fly sheets can be used. Classifications should include provision for data necessary in preparing the fiduciary income tax returns.

Headings for the columns might be somewhat as in Figure 9.

## CASH RECEIPTS

| Date | Explanation | Cash | | Total Principal | | | | Total Income | | | |
|---|---|---|---|---|---|---|---|---|---|---|---|
| | | Detail | Deposit | Real Estate | | Personal Estate | | Real Estate | Personal Estate | Other | |
| | | | | Account | Amount | Account | Amount | | Rents | Account | Amount |

Real Estate Income flyleaf:

| | Interest on Bonds | | | | Dividends on Stock | | | |
|---|---|---|---|---|---|---|---|---|
| | U.S. Gov't | State and Municipal | Corporate | Interest on Mortgages | Public Utility Pfd. | Other Pfd. | Common | Rents |

Personal Estate Income flyleaf (same headings as above)

## CASH DISBURSEMENTS

| Date | Ck. No. | Payee | Vo. No. | Cash | | Total Principal | | | | Total Income | |
|---|---|---|---|---|---|---|---|---|---|---|---|
| | | | | Detail | Daily Total | Real Estate | | Personal Estate | | Real Estate | Personal Estate |
| | | | | | | Account | Amount | Account | Amount | | |

Administration Expenses flyleaf:
(Distributed between Real Estate and Personal Estate periodically on some reasonable and workable basis.)

| | Payroll Deductions | | | | | Other | |
|---|---|---|---|---|---|---|---|
| Salaries and Wages | FICA | Income Tax W/H | Other | Office Expense | Miscellaneous Expense | Account | Amount |

Real Estate Income flyleaf:

| Repairs and Maintenance | Insurance | Light and Power | Fuel | Sundry Supplies | Investment Expense | Miscellaneous Expense | Other | |
|---|---|---|---|---|---|---|---|---|
| | | | | | | | Account | Amount |

Personal Estate Income flyleaf (same headings as above)

**Fig. 9. Cashbook-Journal for Large Estate or Trust.**

Cash accounts should be clearly segregated into principal or income, although the cash may be deposited in only one bank account, if the local requirements so permit. This procedure (1) permits the drawing of only one check for the purchase of a bond (principal) and the interest (income) accrued on it; (2) permits the transfer of cash from income to principal without drawing a check to reimburse principal in amortizing bond premium; (3) permits adjustments between principal and income without the transfer of cash between bank accounts.

Distribution columns in the cashbook should be provided only for those classifications which have a sufficient number of transactions in a month to warrant the use of separate columns. Receipts or expenditures occurring only once or twice a month should be entered in the "Other" column.

**General ledger.** Some of the accounts which the trustee of a large estate or trust may need in his general ledger are as follows:

Principal of Real Estate and
    Principal of Personal Estate (separate accounts for each):
Cash
Bonds
Preferred Stocks
Common Stocks
Mortgages
Real Estate
Gains on Sales or Redemptions of Investments
Losses on Sales or Redemptions of Investments
Balance of Principal

Income of Real Estate and
    Income of Personal Estate (separate accounts for each)
Interest Received on U. S. Government Obligations
Interest Received on State and Municipal Bonds
Interest Received on Corporation Bonds
Interest Received on Real Estate Mortgages
Other Interest Received
Dividends Received on Public Utility Preferred Stocks
Dividends Received on Other Preferred Stocks
Dividends Received on Common Stocks
Rents Received
Other Income Received
Salaries and Wages
Office Expense
Office Rents
Legal Expense
Repairs and Maintenance
Insurance
Real Estate Taxes
Water and Sewer Rents
Sundry Supplies
Light and Power
Fuel
Payroll Taxes
Investment Expense
Miscellaneous Expense
FICA Deductions
Income Tax Withheld
Other Payroll Deductions
Distribution of Income
Balance of Income

In addition, an executor or administrator may need the following accounts for principal:

| | | |
|---|---|---|
| After-Discovered Assets | Debts of Decedent | Administration Expenses |
| Funeral Expenses | Taxes | Distribution of Principal |

An account for amortization of bond premiums may also be set up for each of the foregoing "interest received" accounts. Amortization may be posted as a charge direct in the interest received accounts, but separate amortization accounts avoid the necessity for analyzing each account in the preparation of fiduciary income tax returns and accounts for the court.

# 20

# Estates and Trusts—Corporate Fiduciary

by

**EDWIN McINNIS**

Vice President, Bank of America National Trust and Savings
Association, San Francisco

---

## Characteristics of trust accounting by corporate fiduciaries

**Nature of a corporate fiduciary.** This section treats accounting for an individual estate or trust [1] and for other trust operations performed by a corporate fiduciary—that is, a trust company or trust department of a bank. In administering an estate or trust, a corporate fiduciary, whether a separate institution or a department of a bank, will generally follow the legal principles and procedures discussed in Section 19, "Estates and Trusts—Individual Fiduciary." However, since a corporate fiduciary has additional responsibilities, it must observe additional principles and procedures as well as variations in state laws.

A corporate fiduciary must conduct its operations in such a way as to conform to the high responsibilities expected of a bank or trust company. Courtesy, service, promptness, accuracy, full disclosure, and the other usual attributes of a fiduciary relationship are expected of trust companies. Although individual fiduciaries should likewise perform their duties in an exemplary manner, more seems to be expected of a corporate fiduciary. The public especially expects greater skill from specialists employed by a bank or trust company. Corporate fiduciaries therefore make a great effort

---

[1] In trust company terminology, the word "estate" is usually applied only to the property left by a decedent during the period of administration. Upon completion of the administration, the estate becomes a "trust" under the decedent's will. The word "administration" is applied during the period in which assets are being assembled and debts and taxes of the decedent's estate are being ascertained and paid, and up to and including the time of final distribution.

The word "trust" also includes a fund left under a lifetime or inter-vivos trust, usually called a "living trust." For practical purposes, the word "trust," when used in this article, also includes agencies and custodianships. Although such accounts are not actually trusts, they are managed in about the same manner as trusts.

to develop and use every type of operational and mechanical device that will help achieve the desired result, and for the same reason they undertake extensive staff training programs.

Banks and trust companies perform for corporations several types of service that are not discussed here.  These corporate services include acting as transfer agent and registrar for stock, as paying agent for bonds and coupons, as trustee under an indenture, and as depositary in a corporate reorganization and performing other special duties for corporations.

The trust accounts discussed in this article consist of properties under administration as estates and properties which fiduciaries hold for management as trustees under wills as well as under agreements.

**Types of trust business.**  *Administration of estates.*  A bank or trust company may act in the following capacities: As executor, if named in the will; as co-executor, if named to act with one or more other executors— usually individuals; as administrator, on nomination of the heirs if there is no will; as administrator with the will annexed, if the executor named in the will cannot or will not act and the nomination of the heirs is obtained.

The process of administering an estate varies to some extent with the laws of the state in which the property is being administered.  Some states provide a longer period for administration than others, and some require more supervision over the actions of the administrators than do others. There are also many variations in procedural matters among the states. The imposed procedures are generally the same whether the estate is handled by a corporation or by an individual.  However, a corporate fiduciary generally need not file a bond with the court, for it has usually filed a bond with the state to assure the faithful performance of all trust duties as a condition precedent to doing a trust business within the state.

Basically, administration involves the gathering together of all of the assets, the payment of just debts and claims, the settlement of Federal and state death and inheritance taxes, and the ultimate distribution of the estate to the heirs.  (See Section 19, page 542, for further details regarding the duties of an executor or administrator.)

An executor or administrator does not engage in many of the investment operations of a trustee.  He will only sell such assets of the estate as he is directed to sell in the will, and such assets as he may select that are not disposed of by the will, to raise funds for the payment of debts, costs, and taxes.  Ordinarily, he does not invest.  Often he is limited to placing cash in savings accounts or buying Government or municipal bonds.  He is expected, however, to sell or dispose of perishable property and to be aware of conditions that might result in losses to the estate under his care.  Although he has no duty to invest funds, he has a duty to protect the estate and the heirs by the sale of property that would otherwise result in a loss.

*Trusts under wills.* When administration of the estate is complete, if the will provides that some or all of the property is to be held in trust for a period of time, a testamentary trust or trust under will is created. Such a trust may last for years, or for the life of a person or persons, or even in perpetuity if it is a charitable trust.

The operation of a testamentary trust usually involves receipt and disbursement of income, purchase and sale of trust assets, disbursement of income or regular payments to heirs and beneficiaries, and regular accountings to the court. The assets of a trust may consist of stocks, bonds, real estate, notes, and other property of any kind.

Accounts are furnished in many instances to all those who are receiving payments from the trust, to show the amount of income and the disbursements from it. This account may be a copy of the one filed with the court. The account rendered to a court must be clear and complete, starting with the property on hand at the close of the former account and showing all receipts and disbursements, all changes in assets (such as stock splits, and so forth), all purchases and sales, and the total of the assets on hand at the end of the current accounting period.

*Living trusts.* A living trust, also called a voluntary trust or an inter-vivos trust, is one established during the lifetime of the maker of the trust, who is known as the donor, trustor, or settlor. An agreement is prepared, executed by the trustor, and accepted by the bank or trust company as trustee. Such a trust may be made revocable or irrevocable. It may operate only during the lifetime of the trustor, or it may continue after his death. If the trust terminates at death, the assets held may be delivered to the personal representative of the estate of the deceased trustor, or, if so directed by the trust instrument, may be delivered directly to the persons named in the trust. A living trust may also be designed to continue after the death of the trustor during the minority of a child, for the period of survivorship of a family member, such as a wife, or in perpetuity for a charity.

The trustee extends care and custody of the property placed in trust, accounts for dividends and interest, rentals, and business profits, and makes purchases and sales of property as deemed proper. If the trustee is given full investment supervision, the decisions are made by the trustee and are carried out. If some or all of the supervision over the investments is retained by the trustor, he may direct purchases or sales, or may approve or disapprove of the recommendations of the trustee. In other words, the trustor may give the trustee full authority, or may reserve some to himself, or may even require the trustee to get the approval of another person, such as a family member, before purchases or sales are made.

As in other types of trust operations, the income which is earned is disbursed or reinvested, as may be directed in the trust agreement. Payments from the trust may be a part of the income, all of it, or all plus additional sums from principal to provide a minimum periodic payment and additional amounts for emergencies and for the needs of the beneficiaries as well.

*Guardianships.* The duty of a guardian is to conserve and manage assets. When a trust company is appointed as guardian, it will set up the assets and receive the income, make payments in accordance with court order for the support and care of the ward, invest funds available and make such purchases and sales of assets as may be ordered by the court or authorized by statutes.

Guardianships are over minors and incompetent persons. When a minor reaches his majority, the property is transferred to his name, the guardian making a final accounting to the court. When an incompetent is restored to capacity, the same procedure prevails. When a ward dies, the property passes to the personal representative of his estate for disposition under his will, or to his heirs. (See Section 19, page 543, for an enumeration of the functions of a guardian.)

*Management accounts.* A bank or trust company also offers full investment services without taking title to the assets. In rendering management agency services, the bank furnishes each management account with the care and custody of the property placed in the account and provides accountings and reports. This service may be on a limited advisory basis, with approval of the principal being obtained before action is taken, or on a full discretionary basis, with the bank being authorized to carry out its Investment Committee's recommendations without such approval.

As agent, a bank or trust company will also take over the care and management of real estate, collecting rents, making repairs, negotiating leases, paying taxes, and arranging for and maintaining insurance protection.

*Safekeeping and custodianship.* This type of service includes care, custody, and accountings, but not investment recommendations.

*Depositary agent.* Very often a trust company will manage properties or perform the accounting and care and custody of an estate or trust for an individual executor, administrator, guardian, or trustee. The duties assumed by the bank or trust company may comprise full management or only partial management. In some cases, this type of appointment may be for the purpose of reducing the bond of the individual fiduciary. In that event, the property placed with the bank or trust company can be withdrawn only on court order.

*Retirement trusts.* Pension and profit-sharing trusts operate similarly to other trust accounts, except that the income is accumulated and invested. When an employee retires, cash on hand or proceeds of sales provide the funds to pay the employee the amount of his pension or the share of his allocated profits to which he is entitled.

*Thrift or savings trusts.* In this type of trust account, which is often designed to augment retirement benefits, both the employer and the employee contribute funds, which the trustee then invests. There are many different types of thrift and savings trusts. They vary as to the percentages which may be contributed by the employee, the amount and source of the employers' contributions, the form of investment, and the time or times at which savings may be withdrawn.

**Government control.** About 2,000 banks and trust companies are engaged in trust business, chartered under either National or State law. These banks may be members of the Federal Reserve System or not, but all national banks must be members of the Federal Reserve. National banks must be members of the Federal Deposit Insurance Corporation and State banks may or may not be members of this corporation. Each of four authorities—the Federal Reserve System, the Federal Deposit Insurance Corporation, the Comptroller of the Currency, and State banking departments—has the right to examine the banks under their respective supervision. The examinations of one agency may, however, in some cases, be acceptable to the others.

A discussion of governmental control of banks appears in Section 11, "Commercial Banks," in Volume I of this Encyclopedia. The statutory and common law control of estates and trusts described in Section 19, page 532, applies as well to estates and trusts administered by corporate fiduciaries.

**Taxes, licenses, and fees.** For a discussion of taxes and fees payable by estates and trusts, see Section 19, page 534. For a discussion of taxes and fees of commercial banks, see Section 11, Volume I, page 284.

A going business operated as a part of an estate or trust will, of course, be subject to the same taxes, licenses, fees, and charges as other such businesses not held in an estate or trust.

**Financing.** A trust department of a bank may borrow from its bank or other banks sufficient funds to cover advances made to individual trusts. As to other occasions for financing the operations of an estate or trust, see Section 19, page 534.

**Principal accounting problems.** The principal problem area of trust accounting by corporate fiduciaries lies in the mass of detail required in the conduct of the business. All transactions, even those that seem inconsequential, must be thoroughly and completely described on all the books, records, and accounts of the particular estate or trust. In addition, all reports and records must be made promptly. Tax returns, reports to court, and accountings to heirs must be presented on time to avoid penalties, criticisms, and explanations. Discounts are sometimes given on state inheritance taxes if paid on time, but interest is charged if payment is late. Other accounting problems are the same as the individual fiduciary's. They are enumerated and explained in Section 19, pages 534–542.

## Functional organization

**Division of operations.** Two basic divisions are found in the performance of the trust functions of a bank or trust company: (1) the administrative division, and (2) the accounting and operating division. The administrative division, staffed with trust officers who deal directly with the trust customers, is charged with the administration and management of the estates and trusts. The operating and accounting division provides specialized services and skills and maintains the records of each estate and trust.

**Functions of the administrative division.** The administrative work is often separated into two divisions: personal trusts, and corporate trusts. Personal trusts include all court and private trusts handled for individuals, alive or deceased. Corporate trusts include the activities mentioned at page 561.

Sometimes the personal trust division is further subdivided into two sections: one handling accounts that are under court supervision, such as executorships, trusteeships under will, and the like, and the other handling living trusts and management accounts. If volume requires it, there may be separate guardianship and/or management sections. Each section is in the charge of an officer skilled and experienced in the type of trust service performed.

Retirement trusts and thrift or savings trusts are usually handled by a separate section. Sometimes these functions are included in the corporate trust division because they are usually trusts for corporations. However, it is just as reasonable to place these activities in the personal trust division because they operate like private trusts in their investment procedures and reports.

Supporting the administrative division are various specialized sections—investment, tax, real estate, and other sections that may be necessary for the particular type and volume of business of the bank or trust company. Each section is in the charge of an officer thoroughly trained and experienced in his field. These sections, though administrative in nature, are under the supervision of the accounting and operating divisions as far as the records maintained there and the bookkeeping done there are concerned.

The *investment section* provides research and analysis and data on suitable investments; arranges for the regular reviews required by law; and carries out the recommendations of the Trust Investment Committee on purchases and sales for estates and trusts. The receipt of income, the completion of purchases and sales, and other details are handled by the accounting division.

The *tax section* keeps the records of all estates and trusts necessary to enable it to file all tax returns. For this purpose, it must maintain a record of cost prices of securities and must be informed of any purchases and sales. It is supplied with income reports for the various estates and trusts for the taxable year. The section must also work with the administrative officers on the non-recurring types of returns, such as the income tax returns of the decedent not filed at death, returns for an estate, and returns for inheritance and estate taxes.

The *real estate section* handles appraisals of property, rentals, and leases, maintains insurance, and pays the real estate taxes for all estates and trusts. As soon as a new estate or trust is set up, the real estate section receives from the administrative division a complete work sheet on all real properties involved, showing the location and the rental information required to set up the necessary records. The section receives instructions from the administrative officers as to whether an appraisal is to be made, what repairs can be made without prior approval of the court or trustor, and what insurance is to be maintained.

**Functions of the accounting and operating division.** The accounting and operating division is also divided into various sections, such as the securities, vault, remittance, and income accounting sections, and the tabulating section, where punch-card equipment is provided. These units operate under the head of the accounting division, who may also supervise the sections which support the administrative division. He is responsible for the maintenance of all necessary records and for personnel of all sections, and is charged with outlining the methods of operation, the flow of work, and the like. He co-ordinates the work of all of the sections.

The *securities section* handles purchases and sales and the receipt and delivery of all securities, after approval of the transaction by the administrative officer. It initiates the recording of the related cash and security transactions.

The *vault section* is responsible for safeguarding securities, releasing them only to duly authorized persons. Trust securities must be segregated from the bank's assets.

The *remittance section* arranges for the distribution of periodic payments to beneficiaries of trusts and other accounts. It maintains diaries of the dates on which payments are to be made, address files of the distributees of these payments, and other records.

The *income accounting section* controls the receipt of dividends, the collection of interest on bonds and coupons, rents, and so on, and performs other similar duties necessary to collect all income on all trust properties and to channel such income to the proper trust account.

Generally, the daily journals and ledger records are maintained in the bookkeeping department, together with the asset records of the securities held in the trust accounts.  This department also arranges for the preparation of the accounts and reports that are submitted to the courts and to the beneficiaries.

**Organization chart.**  An organization chart showing the various divisions and sections and the officer to whom they are responsible is shown in Figure 1.  The broken line from the Trust Investment Committee to the

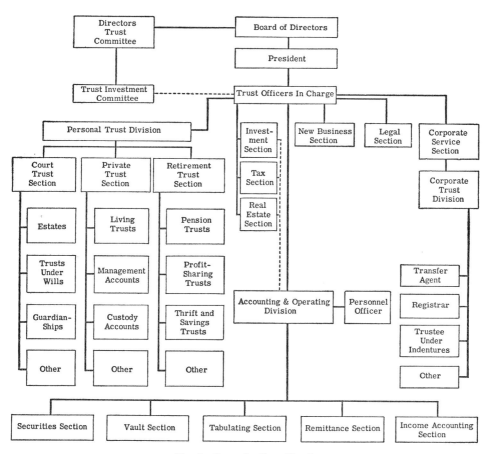

**Fig. 1. Organization Chart.**

The broken lines indicate the supervisory relationships mentioned in the text.

trust officer in charge shows the responsibility of that committee to the trust officer and the latter's responsibility for keeping the Trust Investment Committee functioning for initial and periodic reviews of investments, and the like.  The broken line from the investment, tax, and real estate sections to the accounting and operating division shows the supervision exercised over these sections by the accounting and operating division.

## Classification of accounts and books of account

**Estate and trust accounts.** Usually a minimum of three accounts are maintained for each estate or trust: (1) Income Cash; (2) Principal Cash; and (3) Invested Principal (of the estate or trust).

*Income Cash.* This account shows the income received and the disbursements made for expenses and to beneficiaries.

*Principal Cash.* This account shows the cash received at the inception of the trust, the sales and reinvestments of funds that are part of the corpus of the trust, as well as the amount of principal withdrawn or disbursed, if the account permits revocations or encroachments.

*Invested Principal.* This account shows the properties of the trust, whether stocks, bonds, real estate, or other kind of property. Like the other accounts, it shows receipts and disbursements applicable to the account.

Figures 2, 3, and 4 show the ledger accounts for *Income Cash, Principal Cash,* and *Invested Principal.* The postings to these accounts are often made in triplicate; the first copy furnishes a statement to the beneficiary or the court, the second copy is for the tax section, and the third copy is for the file.

Figure 4 shows how the Principal Account, which is made up of Principal Cash and properties other than cash, may be maintained on one sheet called "Principal Account." Whenever the Principal Cash column shows a decrease because of a purchase of an investment security, the Investments column shows an increase, which is then added to the balance of the other investments. Upon the sale of an investment security, the Principal Cash column shows an increase and the Investments column a decrease.

The necessity for maintaining separate accounts for principal and income is due in part to the long-established practice of creating trusts in which one person, the life tenant, receives the income, and the principal is held for another person, the remainderman. Trust arrangements are as varied as the wishes of the trustors. More than one person may share the income, only some of the income may be paid out, or there may be several remaindermen who will share in the principal on termination of the trust.

Sometimes there is no need to distinguish between income and principal. This may be true in the case of estates under administration to be distributed outright and guardianship. Nevertheless, the separation of income and principal is ordinarily maintained either to meet legal requirements or, in some instances, because the trust customer has requested that the income and principal be separated.

**Detail required in estate and trust accounts.** Each item of income must be sufficiently described to show the source and nature of the item. Sometimes abbreviations may be used when the volume is heavy, as in the case of trusts with numerous holdings of stock.  A payment received of interest on a note must show the date to which the interest is paid and the rate. Similarly, all items of expense must be carefully described to show the person to whom the payment is made, the purpose, the location of real estate if the payment represents an item such as a repair, and so on.

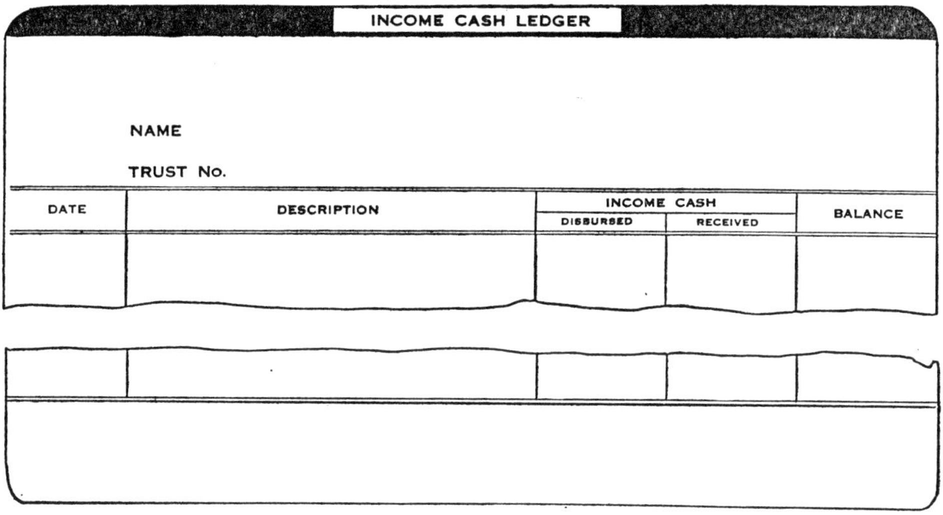

**Fig. 2. Income Cash Account (Income Cash Ledger).**

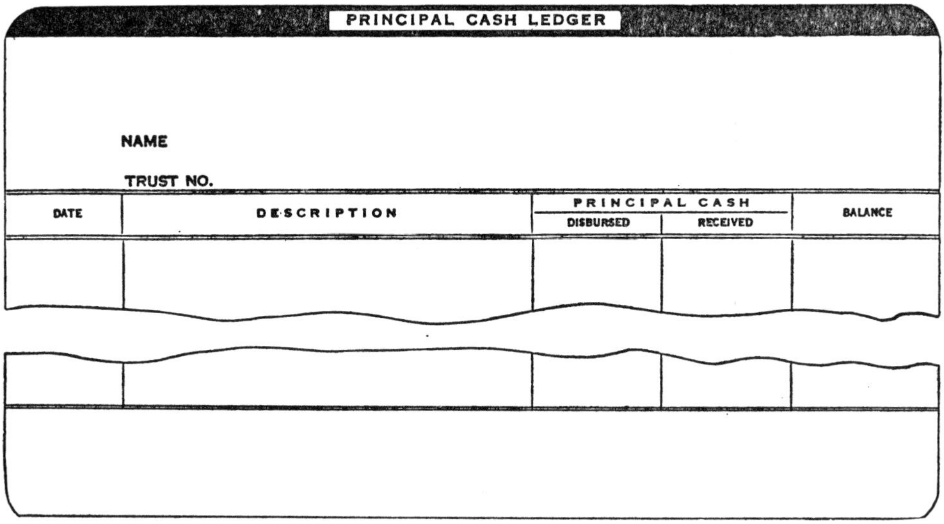

**Fig. 3. Principal Cash Account (Principal Cash Ledger).**

Principal transactions, too, must be completely described.  Entries for purchases and sales of securities must show the actual amount received for the security at market price, brokerage charges, stamp taxes, and accrued interest adjustments.

PRINCIPAL ACCOUNT

PAGE NO.

TRUST NAME

TRUST NO

NUMBER OF COPIES

CLASSIFICATION

PRINCIPAL ACCOUNT

ADMINISTERING OFFICER

| | | | PRINCIPAL CASH | | | INVESTMENTS | | |
|---|---|---|---|---|---|---|---|---|
| DATE | TRUST NO. | EXPLANATION | DECREASE | INCREASE | BALANCE | DECREASE | INCREASE | BALANCE |
| | | BALANCE FORWARD | | | | | | |
| | | | | | | | | |

Fig. 4. Principal Account (Invested and Uninvested Principal Ledger).

**Originating entries for estate and trust accounts.** Each day's entries usually originate with a tag, ticket, or card which describes the transaction fully and indicates the name of the customer and the basic accounts affected. Running records of these original data constitute the journals of the daily estate and trust transactions.

Several examples of tickets for originating entries are illustrated below. Figure 5 is used for originating entries for amounts of *Income Cash* dis-

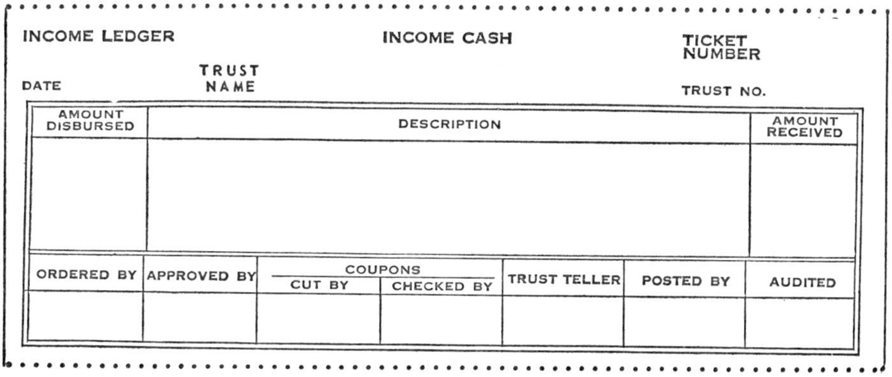
INCOME LEDGER
INCOME CASH
TICKET NUMBER
DATE
TRUST NAME
TRUST NO.

| AMOUNT DISBURSED | DESCRIPTION | AMOUNT RECEIVED |
|---|---|---|
| | | |

| ORDERED BY | APPROVED BY | COUPONS CUT BY | COUPONS CHECKED BY | TRUST TELLER | POSTED BY | AUDITED |
|---|---|---|---|---|---|---|
| | | | | | | |

**Fig. 5. Originating Entry Ticket for Income Cash.**

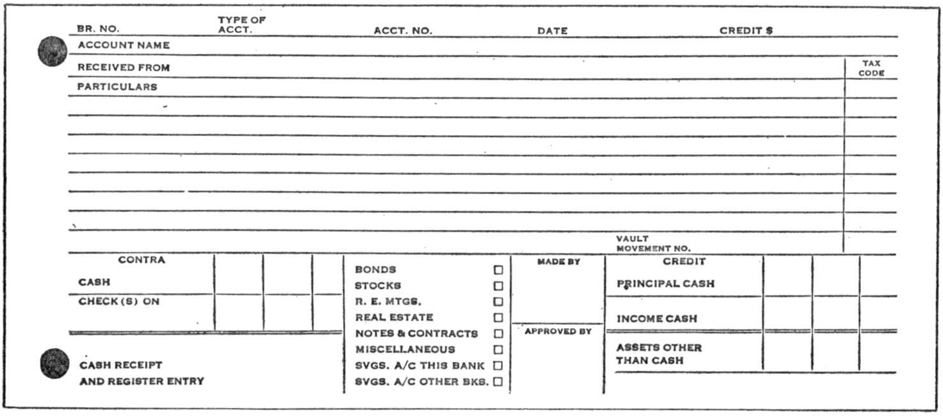
BR. NO.
TYPE OF ACCT.
ACCT. NO.
DATE
CREDIT $
ACCOUNT NAME
RECEIVED FROM
TAX CODE
PARTICULARS
VAULT MOVEMENT NO.
CONTRA
CASH
CHECK (S) ON
BONDS
STOCKS
R. E. MTGS.
REAL ESTATE
NOTES & CONTRACTS
MISCELLANEOUS
SVGS. A/C THIS BANK
SVGS. A/C OTHER BKS.
MADE BY
APPROVED BY
CREDIT
PRINCIPAL CASH
INCOME CASH
ASSETS OTHER THAN CASH
CASH RECEIPT AND REGISTER ENTRY

**Fig. 6. Credit Ticket for Cash Receipt and Register Entry.**

bursed or received. A similar form is used for entries in the *Principal Cash* account, but it is printed in red to distinguish it from the *Income Cash* ticket.

Figure 6 is a credit ticket covering a cash receipt and register entry. Figure 7 is a debit ticket (printed in red) for cash disbursement and register entry. Figure 8 is a ticket covering a journal entry where assets are adjusted without cash changes.

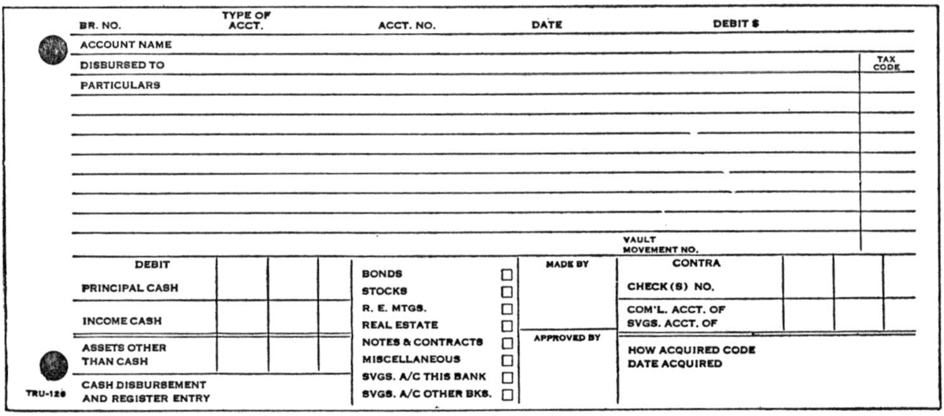

BR. NO. | TYPE OF ACCT. | ACCT. NO. | DATE | DEBIT $
ACCOUNT NAME
DISBURSED TO | TAX CODE
PARTICULARS
VAULT MOVEMENT NO.
DEBIT
PRINCIPAL CASH
INCOME CASH
ASSETS OTHER THAN CASH
CASH DISBURSEMENT AND REGISTER ENTRY
BONDS ☐
STOCKS ☐
R. E. MTGS. ☐
REAL ESTATE ☐
NOTES & CONTRACTS ☐
MISCELLANEOUS ☐
SVGS. A/C THIS BANK ☐
SVGS. A/C OTHER BKS. ☐
MADE BY
APPROVED BY
CONTRA
CHECK (S) NO.
COM'L. ACCT. OF
SVGS. ACCT. OF
HOW ACQUIRED CODE
DATE ACQUIRED
TRU-128

**Fig. 7. Debit Ticket for Cash Disbursement and Register Entry.**

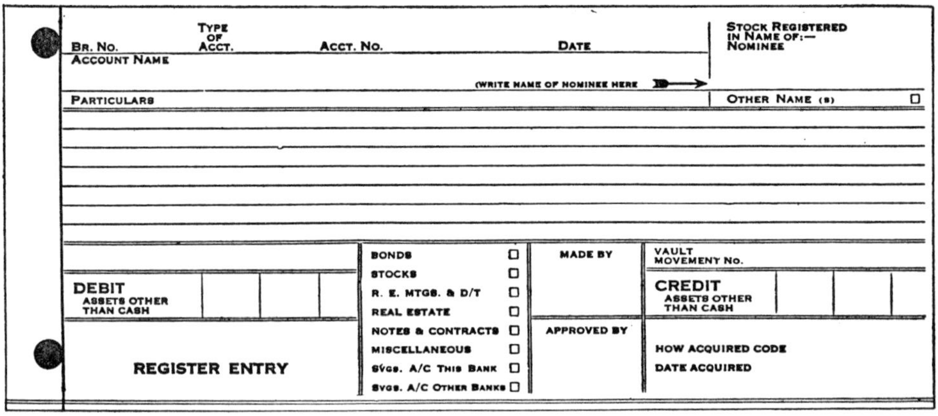

BR. NO. | TYPE OF ACCT. | ACCT. NO. | DATE
STOCK REGISTERED IN NAME OF:— NOMINEE
ACCOUNT NAME
(WRITE NAME OF NOMINEE HERE
PARTICULARS
OTHER NAME (S) ☐
BONDS ☐
STOCKS ☐
R. E. MTGS. & D/T ☐
REAL ESTATE ☐
NOTES & CONTRACTS ☐
MISCELLANEOUS ☐
SVGS. A/C THIS BANK ☐
SVGS. A/C OTHER BANKS ☐
MADE BY
APPROVED BY
VAULT MOVEMENT NO.
DEBIT ASSETS OTHER THAN CASH
CREDIT ASSETS OTHER THAN CASH
REGISTER ENTRY
HOW ACQUIRED CODE
DATE ACQUIRED

**Fig. 8. Ticket Covering Register Entry (No Cash Changes).**

Figure 9 is the triplicate copy of a combination tag that is used in connection with collection of installments due on a note. The original and duplicate are sent to the payor, who returns the duplicate with the payment. The directions for posting shown in the illustration do not, of course, appear on the copies sent to the payor.

Sometimes a copy of a check or voucher is the originating tag. For example, when a transaction originates with the expenditure of funds, a copy of the check drawn is the originating tag. Figure 10 is the duplicate voucher of a check drawn, showing the entries to be made to cover the remittance.

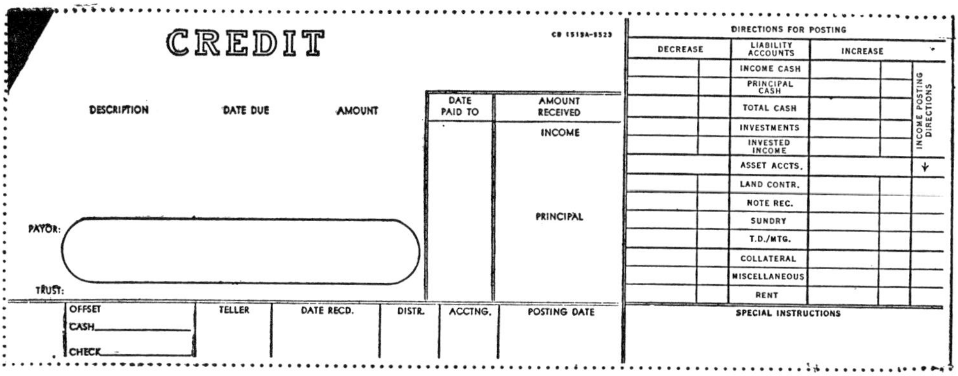

CREDIT

CB 1519A-5523

| DESCRIPTION | DATE DUE | AMOUNT | DATE PAID TO | AMOUNT RECEIVED |
|---|---|---|---|---|
| | | | | INCOME |
| | | | | PRINCIPAL |

PAYOR:

TRUST:

| OFFSET CASH CHECK | TELLER | DATE RECD. | DISTR. | ACCTNG. | POSTING DATE |
|---|---|---|---|---|---|
| | | | | | |

DIRECTIONS FOR POSTING

| DECREASE | LIABILITY ACCOUNTS | INCREASE |
|---|---|---|
| | INCOME CASH | |
| | PRINCIPAL CASH | |
| | TOTAL CASH | |
| | INVESTMENTS | |
| | INVESTED INCOME | |
| | ASSET ACCTS. | |
| | LAND CONTR. | |
| | NOTE REC. | |
| | SUNDRY | |
| | T.D./MTG. | |
| | COLLATERAL | |
| | MISCELLANEOUS | |
| | RENT | |

INCOME POSTING DIRECTIONS

SPECIAL INSTRUCTIONS

**Fig. 9. Triplicate Copy of Combination Tag Used for Collection of Payment Due on Note.**

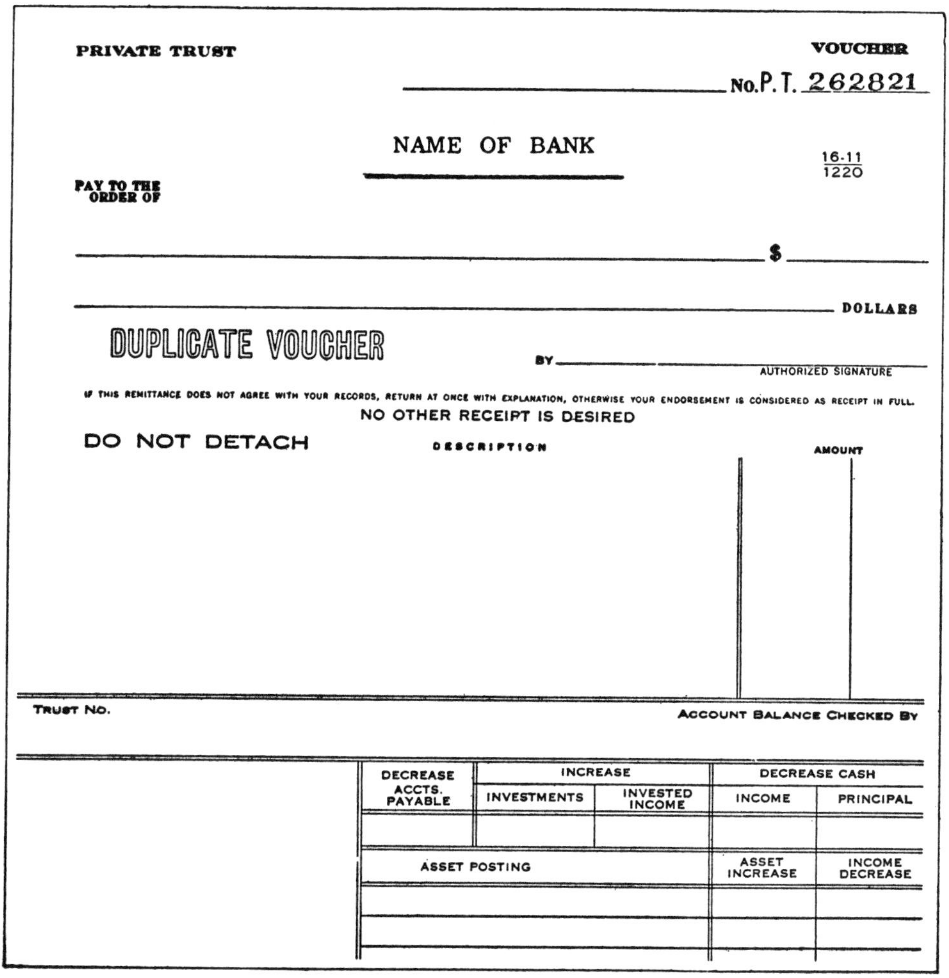

PRIVATE TRUST

VOUCHER

No. P.T. 262821

NAME OF BANK

16-11
1220

PAY TO THE ORDER OF

$

DOLLARS

DUPLICATE VOUCHER

BY

AUTHORIZED SIGNATURE

IF THIS REMITTANCE DOES NOT AGREE WITH YOUR RECORDS, RETURN AT ONCE WITH EXPLANATION, OTHERWISE YOUR ENDORSEMENT IS CONSIDERED AS RECEIPT IN FULL.

NO OTHER RECEIPT IS DESIRED

DO NOT DETACH

| DESCRIPTION | | AMOUNT |
|---|---|---|
| | | |

TRUST NO.

ACCOUNT BALANCE CHECKED BY

| DECREASE ACCTS. PAYABLE | INCREASE | | DECREASE CASH | |
|---|---|---|---|---|
| | INVESTMENTS | INVESTED INCOME | INCOME | PRINCIPAL |
| | | | | |
| ASSET POSTING | | | ASSET INCREASE | INCOME DECREASE |
| | | | | |
| | | | | |

**Fig. 10. Duplicate Voucher of Check Drawn.**

All entries shown on the originating tag, ticket, or card are posted to the ledger record of the individual estate or trust. This ledger, in many cases, is a columnar record showing the three basic accounts. By this arrangement, one description serves for the three accounts. When punch-card equipment is used, the ledger may be no more than a file of copies of the separate daily journal entries.

**Supplementary records.** In a large organization, supplementary records, not necessarily a part of the accounting system but important in the management of estates and trusts, are maintained covering trust properties. A few of these records are described below; the use of some of them is referred to in the procedures section at pages 588 et seq.

*Investment records.* In addition to the Invested Principal Ledger described at page 568, two other investment records are maintained:

1. A record of holdings of each issue of bonds, each type of stock, real property, and so on, held in a particular trust account. This record consists of a group of sheets, usually multi-colored but different in design, grouped together for the particular account. If tabulating equipment is used, this investment record may be maintained on punched cards. By whatever method the record is kept, it shows immediately what assets the trust holds at any one time, without the necessity for analyzing the Invested Principal ledger account. Thus there might be a sheet or card on which are recorded the purchases and sales of American Telephone and Telegraph stock, ending with the total shares held at the close of the semi-annual period and their carrying value. The total of all of the values on all of the sheets or cards would agree with the balance of the Invested Principal account.

2. The investment section usually maintains a record of all the bonds of a particular issue and of all stocks of a particular company held in all trusts. Sometimes these records are classified into trust accounts with full, partial, and limited responsibility for investments and those with no such responsibility. These records serve many purposes. An item of interest regarding one particular issue of bonds or stock may be of value to all estates and trusts holding the particular security. Furthermore, if tabulating machines are used, pre-cut entries for dividends can be made up as soon as the dividends are declared for all of the estates and trusts affected. These records provide data on the trusts that hold securities on which the dividend is to be received.

*Real estate records.* Records pertaining to real estate may be maintained on the basis of location, type of building, duties to be performed, and so on. In a large trust company, it may be necessary to carry a record of balances on loans on any real property held in trust. The real estate department also keeps rent ledgers, records of insurance carried on each parcel of property, insurance ticklers for expiration of policies, and ticklers of real estate tax due dates.

*Tax records.* The tax section maintains records of the due dates of tax returns, especially if the trust company reports on a fiscal-year basis.

*Loan records.* An estate or trust may own real property on which there is a mortgage, or it may own a note secured by real estate. In either case, supplementary records may be maintained to keep track of the payments to be made on the obligation owed or owned. These records may consist of cards that carry all of the data regarding the particular liability or asset. In the case of a note, for example, the cards may show information about the documents held in the vault, such as the note itself, deed of trust, appraisal, fire insurance policies, title insurance, and the like. The card record is merely for convenience.

*Progress records.* The administrative officer may keep a progress record of each estate that he handles. This record, often in loose-leaf form, lists the steps the officer must take to gather the assets, pay debts and claims, and distribute the estate. The form shows the days on which tax returns are due, provides space for listing of claims, and has columns to show approval, disapproval, and ultimate payment.

**Valuation of assets.** This subject, as well as the difference in value of assets for court and for tax accounting, has been treated in Section 19, pages 540–542. The discussion found there is equally applicable to estates and trusts administered by corporate fiduciaries. Other points of interest to a corporate fiduciary are mentioned below.

When the assets of an estate are received, and before they are appraised for tax purposes, it is customary to set them up at nominal values. Sometimes a bond is set up at par and a stock at $1.00 per share, or the total par value is used. After the estate has been appraised by state taxing authorities, the assets may be adjusted to show the appraiser's valuation.

The ultimate valuation by Federal taxing authorities may not agree with that of the state, but the value finally established by the Federal authorities must be used in determining capital gains or losses on sales for Federal income tax purposes.

Valuation of estate properties is further complicated by the fact that, for Federal estate tax purposes, the executor may choose the value of the securities in the estate at the date of death or one year after death.

A trust company must know the cost basis of each asset in a trust, for the purpose of determining capital losses or capital gains tax liability on a sale, as well as depreciation. In a revocable trust, cost values are requested of the trustor. In the case of safekeeping and custody accounts, however, the trust company may set up the securities at a nominal value, not at cost or market, because in this type of account the customer determines when sales are to be made and merely issues instructions to the trust company. When the income tax liability is of great importance to the customer or to the estate or trust, additional records must be available to show the cost of each certificate or share as well as of the total holdings of the stock.

It is not customary to present to the court detailed listings of assets with their market valuations unless the court requires such information. But market value must be known when fees are based on the value of the trust fund. A trust company will on request, but sometimes only for an additional fee, submit a statement of market value with its periodic reports.

**Trust company accounts.** The properties held in trust accounts by an independent trust institution or a trust department of a bank are not included in their balance sheets or financial statements.

Only two trust accounts are incorporated in the annual or semiannual statement of a trust company or a trust department of a bank—Uninvested Funds and Advances to Trusts. The accounts are explained below:

*Uninvested Funds.* This account represents uninvested or undistributed cash or savings accounts covering cash held for costs or emergencies for the various estates and trusts.

It is customary to prepare a daily adjustment of the uninvested cash on hand. Figure 11 illustrates a form used to make the adjustments for all cash and asset transactions of the day in all of the individual estate and trust accounts. The reverse side of the form (Figure 12) is used to recapitulate the resource changes.

The law requires that the banking department of National and State banks deposit with or place under the control of the trust department, securities—usually government and municipal bonds—to secure these deposits.

*Advances to Trusts.* The statement of condition of a trust company or a trust department of a bank must give effect to the bank funds that have been advanced to the trust department to cover overdrafts of cash in trust accounts.

**Fiduciary financial statement.** The fiduciary financial statement is a recapitulation of all of the individual trust accounts. It is often arranged in a form similar to the reports required by supervisory authorities, such as that which the Comptroller of the Currency requests for national banks. Figure 13 illustrates a fiduciary financial statement.

*Resources.* The resources shown on the fiduciary financial statement are the various types of properties held—bonds, stocks, notes, real estate, savings accounts, and miscellaneous assets. These resources are usually separated into court trusts and private trusts. In addition, the financial statement includes the accounts that describe the overdrafts created in the trust accounts and the uninvested cash held by the banking department, secured by bonds, which is not in the form of savings accounts.

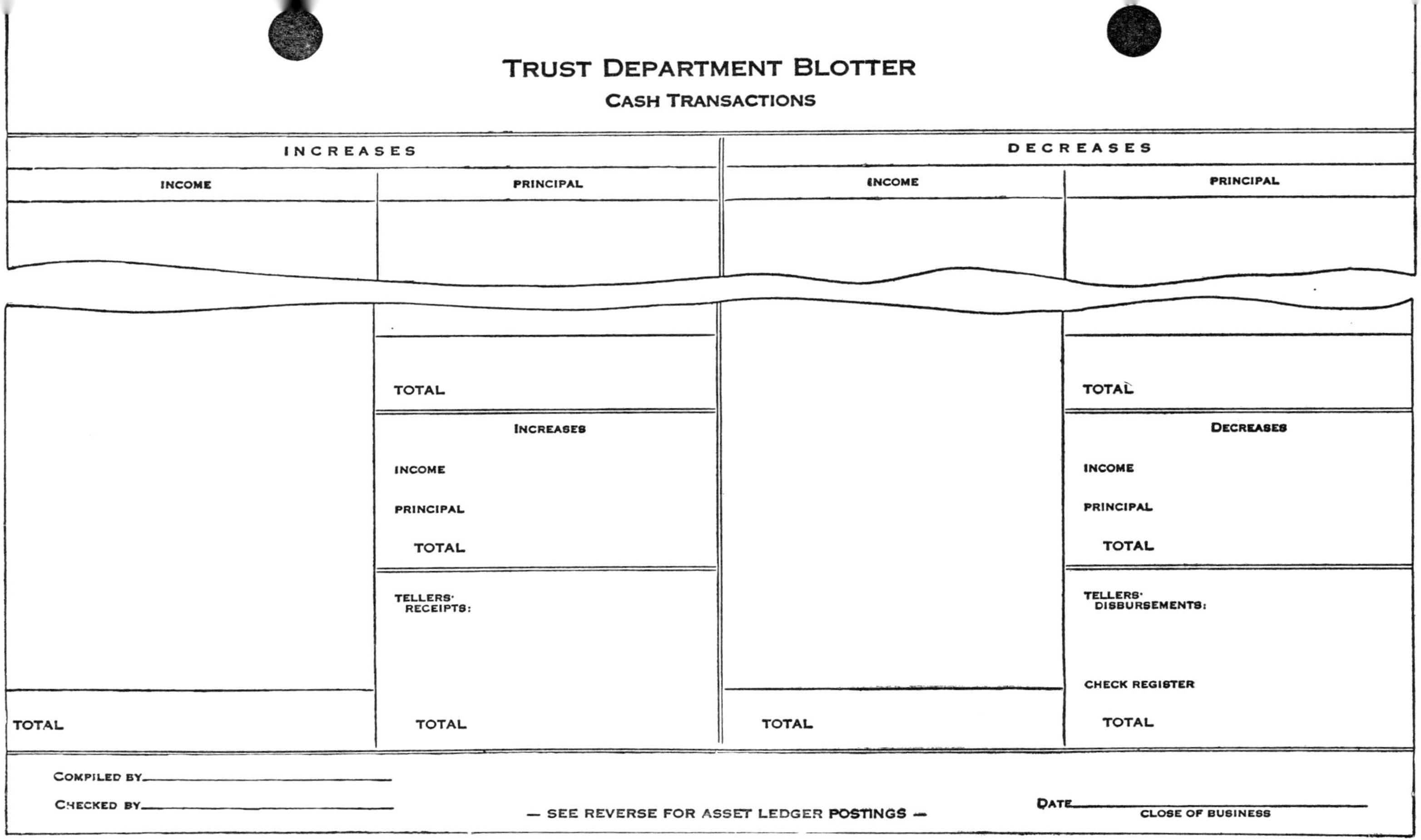

# Trust Department Blotter

## Cash Transactions

### INCREASES

| INCOME | PRINCIPAL |
|--------|-----------|

TOTAL

**INCREASES**

INCOME
PRINCIPAL
TOTAL

TELLERS' RECEIPTS:

TOTAL

TOTAL

COMPILED BY _____
CHECKED BY _____

### DECREASES

| INCOME | PRINCIPAL |
|--------|-----------|

TOTAL

**DECREASES**

INCOME
PRINCIPAL
TOTAL

TELLERS' DISBURSEMENTS:

CHECK REGISTER

TOTAL

TOTAL

— SEE REVERSE FOR ASSET LEDGER POSTINGS —

DATE _____ CLOSE OF BUSINESS

577

**Fig. 11. Trust Department Blotter—Cash Transactions.**

## TRUST DEPARTMENT BLOTTER
### ASSET LEDGER POSTINGS

| CONTROL | | | | | | INCREASES | | | | | |
| INCREASES | DECREASES | BONDS | STOCKS | MORTGAGES & TRUST DEEDS | REAL ESTATE | NOTES RECEIVABLE | BLDG./SAVINGS & LOAN ACCTS. | SUNDRY DEMAND DEPS. | TIME DEPOSITS | MEMO. ACC'TS |
| INVESTMENTS | | | | | | | | | | COLLATERAL CONTROL |
| | | | | | | LAND CONTRACTS | SUNDRY ASSETS | DEMAND DEPS. OTHER BANKS | TIME DEPS. OTHER BANKS | ACCOUNTS PAYABLE |

TOTAL INCREASES    $ _____

### DECREASES

| | | BONDS | STOCKS | MORTGAGES & TRUST DEEDS | REAL ESTATE | NOTES RECEIVABLE | BLDG./SAVINGS & LOAN ACCTS. | SUNDRY DEMAND DEPS. | TIME DEPOSITS | MEMO. ACC'TS |
| | | | | | | | | | | COLLATERAL CONTROL |
| INVESTED INCOME | | | | | | | | | | |
| | | | | | | LAND CONTRACTS | SUNDRY ASSETS | DEMAND DEPS. OTHER BANKS | TIME DEPS. OTHER BANKS | ACCOUNTS PAYABLE |
| MEMO ACCOUNTS | | | | | | | | | | |
| RE CAP | | | | | | | | | | |
| TOTAL INCREASES | TOTAL DECREASES | | | | | | | | | |

TOTAL DECREASES    $ _____

COMPILED BY _____

CHECKED BY _____

DATE _____    CLOSE OF BUSINESS _____

**Fig. 12. Trust Department Blotter—Asset Ledger Postings (Reverse side of Fig. 11).**

## FIDUCIARY FINANCIAL STATEMENT

| | | | | | | | | | | | | | |
|---|---|---|---|---|---|---|---|---|---|---|---|---|---|
| COURT TRUST RESOURCES: | | | | | | | | | | | | | |
| Bonds: Court Trusts | 500 | | | | | | | | | | | | |
| Stocks: Court Trusts | 501 | | | | | | | | | | | | |
| Real Estate Mortgages: Court Trusts | 502 | | | | | | | | | | | | |
| Notes and Contracts | 503 | | | | | | | | | | | | |
| Real Estate: Court Trusts | 504 | | | | | | | | | | | | |
| Miscellaneous Assets: Court Trusts | 505 | | | | | | | | | | | | |
| Savings Accounts — This Bank: Court Trusts | 506 | | | | | | | | | | | | |
| Savings Accounts — Other Banks: Court Trusts | 507 | | | | | | | | | | | | |
| 509    Sub-Total | S | | | | | | | | | | | | |
| | 510 | | | | | | | | | | | | |
| Overdrafts — Corpus: Court Trusts | 513 | | | | | | | | | | | | |
| Overdrafts — Income: Court Trusts | 514 | | | | | | | | | | | | |
| 519    Total Court Trusts Resources | T | | | | | | | | | | | | |
| PRIVATE TRUST RESOURCES: | | | | | | | | | | | | | |
| Bonds: Private Trusts | 550 | | | | | | | | | | | | |
| Stocks: Private Trusts | 551 | | | | | | | | | | | | |
| Real Estate Mortgages: Private Trusts | 552 | | | | | | | | | | | | |
| Notes and Contracts | 553 | | | | | | | | | | | | |
| Real Estate: Private Trusts | 554 | | | | | | | | | | | | |
| Miscellaneous Assets: Private Trusts | 555 | | | | | | | | | | | | |
| Savings Accounts — This Bank: Private Trusts | 556 | | | | | | | | | | | | |
| Savings Accounts — Other Banks: Private Trusts | 557 | | | | | | | | | | | | |
| 559    Sub-Total | S | | | | | | | | | | | | |
| Due from Local Branch: Demand Deposits | 560 | | | | | | | | | | | | |
| Due from Local Branch: Savings Deposits | 561 | | | | | | | | | | | | |
| Overdrafts — Corpus: Private Trusts | 563 | | | | | | | | | | | | |
| Overdrafts — Income: Private Trusts | 564 | | | | | | | | | | | | |
| Escrows: Assets Other Than Cash | 565 | | | | | | | | | | | | |
| | 566 | | | | | | | | | | | | |
| 569    Total Private Trusts Resources | T | | | | | | | | | | | | |
| TOTAL TRUST RESOURCES | * | | | | | | | | | | | | |

**Fig. 13. Fiduciary Financial Statement.** (*Continued on next page.*)

| | |
|---|---|
| Executorships, Etc. — Invested Corpus | 620 |
| " — Uninvested Corpus (O/D $................) | 621 |
| Depositaryships — Invested Corpus | 622 |
| " — Uninvested Corpus (O/D $................) | 623 |
| | 624 |
| | 625 |
| | |
| 629    Total Corpus (620 to 628) | S |
| | |
| Executorships, Etc. — Invested Income | 630 |
| " — Uninvested Income (O/D $................) | 631 |
| Depositaryships — Invested Income | 632 |
| " — Uninvested Income (O/D $................) | 633 |
| | 634 |
| | 635 |
| | |
| 649    Total Court Trust Liabilities | T |

PRIVATE TRUST LIABILITIES:

| | |
|---|---|
| Corporate Trusts — Invested Corpus | 670 |
| " — Uninvested Corpus (O/D $................) | 671 |
| Subdivision Trusts — Invested Corpus | 672 |
| " — Uninvested Corpus (O/D $................) | 673 |
| Other Private Trusts — Invested Corpus | 674 |
| " — Uninvested Corpus (O/D $................) | 675 |
| Common Trust Fund — Invested Corpus | 676 |
| Common Trust Fund — Uninvested Corpus | 677 |
| 679    Total Corpus (670 to 678) | S |
| | |
| Other Private Trusts — Invested Income | 684 |
| " — Uninvested Income (O/D $................) | 685 |
| | |
| (Memo: O. D. $................) | |
| Due to Local Branch for Advances to Trusts | 690 |
| Foreclosures: Money Received | 691 |
| Oil Royalties: Money Received | 692 |
| Escrows: Money Received | 693 |
| Escrows: Other Personal Property Received | 694 |
| | 695 |
| | |
| 699    Total Private Trust Liabilities | T |
| TOTAL TRUST LIABILITIES | * |

———————— 19———— ———————————— ( BCH. No. ——————— )

———————————————————————
General Bookkeeper

**Fig. 13.** (*Continued from page 579.*)

*Liabilities.* The liabilities are also divided into court trusts and private trusts, and accounts are maintained to show the Uninvested Income and the Uninvested Principal (also designated "Uninvested Corpus") and the Invested Principal (also designated "Invested Corpus"). The advances to trusts are shown as a liability of the trust department to the banking department for the funds advanced.

Sometimes the income of a trust is not paid out, but under the terms of the instrument, or by reason of inability to disburse the earnings, the income is invested but not made a part of principal. The item is shown as Invested Income in the liabilities section.

## Procedures of the accounting and operating division

**Comment on procedures.** Procedures for originating entries in individual trust accounts vary with the size of the trust institutions, the volume of trust business, and the activity in the individual trust accounts. A few variations occur because of differences in state laws. In large institutions, punch-card accounting and Addressograph plates may be used for many of the operations. In a small trust department of a bank, manual records are usually prepared on printed forms. To reduce clerical costs, duplicate copies of the manual records often serve as originating entries for the individual trust accounts.

In the following paragraphs, the procedures for the usual types of transactions and activities that affect the individual trust accounts are explained. They include:

1. Receipt of assets of the estate or trust.
2. Receipt of dividends, interest, and other income.
3. Purchase and sale of securities.
4. Exercise of subscription rights.
5. Sale of property.
6. Payment of debts and fees.
7. Distributions of current income.
8. Distributions of principal during the life of the trust or estate.
9. Distributions on termination of the trust or estate.

**Receipt of assets of the estate or trust.** As executor or administrator, a corporate fiduciary is entitled to take possession of the assets of the estate immediately upon appointment. However, in many other trust accounts, the trustor or another person makes delivery of the assets and a receipt is issued for them. The receipt should describe each item in detail. For example, each certificate of stock should be fully identified by name of company, certificate number, class of stock, number of shares, and so on. In the case of bonds, the receipt should also identify the coupons attached to the bond.

Other necessary originating records may be prepared when the receipts are issued. Sometimes duplicate copies of the customer's receipt are used as originating entries for the security record, for the real estate division's records, for the vault deposit record, and for the auditing department.

Figure 14 illustrates an originating record used when assets are delivered to the trustee. Six copies are prepared simultaneously and distributed as indicated on the form.

| DISTRIBUTION OF COPIES:<br>#1 - AUDITOR<br>#2 - INVESTMENT DIVISION<br>#3 - ACCOUNTING DIVISION<br>#4 - NUMBER SEQUENCE FILE<br>#5 - SECURITIES DIVISION<br>#6 - ADMINISTERING OFFICER | NAME OF BANK<br>Trust Department<br>NOTIFICATION OF ASSETS RECEIVED    (VAULT) | No. **2548** |

( ) BONDS    ( ) BLDG/SAVINGS/LOAN ACCTS    ( ) POSTAL SAVINGS C/D'S    ( ) STOCKS    ( ) SUNDRY

Trust No.                 Trust Name                                  Capacity

If Decedent, Date of Death

Will Federal Optional Valuation be Used? ( ) Yes. ( ) No. ( ) Uncertain

Received From                                                    Date

| DESCRIPTION | DUE DATE &<br>REDEEM. DATE<br>(OF BONDS) | BOND<br>OR CTF<br>DATED | DENOM.<br>OF EACH<br>BD./CTF | NUMBERS | 1ST. &<br>SUBSEQ.<br>COUPONS<br>ATTCHD. | INCREASE<br>ASSETS |
|---|---|---|---|---|---|---|
|  |  |  |  |  |  |  |
|  |  |  |  |  |  |  |

ASSETS DEPOSITED IN VAULT            ASSETS RECEIVED FOR DEPOSIT        APPROVED FOR DEPOSIT

Date _____ By _____            Date_____
In presence of                                                       ADMINISTERING OFFICER
_____            SECURITIES DIVISION    LISTED BY
_____            COPY NO. _____ **1**

**Fig. 14. Notification of Assets Received.**

After the originating records have been prepared, the various other departments prepare the supplemental records, using additional data obtained from the administrative officer who handles the account. Such data include information as to cost prices, insurance policies, rental dates, and other information.

If dividends have been declared but not received on securities at the time the assets are set up, it may be necessary to distinguish between principal and income. In the case of a decedent's estate, such fine distinctions are necessary for tax purposes, for inventory, or, in the case of trusts, to maintain accurate records of the interests of life tenant and remaindermen.

**Receipt of dividends, interest, and other income.** *Ticklers.* In setting up the initial records of a trust account, ticklers are prepared for all income and principal payment dates as well as for other important dates. Thus, for bonds, ticklers are established for the due dates of interest coupons and the maturity of the bond; for stock, the expected dividend dates based on company policy; for notes, the due dates of interest and installments of principal, the maturity date, and the outlaw date fixed by the state's statute of limitations. The rent ledger carries the dates to which rents have been collected.

*Credit tickets and notices.* Prior to the due dates, credit tickets may be made up. Addressograph plates covering securities held may be used for the purpose. If tabulating equipment is used, the tickets may be pre-cut for regularly recurring items. Notices for rental due or note payments are likewise prepared in advance. From these records, coupons are clipped and credited and receipts of dividends, rents, and note payments are checked. In some companies, a duplicate of the notice to tenants or debtors serves as an originating entry.

In addition to the above verification of all items of income, the trust company checks notices of dividend declarations, redemptions of preferred stock and bonds, and other pertinent information reported by the various security services to which it subscribes.

*Additional safeguards.* In the case of a decedent's estate, additional safeguards are often employed. The postmaster may be notified to send all mail addressed to the deceased to the trust company so that dividend checks will not be lost. A similar notice is sent to corporations whose shares or registered bonds are included in the estate. Sometimes the stock certificates are transferred to the name of the trust company in its fiduciary capacity.

A corporate fiduciary has the right to use a nominee as the registered holder of securities. This right is not always given to individual fiduciaries. The use of a nominee speeds purchases and sales by eliminating the need for documents that would otherwise have to be delivered to show the authority of the fiduciary to make the sale.

*Entries.* The receipt of income, whether bond interest, dividends, rents, or note interest, usually involves only entries to the income account of the trust. Stock dividends or dividends payable in stock may involve principal entries as well. Payment of principal on a note is, of course, credited to the Principal Cash account.

**Purchase and sale of securities.** Many methods have been devised to make the originating entry for purchases and sales of securities accomplish several purposes. For example, when instructions for the purchase or sale have been received from the Investment Committee or the trustor, the administrative officer may originate an entry consisting of several parts. These parts may serve as an order to the securities cashier to buy or sell; as a credit or debit to the trust account for income or principal; as an adjustment to the ledgers of assets other than cash; and as an order on the vault for the receipt of a security purchased or the withdrawal of one sold.

The purchase or sale of a security may involve entries to *Income Cash, Principal Cash,* and *Invested Principal.* Although the purchase or sale of a common stock usually does not involve entries to the income account, the purchase or sale of a bond usually entails a payment or receipt of accrued interest which must be debited or credited to the income account. Expenses of the sale, such as stamps and brokers' commissions, are usually considered principal transactions entering into the basis for tax purposes.

**Exercise of subscription rights.**   The exercise of rights to buy securities depends on the decision of the Investment Committee or of the trustor if investment authority has been retained by him.   After a decision has been made, the administrative officer directs the securities cashier to complete the transaction.   In originating transactions of this type, it is customary to issue a letter of instructions, copies of which are held in pending files in the vault department or by the auditor until the transaction is completed. If rights are sold, credits are made to income or principal on the basis of information received from the company issuing the rights, or of instructions given by the tax division.

**Sale of real property.**   The sale of real property may arise from a decision of the Investment Committee or from directions of the trustor or heirs.   After selection of the best bid and court approval, or upon written instructions of the trustor or heirs, the proceeds are charged or credited to the accounts affected.   For example, the funds from an escrow may be applied as follows: *Charges:* (1) to *Income Cash* for rents collected in advance and prorated to the purchaser; (2) to *Principal Cash* for payment of the outstanding mortgage (principal due) and real estate commission; (3) to *Invested Principal* to eliminate the property sold from the list of assets. *Credits:* (1) to *Income Cash* for insurance and tax prorations received; (2) to *Principal Cash* for the full amount of the sale price.   In some companies, all of these entries appear on one tag or record, which is then used as the originating entry for all of the accounts specified.

**Payment of debts and fees.**   Debts of the estate or trust are paid upon proper authorization.   After approval of the administrative officer who handles the account, the record containing the entries is passed to the accounting department.   A check is issued and given to the administrative officer for delivery to the payee.   In the case of a decedent's estate, very often court approval must also be obtained.

*Determination of fees.*   Fees for an executor or administrator are often based on the value of the assets and the income therefrom, plus gains on sales above inventory value, minus losses on sales below inventory value. In most states, the fees are fixed by law and are graduated percentages of the estate thus accounted for and the percentages are the maximum allowed. In some cases, the court determines what portion of the maximum fee is to be paid. Extraordinary fees may be allowed in an estate for extraordinary services after such services have been explained to the court.

Trust accounts are operated on an agreed-fee basis or under the direction of the court. The agreed fee may cover the lifetime of the trust customer, or may even go beyond that period, as in the case of fees for the operation of a living trust after the death of the trustor. In some parts of the country, the fees are set out in the trust instrument; in others, the instrument provides for reasonable fees which are negotiated from time to time. In some instances, fees are based on income received rather than on current value of properties held. (See page 592.)

In the case of court trusts, on filing an account the trustee requests an allowance for the period covered. Extraordinary fees, if any, are also subject to court jurisdiction.

*Entries for fees.* Entries for fees may originate in ticklers, punched cards, or tags previously prepared from Addressograph plates, or in directions from the administrative officer. In states where the law so provides, a portion of the fee may be charged to principal if funds are available, or otherwise as the court may direct.

*Billing and charging.* The fees of the fiduciary may be billed to a trustor or customer, or, if custom or the law of the state so permits, the fees agreed upon or allowed may be deducted from the trust account. Where the customer is billed, the trust company may or may not show the receipt of the fee as a credit to the account and a debit to transfer the fee to earnings, for the fee is sometimes credited directly to earnings. Where the fee is deducted, the customer or court is informed when the account is mailed or presented to the court. In some jurisdictions, the trust company may deduct payments monthly, later calling the attention of the court to the allowances and asking approval.

*Adjustments of fees.* Adjustments must be made with co-executors and co-trustees. Sometimes the fee of the individual co-fiduciary is in addition to and not a part of that of the corporate fiduciary.

*Other charges to trust accounts.* It is customary to charge the trust account for special out-of-pocket expenses such as cost of traveling beyond the local area, long-distance telephone calls, expenses of sales of properties, and similar costs. All such deductions will, of course, be described in the account.

Certain costs are by custom or by law not charged to the trust account as a whole, but to the respective shares of the heirs. Examples are inheritance taxes payable by heirs and the expenses and taxes on a devised parcel of realty. Ordinarily, in the absence of directions in the instrument, income from shares of stock or rentals of realty accrue to the person to whom the shares or realty is bequeathed or devised. Therefore, it is proper that costs and expenses attributable to such shares or property be borne by the heirs. However, many costs are not so simply allocated, for numerous special situations have never been finally determined by the courts. Certain expenses, such as debts, claims, and fees of the executor and attorney, will, in the absence of other directions, be charged to the residuary estate.

When a cost item comes to the attention of the administrative officer, he originates the entry and makes the allocation if any is to be made. In the event of any uncertainty, he may ask the court for instructions on the presentation of the account. Costs which arise in the handling of trusts and management accounts present few allocation problems.

**Distributions of current income.** The administrative officer determines the dates when income is to be distributed and whether payment is to be made by check directly or deposited in a designated bank account of the beneficiary. Thereafter the payment is made automatically by the accounting division. Upon receipt of instructions from the diary clerk to make the disbursement, the remittance clerk prepares the originating entry or uses a previously prepared tag or punched card. He examines the account and sets aside any necessary reserves for fees, taxes, and the like, and issues a check or makes the deposit. Only in the event of some special situation does he consult with the administrative officer. In cases where the beneficiaries desire equal monthly allowances, the income for the year is estimated, reserves are set aside, and one-twelfth of the estimated income is paid each month. An annual adjustment is made, if necessary.

In cases where it is necessary to file with the court a receipt for each disbursement, a copy or stub of the check, countersigned by the payee, serves that purpose. If the remittance is made by a deposit, a request for a voucher receipt accompanies the duplicate deposit tag that is sent to the beneficiary.

**Distributions of principal during the life of the trust.** In some instances, principal disbursements are also made, or enough principal is used to bring the periodic income up to a certain amount. In these cases it is customary to use the available income first and then principal. As the entire trust is ordinarily invested, the remittance clerk brings to the attention of the administrative officer the necessity for selling assets to raise funds.

Many trust accounts provide for disbursements which in the opinion of the trustee may be necessary for the care and support of the beneficiary. Usually a determination effective for a period of six months or more is made, and during that period the remittances follow the procedures outlined. Banking regulations request that such payments be discussed by the proper officer's committee and that a record be made of the decision.

**Distributions on termination of the estate or trust.** When an estate is to be distributed, or a trust is to terminate, after final determination has been made that all taxes have been paid or provided for, the administrative officer informs the securities cashier of the manner in which the securities are to be reissued, giving the names and addresses of the heirs or beneficiaries. The securities cashier also records whatever documents are necessary to transfer title to real estate, endorses or assigns notes, and requests checks from the accounting department for the shares distributable in cash. Sometimes it is necessary to order the sale of a number of shares of stock to permit a fractional distribution to an heir or to effect partial distributions when beneficiaries attain a certain age.

The property to be distributed is delivered to the administrative officer for distribution to the heirs. On distribution, the officer obtains receipts, which he files with the court when necessary. It is customary to include in the receipt an acceptance of the property distributed in full or partial discharge of the bank in its fiduciary capacity, releasing the bank or trust company from further responsibility to that extent.

**Control of securities in vault.** Two forms are used in controlling all changes in the securities kept in the vault for safekeeping. One is a deposit ticket (Figure 15); the other is a withdrawal ticket, similar to Figure 15 but printed in a different-colored ink. These forms are made up in pads and numbered consecutively. They are kept in the securities section, which handles all receipts and deliveries of securities. When securities are

| Name and Address Of Bank | *SECURITIES DEPOSITED IN VAULT* | | | No. D 12486 | |
|---|---|---|---|---|---|
| *TRUST NO.* | *NAME* | | | *DATE* | |
| QTY. | DENOM. (EACH) | DESCRIPTION | | NUMBERS | FIRST ATTACHED COUPON DATED |
| | | | | | |
| | | | | | |
| | | | | | |
| | | | | | |
| | | | | | |

| HOW ACQUIRED | | | | |
|---|---|---|---|---|
| DEPOSITED BY | ENTERED BY TRUST INVESTMENT DIVISION | OFF SET TICKET No. W | ENTERED BY ACCT'G DIVISION | |
| IN PRESENCE OF | | AUDITED BY | PREPARED FOR DEPOSIT BY: | |
| | | | | |

Fig. 15. Vault Deposit Ticket.

to be taken to the vault (or withdrawn from it), the securities section makes out the deposit ticket (or the withdrawal ticket) for each security to be deposited (or withdrawn).

The vault deposit and withdrawal tickets are made up in as many copies as may be required for notification of the various interested sections or departments. For example, a four-part form might be used as follows: the original to be kept in the vault as a record of all vault withdrawals and deposits, the duplicate to be sent to the individual trust file, the triplicate to be sent to the tax section, and the quadruplicate to be sent to the auditor.

In some trust departments, the vault deposit and withdrawal forms are a part of the purchase and sale order form. Thus, the preparation of an order to sell a security operates as an order to withdraw the security, and the preparation of an order to purchase provides a form that is used as a follow-up and ultimately as the actual ticket directing the deposit of the new security in the vault.

## Procedures of the administrative division

**Non-automatic procedures.** The administrative division, as explained at page 565, maintains the contacts with trustors, courts, heirs, and beneficiaries. It is charged with the careful and efficient operation of the trust accounts. The part played by the administrative division in the numerous transactions of an automatic type was explained in the procedures of the accounting and operating division. Many other situations arise during the administration of an estate or trust, or in the handling of a living trust or management account, which call for non-automatic procedures. Some of these situations are explained below.

**Investment section procedures.** *Originating transactions in securities.* A periodic review of securities (at least annually) is conducted by the Trust Investment Committee which may result in the ordering of sales or purchases. In many cases, however, the administrative officer must originate transactions in securities for the trust account. Cash may have to be raised to pay debts, claims, and taxes, to make payments to beneficiaries, to pay for new shares on the exercise of rights, and in like cases. The administrative officer instructs the investment division to select the security to be sold or to determine whether rights are to be exercised or sold. The investment section informs the administrative officer, who, in turn, informs the court, or asks the court's permission, or advises the customer, and then completes the transaction.

*Review of assets.* The investment section presents the Trust Investment Committee with the list of assets of each trust for review in accordance with regulations of state and national supervisory authorities.

## SYNOPTIC RECORD OF FIDUCIARY POWERS

BR. No. _____ TYPE ACCT. _____ ACCT. No. _____ APPROX. VALUE _____ TESTAMENTARY TRUST _____

ACCT. NAME _____ DATE APPMT. _____ DATE DEATH _____ LIVING TRUST _____

I. DO WE ACT IN SOLE CAPACITY? _____ NAME OTHERS, IF ANY _____
(YES OR NO)

II. IS THIS TRUST REVOCABLE? _____

III. HAS TRUSTEE DISCRETION AS TO PMT. OF PRINCIPAL? _____ FOR BENEFICIARIES _____ FOR FEES OR EXPENSES _____

IV. ARE PAYMENTS TO BENEF. LIMITED TO SPECIFIC AMOUNTS OR PARTICULAR PURPOSE? _____

_____

V. WHEN DOES TRUST TERMINATE? _____

_____

VI. TO WHOM IS INCOME PAYABLE?

| NAME | RELATIONSHIP | APPROX. DATE OF BIRTH | PERCENTAGE OF INCOME |
|------|--------------|------------------------|----------------------|
| | | | |
| | | | |
| | | | |
| | | | |

VII. REMAINDERMEN:

| NAME | RELATIONSHIP | APPROX. DATE OF BIRTH | PERCENTAGE OF CORPUS |
|------|--------------|------------------------|----------------------|
| | | | |
| | | | |
| | | | |
| | | | |

VIII. CONCERNING INVESTMENT MANAGEMENT POWERS AND RESPONSIBILITIES:

| ACTIONS CONCERNING ASSETS | DO WE HAVE POWER TO TAKE ACTION SET FORTH, EVEN THOUGH IT MAY BE SUBJECT TO SOMEONE'S APPROVAL? (YES OR NO) | PERSONS, IF ANY, WHOSE MANDATORY CONSENT OR APPROVAL IS REQUIRED TO SUCH ACTION. (IF NONE, SO STATE.) | PERSONS, IF ANY WHOSE DIRECTIONS IT IS MANDATORY THAT WE FOLLOW. (IF NONE, SO STATE.) | IS COURT ORDER REQUIRED FOR SUCH ACTIONS? (YES OR NO) |
|-----|-----|-----|-----|-----|
| SALES | | | | |
| PURCHASES | | | | |
| DEPOSITS | | | | |
| EXCHANGES | | | | |

1. WHOM, IF ANYONE, DO WE CONSULT REGARDING ASSETS, AS A COURTESY? _____

2. ARE PURCHASES RESTRICTED TO LEGALS FOR SAVINGS BANKS? _____ YES OR NO

3. DOES INSTRUMENT EXPRESSLY AUTHORIZE INVESTMENT IN OUR COMMON TRUST FUND? _____ YES OR NO

4. STATE OTHER INVESTMENT RESTRICTIONS NOT SHOWN ABOVE: •


IX. ALLOCATION OF STOCK DIVIDENDS, RIGHTS AND WARRANTS, AND OTHER POWERS:

1. STOCK DIVIDENDS DIRECTED AS   PRINCIPAL _____ INCOME _____ DISCRETION _____ SILENT _____

2. RIGHTS AND WARRANTS DIRECTED AS   PRINCIPAL _____ INCOME _____ DISCRETION _____ SILENT _____

3. AUTHORITY TO VOTE STOCK   PROHIBITED _____ FULL _____ LIMITED _____ SILENT _____

4. AMORTIZATION REQUIRED   YES _____ OR   NO _____

5. USE OF NOMINEE   PROHIBITED _____ PERMITTED _____

ADDITIONAL INFORMATION


DATE _____          _____
                                            ASSISTANT TRUST OFFICER

(TRUST DATA CARD MUST ACCOMPANY THIS FORM)

**Fig. 16. Synoptic Record of Fiduciary Powers.**

Determinations for sale, retention, and reinvestment are made after full consideration of all aspects of the account and all needs of the beneficiaries. In many trust companies, the information is given to the committee in the form of a synoptic record of fiduciary powers of each trust account (see Figure 16). From the records an immediate determination can be made of the income of the beneficiary, his tax status, his dependence on the funds paid from the trust account, the necessity for approval of any changes, and the cost basis for permitting the determination of possible gains or losses.

*Common trust funds.* State law may permit the pooling of investments of many trusts in a common trust fund, with each participating account owning its proportionate share of the fund. (Federal Reserve regulations permit such common trust funds with certain limitations. Under present regulations, only bona fide trust accounts may participate in a common trust fund, and then only to the extent of $100,000.) When a trust account is to be placed in the fund, the Investment Committee's direction results in automatic diversification of the funds. Otherwise, the committee must arrange for the selection of investments which will give the account proper diversification of investments.

If funds are needed for payments to beneficiaries, units of the common trust can be redeemed. The administrative officer informs the investment section of the need, and that section authorizes the sale of sufficient securities from the fund on the regular valuation date to satisfy requirements.

*Other investment section activities.* Other investment matters can be arranged by the administrative officer directly with the particular departments affected. For example, legal requirements or provisions of the trust instrument as to amortization of premiums on bonds are handled by the accounting division. In directive accounts, such as retirement trusts, the instructions are given to the securities cashier for completion, and the investment section is merely advised of the change.

**Real estate section procedures.** The Investment Committee reviews the real estate in the account to determine whether it should be retained or sold, whether rental income is adequate, what repairs are necessary, whether approval of contractors' bids is required, and whether adequate insurance is carried. Under the direction of the administrative officer, a reserve fund may be maintained and operated.

The real estate section originates the tags for the ordinary entries. If the administrative officer has occasion to originate an entry affecting the real estate, he informs the real estate section of the entry if it affects the records of the section. The administrative officer also reviews the statement of receipts and disbursements before the statement of the account is mailed or presented to the court.

**Tax section procedures.** The tax section must receive and maintain complete data on all transactions having any tax effect. Ordinarily, the tax section can compile totals of income received from its records, or such information may be furnished by the accounting division. The information is often coded on a punched card. The cards carrying the income information can be re-sorted and totals easily obtained for each type of income: dividends, rents for special schedules, tax-exempt income, and other classes of income. For gains and losses, the tax section must have the cost or inventory value as soon as the account is established or appraised. (As indicated at page 575, the value for Federal estate tax purposes may be used.)

The tax section must be informed when purchases are made, when sales occur, and when principal or liquidating payments are made. Prompt receipt of the necessary information is essential where some or all trusts and estates are on a fiscal-year basis. In some companies, a copy of the originating entry, a copy of the instructions of the administrative officer, or a copy of the daily journal of entries to trust accounts is sent to the tax section.

From the information thus furnished, the tax section prepares and files information or fiduciary returns. Copies are sent to the administrative officer to be used in assisting beneficiaries in preparing their returns. In some instances, such as estates, a return is filed and the tax paid. Where a trust or estate includes a going business, the tax division looks after the payment of taxes and the filing of tax reports, as well as such other reports as personal property taxes, sales tax, and Social Security and withholding returns of employees.

**Going businesses.** It is quite proper for the trustee to obtain the authority of the court to continue operation of a going business if, in the opinion of the fiduciary and in the light of any provisions of the will, continuation is advisable and for the best interests of the trust and the heirs. If the business is a sole proprietorship, it may be incorporated for the reasons noted in Section 19, page 533. If it is a partnership, in the usual case it will be terminated by the surviving partner or partners, with the corporate fiduciary verifying the receipt of the proper share of the decedent's interest.

All of the records of the business are under the supervision of the trust company. The administrative officer outlines the duties of the officers or employees who are to carry on the business. The administrative officer must see that the business maintains proper insurance coverage. A separate bank account is maintained for the business, with the administrative officer countersigning checks.

The income available as profits, or dividends in the case of a corporation, are paid into the trust or estate, and they appear in the statement of the account. When reporting to the court, it is often advisable to include a balance sheet and profit and loss statement of the business as exhibits appended to the account.

Many special accounting problems arise on the incorporation, liquidation, or sale of a going business, and many special tax problems are encountered that cannot be discussed here because of space limitations.

## Costs

**Costs covered.** Fees and other costs charged to the trust customer have been covered at page 584. Two additional cost areas are considered here: (1) trust company costs, and (2) cost studies to establish the basis for fees.

**Trust company costs.** The income of the trust company comes from fees. If the trust operation is performed by a separately capitalized corporation, as distinguished from a trust department of a bank, there may be earnings on invested capital as well. Usually, separate accounts are provided to accumulate the different classes of fees received during the accounting period.

The expenses of the trust department or trust company include the usual expenses for salaries, rents, supplies, and the like. In addition, there may be examination costs paid to state and national authorities. It is customary, in many companies, to budget expenses for at least semiannual periods.

Figure 17 illustrates an expense report which lists the classification of expenditures. Figure 18 (page 595) shows how the expenses are summarized in the statement of income and expense.

**Cost studies to establish fees.** For many years trust companies, independently or under the sponsorship of the American Bankers Association, have been making studies of costs of trust operations. A number of publications have reported these studies. The studies have made it possible in many cases for the trust company to establish fee schedules that will properly compensate the company for its services and permit a profit from operations. Ordinarily, these studies establish transaction costs for the various types of common entries.

Many trust accounts are still operating under fee arrangements established years ago, some of which are based on income. Today, however, the trend is to base charges on principal under management, increased or decreased by factors that take into consideration the kind or number of items varying from a typical account. In other words, the fee will be a percentage of the value of the assets, perhaps more for improved real estate than for securities. However, as one account may consist of a small number of securities and another of the same value may consist of a large number of

| | | ACCOUNTING DEPARTMENT | | EXPENSE REPORT | | No._____ |

<table>
<tr><td colspan="2">☐ ACCOUNTING DEPARTMENT<br>TO: ☐ _____<br>District Operations Officer<br>AT_____<br>Branch</td><td colspan="2">EXPENSE REPORT<br><br>Original and 1 copy to Accounting Dept.<br>Forward 1 copy direct to District Operations Officer. List all items by classification on reverse side.</td><td colspan="2">_____ No._____<br>(Branch)<br>Month Ending_____ 19___<br><br>Bank Operations District No._____</td></tr>
</table>

| | CLASSIFICATION | | CURRENT MONTH (Include Trust) | TOTAL TO DATE | BUDGET· CURRENT PERIOD | |
|---|---|---|---|---|---|---|
| | | 1 | | | | 1 |
| | Contracts: Janitorial & Fluor. Ser. Wages: Bldg. Employes | 2 | | | | 2 |
| | Heat—Fuel | 3 | | | | 3 |
| | Light and Power | 4 | | | | 4 |
| | Water | 5 | | | | 5 |
| | Rubbish and Supplies | 6 | | | | 6 |
| ★ | Repairs, Maintenance and Alter. | 7 | | | | 7 |
| ★ | Tenant Space, Maint. and Alter. | 8 | | | | 8 |
| # | Salaries | 11 | | | | 11 |
| # | Extra Hours Compensation | 12 | | | | 12 |
| ★ | Other Staff Expense | 13 | | | | 13 |
| | Advisory Board and Directors' Fees | 14 | | | | 14 |
| | Legal | 15 | | | | 15 |
| | Repairs—Furniture, Mechanical and Safe Deposit Equipment | 16 | | | | 16 |
| | Equipment Rental | 17 | | | | 17 |
| | Imprinted Checks and Endorsement Stamps | 18 | | | | 18 |
| ★ | Stationery and Office Supplies | 19 | | | | 19 |
| | Advertising—General (for Admin. Depts. use only) | 20 | | | | 20 |
| ★ | Advertising—Miscellaneous; Neon Sign Maintenance | 21 | | | | 21 |
| ★ | Dues | 22 | | | | 22 |
| ★ | Donations | 23 | | | | 23 |
| | Telephone—Local Service | 24 | | | | 24 |
| | Telephone—Long Distance | 25 | | | | 25 |
| | Telegrams and Cables | 26 | | | | 26 |
| | Postage and Mail Insurance | 27 | | | | 27 |
| ★ | Travel and Auto | 28 | | | | 28 |
| | Credit Reports, Reports of Legal Documents Recorded, etc. | 29 | | | | 29 |
| ★ | Newspapers, Publications, etc. | 30 | | | | 30 |
| | Armored Car Services | 31 | | | | 31 |
| ★ | Miscellaneous | 32 | | | | 32 |
| † | Fees and Legal Expense: Charged-off Loans | 33 | | | | 33 |
| | Fixed Interbranch Charges | 34 | | | | 34 |
| | Totals (CURRENT MONTH AND TOTAL TO DATE MUST AGREE WITH GL-20) | | | | | |

★ Opposite listing on reverse, enter description of all items of $10.00 or more. Opposite items budgeted in preceding period, also enter: "Budgeted in preceding period."

# Total of classifications 11 and 12 must agree with total of lines 861 and 863 of GL-20.

† Opposite listing on reverse, indicate debtor's ACCOUNT number.

All expenditures detailed in this report have been reviewed by me and have my approval.

_____
Assistant Cashier - Manager

**Fig. 17. Expense Report.**

593

securities, the charges will be increased to take into account the additional duties required in the latter type of account.

In addition to the annual fees, charges usually include fees for additions to trusts, amendments thereof, revocations, and distributions.

## Accounting to courts and clients

**Procedures for preparing accountings.** The trust company prepares the account to the court or to the customer or beneficiary from the account ledger. In many cases the account rendered is a typed transcription from the ledger or a copy of the ledger as it is prepared. If punch-card equipment is used, when a statement is necessary, the cards covering the income and principal entries since the last report are run through the tabulating machine to prepare the statement.

Accounts to court may follow the forms illustrated in Section 19, "Estates and Trusts—Individual Fiduciaries" (see pages 549–554). They are often typed in the office of the attorney from the forms furnished by the trust company. In many jurisdictions, the typed or machine-run statements of the trust company, in chronological form, are accepted as an exhibit attached to the report submitted to the court. Photostats or duplicates of ledgers and many other forms of statements have been used.

Accounts to customers should be readily understandable. The statements should, of course, start with the cash, income, and principal on hand at the end of the last report and should show the figures for the current period. In addition, it is customary to list the assets other than cash on hand. Sometimes this is accomplished by running a list of the Addressograph plates describing each security which were set up as ticklers or interest-coupon credit entries, or by a run of the punched cards covering each asset, if such equipment is available.

To spread the work load, efforts are often made to stagger the preparation and presentation of statements. For example, statements for trusts under wills may be filed on the anniversary of the distribution of the estate into trust. In management accounts, the larger volume of statements, however, may have to coincide with the taxable year of the customer.

## Reports to management

**Types of reports to management.** Many reports of various types reach management, in addition to the usual statement of income and expenses (see Figure 18). A number of reports are required either by reason of supervisory regulations or by established practice.

Reports must be made of all new accounts accepted and old accounts relinquished. The investment section must prepare reports for the initial review of all new trusts and the periodic review of all existing trusts.

Usually, these reports are prepared to record the action of the Trust Investment Committee; they are signed by each member of the Committee and are filed for review by the trust examiners.

A report is also submitted monthly to the Directors' Trust Committee. It includes a list of all purchases and sales of trust assets, new business

## STATEMENT OF INCOME AND EXPENSES

*Income*

| | |
|---|---|
| Court trust fees .................................................................... | $ ........ |
| Private trust fees .................................................................. | ........ |
| Pension and profit-sharing trust fees ............................................ | ........ |
| Corporate trust fees ............................................................... | ........ |
| Escrow fees ........................................................................ | ........ |
| Trust deed, foreclosure, and reconveyance fees ................................... | ........ |
| Other earnings ..................................................................... | ........ |
| Interest paid by bank on uninvested funds ........................................ | ........ |
|     Gross Earnings ............................................................ | $ ........ |

*Expenses*

| | |
|---|---|
| Salaries ........................................................................... | $ ........ |
| Rent ............................................................................... | ........ |
| Postage, telephone, and stationery ............................................... | ........ |
| Other expenses ..................................................................... | ........ |
| General overhead ................................................................... | ........ |
|     Total Expenses ............................................................ | $ ........ |
|     NET EARNINGS ............................................................. | $ ........ |

**Fig. 18. Statement of Income and Expenses.**

received, business relinquished, number of accounts on hand, and so on.

Many reports are furnished by the accounting and operating division to the administrative officers, containing such information as advances to trusts (overdrafts), cash awaiting investment, maturity of bonds and notes, and other reports of this type.

## Conclusion

This article suggests procedures that can be used by small as well as large institutions; it does not portray the procedures of any single institution. Because of space limitations, it has not been possible to cover all of the excellent procedures that have been developed, or to treat the many complex, though interesting, problems that arise in the administration of trusts and estates.

Many new systems and ideas, aimed at simplification of trust accounting, are currently being studied, particularly under the sponsorship of the American Bankers Association. The development of accounting machinery has been, and will continue to be, helpful in reducing costs and in providing customers with prompt and efficient management of their accounts.

# 21

# Exporters and Importers

by

CURTIS D. EPLER

Certified Public Accountant, New York, N. Y.

---

## Characteristics that affect the accounting system

**Nature of foreign trade.** *Exporting.* Exporters encounter numerous restrictions and formalities when selling merchandise abroad. They have to employ unusual selling methods and must face intricate financing problems. Even the shipping of goods requires special knowledge.

Selling abroad poses a question of how to sell. The answer depends upon the size and condition of the market, the purchasing power of the community as a whole, the volume that the smaller seller has to offer, his financial resources, and the available channels of selling. An exporter may (1) sell direct to and in foreign countries; (2) sell abroad indirectly through domestic export firms, domestic agents, and export associations; or (3) sell to foreign purchasing agents. "Direct selling" is selling to foreign buyers in foreign countries. It means having a salesman or sales representative (he handles lines for a number of sellers, and usually pays his own expenses) in the market. Such salesmen are paid on a commission basis and very rarely act as agents. "Indirect selling" is carried on through export middlemen; it is the least expensive method of selling abroad. There are four important types of middlemen: (1) export merchants, (2) export commission houses, (3) manufacturer's export agents, and (4) export-and-import brokers.

*Export merchants* are international-trade middlemen who purchase outright and sell for their own account abroad. They offer the advantage of assuming all the risks, and the seller practically is engaged in domestic commerce. The main disadvantage of this method is that the seller has no opportunity to promote sales.

*Export commission houses* operate on a commission, acting as agent for the buyer. This type of organization is far more prevalent abroad. The commission house is actually a resident buyer for overseas customers, and, as such, merely acts as a channel through which orders pass. These houses do not ordinarily assume credit risks.

*Export agents* function similarly to export commission houses, except that the agent acts as an agent for the seller and attempts to promote and sell actively the manufacturer's products. On some occasions, he assumes all credit risks.

The *export broker* is customarily a commodity specialist in one or two products. He acts principally for a commission as a go-between, and is essentially a contact man between those who wish to buy and those who have commodities for sale.

*Importing.* Buying abroad, like selling abroad, has its problems of government restrictions, financing, and choosing buying channels.

Two general channels of buying are open to the importer: (1) direct buying, and (2) indirect buying. Importers can buy through import merchants, indent houses, import commission houses, import brokers, and other types of middlemen. *Import merchants* buy abroad and import on their own account. The import merchant may process the imported goods, perform storage functions, and assume all risks. Actually, the buyer who consumes goods imported through an import merchant is engaged in domestic commerce. The *indent house* is an import merchant who buys only on order for domestic customers who use him because he has a thorough experience with foreign exchange and can secure lower transportation costs. He assumes no risks. An *import commission house* usually sells on commissions received from the foreign producer. An *import broker* buys foreign goods for the account of the purchaser, but may be paid by either purchaser or seller. His primary function is to bring buyer and seller together. He never takes title to the goods, nor does he perform shipment services. Often he receives a commission from both the buyer and seller for his service.

Obviously, it is impossible to present a complete accounting system for all types of enterprises which import or export, or even for all types of export and import middlemen. This section has therefore been limited to a discussion of various characteristics of foreign trade, accounts, and records which may be useful in establishing a system of accounts for a business that engages in some form of export or import trade.

The Drug Manufacturing section in this volume should be referred to for additional information on accounting for export sales. The Index in Volume V should be referred to for other industries in which export or import transactions are integrated with a general accounting system.

**Government control.** Political and economic conditions in the United States and in foreign countries affect both export and import trade. Few businesses are as hemmed in with restrictive control as is foreign trade.

All foreign trade practice is subject to supervision by the State and Commerce Departments of the Federal Government. Disgruntled overseas suppliers or customers invariably take their complaints, justified or otherwise, to the nearest American Consulate. In due course, the American importer or exporter is called before the regional office of the Department of Commerce to offer a satisfactory reply for transmittal to the overseas complainant.

*Export restrictions and control.* Every commodity shipped from the United States is subject to export control. Although this control has been relaxed in recent years to permit shipments to specified areas without individual licenses, every outgoing cargo requires an export declaration (known as a "deck"), which is ostensibly used for statistical purposes only but without which no carrier can accept any export.

In addition, exporting may encounter any or all of these regulations of the country to which the goods are shipped: tariffs, quotas, import licenses, foreign exchange controls, quarantine regulations, patent or trademark regulations, import restrictions, monopolies, and reciprocal trade agreements. Of these, foreign exchange controls are especially important. Most countries have set up some form of currency control which prohibits payments to other countries without licenses. An official rate of exchange and a free-market or black-market rate have been known to exist side by side.

*Import restrictions and control.* Most of the problems that the importer faces arise from customs procedure, determination of duty, customs clearance, foreign trade zones, and the use of licensed customs brokers.

Most imports require a special invoice, legalized by the United States Consul at the point of origin, certifying to the accuracy of the price and quality data. Imports are also carefully controlled by the Treasury Department to ascertain that proper duties are paid. Duties are "ad valorem" (a percentage of the value of the goods), or "specific" (levied by number, weight, or volume), or a combination of both. There is no official source of all rates of duties. Often, because of their individuality or newness, articles are not classified, and rulings must be obtained from the United States Customs Service, which has offices in every port.

Each import cargo must be entered through a customs house by a licensed customs broker. These specialists in customs procedures act for importers on a fee basis. They take care of all details of clearance of goods through customs and are licensed by the Treasury Department.

The transactions in clearing merchandise through customs at ports of arrival are called "entries." There are several types of entries, among which are the following: consumption entry, warehouse entry, and bonded manufacturing warehouse entry.

The free consumption entry is merely a permit authorizing the entry of duty-free goods into this country. The dutiable consumption entry author-izes the entrance of merchandise by a permit after the payment of duties. The six-months-bond entry applies to special goods that are admitted to the country; the collection of duties is suspended for six months, until merchandise is withdrawn for consumption.

Warehouse entries do not require the immediate payment of duties. Upon arrival, the importer is required to post a bond and place the mer-chandise in a bonded warehouse. Whenever merchandise is taken from the warehouse, for whatever reason, an entry must be obtained and duties paid. Warehouse entries are not issued, however, for duty-free goods, explosives, and perishables. But certain exceptions are allowed in the case of perishables, depending upon the nature of the goods and the type of warehouse that will store the goods.

When materials are imported for use in the manufacture of finished goods destined for export, they may be admitted under the bonded manu-facturing warehouse entry.

**Financing peculiarities.** *Exporters.* Sales are generally made on the basis of (1) an export letter of credit executed in favor of the seller by the buyer abroad, (2) drafts drawn by sellers on buyers abroad, and (3) an open account.

Export letters of credit eliminate credit risks and the risk of obtaining dollar exchange, since the seller receives dollars upon presentation of the proper shipping documents. The documents are usually a commercial invoice, consular invoice (when the country of destination demands it), bill of lading or certificate of manufacture, and insurance certificates. In addition, special documents, such as certificates of origin and weight lists, may be required. See also Figure 3 for enumeration of documents.

Dollar drafts are the most commonly used financing device in exporting despite the seller's assumption of the risk and the fact that dollars are not available until funds have been returned from abroad. Sellers sometimes discount their drafts with their banks, thereby raising funds to assist them in financing their business.

Under an open-account arrangement, the seller sends shipping docu-ments directly to the buyer, who will remit the value of the goods at the expiration date of the bill. Usually, in sales made against draft, the docu-ments are attached to the draft. If the draft is drawn at sight, the buyer obtains the documents at the time he pays for the draft. If the sale is made at 30 or 60 days, the documents are released to the drawee (buyer) when he accepts the draft. Payment is effected the day the draft matures.

*Importers.* Payment is made by sight or time drafts, open account, or letters of credit. The import letter of credit assures payment to the foreign seller at the time or shortly after the goods are shipped. Since the sight draft calls for payment in the United States, foreign sellers are often unwilling to accept this method of payment unless the importer has a high credit rating. Under this arrangement, the importer pays when the draft with the shipping documents is presented to the importer for payment by the collecting bank.

Open accounts are granted to well-known importers with sufficient financial resources to meet their obligations. The shipping documents are sent to the buyer, who honors the obligation on the expiration of the terms of sale.

*Receipt or payment in foreign currencies.* Exporters and importers will sometimes have to accept or make payment in foreign currencies. When an export sale is payable in a foreign currency, the seller does not know exactly how much he will receive for the goods sold because he does not know what the rate of exchange will be on the day he converts the foreign currency into dollars. Similarly, an importer who must pay at a future date in foreign currency does not know how much he will have to pay for the foreign currency in dollars when he has to make payment. In order to avoid speculation in currency, the amounts involved should be covered immediately by purchase or sale of the amount of foreign currency against United States dollars. Unfortunately, however, it is not always possible to effect such purchases and sales because futures in some currencies are not readily available or salable in this country. This situation presents the necessity for the two accounts explained at page 605, Profit or Loss on Exchange—Non-Regulated Currencies and Profit or Loss on Exchange—Regulated Currencies.

In the purchase of exchange futures, the importer obligates himself to accept a certain amount of foreign exchange at a rate a few points in advance of the spot (immediate delivery) rate for the deferred delivery of the needed foreign currency. If the credit standing of the importer is particularly good, a contract to pay dollars and receive future exchange is sufficient; otherwise, he must post a cash margin with the foreign exchange banker and immobilize a portion of his working capital. If no cash margin is required, this purchase of exchange requires merely a statistical record of the amount, the rate obtained, and the due date of the purchase. If a margin is required, the entry of the deposit on margin on futures bought is simply a debit to the foreign exchange banker and a credit to cash.

**Principal accounting problems.** The most important problem is to furnish management with an accurate and up-to-date picture of every foreign transaction involving the payment or receipt in foreign currency. These data will enable management to take any necessary steps to hedge against any possible losses and to consolidate any profits already made into American currency.

It is important to watch receivables for which clients have paid in local currency but which cannot be converted to dollars because of exchange shortages and consequent currency restrictions.

It is also important to maintain properly the numerous special records described at pages 606 et seq.

## Functional organization

**Departments concerned with foreign transactions.** *Selling.* The selling department keeps close contact with customers, branch offices, commission agents, and ultimate consumers. The responsible individuals in this department must select the firms with which they will deal and must meet the firms' representatives. In exporting, the contacts are generally with firms located abroad. In importing, the selling department's contacts are with domestic firms.

*Purchasing.* The purchasing department maintains contacts with suppliers in order to be informed about prices, availability of materials, and the like. This information enables the responsible individuals to make purchase commitments and to inform the selling division about possibilities in the field for circularizing customers and for advertising. If numerous products are imported, there may be commodity specialists to do the buying.

Large establishments usually divide their selling and purchasing organization into smaller units, either (1) on a geographical basis, such as Canada, Cuba, Mexico, and United States territories; Latin America and Europe; South and Central Africa; Middle East; Far East; and British Commonwealth (Australia and British Africa); or (2) on the basis of product classifications.

*Shipping department.* The shipping department takes care of all transportation, obtaining export and import licenses and the like. Many firms use specialized forwarders who perform numerous import-export functions.

*Accounting department.* In addition to performing its regular functions, this department watches expiration dates of letters of credit.

## Classification of accounts and books of account

**Comment on classification of accounts.** Although this section does not purport to present an accounting system for a particular type of foreign trader, a chart of accounts is presented to indicate the usual accounts of a merchant who buys or sells in domestic and foreign markets and pays and earns commissions on purchases or sales. The income and expense accounts are presented in the order in which they would appear on a profit and loss statement.

## Balance sheet accounts.

| | Debits from | Credits from |
|---|---|---|
| *Current Assets* | | |
| Cash in United States Banks ......... | Cash Receipts Journal | Cash Disbursements Journal |
| Cash in Foreign Countries—Non-Regulated Currencies ................. | Do | Do |
| Cash in Foreign Countries—Regulated Currencies ....................... | Do | Do |
| Cash on Deposit .................... | Do | Do |
| Petty Cash ....................... | Cash Disbursements Journal | General Journal or Petty Cash Book |
| Marketable Securities—United States.. | Do | Cash Receipts Journal |
| Marketable Securities—Foreign ...... | Do | Do |
| Accounts Receivable—Domestic ...... | Sales Journal, General Journal | Do |
| Accounts Receivable—Foreign ....... | Do | Do |
| Notes Receivable—Domestic ......... | General Journal | Cash Receipts Journal, General Journal |
| Notes Receivable—Foreign .......... | Do | Do |
| Allowance for Doubtful Accounts ..... | Do | General Journal |
| Claims Receivable ................. | Do | General Journal or Cash Receipts Journal |
| Merchandise Inventory .............. | Do | Do |
| *Fixed Assets* | | |
| Furniture and Fixtures .............. | Cash Disbursements Journal | Do |
| Allowance for Depreciation—Furniture and Fixtures ..................... | General Journal | Do |
| *Current Liabilities* | | |
| Accounts Payable .................. | Cash Disbursements Journal | Purchase Journal |
| Notes Payable ..................... | Do | General Journal |
| Trade Acceptances Payable .......... | Do | Do |
| Deposits from Customers ............ | Do | Cash Receipts Journal, Sales Journal, General Journal |
| Duty Adjustment ................... | Cash Disbursements Journal, General Journal | Cash Receipts Journal, General Journal |
| F.I.C.A. Tax Payable ............... | Cash Disbursements Journal | Cash Disbursements Journal or General Journal |
| Withholding Tax Payable ............ | Do | Do |

|  | *Debits from* | *Credits from* |
|---|---|---|
| Other Payroll Taxes Payable ......... | Cash Disbursements Journal | Cash Disbursements Journal or General Journal |
| Accrued Expenses ................. | Cash Disbursements Journal or General Journal | General Journal |
| Commissions Payable ............... | Cash Disbursements Journal | Sales Journal |
| Federal Income Tax Payable ........ | Do | General Journal |
| *Capital Accounts* | | |
| Capital Stock ...................... | | Cash Receipts Journal or General Journal |
| Earned Surplus ................... | General Journal | General Journal |

## Income and expense accounts.

| | | |
|---|---|---|
| Export Sales ....................... | | Sales Journal |
| Domestic Sales ..................... | | Do |
| Income from Commissions .......... | | Cash Receipts Journal, Sales Journal |

*Cost of Goods Sold*

| | | |
|---|---|---|
| Purchases ..................... | Purchase Journal | General Journal |
| Duties Paid .................... | Cash Disbursements Journal, Purchase Journal | Do |
| Freight Inbound ................. | Do | Do |
| Freight Outbound ............... | Purchase Journal, Cash Disbursements Journal, Sales Journal | Do |
| Discounts and Allowances ........ | Cash Receipts Journal | Do |
| Shipping Expenses ............... | Sales Journal | Do |
| Storage and Warehousing ........ | Cash Disbursements Journal (for first month) | Do |
| Marine Insurance ............... | Cash Disbursements Journal, or Purchase Journal | Cash Disbursements Journal |

*Expenses*

| | | |
|---|---|---|
| Officers' Salaries ................. | Cash Disbursements Journal | |
| Salesmen's Salaries and Commissions | Do | |
| Office Salaries ................... | Do | |
| Shipping Salaries ................ | Do | |
| Commissions .................... | General Journal, Cash Disbursements Journal | |
| Travel and Entertainment ........ | Cash Disbursements Journal | |
| Advertising ..................... | Purchase Journal, Cash Disbursements Journal | |

|  | *Debits from* | *Credits from* |
|---|---|---|
| Selling Expenses | Purchase Journal, Cash Disbursements Journal | |
| Buying Expenses | Do | |
| Storage and Warehousing | Do | |
| Trucking | Do | |
| Rent | Do | |
| Stationery and Supplies | Do | |
| Professional Fees | Do | |
| Telephone and Telegraph | Do | |
| Samples | Do | |
| Postage | Do | |
| Cables | Do | |
| Office Expense—Domestic | Do | |
| Office Expense—Foreign | Do | |
| Packing | Cash Disbursements Journal, Sales Journal | |
| Insurance Premiums | Do | |
| Payroll Taxes | Cash Disbursements Journal | |
| State Income Taxes | Do | |
| Miscellaneous Taxes (broken down). | Do | |
| *Other Income and Expenses* | | |
| Freight Income | Do | Purchase Journal |
| Insurance Income | Do | Do |
| Interest Income | | Cash Receipts Journal, General Journal |
| Interest Expense | Do | |
| Profit or Loss on Exchange—Non-Regulated Currencies | General Journal, Cash Receipts Journal, Cash Disbursements Journal | General Journal, Cash Receipts Journal, Cash Disbursements Journal |
| Profit or Loss on Exchange—Regulated Currencies | Do | Do |

**Accounts peculiar to export and import trade.** *Cash in Foreign Countries—Non-Regulated (or Regulated) Currencies.* This account represents funds in foreign countries which may be the result of a transaction in a foreign country, or which may be in the hands of the firm's agent or representative to be used for expenses.

*Cash on Deposit* and *Deposits from Customers.* The firm may deposit cash in order to obtain merchandise. Similarly, advances or deposits are made by customers in order to obtain merchandise or for future use.

*Marketable Securities—Foreign.* Sometimes foreign countries request deposits for customs duties or other charges, and it may be advantageous to buy foreign government securities for this purpose. The account, however, may also reflect the ownership of shares in a foreign corporation.

*Duty Adjustment.* Ad valorem duties are based on value, but the Tariff Act supplies at least five possible definitions of "value." Customs appraisers are known to be rather arbitrary in determining the value at which goods were freely offered in the foreign market on the date the on-carrying vessel last touched a port in the exporting country. This value is converted to dollars at a foreign exchange rate indicated daily by the Federal Reserve Board. Where the importer's estimate of dutiable value differs from that of the customs appraiser, the importer is given an opportunity to amend his customs entry and pay the correct duty without penalty. But all duty payments are provisional, the final and correct amount not being determined until the entry is liquidated by the Customs House. Liquidation may occur long after the merchandise has been sold and payment received; it seldom occurs less than a year after the provisional payment of the duty.

The common practice is to use a Duty Adjustment account to which refunds from the Treasury Department of duty overpayments can be credited and demands for additional duty debited. Such debits and credits often run into large percentages of respective cost and selling price, leaving the importer in a financially unsettled position profit-wise until entries are liquidated.

*Profit or Loss on Exchange—Non-Regulated (or Regulated) Currencies.* If goods exported by an American company are sold for dollars, the foreign exchange required to supply these dollars is provided by the purchaser, who sustains any resulting exchange loss or profit. Conversely, if the goods are sold payable in the currency of the purchaser (and this is still customary in many parts of Western Europe and the British Commonwealth), the seller receives payment in foreign currency and sustains any loss or profit arising from the difference between the dollar invoice value of the goods and the market value of the foreign money received in payment. This plus or minus difference is respectively credited or debited to the Profit or Loss on Exchange—Non-Regulated (or Regulated) Currencies account. Of course, if all foreign currency transactions are immediately covered through purchase or sale of futures, there is no need for these accounts.

The settlement of foreign accounts payable, when due in the foreign currency, is accomplished by the purchase in the United States of the required number of units of the foreign currency, which are then sent abroad. This purchase causes a draft, drawn by someone in the United States upon a bank in a foreign country, to be handed to the foreign creditor. Entry of the check drawn to the foreign exchange banker for this purchase is made in the Cash Disbursements Journal as usual. If an obligation to pay £1000 was set up in the initial accounts payable entry at the rate of $2.80

per £, and these £s are ultimately purchased at $2.82, there is a $20 exchange loss on the transaction. The entry is:

| | | |
|---|---|---:|
| Dr. | Foreign Account Payable ................................. | $2,800 |
| Dr. | Profit or Loss on Exchange—Non-Regulated Currencies...... | 20 |
| Cr. | Cash .................................................. | $2,820 |

For settlement of foreign obligation of £1,000 by purchase of draft at exchange rate of $2.82.

*Miscellaneous Income—Insurance, Freight, Interest.* In the export trade, profits on such expenses as insurance, freight, and interest result from the fact that the exporter may be in a position to obtain a lower overall rate for his entire volume, or because of strong competition in the field. These profits reduce the expenses of insurance, freight, and interest. However, it is advisable to maintain separate accounts for Insurance Income, Freight Income, and Interest Income. They are shown as Other Income at the bottom of the profit and loss statement.

*Trading accounts.* Each deal, whether it is an import or an export transaction, is given a contract number, and an account is opened for the deal, identified by the number of the contract. The accounts are kept in one or more subsidiary ledgers, such as coffee, cotton, and the like, or Australia, Canada, and so on, depending upon whether the organizational setup is by product or by geographical unit. Each subsidiary ledger is controlled through a general ledger account called Contracts or Merchandise. All costs or expenses applicable to the particular transaction, such as freight, insurance, and the like, are recorded in the account set up for the transaction. Generally, only the first month's warehousing expenses are charged to a specific deal. Charges after the first month for warehousing and insurance should be treated as general expenses. All general expenses must be allocated to their proper expense categories.

The trading accounts are reflected in the inventory account in the balance sheet. In order to arrive at the proper inventory figure, the prepaid expenses in the trading accounts must be separated.

**Records peculiar to export and import trade.** *Shipping folder.* A shipping folder is prepared as soon as a sale for export is contracted, in order to house all documents and other papers relating to the particular contract. The outside of the folder should be imprinted as shown in Figure 1, in order to eliminate the necessity for scanning through many papers for information. A similar folder is set up when a purchase for import is made.

*Exporter's draft register.* A draft register is maintained to provide a constant check on due dates of notes receivable and trade acceptances set up against drafts on overseas accounts and loans or advances by banks or other lending institutions (see Figure 2). This running record is kept up to date as information is received from the overseas collecting bank rela-

Customer _____ Order _____

_____ Date _____

_____ Indent _____

Export License _____ Expires _____ Case No. _____

Import License _____ Expires _____

Supplier _____

Commodity _____ Quantity _____

Delivery Date _____ Delivery To _____

Customer Terms: Letter of Credit

Advice # _____ New York Bank _____

Credit # _____ Foreign Bank _____

Amount $ _____ Ship Expiration _____ Doc. Expiration _____

Other _____

CIF COST ANALYSIS

( )FOB ( ) FAS _____ Agent _____

Inland Freight _____ Commission _____

Export Packing _____ Other _____

Ocean Freight _____ SPECIAL INSTRUCTIONS :

Consular Fee _____

Insurance _____

Commission _____

Other _____

Total CIF COST _____

Total CIF SALES _____

GROSS PROFIT _____

**Fig. 1. Imprinted Shipping Folder.**

tive to the dollar payment. The transaction is closed out when the client's payment and the corresponding bank loan are noted in the last column.

EXPORTER'S DRAFT REGISTER

| Invoice Date | Inv. No. | Draft No. | Customer's Name & Address | Terms | Draft Maturity Date | Draft Amount | Observations |
|---|---|---|---|---|---|---|---|
| 1/2/5- | 503 | 15 | Ricardo Gonzales, San José, Costa Rica | 90 d. | 4/2/5- | 1,200 — | Accepted to mature 4/2/5- |
| 1/12/5- | 508 | 16 | Enrique Martinez, San Juan, Puerto Rico | 60 d. | 3/12/5- | 1,850 — | Not yet accepted. |
| 4/10/5- | 519 | 17 | José Rivera S., Bogotá, Colombia | Sight | — | 6,000 - | Awaits arrival of merchandise per bank notice 4/20/5- |

**(CONTINUATION OF ABOVE)**

| Report of Collecting Bank | Amount Borrowed Against This Draft | | Lending Institution | Loan Due | Payment Effected by Customer | Payment Effected to Bank |
|---|---|---|---|---|---|---|
| Paid in local currency 3/1/5- now awaiting exchange authorization to transfer proceeds to U.S.A. | 900 — | 75% | N.H.M. | 4/2/5- | 3/30/5- | 4/2/5- |
| Client out of town | 1,480 — | 80% | B/M | Demand | | |
| Bank reports client unwilling to liquidate draft unless insurance premium is waived as he covered locally. Matter referred to local agent named in collection instructions. | 4,500 — | 75% | N.H.M. | 6/10/5— | | |

**Fig. 2. Exporter's Draft Register.**

*Importer's draft register.* The American importer who buys on draft terms keeps a register of draft maturities similar to that shown in Figure 2. Even importers who establish letters of credit to pay for their merchandise normally receive the documents from their bank on a trust-receipt basis, signing a 30- or 60-day note. Under these circumstances, importers keep registers of maturities somewhat as follows:

| Date | Reference Number | Supplier | Amount | Matures on | Due to |
|------|------------------|----------|--------|------------|--------|
| 1/4/5– | 4395 | John Smith London, England | £1,380 | 4/4/5– | Resource |
| 1/5/5– | 075 | Hideki Suzuki | $8,975 | 3/15/5– | NCB |
| 1/13/5– | 1395 | Herman Muller Hamburg, Germany | $6,350 | 3/13/5– | Resource |

The indication "Resource" in the last column indicates that the foreign resource has drawn the time draft, in local currency or United States dollars as indicated, and that payment is due, through the presenting bank, to the overseas supplier. The initials NCB indicate that a dollar letter was opened by the importer through the National City Bank. When title documents were presented against the credit, the opening bank paid the supplier and released the documents on trust receipt to the importer for repayment 3/15/5–.

*Insurance register.* Insurance against all risks of sea transport must be undertaken if the sales contract requires it. Details of all shipments are entered in the Insurance Register from the shipping documents. The register includes the following columns:

> Insurance Certificate Number
> Date of Bill of Lading
> Invoice Number
> Description of Merchandise (Marks)
> Name of Boat
> Name of Ports
> Insured Value
> Premium Rate

It is customary to insure goods for from 10 to 20 per cent more than their landed invoice value, and to have claims payable prorata for this insured percentage. Duty amounts are insurable at a fraction of the marine insurance cost, for goods must have safely completed their voyage before duty is payable.

*Letters of credit register.* Since no entries are made in the regular books of account for letters of credit opened or received, a register for both categories should be maintained.

When arrangements have been made with a local bank for an import credit to be established, a carbon copy of the credit application provides the essential information of amount, beneficiary, merchandise, expiration date, and percentage of total paid out to the foreign shipper against his title documents. It is convenient to file the copies of the credit application in a loose-leaf book, with the following columnar headings mimeographed on the reverse side of the form:

Letter of Credit Number Assigned
Amount of Draft Drawn:
    In Dollars
    In Foreign Currency
Date Drawn
Vessel Shipped
Date Shipped
Date of Expected Arrival
Date Documents Were Received Under Trust Receipt
Date T/R Matures
Balance Undrawn on Credit

If the credit is opened in a foreign currency, extra columns are added to express the amount of that currency under the Amount of Draft Drawn column and the Balance Undrawn on Credit column, as well as the dollar equivalents and the rate at which exchange was covered.

Incoming letters of credit are filed with the credit and collection section of the accounting department, which must check all documents and present them for collection. A photostated copy of the letter of credit is placed in the shipping folder for the guidance of the traffic and invoicing sections of the shipping division. The incoming letters of credit book has the columns:

Shipment Reference Number
Customer Name and Address
Amount
Merchandise
Notified by (Which Local Bank)
Opened by (Which Foreign Bank)
Last Date for Shipment
Last Date for Negotiation
Partial Shipment Permitted
Date Draft Presented Against L/C
Date Payment Received

*Claims register.* This register contains the record of claims made for short shipment, damages to merchandise, or loss in transit and supports the Claims Receivable account. Claims should be sent immediately to the supplier, insurance company, and common carriers against which they are made. A form is usually filled out in duplicate with the necessary data. The copy of the form is numbered, placed in a binder, and entered in the claims register. Entries from the claims register are debited to Claims Receivable and credited to the contract account or individual contract (depending upon the method of recording contracts), or other appropriate account.

If the claim is settled in full, the Claims Receivable account is cleared through the cash receipts book or by general journal entry. After the claim it settled, the claim form is removed from the binder and filed, and an appropriate entry is made in the claims register.

Short settlements on open contracts, as well as overs, are credited or charged to the contract account or to the individual contracts, again depending upon the system used. Overpayments and short payments on closed contracts are best shown as General Expense or Other Income.

If there are numerous claims which occur regularly, the claims register may be used as a book of original entry.

*Commitment register.* If the number of transactions warrants it, a commitment register may be used to record the purchases or commitments to purchase from foreign suppliers and the sales made from such merchandise. This record enables the trader to see, from the open balances, what merchandise is still available for sale. The columns in the register are as follows:

| *Purchases or Commitments to Purchase:* | *Sales* |
|---|---|
| Shipping Folder Number | Shipping Folder Number |
| Date of Purchase Contract | Date Sold |
| Merchandise Description | Merchandise Description |
| Quantity | Quantity |
| Unit Price | Unit Price |
| Delivery Date | Delivery Date |
| Payment Terms | Payment Terms |
| Date Vendor's Invoice Received | Date Invoiced |
| | Amount Invoiced |

## Procedures for export and import transactions

**Export transaction.** *Receipt of order.* A customer abroad will place his order directly or indirectly, as explained at page 596. When the order is received, it is immediately given an order number and a shipping folder for the order is set up. An account is opened for the transaction in the subsidiary ledger. Since almost all goods require an export license, it is practical to make purchase commitments to fill the order subject to obtaining the necessary license.

*Application for export license.* An Application for Export License, Form IT-419 (Department of Commerce, Office of International Trade), is prepared in triplicate. The original and a copy are filed with the Office of International Trade, Washington, D.C., and the triplicate is retained by the applicant. All parties in interest must be disclosed. In many cases, certain documents must accompany the application.

A Single Transaction Statement by Consignee and Purchaser, Form FC-842, must be submitted by the overseas buyer and importer to the United States seller or United States exporter, who sends it to the Office of International Trade along with the Application for Export License.

One set (two cards) of Form FC-116 must be attached to the Application for Export License when it is filed. The applicant's copy and the OIT file copy must be self-addressed. The applicant's copy is returned to him showing the OIT case number for future reference in inquiring about the application.

An import license issued by the country of destination must be obtained if payment is to be made after arrival in the foreign port. Application for an AEC (Atomic Energy Commission) license, on Form AEC-17, is necessary for export of materials to be used for the production of fissionable material.

*Shipping.* Shipping space is secured by the shipping or traffic department as soon as the order is received. The necessary documents are sent to the steamship line or a forwarding agent. Figure 3 illustrates the instruction to effect shipment.

*Sales invoices.* The exporter needs a great number of copies of invoices for goods shipped. Photostat or some other reproducing process can be used to facilitate production of an ample supply of identical copies. Besides the usual copies for internal use, additional copies are required for various purposes. For example, invoices must be included with other documents in instructions to steamship lines of forwarding agents to effect shipment; they must also be included with other documents in instructions to banks to make collections. Invoices should be prenumbered and copies for internal use should be on colored paper.

*Collection against letter of credit.* To obtain payment against a letter of credit, the documents mentioned on Figure 4 are presented to the bank along with the draft. If collection is to be made abroad, the receiving documents with the draft are sent to an American bank, which collects through its branch or agent abroad. The bank's responsibility is clearly stated on the back of the "request for collection" letter furnished by the bank and signed by the firm.

*Export sales journal.* An export sales journal form is illustrated in Figure 5 (page 615). Postings are made monthly to the proper general ledger accounts.

Sales allowances or discounts can be recorded in a separate journal or in the export sales journal, in which case additional columns would be provided therefor.

Commissions are not paid on overseas sales until payment in full is

To:                                    Date:

                                       Ref:

Gentlemen:

Please effect shipment per_____ Booking No. _____

from_____to_____via _____

| MARKS | DESCRIPTION | |
|---|---|---|
| | No. of Pcs : <br> Quantity : <br> Dec. Descp: <br><br> B/Lading Description | Gross Wt.    lbs <br>      kilos <br> Legal Wt.    lbs <br>      kilos <br> Net Wt.    lbs <br>      kilps <br><br> Cubic feet: <br><br> FAS VALUE: |

( ) Issue Dock Receipt with delivery instruction to:

( ) Delivery being effected on D/R issued by this office.

| | |
|---|---|
| ( ) Exp. Lic. No.      attached. | |
| ( ) Imp. Lic. No.      attached. | |
| ( ) Exp. Lic. No.      on file with | |
|      customs. | |
| ( ) Commercial Invoice attached for consular documentation. | |

( ) 3 Clean Original B/L <br>    ( ) On Board <br>    ( ) Prepaid <br>    ( ) Collect <br> ( ) Non-Nego B/L Copies <br> ( ) Consular Invoices <br> ( ) Cert. of origin <br> ( ) Forwarders Receipt <br> ( ) Legalized Invoice <br> ( )

Bills of Lading to be issued as follows:

SHIPPER                 :

Consigned to            :

Notify Party            :

Ultimate Consignee      :

SPECIAL INSTRUCTIONS:

Fig. 3. Letter to Effect Shipment.

received. This practice is based on the unusual delays and risks of the export business and the need for tying the overseas sales agent to the transaction until dollars have been received in the United States. The export sales journal shows the liability.

**Import transaction.** The procedures used in making domestic purchases apply equally to import purchases, with the following exceptions: (1) In

Date:

Advice:

Our Ref:

To:

Gentlemen:

We submit herewith the following documents under above mentioned advice and request that you acknowledge receipt by stamping attached copy.

Draft ( ) #_____ $_____

Original Bills of Lading ( ) #_____

Non-Negotiable Bills of Lading ( ) #_____

Insurance Certificates ( ) #_____

Commercial Invoices ( ) #_____

Consular Invoices ( ) #_____

Certificate of Origin ( ) #_____

Packing List / Weight Notes ( )

Inspection Certificate ( )

( )

Covering Shipment of _____

Per S/S _____ from _____ to _____

Drawn on _____

( ) Please mail check

( ) Advise when ready-will pick up

( ) Credit Loan No. _____

( ) Credit our account　　　Very truly yours,

Export Department

**Fig. 4. Instructions to Collect.**

rare cases import licenses must be obtained from the Department of Commerce, (2) the merchandise must be passed through customs, (3) a consular invoice is required, as well as several copies of the commercial invoice from the seller.

| EXPORT SALES JOURNAL | | | | | | | |
| --- | --- | --- | --- | --- | --- | --- | --- |
| Date | Invoice # | Name | Description | | Order # | Amount (charge to A/R) | |
| | | | Quantity | Kind | | | |
| | | | | | | | Continued Below |

| | Expense | | Other Charges | | Commission | |
| --- | --- | --- | --- | --- | --- | --- |
| Merchandise | Freight | Insurance | Item | Amount | Name | Amount |
| | | | | | | |

Fig. 5. Export Sales Journal.

Shipping space is arranged for by the seller abroad or by the purchaser in this country, and insurance is effected as agreed upon between the seller abroad and the importer.

Upon receipt of the invoices, an entry is made in the Import Purchase Journal, and the trading account covering the deal is set up in the subsidiary ledger.

Payment of the invoice is made by sight or time draft or letter of credit, as explained at page 599.

## Reports to management

**Financial and operating reports.** Balance sheets and income statements are prepared periodically as in any other business.

Firms engaged in buying and selling abroad are particularly interested in knowing from day to day what funds are available, what commitments have been made, and what buying and selling are required. How these reports are prepared depends somewhat upon how active the owners of the business are in effecting deals in foreign markets.

Management must be kept informed constantly of all deals made in a foreign currency that are not covered by exchange futures.

# 22

# Farming ("Family Type")

by

**EARL W. KEHRBERG**

Assistant Professor, Department of Agricultural
Economics, Purdue University

## Characteristics that affect the accounting system

**Nature of the business.** The farm business is often a family affair. It is operated as much with a view to providing a home as to conducting a business operation for profit. The farmer draws on the same bank account to pay for his childrens' school supplies as he does to buy fertilizer. In fact, he may pay for both items with the same check. When he sells eggs, a part or all of the proceeds may be used to buy groceries for the farm household.

The entire family often takes part in operating the farm. The farmer's wife may take care of the poultry and help clean milking equipment while the children "do chores." Farm produce, such as eggs, milk, cream, vegetables, and meat, goes directly into the household. This situation complicates record-keeping from a business viewpoint.

The operator of a diversified farm services, operates, and often repairs his own farm machinery. He carries on a number of farming operations, such as dairying, hog raising, and crop raising. Besides these, he makes the over-all management decisions for the farm and acts as his own buyer and seller. If any records are kept, he and/or his wife is the bookkeeper. Farmers ordinarily cannot afford a full-time bookkeeper or accountant, and most of them lack specialized knowledge of accounting and record analysis. They like their facts simple and do not appreciate complicated accounting procedures. Because they do the farming as well as the bookkeeping, they demand record systems that require a minimum of effort and time. Single-entry bookkeeping systems best meet these requirements. The system presented, therefore, is in terms of single-entry accounts.

The farm business, however, is extremely complex, with many products being produced on the same farm. Some are marketed, while others are used as input factors in other stages of the business. Many enterprises compete for limited labor, capital, and equipment. The production processes are subject to vagaries of the weather, disease, insect damage, and the like. Furthermore, farming methods have been changing rapidly in recent years.

Although the use of bookkeeping in agriculture predates the Industrial Revolution, standardized procedures have not been so well defined for as long a time as in other industries. Methods of analyzing and setting up records are still in a relatively early stage of development.

**Types of establishments.** Farms and farming areas are classified according to their major enterprises. For example, dairy-hog farms, wheat farms, a Dairy Belt, and Corn Belt are common terms. Each type requires a slight modification of records. The records discussed in this section are practical for the general diversified farm especially prevalent in the Midwest. However, by changing the accounts to conform with the products and corresponding expenses of other areas, these records should fit in well with most of the needs of "family-type" farms. Large-scale farms that can afford bookkeepers may find it profitable to use more complex and complete records.

Some indication of how farms vary in gross income can be obtained from the United States Census estimates of farms by economic classes. In Table I, adapted from the Census figures, it may be noted that over 90 per cent of all farms sold farm products valued at less than $10,000 per farm. Over 85 per cent of the commercial farms sold products valued at less than $10,000. Small business is the dominant form in agriculture.

TABLE I

Percentage of Farms Selling Different Values of Farm Products for the United States, 1950

| Value of Product Sold | Percentage of All Farms | Percentage of Commercial Farms |
|---|---|---|
| Commercial Farms: | | |
| $25,000 or more .......................... | 1.9% | 2.8% |
| 10,000 to 24,999 ......................... | 7.1 | 10.3 |
| 5,000 to 9,999 ......................... | 13.4 | 19.5 |
| 2,500 to 4,999 ......................... | 16.4 | 23.8 |
| 1,200 to 2,499 ......................... | 16.8 | 24.3 |
| 250 to 1,199 ......................... | 13.3 | 19.4 |
| Other Farms: * | | |
| Part-time ............................. | 11.9 | |
| Residential ............................. | 19.1 | |
| Abnormal, i.e., experimental, etc.......... | 0.1 | |

* Except for abnormal farms, the value of product sold per farm under this classification was less than $2,000.

**Governmental controls and taxes.** While price supports, marketing quotas, and acreage allotments are familiar terms in agriculture, they do little to alter the bookkeeping. Income taxes, however, affect farm record-keeping. Few farmers even kept records until the early 1940's. The widening of the Federal income tax base and increased income levels began to necessitate better records. The farm business and the farm household are so interrelated that income taxes have a direct effect on farm record-keeping, even though the Federal income tax paid by farmers is a personal and not a business tax. The Federal Internal Revenue Service has never required that the farmer keep records in any particular way, but the nature of the reports which the farmer must make and the required forms and suggested forms that he uses (Form 1040F in particular) have a great impact on the farmer's records. Although a complete set of records kept for management purposes can be used to fill out an income tax report, the farmer dislikes the sorting and rearranging of records that must occur unless his records are set up to give him his income tax information directly. Since many farmers keep records only for use in filling out income tax reports, it is practical to consider records first with regard to the ease with which they satisfy this requirement.

**Functional peculiarities.** *Length of the production period.* Farm production is not a continuous process. Instead, plans are made months in advance of the harvest. Although there are some exceptions, such as dairying, most crops are planted with no product forthcoming for several months, and then it all comes at once. Monthly summaries do not mean much to the farmer under these conditions. Once the production process is under way, little can be done to slow it or stop it. A few of the more ambitious farmers may wish quarterly summaries to use in checking their budgets (plans) and in filling out social security and withholding tax forms.

*Risk and uncertainty.* Although most industries are faced with a certain amount of risk and uncertainty, farming faces more than most. Weather, disease, and insects change the farming picture almost overnight. What was planned as an adequate feed supply at the beginning of the cropping year may turn out to be a great deal more or less than required. Records are of little use in controlling this situation, although an analysis of records may help in designing a farming system that is more flexible. The prices received by farmers are subject to relatively violent fluctuations, but the farmer can make only limited adjustments in production, once the production processes are under way.

*Complexity of production relationships.* Detailed cost accounts are often too difficult for the average farmer to keep and analyze. Livestock furnish manure for crops, and some crops, such as alfalfa, may harbor nitrogen-fixing bacteria from which other crops benefit. The extent of such benefits is difficult for even experts to evaluate, and any arbitrary valuations for bookkeeping purposes affect management decisions. Most farmers accept as the goal of their accounting an over-all picture of their business rather than detailed cost analysis. In some areas, such as Illinois and Minnesota, very detailed records are kept. However, fieldmen assist with the record-keeping. There are record-keeping associations in a number of states. Extension personnel usually assist these groups in varying degrees. Information along these lines may be obtained from the nearest agricultural experiment station or extension service.

**Ownership peculiarities.** In the United States, 26.8 per cent of the farms are leased. Leasing systems vary in their terms of payment from straight cash to payment in kind, that is, share of the crops. Wherever the forms of share-leasing are in effect, the landlord usually takes some part in the management of the farm. Hence, two sets of records are often kept. These records serve as a basis for division of expenses and returns under the lease, as well as other purposes. Ordinarily some adaptation of the records to this situation is required. A simple procedure is to include three columns in the income statement: one for the farm as a whole, one showing the tenant's expenses and share of returns, and the third, those of the landlord. Similarly, throughout depreciation schedules, receipts accounts, and expenditures accounts, two columns may be kept showing the share received or contributed by each of the two parties. The crop record may have a column added indicating the landlord's and tenant's shares of crops under the lease. Various forms (record books) are available at agricultural experiment stations in areas where crop-share and livestock-share leases are prevalent. The latter especially involve the sharing of a number of the factors of production as well as of the various crops and livestock sold.

## Objectives of the system

**Specific objectives of the system.** Seven reasons why the farmer keeps records are as follows:

1. To furnish information for filing income tax reports.

2. To furnish information about weak and strong points of the farm business.

3. To furnish physical production information useful in making plans (budgets).

4. To help establish credit rating.

5. To help in settling estates and in transferring the farm property from father to son.

6. To prevent duplicate payment of bills.

7. To serve as a basis for dividing expenditures and returns under share-leasing arrangements.

Of these, information for filling out income tax reports is most important in the eyes of the farmer. Many farmers keep records for no other purpose.

In spite of the farmer's preoccupation with income taxes, the importance of records for management purposes and other objectives should not be discounted. The better farmers in the community tend to find many ways of utilizing their records. However, most farmers prefer records that culminate directly in income statements that satisfy the federal income tax forms.

## Types of records and accounts

**Required records.** The records needed by farmers are (1) inventories, (2) capital accounts and depreciation schedules, (3) records of receipts and expenditures, and (4) production and performance records. When the records are kept solely for income tax purposes, the whole system may be reduced to a few financial records. Farmers have the option of reporting income on the cash receipts and disbursements basis, which requires no inventories, although a depreciation schedule is recommended for such items as machinery and purchased breeding stock. However, by the addition of a few inventories and physical production records, some indication of costs and returns of various enterprises and farming practices can be obtained. Hence, these records will be presented, although the actual extent to which the individual farmer keeps them depends upon his ability to utilize and interpret such information.

### A. Inventories and Capital Accounts

**Farm inventories.** Farm inventories are relatively simple records that furnish a great deal of valuable information for the little time required to assemble them. Many farmers are surprised to find their financial position different from that which they had supposed before keeping inventories and preparing a net worth statement. Farmers are often engaged in trying to gain ownership of a farm. Whether their equity in the business is increasing or decreasing is of prime importance. The whole farm family may be sacrificing some of its time and living standards in order to accomplish this end.

Banks and credit agencies in many instances require information accumulated through inventories before lending money to farmers. With modern machinery and expensive equipment, capital requirements in agriculture have increased. Consequently, inventories and net worth summaries are becoming more important as the farmer tries to attract outside capital into his business.

Although the farmer is not required to have inventories if he reports income on the cash basis for tax purposes, he often finds them useful. On the other hand, if he chooses to use the accrual method of reporting income for tax purposes, he needs a complete set of inventories. Under either system, lists of depreciable property and depreciation schedules are required if the farmer wishes to exercise his privilege of charging depreciation as an expenditure.

**Inventory forms.** A list of inventories such as are used on a Midwest farm would include:

1. Inventory of feeds
2. Inventory of seeds and supplies
3. Hog inventory
4. Cattle inventory
5. Poultry inventory
6. Sheep inventory
7. Horse inventory

Capital lists and depreciation schedules include:

1. Machinery and equipment
2. Buildings
3. Land and permanent improvements to land

As would be expected, the farmer's house and household equipment other than office are not included in the business inventories.

A typical livestock inventory follows the general form suggested for cattle (Figure 1).

| Item | First of Year, 19— | | | | End of Year, 19— | | | |
|------|-----|--------|-------|-------------|-----|--------|-------|-------------|
|      | No. | Weight | Price | Total Value | No. | Weight | Price | Total Value |
| Milk cows ..... | | | | | | | | |
| Beef cows ..... | | | | | | | | |
| Bulls .......... | | | | | | | | |
| TOTAL ..... | | | | | | | | |
| Calves ......... | | | | | | | | |
| Heifers ........ | | | | | | | | |
| Feeder cattle .. | | | | | | | | |
| TOTAL ..... | | | | | | | | |
| TOTAL FOR ALL CLASSES .. | | | | | | | | |

**Fig. 1. Cattle Inventory.**

Such inventories and capital accounts are summarized easily and brought together by the farmer into a statement of net worth. No special form is required, although practically every agricultural experiment station and the United States Department of Agriculture have available single-entry record books that include some form of net worth statement. A net worth summary such as is shown in Figure 2 is satisfactory.

| ASSETS: | 19—<br>Beginning of Year | 19—<br>End of Year |
|---|---|---|
| Cash ........................................ | | |
| Accounts and notes receivable ............... | | |
| Feeds ...................................... | | |
| Supplies ................................... | | |
| Sheep ..................................... | | |
| Poultry ................................... | | |
| Hogs ...................................... | | |
| Cattle .................................... | | |
| Machinery ................................. | | |
| Buildings ................................. | | |
| Land ...................................... | | |
| Total assets ........................... | | |

LIABILITIES:

| | | |
|---|---|---|
| Accounts payable .......................... | | |
| Notes payable ............................. | | |
| Mortgage on farm ......................... | | |
| Other ..................................... | | |
| Total liabilities ....................... | | |
| Net worth ............................ | | |
| Increase or decrease in net worth ........ | | |

**Fig. 2. Net Worth Summary.**

**Valuation of assets.** Farm assets are commonly evaluated by one of the following methods:

1. Market value less cost of marketing
2. Cost or cost less depreciation
3. Replacement value
4. Capitalized value

The farmer chooses the methods which best suit his purposes. However, if the records are used for income tax reporting purposes, permission from the Internal Revenue Service is required before changing methods. In general, the farmer desires a true net worth statement and an income statement that reflects the relative profits and losses of different accounting periods. Given goals of simplicity, income tax reporting, and management analysis, the method that is best for one purpose is frequently not best for the others.

Products such as corn and market hogs are usually valued at market value less cost of marketing. Since a ready market exists for such items, this price reflects their true value to the business at any time. Machinery and other depreciable property are valued at cost less depreciation. The farmer is not usually interested in "paper losses or profits" from those items which are not intended for sale. In some instances, the original cost of a machine or building is unknown. A replacement value based on present costs and use is then used to approximate the value. That value may be depreciated to compare with the remaining years of service expected of the asset in question.

When assets are valued at cost, their true net worth is not always shown, for example, during periods of rising or falling price levels. It is sometimes suggested that in such cases the farmer should make adjustments in the values of machinery or land between accounting periods. Such a method has the merit of giving an accurate estimate of the net worth of the business. Any gains in the value of assets which accrue to the farmer through no credit to his operating management are kept out of the profits attributed to each accounting period. However, two sets of records are required, one for income tax purposes and one for management. Unless the farmer is very desirous of having the corrected net worth values to accomplish his objective, he usually compromises accuracy for the sake of simplicity and the availability of income tax information.

Similarly, in order to obtain an accurate value for land, it is often advocated that land value be estimated as a capitalized value of the stream of expected returns. However, the farmer is permitted capital gains privileges from the sale of his farm and needs the original records of purchase and improvement. Furthermore, he does not want his income statement to reflect changes in land values that would increase his taxable income. Hence, the cost basis for valuation is ordinarily used despite the resulting inaccuracy of present net worth.

In general, it may be noted that items with a ready, well-established market can be valued directly by means of market price less cost of marketing. Longer-lived assets fit into the cost or replacement framework. For some items, such as silage, corn stalks, and the like, there is no well-established market value, and costs are difficult to compute. Such items can usually be evaluated indirectly through an estimate of other feeds or items which they can replace. For example, three pounds of silage is often valued as the equivalent of one pound of hay.[1]

**Depreciation.** Depreciation is easily calculated for farm assets by the straight-line method. For example, a $1200 tractor may be estimated to have a salvage value of 10 per cent of the cost, or $120. The difference, $1080, is prorated over some estimated life such as 10 years. Farm machinery averages a life of around 15 years, while buildings average about 40 years of life. The Internal Revenue Service publishes *Bulletin F,* which lists reasonable depreciable life for various farm assets. Although other methods of depreciation are sometimes used, their advantages seldom offset the added complications of calculation.

Pages from the *Indiana Farm Depreciation Book* illustrate the general form which the capital accounts and depreciation schedules usually take (Figures 3 and 4). Note the illustrative entries designed to aid the farmer in using the book.

---

[1] For a complete list of valuation procedures acceptable for income tax reporting, see J. K. Lasser, *Farmer's Tax Handbook,* 2nd ed., Englewood Cliffs, N. J.: Prentice-Hall, Inc., 1951.

## LAND AND OTHER NON-DEPRECIABLE IMPROVEMENTS

| Property Item | Date Acquired | Cost or Value | Subsequent Nondepreciable Costs to Jan. 1, 19___ Date | 19___ | | |
|---|---|---|---|---|---|---|
| | | | | Investment at Beginning of Year | Increase or Decrease In Investment During Year[1] | Nature of Investment or Sale |
| (Example) 160 Acres Land | 1/10/42 | $20,000 | $300 | $20,300 | $ | |
| Residence | 1/10/42 | 3,500 | 100 | 3,600 | | |
| 40 Acres Land | 11/15/54 | 6,000 | | | | |
| 1 | | | | | | |
| 2 | | | | | | |
| 3 | | | | | | |
| 4 | | | | | | |
| 5 Total | X X | | | | | |

[1]Use an Additional Line for Purchases of Land. Also When Part of the Farm is Sold Enter the Number of Acres Remaining, Cost, Etc. On A New Line.

## BUILDINGS AND OTHER DEPRECIABLE IMPROVEMENTS

| Buildings and Improvements | Date Acquired | Cost or Other Basis | Est. Years Life | Annual Depreciation | 195— | | | |
|---|---|---|---|---|---|---|---|---|
| | | | | | Depreciation Allowed or Allowable in Prior Years | Unrecovered Cost at Beginning of Year | Increase or Decrease in Investment During Year | Depreciation This Year |
| (Example) Barn No. 1 | 1/10/42 | $4,800 | 40 | $120 | $1,080 | $3,720 | $ | $120 |
| Poultry House | 1/10/42 | 2,100 | 30 | 70 | 210 | 1,890 | | 70 |
| Fencing A | 1/10/42 | 1,280 | 20 | 64 | 576 | 704 | | 64 |
| Barn No. 1 (Overhauled) | 11/1/54 | 5,260 | 35 | 150 | | | | |
| Fencing B | 6/20/52 | 450 | 15 | 30 | | | | |
| Line X X X | X X | X X | X X | X X | 19___ | | | |
| 1 House For Tenant | $ | | $ | $ | $ | $ | | $ |
| 2 House For Hired Man | | | | | | | | |
| 3 Barn | | | | | | | | |
| 4 Corn Crib | | | | | | | | |
| 5 Garage | | | | | | | | |
| 6 Hog House (Perm.) | | | | | | | | |
| 7 Machine Shed | | | | | | | | |
| 8 Poultry House | | | | | | | | |
| 9 Water System | | | | | | | | |
| 10 Fencing | | | | | | | | |
| 11 Tiling | | | | | | | | |
| 12 Lime or Rock Phosphate | | | | | | | | |
| 13 | | | | | | | | |
| 14 | | | | | | | | |
| 15 | | | | | | | | |
| 16 | | | | | | | | |
| 17 | | | | | | | | |
| 18 | | | | | | | | |
| 19 Total | X X | | X X | | | | | |

**Fig. 3. Land and Buildings Depreciation Schedules. (From *Indiana Farm Depreciation Book*, prepared by Department of Agricultural Economics, Agricultural Extension Service, Purdue University.)**

| Machine or Equipment Item | Date Acquired | Cost or Other Basis | Est. Years Life | Annual Depreciation | Depreciation Allowed or Allowable in Prior Years | Unrecovered Cost at Beginning of Year[1] | Bought or Sold During Year[2] | Depreciation This Year |
|---|---|---|---|---|---|---|---|---|
| | | | | | | 195— | | |
| (Example) Combine | 1/12/42 | $1,200 | 10 | $120 | $1,080 | $ 120 | $ Traded in on new one | $ 60 |
| Combine | 6/20/51 | 1,720 | 10 | 172 | | (60) | 1660 | 86 |
| Tractor No. 1 | 1/10/46 | 1,850 | 10 | 185 | 925 | 925 | Sold 12/20/51. 600 | 185 |
| Tractor No. 2 | 10/15/48 | 2,250 | 10 | 225 | 506 | 1,744 | | 225 |
| Tractor No. 3 | 12/20/51 | 2,405 | 10 | 240 | | | 2,405 | |
| Tractor No. 2 (Overhauled) | 3/10/54 | 1,731 | 6 | 288 | | | | |
| Line   X X | X X | X X | X X | X X | | 19____ | | |
| 1 Auto (farm share)—% | | $ | | $ | $ | $ | $ | $ |
| 2 Belts | | | | | | | | |
| 3 Breaking Plow | | | | | | | | |
| 4 Brooders (chick) | | | | | | | | |
| 5 Brooders (pig) | | | | | | | | |
| 6 Brooder House | | | | | | | | |
| 7 Buck Rake | | | | | | | | |
| 8 Cans, Buckets, Etc. | | | | | | | | |
| 9 Chicken Feeders-Fount. | | | | | | | | |
| 10 Combine | | | | | | | | |
| 11 Corn Binder | | | | | | | | |
| 12 Corn Picker | | | | | | | | |
| 13 Corn Planter | | | | | | | | |
| 14 Corn Sheller | | | | | | | | |
| 15 Cream Separator | | | | | | | | |
| 16 Cultipacker or Roller | | | | | | | | |
| 17 Cultivator | | | | | | | | |
| 18 Dirt Scoop | | | | | | | | |
| 19 Disc | | | | | | | | |
| 20 Electric Fence Charger | | | | | | | | |
| 21 | | | | | | | | |
| 22 | | | | | | | | |
| 23 | | | | | | | | |
| 24 | | | | | | | | |
| 25 | | | | | | | | |
| 26 | | | | | | | | |
| 27 | | | | | | | | |
| 28 | | | | | | | | |
| 29 | | | | | | | | |
| 30 | | | | | | | | |
| 31 | | | | | | | | |
| 32 | | | | | | | | |
| 33 | | | | | | | | |
| 34 | | | | | | | | |
| 35 Total | X X | | X X | | | | | |

[1]In case of trade-in or overhaul, show unrecovered cost as of the date of trade or overhaul. Circle this figure.
[2]Enter the amount paid or received. For traded items, enter the cash difference paid or received.

**Fig. 4. Machinery and Equipment Depreciation Schedule. (From *Indiana Farm Depreciation Book*, prepared by Department of Agricultural Economics, Agricultural Extension Service, Purdue University.)**

When income is reported on the cash basis, the breeding stock, dairy stock, and draft animals that were purchased and not raised on the farm are depreciated. Farm-raised animals are not depreciated when the cash basis is used. Under the accrual system, all animals are ordinarily recorded in the regular inventories, since extra posting and bookkeeping are required to transfer farm-raised animals to capital accounts when they become old enough to be considered producers or breeding stock. Any depreciation is taken care of automatically in the inventory valuation procedures.

### B. Income Statements

**Cash income statement.** When a farm cash income statement is being made up, only those transactions completed during the year are included in the figuring of income or expense. No account is taken of inventory changes in the cash income statement. Depreciation is charged on assets such as buildings, machinery, and equipment. Depreciation is also charged on purchased work animals, as previously explained. The cost of purchased animals and equipment is accounted for at the time of sale. For example, feeder cattle purchased this year may not be sold until next year. Consequently, the income statement for next year includes the profit from the sale (sale prices less purchase price less cost of sale). Nothing about the transaction appears in this year's statement.

This procedure has important implications from an income tax standpoint. Farmers receive capital gains privileges on returns from the sale of breeding stock (except poultry), dairy stock, and draft animals held for twelve months or more for use on the farm. A farmer reporting on the cash basis includes the entire net sale value (sale value less cost of sale) in the case of farm-raised breeding stock. When the animals were purchased rather than raised the original cost is subtracted from this amount. Farmers reporting income on the accrual basis receive capital gains privileges on the sale price less the beginning inventory value or a capital account value for the year of sale. The farmer on the cash basis has a definite advantage in the case of farm-raised stock.

When the cash income statement is used for income tax purposes alone, as is often the case, the value of farm produce used in the household and capital gains items are not counted as income. These items are easily added in when the statement is used for management purposes. Since farmers who report their incomes on the cash receipts and disbursements basis are required to use Federal income tax form 1040F, an income statement that closely approximates it is needed (Figure 5).

**Accrual type of income statement.** The second type of statement used for reporting income is designed to reflect more accurately the production and business activities for a particular accounting year. It is similar to the cash income statement but with the addition of inventory changes. Income

## INCOME TAX SUMMARY ON CASH RECEIPT AND DISBURSEMENT BASIS

Farm Income For Taxable Year (Enter Totals From Pages Indicated)

| Line | 1. Sale of Livestock Raised | | | | 2. Sale of Produce Raised | | | | 3. Other Farm Income | | |
|---|---|---|---|---|---|---|---|---|---|---|---|
| | Kind | Page Col. | No. | Amount | Kind | Page Col. | Amount | | Items | Page Col. | Amount |
| 1 | Cattle | 52 3 | | | Grain | 53 14 | | | M'dse Rec'd for Produce | 53 23 | |
| 2 | Horses/Mules | 52 5 | | | Hay—Straw | 53 15 | | | Machine Work—Teams Hire | 53 24 | |
| 3 | Sheep | 52 7 | | | Tobacco | 53 — | | | Breeding Fees | 53 25 | |
| 4 | Hogs | 52 9 | | | Potatoes | 53 16 | | | Cash Rent | 53 26 | |
| 5 | | | | | Sugar Beets | 53 — | | | Work Off Farm | 53 27 | |
| 6 | Poultry | 52 11 | | | Fruits, Vegetables, Nuts | 53 16 | | | Forest Products | 53 28 | |
| 7 | | | | | Eggs | 53 19 | | | Agr. Program Payments | 53 29 | |
| 8 | | | | | Dairy Products | 53 20 | | | Patronage Dividends | 53 30 | |
| 9 | Bees | 52 13 | | | Meat Products | 53 17 | | | Other | 53 30 | |
| 10 | | | | | Dressed Poultry | 53 17 | | | | | |
| 11 | | | | | Wool | 53 18 | | | | | |
| 12 | | | | | | | | | | | |
| 13 | Total | | | $ | Total | | $ | | Total | | $ |

### 4. Sale of Livestock and Other Items Purchased

| Line | Description | 1 Page Col. | 2 Date Acquired | 3 Gross Sales Price | 4 Cost Price | 5 Depreciation Allowed in Prior Years | 6 Profit Col. 3 + Col. 5 — Col. 4 |
|---|---|---|---|---|---|---|---|
| 14 | Cattle | 52 4 | | | | | |
| 15 | Horses/Mules | 52 6 | | | | | |
| 16 | Sheep | 52 8 | | | | | |
| 17 | Hogs | 52 10 | | | | | |
| 18 | Poultry | 52 12 | | | | | |
| 19 | Machinery | 53 31 | | | | | |
| 20 | | | | | | | |
| 21 | | | | | | | |
| 22 | Improvements | 53 31 | | | | | |
| 23 | | | | | | | |
| 24 | | | | | | | |
| 25 | Total (Enter on Line 55) | | | | | | |

### 5. Expenses for Taxable Year

| Line | Items | Page Col. | Amount | Line | Items | Page Col. | Amount |
|---|---|---|---|---|---|---|---|
| 26 | Labor Hired | 52 33 | $ | 37 | Total of Line 36 | xxx | $ |
| 27 | Feed Purchased | 52 34 | | 38 | Taxes | 53 44 | |
| 28 | Seeds, Plants | 52 35 | | 39 | Insurance | 53 45 | |
| 29 | Machine Hire | 52 36 | | 40 | Interest on Farm Debts | 53 46 | |
| 30 | Supplies | 52 37 | | 41 | Electricity & Telephone | 53 47 | |
| 31 | Repairs & Maintenance | 52 38-39 | | 42 | Cash Rent | 53 48 | |
| 32 | Breeding Fees | 52 40 | | 43 | Freight, Yardage, Trucking | 53 49 | |
| 33 | Fertilizer | 52 41 | | 44 | Auto (Farm Share) | 53 50 | |
| 34 | Veterinary and Medicine for Livestock | 52 42 | | 45 | Miscellaneous | 53 51-52 | |
| 35 | Fuel, Oil, Grease, etc. | 52 43 | | 46 | | | |
| 36 | Total To Line 37 | | | 47 | Total Expense | | |
| 48 | Depreciation on Purchased Work & Breeding Stock, Page 56, Line 30 | | | | | | |
| 49 | Depreciation on Machinery and Equipment, Page 55, Line 90 | | | | | | |
| 50 | Depreciation on Improvements, Page 55, Line 30 | | | | | | |
| 51 | Total Depreciation | | | | | | |

### Summary of Income and Deductions — Cash Basis

| Line | | | Line | | |
|---|---|---|---|---|---|
| 52 | Sale of Livestock Raised, Table 1, Line 13 | $ | 57 | Total Expense, Line 47 | $ |
| 53 | Sale of Produce Raised, Table 2, Line 13 | | 58 | Total Depreciation, Line 51 | |
| 54 | Other Farm Income, Table 3, Line 13 | | 59 | Total Deductions, Line 57, 58 | |
| 55 | Sale Liv'st'k. & Other Items Bought, Line 25, Col. 6 | | 60 | Net Farm Profit (Line 56 minus Line 59.) Report on Income Tax Form. | |
| 56 | Gross Profits: Total Lines Above | | | | |

**Fig. 5. Cash Income Statement. (From *Indiana Farm Record Book*, prepared by Department of Agricultural Economics, Agricultural Extension Service, Purdue University.)**

627

# INCOME TAX SUMMARY ON AN ACCRUAL BASIS

| # | Description (Kind of livestock, crops, or other products) | On Hand First of Year | | Purchased During Year | | Raised During Year | | Consumed or Lost During Year | | Sold During Year | | On Hand at End of Year | | |
|---|---|---|---|---|---|---|---|---|---|---|---|---|---|---|
| | | Quantity | Inventory Value | Quantity | Amount Paid | Quantity | Inventory Value | Quantity | Inventory Value | Quantity | Amount Received | Quantity | Inventory Value | |
| 1 | Cattle | | | | | | | | | | | | | |
| 2 | | | | | | | | | | | | | | |
| 3 | Horses and Mules | | | | | | | | | | | | | |
| 4 | Sheep | | | | | | | | | | | | | |
| 5 | Hogs | | | | | | | | | | | | | |
| 6 | | | | | | | | | | | | | | |
| 7 | Poultry | | | | | | | | | | | | | |
| 8 | | | | | | | | | | | | | | |
| 9 | Grain | | | | | | | | | | | | | |
| 10 | Hay and Straw | | | | | | | | | | | | | |
| 11 | Seed | | | | | | | | | | | | | |
| 12 | Tobacco | | | | | | | | | | | | | |
| 13 | Potatoes, Vegetables, Tomatoes, Fruits | | | | | | | | | | | | | |
| 14 | Dairy Products | | | | | | | | | | | | | |
| 15 | Eggs | | | | | | | | | | | | | |
| 16 | Dressed Poultry—Meats | | | | | | | | | | | | | |
| 17 | Wool | | | | | | | | | | | | | |
| 18 | | | | | | | | | | | | | | |
| 19 | | | | | | | | | | | | | | |
| 20 | | | | | | | | | | | | | | |
| 21 | Msde. Rec'd. for Produce | | | | | | | | | | | | | |
| 22 | Machine Work, Team Hire | | | | | | | | | | | | | |
| 23 | Breeding Fees | | | | | | | | | | | | | |
| 24 | Cash Rent | | | | | | | | | | | | | |
| 25 | Work Off Farm | | | | | | | | | | | | | |
| 26 | Forest Products | | | | | | | | | | | | | |
| 27 | Agr. Program Payments | | | | | | | | | | | | | |
| 28 | Miscellaneous | | | | | | | | | | | | | |
| 29 | | | | | | | | | | | | | | |
| 30 | | | | | | | | | | | | | | |
| 31 | Silage | | | | | | | | | | | | | |
| 32 | Supplement | | | | | | | | | | | | | |
| 33 | Fertilizer | | | | | | | | | | | | | |
| 34 | | | | | | | | | | | | | | |
| 35 | | | | | | | | | | | | | | |
| 36 | | | | | | | | | | | | | | |
| 37 | | | | | | | | | | | | | | |
| 38 | | | | | | | | | | | | | | |
| 39 | | | | | | | | | | | | | | |
| 40 | | | | | | | | | | | | | | |
| 41 | | | | | | | | | | | | | | |
| | Totals | | XX | | XX | | XX | XXXX | XX | XX | XXXX | XX | XX | XX |
| | | | Enter on Line 4 | | Enter on Line 5 | | | | | | Enter on Line 2 | | Enter on Line 1 | |

## Summary of Income and Deductions Computed on an Accrual Basis

| | | | | | |
|---|---|---|---|---|---|
| 1 | Inventory of Livestock, crops, and products at end of year | $ | | 7 | Expenses (complete Table 5, |
| 2 | Sales of Livestock, crops, and products during year | | | | Page 58 for Total) |
| 2a | Other Miscellaneous Receipts (specify): | | | 8 | Depreciation (on Improvements |
| | | | | | and machinery only) Page 55, |
| | | | | | Lines 30, 90 |
| | | | | 9 | Net operating loss deduction |
| 3 | Total | $ | | | (attach statement) |
| 4 | Inventory of Livestock, crops, and products at beginning of year. | $ | | | |
| 5 | Cost of Livestock and products purchased during year. | $ | | | |
| 6 | Gross-Profits (Line 3—the sum of Lines 4 and 5) | $ | | 10 | Total Deductions | $ |
| 11 | Net Farm Profit (Line 6 minus Line 10). Report on Income Tax Form. | | | | | $ |

**Fig. 6. Accrual Income Statement. (From *Indiana Farm Record Book*, prepared by Department of Agricultural Economics, Agricultural Extension Service, Purdue University.)**

earned during the year is included regardless of when money or value changed hands. Similarly, expenses are included when they are applicable to the year's operations, whether or not the bills were paid that year. Inventory changes are accounted for also. Hence, more complete records are needed in order to summarize income in this manner.

The farmer will find a number of record books that have an income statement closely approximating page 2 of Form 1040F, an optional statement which the Internal Revenue Service furnishes for farmers reporting income on the accrual basis. Farm produce used in the household and the sale of capital items such as machinery and equipment are not entered for tax purposes. However, the inventory summaries and sales of livestock presented in the income statement will include breeding stock, dairy stock, and draft animals. In using the statement for income tax purposes, it is customary to circle or otherwise indicate that these items are not added into the totals used in determining inventory change. Such circled items are included in the form filed with the Director of Internal Revenue and serve as a check on the acquisition and disposal of property. For management purposes, the capital gains items plus produce used in the household may be included in the income figures. The form illustrated in Figure 6 closely approximates the federal income tax form. The expense summary, section 5 of Figure 5, is included with the accrual statement when that is used.

## C. Receipts

**Classification and records of receipts.** Farm receipts fall under one of the following headings:

1. Crop sales
2. Livestock sales
3. Livestock product sales
4. Miscellaneous income

Much of the work involved in routine entries in receipt accounts can be eliminated for the farmer if the accounts are designed properly. For example, a single-entry crop sales account (Figure 7) is easy to use.

| Date | Item and Explanation | Quantity | Price | Total Value |
|------|----------------------|----------|-------|-------------|
|      | Corn                 |          |       |             |
|      | Wheat                |          |       |             |
|      | Oats                 |          |       |             |
|      | Hay                  |          |       |             |
|      | Others               |          |       |             |
|      | TOTAL CROP SALES     |          |       |             |

**Fig. 7. Crop Sales.**

Livestock sales accounts may be handled in similar fashion. Often separate accounts for hogs, cattle, sheep, and poultry prove most convenient. For example, an account for sales of cattle raised on the farm is set up in Figure 8. Note the division in the account to permit easy access to capital gains information. It is easier to make the distincton at the

| Date | Kind and Explanation | No. | Wt. | Price | Breeding Stock and Dairy Stock held for More than 12 months | Market Cattle and Other Cattle not held 12 months |
|------|------|------|------|------|------|------|
| | | | | | Amount | Amount |
| | Dairy cows | | | | | |
| | Dairy heifers | | | | | |
| | Dairy calves | | | | | |
| | Beef cows | | | | | |
| | Beef heifers | | | | | |
| | Feeders | | | | | |
| | Bulls | | | | | |
| | Totals | — | — | — | | |
| | TOTAL SALES FROM FARM-RAISED CATTLE | | | | | |

**Fig. 8. Sales from Farm-Raised Cattle.**

time of entry than to sort these items out of general livestock accounts at the time of summary. Tax has to be paid on only one-half of the gains from such items, with the exception of poultry. This can amount to considerable saving to the farmer who has records available.

Purchased cattle are handled in a duplicate of the above account. This procedure makes information about purchased livestock readily available for making up the cash income statement (Figure 5). Hog, sheep, and poultry sales accounts are of the same type as shown for cattle. A capital gains division is unnecessary for poultry, since no capital gains privileges are allowed on this class of livestock. The major classifications of the animals are often printed into the "readymade" forms (Figure 8). The farmer's recordings are then reduced to a minimum. However, a few extra lines are always needed to permit individual farmers flexibility in recording their specialties and differences. Some farmers stress the sale of breeding stock. A few farmers carry crops and livestock uncommon in their area. For example, a few farms in the Midwest have goats, geese, or ducks.

Livestock product sales accounts in the case of eggs are arranged on the basis of months (Figure 9). Dairy product records are similar, except that provision for recording physical data such as quantity (pounds or gallons

CASH RECEIPTS — EGG SALES — Instructions on Inside of Front Cover

| Date | 1 No. of Doz. | 2 Price Per Doz. | 3 Gross Amount Received | 4 Net Amount Received | Date | 5 No. of Doz. | 6 Price Per Doz. | 7 Gross Amount Received | 8 Net Amount Received | Date | 9 No. of Doz. | 10 Price Per Doz. | 11 Gross Amount Received | 12 Net Amount Received | Month | 13 No. Hens | 14 Total Doz. | 15 Price Per Doz. | 16 Gross Amount Received | 17 Net Amount Received |
|---|---|---|---|---|---|---|---|---|---|---|---|---|---|---|---|---|---|---|---|---|
| Jan. (No. Hens___) | | | XXXX XX | XXXX XX | May (No. Hens___) | | | XXXX XX | XXXX XX | Sept. (No. Hens___) | | | XXXX XX | XXXX XX | Jan. | | | | | Summary for Year |
| | | | | | | | | | | | | | | | Feb. | | | | | |
| | | | | | | | | | | | | | | | Mar. | | | | | |
| | | | | | | | | | | | | | | | Apr. | | | | | |
| | | | | | | | | | | | | | | | May | | | | | |
| Total | | | | | June (No. Hens___) | | | XXXX XX | XXXX XX | Oct. (No. Hens___) | | | XXXX XX | XXXX XX | June | | | | | |
| Feb. (No. Hens___) | | | XXXX XX | XXXX XX | | | | | | | | | | | July | | | | | |
| | | | | | | | | | | | | | | | Aug. | | | | | |
| | | | | | | | | | | | | | | | Sept. | | | | | |
| | | | | | | | | | | | | | | | Oct. | | | | | |
| | | | | | Total | | | | | Total | | | XXXX XX | XXXX XX | Nov. | | | | | |
| Total | | | | | July (No. Hens___) | | | XXXX XX | XXXX XX | Nov. (No. Hens___) | | | XXXX XX | XXXX XX | Dec. | | | | | |
| March (No. Hens___) | | | XXXX XX | XXXX XX | | | | | | | | | | | Total | | | | | |
| | | | | | | | | | | | | | | | | | | | | |
| | | | | | | | | | | | | | | | | | | | | |
| | | | | | Total | | | | | Total | | | XXXX XX | XXXX XX | | | | | | |
| Total | | | | | Aug. (No. Hens___) | | | XXXX XX | XXXX XX | Dec. (No. Hens___) | | | XXXX XX | XXXX XX | | | | | | |
| April (No. Hens___) | | | XXXX XX | XXXX XX | | | | | | | | | | | | | | | | |
| | | | | | | | | | | | | | | | | | | | | |
| | | | | | | | | | | | | | | | | | | | | |
| Total | | | | | Total | | | | | Total | | | XXXX XX | XXXX XX | | | | | | |

ANALYSIS OF EGG PRODUCTION

1. No. Doz. Eggs Sold _____ Value $_____

2. No. Doz. Eggs Home Use _____ Value $_____

3. Total Doz. Eggs Produced _____ Value $_____

4. Eggs Per Hen Per Year _____
   a. Total Doz. x 12 ÷ Av. No. Hens
   b. Av. No. Hens per Year =
      Total Hens by Months ÷ 12

5. Income Per Hen $_____
   Total Value Eggs ÷ Av. No. Hens

Fig. 9. Egg Sales. (From *Indiana Farm Record Book,* prepared by Department of Agricultural Economics, Agricultural Extension Service, Purdue University.)

631

of milk and cream), butterfat test, and the number of cows is usually included.

There are always a few receipts that do not fit into the major categories. Often these are items such as labor off the farm, gas refunds, and dividends from membership in co-operative associations. These items can be entered in a single Miscellaneous Income account. A few of the major headings suggested may be used with a Miscellaneous Income column as a catch-all.

## D. Expenditures

**Classification and records of expenditures.** Farm expenditures may be divided into major classifications and then handled in the same manner as receipts. It is often more convenient, however, to use a multi-column expense account (Figure 10). (Multi-column receipt accounts are also fairly common in practice.) A continuation of expense column headings in Figure 10 and items that would appear under them are as follows:

Seeds and fertilizer
Machine work hired
Crop expenses (other than seed and fertilizer):
    Sprays
    Special harvesting costs, such as twine
    Crop insurance
Livestock expense:
    Breeding fees
    Registration fees
    Veterinary fees and medicine
    Dips
    Sheep-shearing
Farm building repairs
Machinery repairs
Auto and truck repairs (farm share)
Fuel, light, and power (farm share)
Interest paid (farm items only)
Poultry purchased (sometimes handled as one of the livestock purchased accounts)
Miscellaneous expense:
    Advertising
    Farm papers and journals
    Fencing
    Farm organization dues
    Farm business travel

| Cross-Check Column | Date | Explanation | Feed Purchased | Labor Hired | Hauling and Freight |
|---|---|---|---|---|---|
| | | | | | |
| | | | | | |

**Fig. 10. Farm Expenses.**

With one entry per line, by totaling the columns it is possible to check on addition or errors in entry. Each succeeding page is a repetition of the first, with the totals carried forward to a summary page. If totals are brought forward by months, quarterly summaries are easily made if desired. Many farmers find it more convenient to bring forward the page totals and disregard monthly summaries. The monthly or page summaries are aggregated into the yearly summaries of the expenses appearing in the income statements (Figure 5, section 5).

Since inventories are not used in making up the cash income statement, a record of livestock purchases must be kept for use in calculating profit when the animals are sold. This can be a very simple record (Figure 11).

| Date | Explanation | No. | Weight | Price | Total Amount |
|------|-------------|-----|--------|-------|--------------|
|      |             |     |        |       |              |

Fig. 11. Livestock Purchases.

## Management analysis

**Records for management analysis.** Management decisions require more information than is given in the financial records used for income tax reporting. Additional records of the production type helpful in farm management include (1) the farm map (2) crop record, (3) livestock production records, (4) labor record, and (5) feed record. When the farm is relatively small, many of these records are kept in the farmer's head or in a pocket notebook. The man who has operated the same farm for a number of years often knows the acreages in every field, the soil types, slopes, lime requirements, and relative fertilizer responses. However, yields and production information are soon forgotten.

**Farm map.** A farm map need be only a rough outline on squared paper of the farm and its fields. Information regarding field sizes, slopes, types of soil, lime (pH), and fertilizer may be noted or indicated by coloring on the map to aid in planning and maintaining a rotation and fertilization program.

**Crop record.** The cropping record (Figure 12) serves as a source of information regarding the various amounts of home-grown feeds available for livestock. The yields per acre, when combined with information on fertilizer used, soil type, and topography, may be used to check crop production efficiency. Decisions regarding changes in rotations in order to obtain feed supply better adjusted to livestock programs demand crop-yield information. Similarly, when soil-building or other practices are considered, the cropping history may be useful.

| Harvested Feed Crops | Field No. | Acres | Ave. Yield | Total Yield | Value Per Unit | Value Total | Remarks |
|---|---|---|---|---|---|---|---|
| Corn | | | | | | | Fertilizer applications, seeding rates, weather conditions and other pertinent information. |
| Oats | | | | | | | |
| Silage | | | | | | | |
| Hay | | | | | | | |
| Total Crop Acres | | | | | | | |
| Pasture | | | | | | | |
| Permanent | | | | | | | |
| Rotation | | | | | | | |
| Total Pasture | | | | | | | |
| Total Feed Crops | | | | | | | |
| Farmstead | | | | | | | |
| Roads | | | | | | | |
| Waste | | | | | | | |
| Total Acres | | | | | | | |
| Non-feed Crops | | | | | | | |
| Seed: Timothy Clover Other | | | | | | | |
| Total Non-feed Crops | | | | | | | |
| Total of All Crops | | | | | | | |

**Fig. 12. Crop Record.**

**Livestock production.** Combined with feed utilization summaries, livestock production records can be used to discover wasteful feeding practices. When prices and outlook are also taken into account, the livestock performance records serve as a basis for the input-output data needed to make farm reorganization plans or to plan new systems of farming. Production history furnishes information upon which budgets are made up and then serves as a check on the plans when they are carried out. The livestock production record (Figure 13) is a simple summary of livestock produc-

| | Hogs | Cattle | (Other classes of livestock) | | | |
|---|---|---|---|---|---|---|
| Ending Inventory ...... | | | | | | |
| Sales (livestock) ....... | | | | | | |
| Product Sales .......... | | | | | | |
| Household Use ........ | | | | | | |
| Total .................. | | | | | | |
| Beginning Inventory ... | | | | | | |
| Purchases ............. | | | | | | |
| Increase or Decrease .......... | | | | | | |

**Fig. 13. Livestock Production.**

| | Value | | Value |
|---|---|---|---|
| Beginning inventory ......... | | Ending inventory ............ | |
| Purchased feed .............. | | Crops sold ................... | |
| Farm raised feed (from crop record) ......... | | Landlord share ............. | |
| | | Used for seed, etc. .......... | |
| Totals ..................... | | | |
| Difference or Feed Fed to Livestock .......... | | | |

**Fig. 14. Feed Supply Summary.**

tion in value terms. Physical production records, such as the number of litters of pigs farrowed and the size of litters, are also useful. Some farmers find it worth while, especially in selecting breeding stock, to keep detailed records of individual animal performance. Dairy cow production records of this sort are often kept for a short while during the lactation period in order to estimate individual cow performance or herd performance in a physical sense. Feed supply summaries (Figure 14) are used along with the livestock production summaries to analyze feeding efficiency. Again, the physical record system may be carried to greater extent in this area. A few farmers keep records of the feed that is fed to animals, either as individual animals or as classes of livestock, such as hogs, poultry, and the like.

**Efficiency factors.** Several states have record-keeping associations that make available information which permits the farmer to compare his performance with that of similar farmers and farms. A number of efficiency indicators used for this purpose are listed in Figure 15. It must be kept in mind that these are indicators or signals, and not objectives in and of themselves. Having a high return per $100 worth of feed fed and a low in some other area may not be so desirable profitwise as a more balanced arrangement. Over-all efficiency of the farming operations is the desired goal. Furthermore, the ratio-type indicators fail to take into account the other variables of production that may be present. For example, higher returns per $100 worth of feed fed are expected of dairy cattle than of hogs. This is so largely because more labor relative to feed is used in dairying. Hence, the analyst must recognize fundamental relationships that may exist in the background. However, if the farmer has farm business summaries available, he may obtain useful hints as to the efficiency status of his farming operations. Care must be taken to make any such comparisons with farms of the same size, same general organization, same soil type and for the same production period, in order to assure as nearly as possible that factors other than those under examination are as much alike as possible. County agents and other experts often are available for consultation on the interpretation of efficiency factor reports (Figure 15). The standards of performance referred to in the efficiency factor report may be an average of farms or of better farms in the area as presented by farm business associations and/or the Agricultural Extension Service. When such business summaries are not available, the county agent or other extension workers can usually make available average figures for use as rough guide for efficient performance.

| Performance Indicator | This Year | | Last Year | | Standards of Performance | |
|---|---|---|---|---|---|---|
| Net farm income ............ | | | | | | |
| Land utilization: | | | | | | |
|   Total acres ................ | | | | | | |
|   Crop acres ................ | | | | | | |
|   Per cent of land in cultivated crops .................... | | | | | | |
|   Per cent of land in rotation hay and pasture ......... | | | | | | |
|   Per cent of land in high-profit crops .................... | | | | | | |
| | Acres | Ave. Yield | Acres | Ave. Yield | Acres | Ave. Yield |
| Crop acres and Yields: | | | | | | |
|   Corn ...................... | | | | | | |
|   Oats ...................... | | | | | | |
|   Soybeans .................. | | | | | | |
|   Wheat ..................... | | | | | | |
|   Hay: | | | | | | |
|     Alfalfa ................. | | | | | | |
|     Clover ................. | | | | | | |
|     Timothy ................ | | | | | | |
|   Others .................... | | | | | | |
| Livestock Production: | | | | | | |
|   Pigs weaned per litter ....... | | | | | | |
|   No. calves raised per cow bred | | | | | | |
|   Lbs. wool per sheep sheared.. | | | | | | |
|   Lbs. butterfat per cow ...... | | | | | | |
|   Lbs. milk per cow (fat corrected) ................... | | | | | | |
|   Eggs per hen per year ....... | | | | | | |
| Livestock returns: | | | | | | |
|   Livestock returns per $100 feed fed ................ | | | | | | |
|   Returns per $100 feed fed for individual livestock classes when sufficient feeding records are available ........ | | | | | | |
|   Income per dairy cow ...... | | | | | | |
|   Egg income per hen ........ | | | | | | |
| Other factors: | | | | | | |
|   Crop acres per man ........ | | | | | | |
|   Gross income or gross profits per man .................. | | | | | | |
|   Power and equipment cost per acre ................ | | | | | | |
|   Net income per acre ........ | | | | | | |
|   Livestock units per man .... | | | | | | |

Fig. 15. Efficiency Indicators.

# 23

# Flour Milling

by

**PAUL M. GERMAN**

Vice President and Comptroller, Standard Milling Company,
Kansas City, Missouri

## Industry characteristics that affect the accounting system

**Nature of the business.** Flour milling is, for the most part, a reduction of wheat berries to a refined product of varying grades of flour to be used in baking bread and cakes. Other kinds of grain, such as corn, rye, and barley, are milled to various degrees, but this article will be confined to the accounting problems of the wheat milling process.

The industry is engaged in the purchase, storage, and milling of wheat. Its products, flour and feeds, are sold to bakery, grocery, and feed channels. Present-day mills for the most part are a combination of grain storage bins known as *grain elevators,* and processing mills. They vary in size from small mills, capable of producing in a 24-hour day only 400 bags of flour containing 100 pounds each, to mammoth mills in centers like Buffalo, Minneapolis, Kansas City, and other metropolitan areas capable of producing 30,000 bags per day.

The unit of measurement in flour milling is the hundredweight (cwt.) which is 100 pounds of flour no matter how packed. Packaging varies from two-pound paper bags for the home to 200-pound cotton bags for export.

Wheat itself is divided into two main classes—winter wheat, planted in the fall and harvested in June and July in the more temperate states of the Southwest, and spring wheat, planted in early spring for harvest in August and September in the Northwest, where extreme cold weather prevails during the winter. These classes are subdivided into many grades with individual characteristics, but mainly into hard wheat, soft wheat, and Durum wheat. Hard wheat flours are used for the most part for baking bread, rolls, and similar products in either the bakery or the home; soft wheat flours are best for fine cake products; Durum wheat is primarily used in the production of macaroni, spaghetti, and other alimentary pastes. It is estimated that 68 per cent of all flour products go into the commercial bakery channels, about 27 per cent into households in the form of flour and prepared mixes, and about 5 per cent into Durum products.

The number of employees in the average mill is not large when compared with most manufacturing operations, averaging from probably 20 men in a 1,000-cwt.-per-day mill to 175 men in a 15,000-cwt.-per-day mill. This, of course, will vary among mills, depending upon the type of flour produced. One mill may produce nothing but bulk flour; a second mill of the same size may pack half of its production in family-size packages and specialties, which will greatly increase the number of men required to operate the mill.

Normal mill operation is to grind 24 hours a day and pack and ship in an eight-hour daylight shift. This arrangement necessitates facilities for bulk storage so that the flour ground during the 16-hour period from 4 P. M. to 8 A. M. can be stored awaiting arrival of the packing crew. Without such facilities, packing must continue around the clock. There are two reasons for 24-hour grinding: first, most millers feel that the longer the run of a certain grade, the more uniform the finished product becomes and the better the yield: second, because of the need for roll surface, an eight-hour shift would increase capital investment and space requirements to three times the present requirements.

**Government control.** The Federal Government plays an important part in the daily operations of the milling industry. As a result of its farm support program, the Government owns more grain at one time than all the mills in the country. A large portion of grain today is placed in storage immediately after harvest, and the Government parity loan is taken out by the farmer. If at the expiration of the loan period as set by the Commodity Credit Corporation (March 31 under present regulations) the farmer has not redeemed his grain, title passes to the Commodity Credit Corporation, which then assumes all elevation, storage, and conditioning charges. The Commodity Credit Corporation then must continue to store the grain in privately owned elevators or sell it to millers or grain dealers or use it for export purposes.

The Government also enters directly into the milling operation in that under the International Wheat Agreement, or similar programs, it provides a subsidy on flour shipments to foreign countries. The Government occasionally buys huge quantities of flour for direct delivery to impoverished peoples in foreign lands. Of course, it also buys large quantities of flour on a competitive-bid basis for use by the armed forces.

**General features.** *Competition.* Competition in the milling industry is extremely strong. One reason is the excessive capacity of the mills. It is estimated that, on the basis of a five-day work week, there is approximately

25 per cent more capacity available than the maximum needs of the people in the United States require. A large export business is therefore essential, and whenever it fails to materialize, competitive conditions tend to drive domestic profits into a loss pattern. This condition has forced the closing of more than 70 individual milling properties since 1949, representing approximately 65,000 cwts. of daily capacity.

*Seasonal nature.* Wheat, which is the source of all flour, must be harvested at the end of the growing season, generally from about June 1 in Texas to September 15 in Minnesota and Montana. While harvesting is seasonal, production is year-round, but operations vary from three to seven days a week within the year. The industry is constantly striving to reach a Utopian operation of five days a week with continuous grinding around the clock for the entire period, but with packing and shipping being done in the eight-hour daylight period only.

*By-products.* The entire wheat kernel is used in the milling process, but only 71 per cent becomes white flour; approximately 29 per cent of each kernel goes off into the by-product feed. This by-product is generally classified into two categories: bran and shorts. The bran is the heavier part of the wheat kernel and becomes a flaked product during the milling process. Shorts, also known as *feed middlings,* are a result of the separation in the milling process of coarse parts of the endosperm, or white-flour portion of the kernel, from the finer, softer inside portion of the outer bran coating of the kernel. Separation of these two by-products is made during the milling process because the shorts usually sell for a premium of from one to four dollars a ton.

*Research.* Tremendous strides have been made in the field of research insofar as wheat itself is concerned. Such organizations as the Kansas Wheat Improvement Association, the Nebraska Wheat Improvement Association, the Minnesota Rust Prevention Association, and others have, in co-operation with state agricultural schools, done a great deal to improve the milling qualities of wheat thereby producing better flour. Research in milling, however, has lagged in this country, excessive capacity not being generally conducive to research expenditure. In Europe, however, since 1945, great strides have been made in changing antiquated milling processes. Many mills destroyed by the ravages of war have been replaced by push-button and pneumatic operations. New mills in Europe today are using about one-third the manpower used in mills of comparable size in this country.

**Functional peculiarities.** *Buying.* Because of the combination of seasonal harvest and year-round production, the problem of buying grain is one of the most complicated functions in the industry. Commodity markets change from day to day and from season to season. Flour is sold on the basis of current wheat prices at the date of sale—a fact which poses quite a problem for the miller. If he attempts to secure his entire year's grinding requirements during the harvest season, he is faced with a tremendous investment plus the risk of market fluctuation. However, by buying and selling futures on the grain exchanges, the miller is able to hedge his cost of wheat against loss until the date of flour sale. If he buys more wheat on the open market than he needs to produce all orders for flour that he has on hand, he can sell a futures option through a representative on the grain trading floor of the exchanges. At a later date, when he sells more flour, he can buy an option which will cancel in part or whole his original option sale. The reverse is, of course, true if he should sell flour and not have the actual wheat available to grind. He can buy a futures option at the current market price and hold it until he secures his wheat. If the market goes up in the meantime and he has to pay more for his wheat than the price used to figure his flour sale, he is protected by being able then to sell his futures option at the current market, thereby realizing a corresponding profit on the futures transaction that offsets the loss on the wheat purchase.

*Production.* Flour production is a matter of breaking away the outside of the wheat kernel so as to sift the inside—endosperm—into a fine, palatable flour product. There are many variations of sifting and breaking operations. Figure 1 illustrates the milling processes. The finished product varies from an extremely low Ash, very white flour, to a whole wheat flour. The reduction of Ash means less patent-grade flour from a grain of wheat and results in a costlier flour. Theoretically, from each 141 pounds of wheat there results 100 pounds of straight-grade flour and 41 pounds of feed. In milling and bakery parlance, this is approximately a .45 Ash flour. To reduce the Ash, for example, to .41 means that only about 78 per cent of the flour is suitable for separation into this high-grade flour, and the rest of the endosperm is separated into low-grade flours called *first* and *second clears.* These clears will contain from .60 to 1.00 Ash content, depending upon further separation. Obviously, if only 78 per cent of the endosperm is used to make a grade of flour, more wheat is necessary to produce each 100 pounds of this grade, and the remaining flour will be produced as high Ash clears. The clear products sell for $1.00 to $2.00 a cwt. less than the patent, so that the 78 per cent extraction becomes a considerably more expensive flour than a straight-grade, or 100 per cent, extraction.

*Selling.* Two types of sales are made: (1) manufactured products, and (2) elevator service, that is, storage of grain.

For sales of manufactured products, the miller prepares a contract for every sale to the bulk trade, whether for 100 bags or 100,000 bags. Each shipment is applied at the agreed price against the contract until it is exhausted, which may be within anywhere from a week to six months.

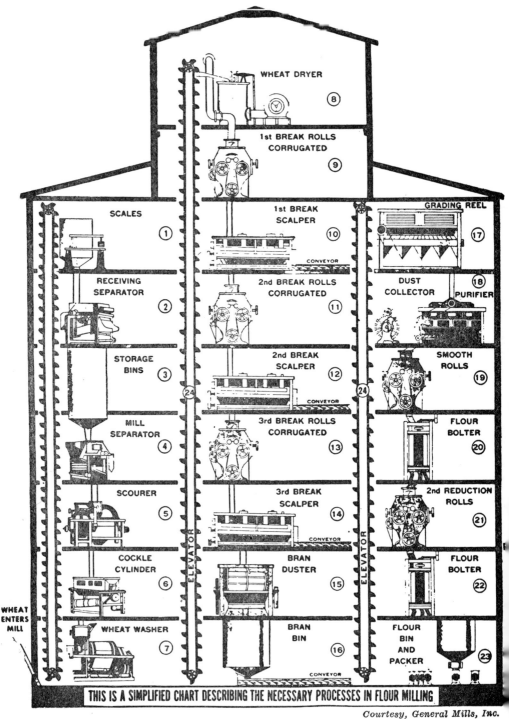

Courtesy, *General Mills, Inc.*

(See page 643 for explanation of circled numbers.)

**Fig. 1. Chart Describing the Necessary Processes in Flour Milling.**

① Scales, for weighing wheat as it is received

② Receiving separator, for separating other kinds of seeds from wheat

③ Storage bins, for reserve supply of wheat in advance of mill requirements

④ Mill separator, for further separating foreign seeds from wheat

⑤ Scourer, for removing dust from wheat kernels

⑥ Cockle cylinder, for removing all round seeds

⑦ Wheat washer, for thoroughly cleansing the wheat

⑧ Wheat dryer, for drying wheat after washing

⑨ 1st break rolls, for rupturing bran, enabling bran and germ to be separated from interior

⑩ 1st break scalper, for sifting middlings through bolting cloth to separate from bran

⑪ 2nd break rolls, for further loosening the middlings from bran

⑫ 2nd break scalper, for separating more middlings from bran

⑬ 3rd break rolls, for further loosening middlings from bran

⑭ 3rd break scalper, for final separation of middlings from bran

⑮ Bran duster, for dusting low-grade flour from bran

⑯ Bran bin, for packing bran for shipment

⑰ Grading reel, for separating middlings by sifting through various sizes of bolting cloth

⑱ Dust collector and purifier for cleaning and purifying middlings by air and sifting

⑲ Smooth rolls, for grinding purified middlings very fine to flour

⑳ Flour bolter, for sifting flour from purified middlings

㉑ 2nd reduction rolls, for further grinding of purified middlings

㉒ Flour bolter, for separating flour from purified middlings of 2nd grinding

㉓ Flour bin and packer, for packing flour for shipment

㉔ Elevator, for raising products to the various machines

**Explanation of Circled Numbers in Fig. 1.**

The contract generally provides that the miller will carry each contract at no additional cost for a predetermined number of days from date of sale, after which time a charge will be made on the unshipped portion until the contract has been completed. For example, a miller may assess one-sixth of a cent per day per cwt. for each bag shipped after the expiration of free time, which means a five-cents-per-month additional charge for each cwt. of flour.

In the sale of elevator service, most millers follow the Uniform Grain Storage Agreement, in effect from year to year with private operators and the Commodity Credit Corporation. This agreement provides for an in-and-out handling charge (called *elevation*) and a per-month storage and conditioning charge. The charges vary by locations and grains as well as by method of receipt—boat, rail, or truck. The storage operator must issue a registered warehouse receipt indicating the bushels received, the date, and the grade characteristics of the grain which he must deliver to the owner when called upon to do so. All charges accrue from the date shown on the receipt but are not necessarily payable until the grain is withdrawn. The Commodity Credit Corporation, however, settles for all accrued charges on September 30, December 31, and June 30 of each year. This arrangement makes it necessary for the miller to accrue large amounts of income at the end of his accounting periods even though he has not issued an invoice for elevator service.

**Ownership peculiarities.**  Flour milling was for a great many years more or less a family enterprise, but with the corporate progress in other industries, a gradual change has also taken place in the milling industry.  Although there are still a great many family-owned mills, mostly located in the smaller communities of the country, the large milling corporations produce the bulk of the industry's output.  These corporations, numbering less than ten, have mills located strategically over the country.  Their daily output varies from 40,000 cwts. to 125,000 cwts.

**Financing peculiarities.**  Because of the pressure of harvest seasons, the problem of providing capital for inventory is always a vital one for the miller.  In most cases, he is able to operate with an open line of credit and must control his physical inventories in order not to exceed his line of credit.  In a great many instances, the miller works with the banks by putting up warehouse receipts, against which the banks loan funds for operations.  In this case, he must pay off the loan and secure the warehouse receipt before he can order the grain out of the warehouse for grinding purposes.  Perpetual inventories must therefore be maintained and accounting controls provided for warehouse receipts by location and for accrued interest and bank loan amortizations.

**Principal accounting problems.**  Accountingwise, the milling industry presents a challenge, owing to the fact that theoretical projection of profit and cost is a large part of the miller's daily work.  Most millers work with a daily netting sheet (Figure 2), on which all sales of flour are recorded and against which is applied the "cost date of sale" factor at the time of sale.  In order to determine this cost, consideration must be given to the price of cash wheat plus protein differential, patent extraction, and feed and grain values.

Grain, as purchased, cannot remain segregated until used.  Therefore, it is stored with grain of like characteristics.  During the time of accumulation within any accounting period, the cost of each purchase may vary considerably.  At the end of the accounting period, it is the practice of the industry to price all wheat inventory at the closing market value by grades.  In order to prevent taking a loss or gain in the grain inventory, it is then customary to calculate a gain or loss in the unfilled flour sales by applying a cost based on the closing market for each grade of flour to be shipped, versus the "cost date of sale" originally applied on the netting sheet.  These figures are accumulated on work sheets such as those illustrated in Figures 3 and 4.

To determine cost rapidly each day for selling and netting-sheet pur-

**DAILY REPORT OF SALES**

SALES OFFICE _____    DIVISION _____    DATE _____    NO. _____

| CUSTOMER | CONTRACT | | H/L No. | GRADE CODE | BULK MILL SELLING PRICE | COST | | | | CON-VER-SION PER CWT | CWT | CONVERSION TOTAL |
|---|---|---|---|---|---|---|---|---|---|---|---|---|
| | NUMBER | DATE | | | | 100% FLOUR | | | | | | |
| | | | | | | WHEAT | FEED | DIFF'L | TOTAL | | | |

TOTAL TODAY

PREVIOUS TOTAL FORWARD

TOTAL MONTH TO DATE                    AVE PER CWT _____

**HEDGE LOT AND CONTRACT CONTROL**

| | REGULAR @ 2.35 | W.W. @ 1.70 |
|---|---|---|
| H/L'S TELETYPED TODAY | | |
| MPLS. | | |
| BFLO. | | |
| L'VLLE | | |
| TOTAL | | |
| PREVIOUS BALANCE CONTRACTS DUE | | |
| TO ACCOUNT FOR | | |
| LESS: ATTACHED-BAK. | | |
| " -GROC. | | |
| " " | | |
| BAL. CONTRACTS DUE | | |

| MIX | CWT | WHEAT VALUE |
|---|---|---|
| CQ | | |
| CC | | |
| CX | | |
| CM | | |
| CF | | |
| CWW | | |
| BQ | | |
| BX | | |
| BM | | |
| BF | | |
| BQW | | |
| BXW | | |
| DS | | |
| DM | | |

**Fig. 2. Daily Netting Sheet.**

STANDARD MILLING CO. – UNFILLED SALES

SALESMAN ______ DATE ______ MILL ______ SALES OFFICE ______

| Date of Contract | Contract Number | Customer | Brand | Unshipped Cwt or Tons | Selling Price | Selling Price Bulk Mill | Net Material Cost Date of Sale | Margin Over Mat. Cost | Net Material Cost Extension | Margin Over Material Cost Extension | MILL GRADES – CWT OR TONS | | | | | | | | |
|---|---|---|---|---|---|---|---|---|---|---|---|---|---|---|---|---|---|---|---|
| | | | | | | | | | | | | | | | | | | | |
| | | | | | | | | | | | | | | | | | | | |
| | | | | | | | | | | | | | | | | | | | |
| | | | | | | | | | | | | | | | | | | | |
| | | | | | | | | | | | | | | | | | | | |
| | | TOTAL | | | | | | | | | | | | | | | | | |

Fig. 3. Territorial Work Sheet for Calculating Gain or Loss on Unfilled Flour Sales.

| GAIN OR LOSS ON Unfilled Sales | | | | | | PAGE NO. | | | |
|---|---|---|---|---|---|---|---|---|---|

**DATE:** _____

Buffalo _____ **MILL OR ELEVATOR** (CONTROL MILL)

**ENTERED BY:** _____ **PRICED BY:** _____ **PRODUCT:** Flour & Feed

**EXTENDED &**
**FOOTED BY:** _____ Inventory **STUB VERIFIED BY:** Stub _____ **BASIS:** DELIVERED

| CONTRACT | | | | | QUANTITY | CONTRACT PRICE | | | MARKET PRICE | | |
|---|---|---|---|---|---|---|---|---|---|---|---|
| DATE | CONTRACT OR CAR NUMBER | NAME | T.W. PROT. | GRADE | | PRICE PER | EXTENSION | | PRICE | EXTENSION | |
| | Flour | | TOTALS FORWARD | | | | | | | | |
| | BX01 | | | | | | | | | | |
| | BX03 | | | | | | | | | | |
| | BX05 | | | | | | | | | | |
| | BX07 | | | | | | | | | | |
| | BX08 | | | | | | | | | | |
| | BX09 | | | | | | | | | | |
| | BM00 | | | | | | | | | | |
| | BFla | | | | | | | | | | |
| | BA03 | | | | | | | | | | |
| | BA07 | | | | | | | | | | |
| | BA08 | | | | | | | | | | |
| | Bg03 | | | | | | | | | | |
| | Bq05 | | | | | | | | | | |
| | Bq08 | | | | | | | | | | |
| | BE05 | | | | | | | | | | |
| | Bqwl | | | | | | | | | | |
| | Bww1-6 | | | | | | | | | | |
| | Bww8 | | | | | | | | | | |
| | BXC1 | | | | | | | | | | |
| | BXC6 | | | | | | | | | | |
| | BXC7 | | | | | | | | | | |
| | BXC9 | | | | | | | | | | |
| | BFC1 | | | | | | | | | | |
| | BRF1 | | | | | | | | | | |
| | | | | | | | | | | | |
| | | | | | | | | | | | |
| | | | | | | | | | | | |
| | NySo Bakery | | | | | | | | | | |
| | NySo Grocery | | | | | | | | | | |
| | Export | | | | | | | | | | |
| | | | | | | | | | | | |
| | | | | | | | | | | | |
| | | | | | | | | | | | |
| | Feed | | | | | | | | | | |
| | | | | | | | | | | | |
| | | | | | | | | | | | |
| | | | TOTALS | | | | | | | | |

DEDUCT CONTRACT VALUE (On Bought to Arrive) ........ X X X X X X X X

DEDUCT MARKET VALUE (On Unfilled Sales) ........ X X X X X X X

GAIN — (BLACK) — Debit Inventory

LOSS — (RED) — Credit Inventory

**Fig. 4. Grade Accumulation for Calculating Gain or Loss on Unfilled Flour Sales.**

poses, a form similar to Figure 5 is generally used. Then, at the end of the accounting period, for positive cost and inventory application, a detailed cost sheet (Figure 6) and its supplements are compiled. Figure 6 demonstrates the variations in wheat mixes due to protein, by-product, and grades, and gross bushels of wheat needed to grind varying grades of flour in view of the patent extraction or Ash requirements.

| DAILY FLOUR COSTS | | | | | | AT CLOSE OF MARKET: 10-11-5 | | | | | | | |
|---|---|---|---|---|---|---|---|---|---|---|---|---|---|
| | CASH WHEAT VALUE PER BUSHEL | | | | BU. PER CWT | 100% FLOUR COST | | | | GRADE DIFFERENTIALS | | | | |
| | MIX | PREM. | FUTURE | CASH WHEAT | | WHEAT | FEED CREDIT | DIFF'L | TOTAL | 01 | 03 | 05 | 07 | 08 |
| BUFFALO MILL | | | | | | | | | | | | | | |
| PEP | Q | 51 | " | 2814 | 2.35 | 661 | 78 | | 583 | | | | -10 | -20 |
| | X | 2878 | " | 2591 8 | 2.35 | 609 | " | | 531 | 10 | 5 | 3 | 0 | ±5 |
| PERFECT | M | 143 6 | " | 345 | 2.35 | 576 | " | | 498 | 10 | 5 | 3 | 0 | -5 |
| N.W. | A | 1178 | " | 2421 8 | 2.35 | 569 | " | | 491 | 10 | 5 | 3 | 0 | -5 |
| FAMILY | F | 0639 | " | 236 5 8 | 2.35 | 556 | " | | 478 | 29 | .11 | 06 | 0 | |
| EXPORT | E | 31 | | 2614 | 2.35 | 614 | | | 536 | | | | | |
| | QW | 51 | " | 2814 | 1.70 | 478 | — | | 478 | | | | BWW8 | BWW9 |
| | XW | 2878 | " | 2591 8 | 1.70 | 441 | — | | 441 | | | | 15 | 15 |
| | | | | | | | | | | | BXC6 | BXC7 | | BXC9 |
| 1ST CLEAR | X | | " | | 2.35 | | " | - | 535 | | -11 | -57 | | -1.15 |
| 1ST CLEAR | F | | " | | 2.35 | | " | - | 440 | | | | | |
| | | | | 2044 | | R.W. | Bflo. | | | | | | | |
| CAKE FLOUR | | Diplomat DSO5 | | | | | | | 461 | 50 | 25 | 0 | -20 | |

| FEED | | MPLS. | | | BFLO. | | | | | | | |
|---|---|---|---|---|---|---|---|---|---|---|---|---|
| | | SACKED | BULK | % | SACKED | BULK | % | | | | | |
| | BRAN | | | 50 | | 38.00 | 35 | | | | | |
| | MIDDS | | | 35 | | 41.00 | 65 | | | | | |
| KC 120 DAY BULK | RED DOG | | | 15 @ .0205 | | | @ .0205 | | | | | |
| 33.38 | AVE. | | | | | 3995 | .778 | | | | | |

Fig. 5. Form for Determining Daily Flour Costs.

The above factors, plus many others within the area of production, hedge position, long or short wheat versus unfilled flour sales, and long or short by-product position, make constant analysis a vital part of the accounting program and a necessity in order to account for the difference between projected profit and actual results at the end of the accounting period.

## Functional organization

**Division into departments or activities.** The following major depart-

## STANDARD MILLING COMPANY

COSTS FOR ― MONTH END INVENTORY     BUFFALO   MILL   PG. 1

| WHEAT MIX COST—PER BU. | BY-PRODUCT VALUES—PER CWT. | DATE AUG 31 19 _ |
|---|---|---|
| FUTURES BASIS: Mpls Sept 2.2938 | MILL FEED ( 39.25 ) | |
| q .51 | 1ST CLEAR 5.35   2ND CLEAR | VIT. ENR. .07   NEW SACKS |
| X .2658   q .044 | Family 4.40     4.00 | S/R .20   S. H. MILL SACKS |
| m .08   S. .0172   mill .2658 | | FEED SACKS |
| A .044   Exp .31   CRW .2458 | | MFG. EXP. PER BUSHEL $ .1745 |

| GRADE | CODE | WHEAT BU. FUT. | WHEAT MIX. PREM. | FEED CWT. 1.9625 | C-1 CWT. 5.35 | C-2 CWT. 4.00 | Fam. CWT. 4.40 | I. M. FRT. | Ingred | NET MATERIAL COST | MFG. EXP. | BULK MILL COST |
|---|---|---|---|---|---|---|---|---|---|---|---|---|
| Pep | BQ05 | 2,350 Q 4.589 | .410 .805 | | | | | | | 5.78 | .41 | 6.19 |
| Perfect Hi-Gluten | BQ08 | 2,235 Q 4.266 | .391 .767 | .050 .200 | | | | | | 5.70 | .39 | 6.09 |
| Heckers Hi-Gluten | BQ09 | 2,115 Q 5.930 | .369 .724 | .100 .400 | | | | | | 5.61 | .37 | 5.98 |
| Farina | BX1F | 3,015 X | .526 | .257 | .026 | | | | | | | |
| Super Heckers | BX01 | 7,718 | 1.032 | 1.375 | .104 | | | | | 5.21 | .53 | 6.74 |
| Red Ball | BX03 | 2,610 X 4.684 | .455 .893 | .089 .476 | .022 .088 | | | | | 5.23 | .46 | 5.69 |
| Best 00 | BX05 | 2,475 X 6.336 | .432 .848 | .032 .171 | .021 .084 | | | | | 5.23 | .43 | 5.66 |
| Staten Island Best | BX07 | 2,350 X 6.016 | .410 .805 | | | | | | | 5.21 | .41 | 5.62 |
| N. W. Giant | BX08 | 1,880 X 4.813 | .328 .644 | .200 1.070 | | | | | | 5.24 | .33 | 5.57 |
| Hi Loaf | BX09 | 1,130 X 3.893 | .198 .389 | .120 .642 | | .400 1.760 | | | | 4.91 | .20 | 5.11 |
| ———— Fam. | BM00 | 3,355 M 7.964 | .585 1.148 | .400 2.140 | .028 .113 | | | | | 4.56 | .59 | 5.15 |
| Perfect Short Pat. | BM01 | 3,015 M 7.157 | .526 1.032 | .257 1.375 | .026 .104 | | | | | 4.65 | .53 | 5.18 |
| Perfect Bakers Pat | BM03 | 2,690 M 4.385 | .469 .920 | .127 .679 | .018 .072 | | | | | 4.71 | .47 | 5.18 |
| | BM05 | 2,475 M 5.875 | .432 .848 | .032 .171 | .021 .084 | | | | | 4.77 | .43 | 5.20 |
| Perfect Std. Pat | BM07 | 2,350 M 5.678 | .410 .805 | | | | | | | 4.77 | .41 | 5.18 |
| Northern ACE | BA01 | 3,015 A 7.044 | .526 1.032 | .104 | .026 1.131 | .257 | | | | 4.78 | .53 | 5.31 |
| Northwest Imperial | BA03 | 2,765 A 6.460 | .482 .946 | .012 .048 | .165 .726 | | | | | 4.74 | .48 | 5.22 |
| ———— Bkg. | BA03N | 2,765 A 6.460 | .482 .946 | .012 .048 | .165 .726 | | | | | 4.74 | .48 | 5.22 |
| Northern Magic | BA07 | 2,350 A 5.490 | .410 .805 | | | | | | | 4.69 | .41 | 5.10 |
| | BA08 | 1,880 A 4.392 | .328 .644 | | .200 .880 | | | | | 4.63 | .30 | 4.93 |
| ———— Bkg. Co. | BG03 | 2,765 G 6.460 | .482 .946 | .012 .048 | .165 .726 | | | | | 4.74 | .48 | 5.22 |
| Heckers Superlative | BF1A | 3.175 F | .554 | | .351 | | | | | | | |
| Pvt. Brand #0 | BF01 | 7.223 | 1.087 | | 1.544 | | | | | 4.59 | .55 | 5.14 |
| Pvt. Brand #1 | BF03 | 2.765 F 6.290 | .482 .946 | .012 .048 | .726 | | | | | 4.57 | .48 | 5.05 |
| Pvt. Brand #2 | BF05 | 2.475 F 5.631 | .432 .848 | .012 .048 | .032 .141 | | | | | 4.59 | .43 | 5.02 |
| Pvt. Brand #3 | BF07 | 2.350 F 5.346 | .410 .805 | | | | | | | 4.54 | .41 | 4.95 |
| Export 95% | BE05 | 2.475 Exp. 6.444 | .432 .848 | .032 .171 | .021 .084 | | | | | 5.34 | .43 | 5.77 |
| Export 100% | BE07 | 2.350 Exp. 6.119 | .410 .805 | | | | | | | 5.31 | .41 | 5.72 |

**Fig. 6. Detailed Cost Sheet Prepared at End of Accounting Period.**

ments are responsible for the functions, departments, and divisions indicated under each:

*Production:*
  Flour milling manufacturing
  Purchasing other than grain
  Capital expenditures
  Laboratory:
    Research
    Product control
  Labor

*Grain:*
  Merchandising—grain
  Purchasing—grain
  Physical elevator operation

*Product sales:*
  Bakery and bulk flour division
  Grocery flour division

  Specialties division
  Mill feed
  Export division

*Accounting:*
  Taxes
  Traffic department
  Warehouses
  Statistics
  Daily grain position
  By-product positions
  Netting sheets
  Sales office
  Banking
  Warehouse receipts
  Elevator control

**Importance of the accounting function.** In the milling industry, the accounting department is a more important segment of organization than it is in most manufacturing industries because it actually helps to direct the daily operation of the business. The importance of the accounting function might best be brought out by describing the position of the president in some of the smaller milling organizations. He is the chief accounting executive. Dozens of times a day this executive of the small mill translates the cost of wheat, plus manufacturing expense, less by-product recoveries, into cost of flour. He relates production needs to available volume when considering a sale. He buys wheat or directs its purchase in accordance with the demand indicated by shipping directions or projected demands. He generally keeps the netting sheet and a projection blotter in front of him at all times, using normal accounting tools for making decisions.

In a large milling company, there is usually an operating committee composed of the president as chief executive officer and the heads of the accounting, production, grain, and product sales departments. The committee setup arises from the urgent need for co-ordination among the various departments. It is important to co-ordinate the procurement of grain, both as to quantity and type, with the product sales, and at the same time to control the flow of this material to production as it is needed. Since the accounting department must maintain perpetual position records for the guidance of each of the departments, the chief accounting executive becomes, in effect, the co-ordinator.

Flour is sold for the most part on a 120-day basis. In other words, the customer has four months in which to take out his merchandise without penalty. Some customers will withdraw weekly; others may wait until the time has almost expired. Shipping directions must therefore be coordinated between the production and grain departments in relation to actual available supplies. Again accounting records make co-ordination possible. The elevator department, operating in most cases under the grain department, maintains perpetual inventories of all grains under its immediate control by kind, grade, protein, moisture, and test weight, and is thus able to mix grain for each individual milling purpose.

The need for co-ordinating and relating the daily cost and supply of wheat to daily flour sales has already been mentioned as a vital accounting problem. The importance of the accounting function will be brought out further in the section dealing with reports to management.

## Principles and objectives of the system

**Principles to be applied in reflecting income, costs, and expenses.** Income from sales of products is a rather easily definable item, as flour, for the most part, is sold on a bulk mill basis. To the sales price are added the cost of packaging and delivery expense. Feed from the milling operation is also sold on a bulk mill basis. Income from elevator operations is generally segregated from milling income.

The principles to be applied in accounting for costs are brought out in the discussion of the cost system at page 660. Brief mention has already been made of the necessity for analyzing the difference between theoretical results at cost date of sale and actual results.

Accounting for expense is much the same as in other manufacturing businesses. Expenses are grouped as (a) selling expense, (b) advertising expense, and (c) administrative expense.

The item of expense most abused and uncontrolled is that of communication. Operating in a commodity market where sales prices are changing constantly and where most deals are made on a haggling basis between seller and buyer leads to abusive use of long-distance telephone calls. It is estimated that communication expense costs the average miller almost two cents per bag of flour sold. Since the average sales price per cwt. is $6.00, the communication cost must be controlled.

Expense control must be set up to point out variable items and to measure the ups and downs in proportion to sales and gross profit.

**Specific objectives of the system.** The ever-pressing objective of the flour milling accounting system is to keep before management current projections of profit or loss on all sales, current cost factors, production schedules, and long and short positions on grain, feed, flour, and futures. These daily controls are essential to enable management to cope with the daily problems of this competitive industry.

## Classification of accounts and books of account

**Comment on chart of accounts.**  The classification of accounts presented here lists the principal ledger accounts.  Subdivisions of the accounts will, of course, vary with the needs of the particular company.  The sources of debits and credits for each of the accounts also vary with the system within the organization and with the preference of the accounting executive.

If the bookkeeping is done on an accounting machine, the tray of ledger cards is divided by the control accounts listed, and in back of each control account are as many supplemental accounts as desired.  In the case of a hand-posted operation, a great many of the control accounts are supplemented by sub-journals or expense ledgers.  Several of the large milling organizations accomplish their entire bookkeeping operation by the use of tabulating equipment.  Basically, however, the ledger controls are fundamental.

### Balance sheet accounts.

*Current Assets:*
   Control—Cash on Hand and in Banks
   Control—Accounts Receivable
      Customers' Accounts
      Elevator Accounts
      Accrued Storage Receivable
      Commodity Credit Corporation—Subsidy Claims
   Control—Notes Receivable
   Reserve for Doubtful Notes and Accounts
   Control—Sundry Ledger
   Control—Personnel Ledger
   Control—Commodity Brokers
   Control—Advances on Grain
   Control—Inventory Clearing Account
   Control—Deferred Charges and Prepaid Expense

*Investments and Other Assets:*
   Membership in Grain Exchanges
   Securities and Real Estate Investments
   Notes Receivable—Long-Term

*Capital Assets:*
   Property, Plant, and Equipment
   Reserve for Depreciation

*Current Liabilities:*
   Notes Payable—Banks
   Notes and Mortgages Payable—Other
   Accounts Payable—General
   Drafts Payable

*Accrued Liabilities:*
  Accrued Payrolls
  Accrued Employee Welfare Expenses

*Reserves:*
  Reserve for Federal Income Taxes
  Reserve for General Taxes
  Reserve for Federal Withholding Taxes
  Reserve for City and State Withholding Taxes
  Reserve for Social Security Taxes
  Reserve for Audit Expense
  Reserve for Legal Expense
  Reserve for Employees' Retirement Income Plan
  Reserve for Shrink—Grain Department

Current Portion Long-Term Debt

Dividends Payable

*Long-Term Debt:*
  Sinking Fund Debentures
  Purchase Money Mortgages
Reserve for Contingencies
Minority Interest in Subsidiaries

*Capital accounts:*
Common Stock:
  Authorized
  Issued
Paid-in Surplus
Earned Surplus
Treasury Stock

## Income and expense accounts.

*Sales:*
  Flour Sales—Bakery Division
  Flour Sales—Grocery Division
  Flour Sales—Export Division
  Millfeed Sales
  Sales—Specialties Division

*Freight Paid on Shipments:*
  Bakery
  Grocery
  Export
  Millfeed
  Specialties

*Exchange and Discounts:*
  Bakery
  Grocery
  Exports
  Millfeed
  Specialties

*Purchases:*

  Wheat Account
  Hedge Account—Wheat
  Miscellaneous Manufacturing Supplies
  Cooperage Supplies
  Sacks and Packages:
    Bakery
    Grocery
    Millfeed
    Specialties

*Mill Expenses:*

  Direct Manufacturing Expense:
    Direct Wages
    Power—Electricity
  Plant Overhead Expenses:
    Indirect Wages
    Repairs
    Amortization—Leasehold Expense
    Rent
    Depreciation
    Taxes
    Insurance
    Heat, Light, and Water
    Supplies
    Employees' Welfare Expense
    Storage and Handling
    Fumigants
    Sundry

*Administrative Expense:*

  Repairs
  Amortization—Leasehold Expense
  Rent
  Depreciation
  Taxes
  Insurance
  Heat, Light, and Water
  Employees' Welfare Expense
  Executive and Office Salaries
  Directors' Compensation
  Audit Expense
  Bank Service Charge on Debentures
  Donations
  Legal Expense
  Memberships and Dues
  Postage
  Registrar of Common Stock
  Stationery and Supplies
  Telephone
  Telegraph
  Teletype
  Travel
  Meetings and Reports—Stockholders
  Sundry

*Selling Expense—Bakery Division:*

  Salaries

Commissions
Travel
Brokerage
Sales Meetings and Conventions
Contests and Prizes
Resale Expense
Telephone
Telegraph

*Selling Expense—Grocery Division:*

Salaries
Commissions
Travel
Brokerage
Sales Meetings and Conventions
Contests and Prizes
Resale Expense
Telephone
Telegraph

*Selling Expense—Specialties Division:*

Salaries
Commissions
Travel
Brokerage
Sales Meetings and Conventions
Contests and Prizes
Resale Expense
Telephone
Telegraph

*Selling Expense—Millfeed Division:*

Salaries
Commissions
Travel
Brokerage
Sales Meetings and Conventions
Contests and Prizes
Resale Expense
Telephone
Telegraph

*Advertising Expense—Bakery Division:*

Trade Papers—Space
Trade Papers—Production
Direct Mail
Samples
Newspaper Space
Customer Relations

*Advertising Expense—Grocery Division:*

Newspaper—Space
Newspaper—Production
Outdoor—Space
Outdoor—Production
Radio
Television

Display
Co-operative
Demonstrator's Expense
Coupons and Postcards—Production
Coupons and Postcards—Redemption
Premiums—Customers
Premiums—Dealers
Warehouse Expense
Special Local Promotion

*Advertising Expense—Specialties Division:*

Trade Papers—Space
Trade Papers—Production
Direct Mail
Samples
Newspaper Space
Customer Relations

*Elevator Income:*

Sales—Wheat
Freight Paid on Wheat Sales
Elevation
Storage
Insurance, Conditioning, and Service Charges
Miscellaneous Income
Purchases—Wheat
Freight Paid on Purchase Wheat
Hedge Account—Wheat

*Elevator Expense:*

Direct Wages
Executive and Office Salaries
Rent
Depreciation
Power and Steam—Electricity
Heat, Light, and Water
Repairs
Supplies
Fumigant
Weighing, Inspection, and Customs Fees
Insurance
Taxes
Demurrage
Travel
Communication Expense
Sundry

Other Income Account

Other Deductions Account

Profit and Loss Account

**Books peculiar to the business.** *Option ledger.* A perpetual record of every futures transaction—purchases and sales—in every trading market by months of future options is maintained in the option ledger (Figure 7). Grain markets trade in the following futures months: May, July, September, December, and March.

This basic record must also be supplemented by a record of all trans-actions by brokers, commission houses, and customers through whom or for whom trades are made.

| | Date | Broker | Bought Of | Bus. | Price | Date | Broker | Sold To | Bus. | Price |
|---|---|---|---|---|---|---|---|---|---|---|
| | | | | | | | | | | |
| | | | | | | | | | | |
| | | | | | | | | | | |
| ◯ | | | | | | | | | | |
| | | | | | | | | | | |
| | | | | | | | | | | |
| | | | | | | | | | | |

STANDARD MILLING COMPANY

Kansas City December Wheat

**Fig. 7. Option Ledger.**

**Accounts peculiar to the business.** *Advances on Grain.* Grain is sold for the most part on a sight draft basis, the shipper drawing a draft for the approximate value of the carload of grain. After the complete inspection, which consists in most cases of Federal or State inspection and checking of unloading weights, protein, moisture, dockage, and grade, a final settle-ment is made between the shipper and receiver. It is the practice to charge the Advances on Grain account with the amount of the draft instead of charging inventories. After the grain has been graded, it is taken into inventory; Purchases—Grain is charged with the amount of the advance and the Advances on Grain account is credited. At the same time, the settlement is charged or credited to the Purchases—Grain Account.

*Commodity Brokers.* In each grain exchange there are brokerage or-ganizations which clear trades between buyers and sellers. It is not prac-tical for each small miller and elevator operator to be a member of all the grain exchanges. The miller, therefore, depends on the brokerage organiza-tions as a means of placing his hedges in the various markets. These brokers handle each trade on the basis of a set fee for brokerage per bushel.

*Hedge Account—Wheat.* The miller always attempts to maintain a hedged position. Therefore, if a sale of flour is made, he must buy either cash wheat or a future. Obviously, cash wheat in the exact quantities and grades needed for manufacturing his flour sales is not a practical solution. So he trades in the futures market as follows:

Oct. 1 Sells 10,000 cwts. of flour—buys 23,500 bu. Dec. Futures
Oct. 12 Buys 10,000 bu. wheat —sells 10,000 bu. Dec. Futures
Oct. 15 Buys 13,500 bu. wheat —sells 13,500 bu. Dec. Futures

In this way he maintains a perfect hedge, having wheat or futures at all times equivalent to his unfilled flour sales (2.35 bushels of wheat are needed to make one cwt. of flour). In actual practice, futures are generally traded in round lots of 5,000 bushels, although 1,000-bushel lots are available at a premium. As the market moves up or down, the price of purchase and sale of a December future will not remain the same. The balance in the individual option ledger—loss or gain—is closed into the Hedge Account—Wheat.

A loss or gain is also calculated on open futures at the end of the accounting period and in turn closed into the Hedge Account—Wheat. These losses and gains are reversal entries at the beginning of each accounting period.

*Inventory Clearing account.* This is the final clearing account for all measured-asset accounts relating to the flour-milling manufacturing operation. Into this account are generally closed the balances from the following subsidiary ledger accounts:

> Wheat Inventory
> Loss or Gain on Unfilled Wheat Sales
> Loss or Gain on Wheat Bought to Arrive
> Flour Inventory
> Millfeed Inventory
> Loss or Gain on Unfilled Flour Sales (market variations)
> Package Inventory
> Mill Supply Inventory
> Miscellaneous Manufacturing Material Inventory

*Loss or Gain on Unfilled Sales—Flour or Wheat. Loss or Gain on Bought-to-Arrive Wheat.* At the close of any accounting period, it is important to measure three items that are part of the over-all hedge position of the flour miller: (1) loss or gain on unfilled flour sales, (2) loss or gain on unfilled wheat sales, (3) loss or gain on bought-to-arrive wheat. In all three instances, cost date of contract is compared with market cost at the close of the accounting period.

Loss or gain on future options is also an integral part of the hedging position of the miller; he must recognize the difference between the closing value at the end of the accounting period and his cost or selling price at date of futures contract.

For example, the miller purchases 100,000 bushels of a certain grade of wheat on October 12 for $2.71 per bushel. On October 31 he still has not received 25,000 bushels of this wheat, and the closing market on that day is $2.75. The miller, therefore, has a profit in his closing inventory of bought-to-arrive wheat of 4 cents per bushel, or $1,000. In view of his marking all inventory to the closing market, this gain on bought-to-arrive wheat is offset by a loss on unfilled flour sales, as he has priced his unfilled sales cost at the closing market value, which reduces his margin in relation to that of the original cost date of sale.

## Peculiarities of procedures: sales-receivables cycle; purchases-payables cycle

**Accounting for sales.** Accounting for sales is a very simple recording of invoices to flour buyers for shipments made against contracts priced at the date of sale. A division of the sales journal by the types of product sold is generally made in order to maintain divisional and product profit and loss control.

**Billing and accounts receivable procedure.** There are no peculiarities in billing and accounts receivable procedures for product sales. Elevator service charges are for the most part billed and collected before the grain is actually shipped from the elevator, except in the case of Government orders. As previously noted, the Government settles all accrued charges three times a year.

**Purchase and payment procedures.** The only peculiarity in the purchase of raw materials is the advances on grain trades, described at page 657. Raw materials are bought for the most part on a cash basis, and normal purchasing and payment procedures apply. Purchases of supplies, repairs, and expense items also follow normal accounting procedures of payment and accrual.

In most milling companies, the purchase of grain is charged directly to the wheat purchase account. All other items are charged direct to their own individual sub-ledger account.

## Distribution cost

**Measurement of distribution costs.** Statistical records for the purpose of determining distribution costs are kept in terms of hundredweights of flour. Where a substantial portion of the miller's business is in family packages varying from two pounds to a hundred and in specialties, a relation of case goods to a hundredweight of flour should be determined in order properly to allocate costs, if such allocation is essential in the miller's operation.

**Allocation of distribution costs.** Since few millers have the same group of men selling bulk products to the baker and family products to the whole-sale grocer and grocery chains, the actual cost of distribution can for the most part be accurately projected and allocated to the individual efforts of the sales force. The cost of delivery can be allocated accurately by the traffic, warehousing, and accounting departments when the charges are paid.

## Cost system

**Use of standard costs.** In view of a constantly changing raw material market, the milling executive must use a standard cost basis to project his up-to-the minute cost into a selling price. From the minute he enters into a contract, he measures his potential profit and loss, and continues to do so through each accounting period until delivery is made. The accountant must be in a position to measure the variations between the standard cost at date of sale and actual results at time of delivery. For years a great segment of the milling industry figured profit and loss on a sales basis rather than on a delivery basis, necessitating many reserve and variation accounts. The majority of mills today operate on a delivery basis.

**Determination of costs.** Systems for determining manufacturing costs are basically the same throughout the industry, although there are many variations in details.

Cost date of sale is determined by taking a theoretical total number of bushels of grain necessary to manufacture the grade of flour sold and multiplying the amount by the market at time of sale. Credit is given for feed and clear flour recovery. A standard manufacturing factor, explained below, is added.

*Example:* Refer to the fifth item in Figure 6, page 649, "Red Ball" BX03. This item shows that, in order to make this particular grade of flour, it is necessary to grind 2.610 lbs. of X-mix wheat at a cost of $2.56 per bushel. From this grind of 156.6 lbs. of wheat, 45.5 lbs. of feed, 8.9 lbs. of first-grade clears, and 2.2 lbs. of low-grade clears will be secured as by-products, leaving 100 lbs. of pure patent flour. By crediting the cost of the wheat value with the value of the by-products, a net material cost of $5.23 results. To this amount is added a manufacturing expense of 46 cents, resulting in a manufacturing cost for 100 lbs. of BX03-grade flour of $5.69.

The standard manufacturing factor which is added is usually determined by dividing the total dollar operating cost of a mill within a set accounting period by the total bushels of flour the mill grinds during that period. This gives a manufacturing cost per bushel ground. The factor is then multiplied by the theoretical number of bushels needed to grind each grade of flour, thus arriving at a standard manufacturing factor. In Figure 6, the factor is shown in the "Mfg. Exp." column; for 2.610 bushels, it is 46 cents per cwt.; for 2.35 bushels, 41 cents; for 2.475 bushels, 43 cents.

When total deliveries are multiplied by cost date of sale, a number of factors, referred to here as *variations,* must be taken into account to arrive at the difference between estimated and actual cost. Figure 8 shows the calculation of the variation between actual yield and expense factors and the standard factors on a packout (cwt.) basis.

The principal variations are covered briefly below. Other variations, such as purchased flour, packing expense on family-size flour, and inter-mill transfer in multiple-unit organizations, must also be considered. Of course, the method of measuring the variation depends a great deal on the daily records available in the organization. It must be kept in mind that records for measuring the variations can become voluminous and expensive. If they are not productive to a point of paying their way, they have no place in a low-margin business such as flour milling.

**Principal variations taken into account in reconciling cost.** The following are the principal variations taken into account in preparing the cost reconciliation:

1. *Yield variation.* Because of variation in growth, some wheat will yield more endosperm per berry than others, so that instead of its taking 141 pounds of wheat to make 100 pounds of flour, it may take only 139 pounds of wheat, thereby providing a gain. If more than 141 pounds is required to make 100 pounds of flour, a loss is noted.

2. *Moisture loss or gain.* Flour is produced at approximately 13.5 per cent moisture. Because of the hard bran coating, wheat must be tempered before it is ground. The grinding process naturally creates heat, which reduces the moisture content. In case of a wet crop, the wheat will take very little temper; exceptionally dry wheat will take additional temper to soften the bran. In the production control reports, total dry wheat versus pounds of products produced is measured and then calculated on a dollar loss or gain basis (See Figure 9, page 666).

3. *Extraction loss or gain.* Again, nature plays an important part, in that in some wheat the endosperm is more easily separated from the bran. In order to reduce Ash, it is necessary to remove more and more specks of bran. It may be estimated that a .41 Ash flour should be made on a 78 per cent extraction basis, but certain mill adjustments by the miller may be necessary that will reduce it to a 76 per cent extraction before he can get a .41 Ash flour.

4. *Feed gain or loss.* As the above factor varies, so does the estimated amount of feed to be taken out of the mill vary. Since feed is normally worth about one-third the value of flour, it is to the advantage of the miller to get a larger percentage of flour out of his wheat.

5. *Clear gain or loss.* Extraction variations will correspondingly increase or decrease the amount of clear flour taken from the mill stream. Since clears are of lower value than patent flour, there is a cost variation factor.

6. *Manufacturing expense.* A 5,000-cwt. mill that will grind 12,000 bushels of wheat a day can set up a per-bushel manufacturing expense, including all direct cost, such as labor, power, and steam, and indirect charges such as depreciation, taxes, insurance, and so forth. As the mill produces more or less hundredweights than the estimate within an accounting period, the actual cost varies from the standard.

| Code | Grade | Net Cwt. Produced (As Ground) | Plus Fed Into This Grade | *Less* Used For Fed in | Net Cwt. Produced (As Packed) | Wheat Used Yield (Bu.) | Tot (Bu |
|---|---|---|---|---|---|---|---|
| DS1A | | 601 | — | — | 601 | 3.890 | 2,3 |
| DS01 | | 116,604 | 5,725 | *6,591* | 115,737 | 3.890 | 456,9 |
| DS03 | | 10,780 | 2,768 | *3,549* | 10,000 | 3.265 | 32,6 |
| DS03 | | 7,113 | 689 | *89* | 7,713 | 3.265 | 25, |
| DS03 | | 1,200 | — | — | 1,200 | 3.265 | 3, |
| DS04 | | 1,791 | 19 | *623* | 1,188 | 2.605 | 3,0 |
| DS04 | [Names of Grades | 1,200 | — | — | 1,200 | 2.605 | 3, |
| DS05 | to be inserted | 200 | — | — | 200 | 2.450 | |
| DS05 | here.] | 33,297 | 2,259 | *2,608* | 32,948 | 2.450 | 80, |
| DM05 | | 230 | — | *3* | 227 | 2.450 | |
| DS08 | | 399 | 61 | — | 460 | 1.960 | |
| DS1G | | 27,014 | — | *3* | 27,011 | 2.450 | 66, |
| DA05 | | 3,200 | — | — | 3,200 | 2.450 | 7, |
| DS45 | | 15,267 | 913 | *181* | 16,000 | 2.450 | 39, |
| DZ48 | | 15,806 | 1,193 | — | 17,000 | 2.450 | 41, |
| DZ41 | | 491 | 160 | *26* | 625 | 1.935 | 1, |
| DSW1 | | 104 | — | — | 104 | 1.850 | |
| TOTAL PATENT FLOUR AND STANDARD YIELDS .............. | | 235,300 * | 13,790 * | *13,673* | 235,416 * | | 766, |
| | Theoretical Yields for 100% Flour: | | | | | | |
| | Regular flour and clears † ....... | | | | 313,551 | 2.450 | 768, |
| | Whole wheat flour ............. | | | | 104 | 1.850 | |
| TOTAL | 100% FLOUR AND THEORETICAL YIELDS ......... | | | | 313,655 | | 768, |
| | Wheat and feed variation, 100% flour basis vs. actual ........ | | | | | (Underage | 3 |
| | | | | | | | Loss 2,1 |
| | Actual Clears Produced: | | | | | | |
| DSC1 | Soft Wheat Cutoff ............. | 64,176 | 5,829 | *3,182* | 66,823 | | |
| DSC9 | Low Grade .................... | 14,178 | 3,819 | *6,367* | 11,630 | | |
| | Total clear flour produced..... | 78,354 | 9,648 | *9,549* | 78,453 | | |
| | Purchased flour used .......... | — | 246 | *461* | *215* | | |
| | Actual Feed Produced: | | | | | | |
| DO91 | Bran ........................ | 25,298 | — | — | 25,298 | | |
| DO97 | Midds ....................... | 118,008 | — | — | 118,008 | | |
| DO93 | Mixed Feed .................. | 1,858 | — | — | 1,858 | | |
| | Total feed produced ......... | 145,164 | — | — | 145,164 | | |
| ACTUAL WHEAT USED AND PRODUCTS PRODUCED ......... | | 458,820 | 23,684 | *23,684* | 458,820 | | 772 |
| | Yield variation—actual used under: produced over standard.. | | | | | | 5 |
| | At average price .............. | | | | | | $ |
| DR. OR *CR.* YIELD VARIATION ADJUSTMENT ACCOUNT (P & L)..... | | | $11,562.05 | NET TOTAL ..................... | | | $13,4 |
| WEIGHOVER ADJUSTMENT (*1,977* BU. @ 2.19) .......................... | | | 4,331.23 | | | | |
| TOTAL *CR.* TO YIELD VARIATION ADJUSTMENT ACCOUNT (P & L).. | | | $15,893.28 | | | | |

* Totals are correct, but fractions in items have been carried to the nearest even figure.

† This chart covers soft wheat flour operations with a theoretical yield of 2.45 bu. per cwt.

**Fig. 8. Calculation of Variation Between Actual Yield and Expense Factors and the Standard Factors on Packout (Cwt.) Basis.**

| First Clear Produced or Used | Second Clear Produced or Used | | Purchased Flour Used | | Feed Produced | | Mfg. Expense At Standard Rates | |
|---|---|---|---|---|---|---|---|---|
| Total Cwt. | Per Cwt. | Total Cwt. | Per Cwt. | Total Cwt. | Per Cwt. | Total Cwt. | Per Cwt. | Total |
| 310 | .112 | 57 | — | — | .746 | 455 | .79 | $ 486.81 |
| 59,582 | .112 | 11,166 | — | — | .746 | 87,687 | .79 | 93,678.18 |
| 2,530 | .093 | 800 | — | — | .626 | 6,259 | .67 | 6,700.00 |
| 1,944 | .093 | 623 | — | — | .626 | 4,828 | .67 | 5,167.83 |
| 293 | .093 | 106 | — | — | .626 | 751 | .67 | 804.00 |
| — | .063 | 74 | — | — | .500 | 594 | .53 | 629.64 |
| — | .063 | 75 | — | — | .500 | 600 | .53 | 636.00 |
| — | — | — | — | — | .470 | 94 | .50 | 100.00 |
| — | — | — | — | — | .470 | 15,486 | .50 | 16,474.49 |
| — | — | — | — | — | .470 | 106 | .50 | 113.66 |
| — | .200 | 92 | — | — | .376 | 173 | .40 | 184.04 |
| — | — | — | — | — | .470 | 12,695 | .50 | 13,505.65 |
| — | — | — | — | — | .470 | 1,504 | .50 | 1,600.00 |
| — | — | — | — | — | .470 | 7,520 | .50 | 8,000.00 |
| — | — | — | — | — | .470 | 7,990 | .50 | 8,500.00 |
| — | — | — | .210 | 129 | .371 | 232 | .39 | 243.75 |
| — | — | — | — | — | .110 | 11 | .38 | 39.69 |
| 64,600 * | | 12,812 * | | 129 | | 146,990 * | | $156,863.74 |
| | | | | | .470 | 147,369 | .50 | $156,775.61 |
| | | | | | .110 | 11 | .38 | 39.69 |
| | | | | | | 147,380 | | $156,815.30 |

(Loss-*Gain*        2,215)

| | | | | | | | | |
|---|---|---|---|---|---|---|---|---|
| 66,823 | — | — | — | — | | | | |
| — | 1.000 | 11,630 | — | — | | | | |
| | | | 1,000 | 215 | | | | |
| | | | | | 1.000 | 25,298— 17.4% | | |
| | | | | | 1.000 | 118,008— 81.3% | | |
| | | | | | 1.000 | 1,858— 1.3% | | |
| 66,823 | | 11,630 | | 215 | | 145,164—100.0% | | |
| 2,163 | | 1,182 | | 85 | | 1,825 | | |
| $ 4.00 | | $ 3.50 | | $ 4.95 | | $ — (Per Ton $—) | | |
| $8,654.80 | | $4,138.40 | | $424.81 | | $ 2,280.19 | | $ 48.44 |

**Fig. 8.** (*Continued.*)

7. *Cash wheat basis.* In cost date of sale, wheat may have been esti-mated at an average of $2.30 per bushel, whereas the accumulated acquisition may actually come to $2.32 per bushel.

8. *Future basis.* When a wheat price is applied to the cost date of sale, the market at time of sale is used. However, it may not be possible to place the future hedge immediately, and the market might change from an eighth of a cent to a cent or more, up or down, before the transaction can be completed.

9. *Futures-spread gain or loss.* At times it is not possible to clear hedges exactly as the cash wheat position or sales by markets would dictate. It then may become necessary to place a hedge in a different month—May instead of December—and even in a different market—Chicago instead of Minneapolis. Since neither the months nor the markets move exactly the same, in lifting these hedges the miller may take a loss or gain.

10. *Wheat premiums.* Cost date of sale estimated premium for protein (see page 668) may be increased or decreased at the time the miller is able to cover with cash wheat.

11. *Wheat position.* If a miller is long or short actual wheat in relation to the amount needed to produce his flour sales, he will have a loss or gain on the basis of such position due to cost at date of acquisition versus closing value (see page 658).

12. *Clear position.* A miller sells clears in the same manner as he sells patent flour: depending entirely on the type of product to be produced by the baker. Seldom, however, is he able to dispose of his clears in the same proportion as they are secured from the grind of his patent flour sales. If his clear inventory is long or short, he will lose or gain with market fluctuations, as he has allowed a fixed credit in his original patent flour sale. However, he is not hedged against his by-product clear inventory position.

13. *Feed position.* What is said of the clear position applies equally to the feed position.

14. *Miscellaneous manufacturing ingredients.* Enrichment, self-rising ingredients, and malt, used in certain types of flour are figured at an average cost per cwt. Physical inventory may indicate variations.

15. *Package variations.* These are due to breakage, fractional cost, and so forth.

**Material control.** Materials are divided into two main categories: (1) raw materials—wheat, and (2) manufacturing supplies, packages, and so forth. Inventory control of raw material—wheat—is discussed at page 668. Control of manufacturing supplies, packages, and the like, is a normal operation of inventory disappearance generally based on a first-in, first-out inventory valuation.

**Labor control.** Since milling is a continuous operation, most employees work in specific categories and do not move from one operation to another, except in the packing department. Labor distribution is therefore fairly well defined. All men employed in the actual manufacturing, packing, and shipping of flour are classified as direct labor, whereas the laboratory and general maintenance labor are considered indirect labor.

**Burden control.** Control of overhead in the milling industry is imperative. Normally, the price of clears is fixed at a price below patent flour, and under the existing industry practice approximately the entire sale price is used as a credit to patent sales, as is the sale price of feed. Therefore, all manufacturing burden must be absorbed by the patent flour. Accordingly, if the average cost of manufacturing is determined to be 50 cents per cwt., the mill must receive this amount in addition to the straight-grade flour cost averaged over all grades.

For standard cost purposes, it is estimated that it will take 2.35 bushels of wheat to grind 100 pounds of straight-grade flour (2.35 $\times$ 60 lb. bushel = 141 lbs., that is, 100 lbs. flour and 41 lbs. feed). When a mill sells a 90 per cent extraction flour, 141 lbs. of wheat will yield 90 lbs. of patent flour, 10 lbs. of clear, and 41 lbs. of feed. Therefore, in order to manufacture 100 lbs. of 90 per cent-extraction flour, the mill must grind approximately 156 lbs. of wheat, or 2.61 bushels. Apportioning total manufacturing cost on a bushel basis ground in the mill means that the 90 per cent patent flour should be assessed approximately .556¢ per cwt. instead of 50¢ per cwt. (See Figure 8).

Variable costs, such as wages, power, steam and electricity, repairs, and so forth, must be watched closely and measured periodically in relation to production in order to test their variation from standard.

Fixed costs, such as salaries of employees, taxes, insurance, depreciation, and so forth, although controlled in total within a period, have a unit variation in direct relation to the number of cwts. produced.

It is extremely difficult to set up and maintain a standard burden because of characteristics already mentioned, namely, the highly competitive nature of the business and the instability of production. From a practical standpoint, the accountant must maintain standards for variable operation, and management must apply such variations in accordance with conditions in the mill at the time of sale.

*Work-in-process.* This term has little meaning in the milling industry. From the time wheat enters the mill until the process is completed, little attention is given to measuring for accounting purposes that part of various grades of products which remains in the process line between start and finish. All product taken off the mill stream automatically becomes a flour or feed product salable in its condition at that time.

**Analysis of costs to establish production control.** Two major factors enter into analysis of costs to establish production control: (1) hundredweights produced in a 24-hour day, and (2) yield to determine hundredweights of flour produced from bushels of wheat ground. Figure 9 is a

| | TODAY | | | | | | MONTH TO DATE | | | | |
|---|---|---|---|---|---|---|---|---|---|---|---|
| | A MILL | B MILL | C MILL | W.W. MILL | TOTAL | | A MILL | B MILL | C MILL | W.W. MILL | TOTAL |
| **WHEAT GROUND—ACTUAL GROSS** | | | | | | | | | | | |
| M   Regular Flour  —Clean Wheat Bu. | 12,063 | | 29,011 | | 41,074 | | 288,612 | | 277,682 | | 661,294 |
|   —Clean Wheat Bu. | | | | | | | | | | 2423 | 2423 |
|   Whole Wheat Flour —Clean Wheat Bu. | 307 | | 1,015 | | 1,322 | | 6,207 | | 9,516 | 77 | 15,800 |
|   Mill Screenings Bu. | | | | | | | | | | 17 | 17 |
|   Elevator Screenings Bu. | | | | | X X X | | | | | | X X X |
|   Toll—Custom. Wheat Bu. | | | | | | | | | | | |
|   Gross Bu. Weighed to Mill | | | | | | | | | | | |
|   Less: Screenings Transferred Bu. | | | | | | | | | | | |
| X   Total Ground—Bushels | 12,370 | | 30,016 | | 42,396 | | 294,819 | | 287,200 | 2517 | 534,536 |
|   Total Ground—Cwt. | | | | | 25,437 | | | | | | 350,721 |
| **PRODUCTS MANUFACTURED—NET** | | | | | | | | | | | |
|   Regular Flour Cwt. | 5,597 | | 12,844 | | 18,441 | | 127,587 | | 122,724 | | 2501,311 |
|   Grits Cwt. | | | | | | | | | | | |
|   Cwt. | | | | | | | | | | | |
| Y   Whole Wheat Flour Cwt. | 5,597 | | | | | | | | | 1424 | 1424 |
|   TOTAL Cwt. | | | | | X X X | | | | | | X X X |
| **BY-PRODUCTS MANUFACTURED—NET** | | | | | | | | | | | |
|   Feed from Reg. Grind—Sacked Cwt. | 61 | | 3,288 | | 3,349 | | 719 | | 30,024 | | 301,743 |
|   Feed from Reg. Grind—Bulk Cwt. | 1,980 | | 1,779 | | 3,759 | | 50,756 | | 19,977 | | 701,733 |
|   Feed from Whole Wht. Grind Cwt. | | | | | | | | | | | |
|   Cwt. | | | | | | | | | | | |
|   Total Produced Cwt. | | | | | 25,549 | | | | | | 353,211 |
|   Gain or Loss Cwt. | | | | GAIN | 112 | | | | | GAIN | 21,490 |
| **OTHER PRODUCTS** | | | | | | | | | | | |
|   —Grain Ground— | | | | | | | | | | | |
|   —Grits Produced—Cwt. | | | | | | | | | | | |
|   —Feed Produced—Cwt. | | | | | | | | | | | |
| **YIELD (BU. PER CWT.)** | | | | | | | | | | | |
| MfY   Regular Flour and Grits —Clean Yield | 2.155 | | 2.258 | | | | 2.262 | | 2.263 | 1.701 | |
|   Whole Wheat Flour —Clean Yield | .055 | | .070 | | | | .049 | | .071 | .066 | |
|   Screenings —Ground | | | | | | | | | | | |
| IfY   —Grits | | | | | | | | | | | |
|   Dirty Wheat Yield | 2.210 | | 2.328 | | | | 2.310 | | 2.334 | 1.767 | |
| **HOURS OPERATED** | | | | | | | | | | | |
|   to | 24 | | 24 | | Hrs. | | 570 | | 239 | 33 | Hrs. |
|   to | | | | | Hrs. | | | | | | |
|   to | | | | | Hrs. | | | | | | |

Days of operation — Fiscal Year to date

Fig. 9. Production Control Report.

relatively simple example of a daily production control report from which manufacturing results can be measured. The majority of mills have more than one grinding unit, and it is important to measure each unit individually, as is indicated by this report. The first section of the report accounts for all wheat put into the milling process. The second section accounts for the finished goods taken from the mill stream, whether flour, feed, or other products. The yield section is one of straight mathematics, but is the important control furnished by the accounting department to top management and the production department. It also provides the accounting department with basic variation information.

**Inventory practices peculiar to the business.** *Measuring inventory.* As stated previously, wheat is traded by grades, insofar as the miller is concerned. He must accumulate a sufficient quantity of the proper type of wheat to mill the various grades of flour demanded by the bakery trade for their many types of baked goods. The baker, being a technician, uses the best grade of flour to produce the best results for each of his baked goods— bread, cakes, pies, cookies, rolls, and the like. To accumulate this wheat, the miller must thoroughly test each lot of wheat received and sort it with similar grades of wheat in his storage bins. A measurement of the number of feet and inches from the top of the elevator bin to the top of the grain can be transposed into the number of bushels in each tank. The calculations are adjusted by the average test weight of the wheat, which varies from 55 pounds to 62 pounds to a bushel under normal conditions.

*Peculiarities of pricing.* Grain is generally purchased in truckloads and railroad carloads. These purchases obviously cannot remain segregated until used, but must be stored with a like quality of grain. During the time of accumulation within any accounting period, the cost by lot can vary considerably. It is the practice of the industry to price all wheat inventories at closing market price by grades at the end of each accounting period.

Pricing varies by tanks of grain in the elevator according to:

Type of wheat ........................................Spring—Winter—Soft
Grade of wheat..............................No. 1 to No. 5 (No. 1 being top)
Protein...........Normally, under 11%; then by quarters or halves up to 17%
Test weight..58 lbs. is the generally normal basis, with plus for over 58 and discount for under 58 on Spring and 60 lbs. for Winter and Red wheats
Moisture .....................................If excessive, a discount is taken
Damage ........................Broken grain, smut or garlic, and so forth

In order to prevent taking a loss or gain in the grain inventory, it is customary to calculate a loss or gain on unfilled flour sales at the close of the accounting period on the basis of the cost date of sale that was applied on the netting sheet and hedged at date of sale against cost to manufacture basis wheat market. This assumes a perfect hedge position, which at times is impractical. Consequently there appears another factor, namely, the long or short position of wheat as applied to unfilled flour sales.

It might be well to point out here that the futures markets are based on ordinary No. 1 wheat. There is a premium factor relating to the per cent of protein in the wheat that cannot be hedged in any way other than by securing the actual grade of wheat necessary to grind the kind of flour the miller has sold. Figure 10 shows the premium for protein that would be paid for actual cash grain where the futures prices indicated prevail.

*Kansas City Market—October 28, 1954—Futures Prices*

March Wheat ................................................2.32¾ per bu.
May Wheat ..................................................2.27⅛ per bu.
July Wheat ..................................................2.13⅛ per bu.
December Wheat ...........................................2.33 per bu.

*Premium (Cents Per Bushel)*

| .Protein | No. 1 Grade | No. 2 Grade | No. 3 Grade |
|---|---|---|---|
| Ordinary (under 11.25) ............... 4 | to 5 | 3 to 4½ | 2 to 4 |
| 11.25–11.40 .......................... 4 | to 15 | 3 to 14½ | 2 to 13½ |
| 11.50–11.70 .......................... 5½ | to 24 | 4½ to 23½ | 3½ to 22½ |
| 11.75–11.90 .......................... 6½ | to 29 | 5¼ to 28½ | 4½ to 27½ |
| 12.00–12.20 .......................... 8 | to 35 | 7 to 34½ | 6 to 32½ |
| 12.25–12.40 .......................... 9 | to 36 | 8 to 35½ | 7 to 33½ |
| 12.50–12.70 ..........................10 | to 37 | 9 to 36½ | 8 to 34½ |
| 12.75–12.90 ..........................11 | to 38 | 10 to 37½ | 9 to 35½ |
| 13.00–13.20 ..........................13 | to 39 | 12 to 38½ | 11 to 36½ |
| 13.25–13.40 ..........................14 | to 40 | 13 to 39½ | 12 to 37½ |
| 13.50–13.70 ..........................15 | to 41 | 14 to 40½ | 13 to 38½ |
| 13.75–13.90 ..........................16 | to 42 | 15 to 41½ | 14 to 39½ |
| 14.00–14.40 ..........................17½ | to 43 | 16½ to 42½ | 15½ to 40½ |
| 14.50–14.90 ..........................19½ | to 44 | 18½ to 43½ | 17½ to 41½ |
| 15.00–15.90 ..........................21½ | to 45 | 20½ to 44½ | 19½ to 42½ |
| 16.00 and up ........................23½ | to 46 | 22½ to 45½ | 21½ to 43½ |

RED WHEAT

| | | | |
|---|---|---|---|
| All protein ........................ 1 | to 2½ | 0 to 2 | 0 to 1 |

**Fig. 10. Premiums for Cash Hard Winter Wheat.**

*Illustration:* If a miller bought 10,000 bushels of 13 protein No. 1, Hard Winter Wheat on October 28, he would have paid cash on the basis of the December futures market of $2.33 per bushel plus a protein premium of 13¢ to 39¢ per bushel. The variation of protein premium is determined by the milling quality of the wheat. The miller knows, by variety of wheat and area grown, the potential milling quality. In many instances, the miller demands delivery of wheat according to technical Farinograph specifications, and he will pay the top price for this wheat—in this case, 39¢ over the December future, or $2.72 per bushel.

*Control of inventory against loss and shrinkage.* This is a physical operation insofar as wheat is concerned and a major function of the elevator organization, which performs, in addition to the duties of unloading and loading out of grain, the service of maintaining grain in proper condition. Grain being a raw commodity, it is subject to in-store damage and must be watched carefully. Loss due to the human element is controlled, since most states maintain a rather rigid control over the public elevator. Weigh-masters and inspectors check all grain that enters and leaves an elevator. In an elevator operated for mill purposes only, all grain is carefully weighed in and out over large 1,000- to 2,000-bushel scales.

## Payroll peculiarities

**Job cards and labor costs.** Most mills have a job card filled out by the employee or foreman and approved by the foreman. It coincides in total time with the time clock card punched in and out each day by the employee. The job card merely indicates hours spent on specific operations.

Cost per cwt. and units produced per man-hour by departments are important. Labor control through a report of plant labor costs (see Figure 11) is particularly important in a multiple mill operation.

## Plant and equipment records—depreciation

**Identification of equipment.** Every piece of equipment installed in a mill should be numbered consecutively with a metal tag in order that it may be identified when equipment is changed, moved, dismantled, or repaired. The number is essential in maintaining the following records.

**Plant and equipment ledgers.** Two ledgers are kept for control purposes and to furnish the accounting department with necessary information for insurance, depreciation, and tax purposes. These ledgers are the location control ledger and the job description ledger.

*Location control ledger.* This ledger is a detailed record of the total cost of all acquisitions, by location of each milling and elevator property. It also provides for the depletion of capital assets due to sale or other disposition. Through this record there is maintained a perpetual balance of all capital assets by physical location. The corresponding depreciation account, by location, is generally maintained in the same ledger.

*Job description ledger.* In the milling industry, a great many of the fixed assets are not totally purchased; they are created by each mill's own maintenance crew. Each job performed on capital additions or repairs is recorded in a job description ledger, generally a loose-leaf binder. Hours and amounts spent on such jobs are entered on the plant labor cost weekly report (Figure 11). When a job is completed, the dollar value is recorded in the location control ledger and cross-referenced to the job description ledger. A cross reference between these ledgers is essential, because many years after the date of installation, it may be necessary to know the original date and cost of installation for depreciation and tax purposes.

PLANT LABOR COST WEEK ENDING _____8-27-_____ 19_____

HOURS OPERATION OF MILLS  A 119:25  B _____  C 118:55    A 1277:40  B 182:05  C 1091:40

D _____  E _____  CW 2:30    D _____  E _____  CW 100:50

| DEPT. NO | OCCUPATION | WEEK | | | | | | CROP YEAR TO DATE | | | | |
|---|---|---|---|---|---|---|---|---|---|---|---|---|
| | | NO. EMP | HOURS | AMOUNT | CWT PER MAN HOUR | NON-PRODUCTIVE HOURS | OVER-TIME PENALTY HOURS | HOURS | AMOUNT | CWT PER MAN HOUR | NON-PRODUCTIVE HOURS | OVER-TIME PENALTY HOURS |
| •100 | MILLERS | 3 | 132 | 259.62 | • | | • | 1638 | 3102.87 | • | • | |
| 101 | GRINDERS | 4 | 160 | 267.60 | • | | | 1526 | 2496.93 | • | 79 | |
| 102 | BOLTERS | 3 | 120 | 190.88 | • | | 8 | 1366 | 2099.08 | • | 70 | 25 |
| 103 | ROLL TENDERS | 6 | 240 | 329.76 | • | | 1 | 2559 | 3531.02 | • | 111 | 56 |
| 104 | OILERS | 8 | 320 | 436.80 | • | | | 3473 | 4742.81 | • | 295 | 56 |
| 105 | SMUTTERS | 6 | 240 | 338.00 | • | | | 2536 | 3581.05 | • | 141 | 32 |
| 106 | SWEEPERS | 7 | 272 | 349.36 | • | | | 3211 | 4175.52 | • | 421 | 76 |
| 107 | SIEVEMEN | 1 | 40 | 68.40 | • | | | 401 | 714.88 | • | 92 | 41 |
| 108 | BELTMEN | 1 | 40 | 68.40 | • | | | 396 | 676.58 | • | 60 | 4 |
| | TOTAL MILLING | 39 | 1564 | 2308.82 | 33.3 | | 9 | 17106 | 25120.74 | 31.9 | 1269 | 290 |
| •110 | HEAD PACKERS | 3 | 132 | 231.90 | • | | | 1638 | 2817.60 | • | | |
| 111 | FLOUR PACKERS | 6 | 235 | 343.40 | • | | | 3377 | 4908.93 | • | | 6 |
| 112 | PIT SEWERS | 2 | 80 | 120.90 | • | | | 888 | 1332.80 | • | | 2 |
| | TOTAL FLR. PKG. LG. | 11 | 447 | 696.20 | 54.4 | | | 5903 | 9059.33 | 85.0 | | 8 |
| | WEEK / PERIOD | | | | | | | | | | | |
| 121 | 2# CWT. 15 / 659 | | 3 | 4.34 | 5.0 | | | 158 | 227.92 | 4.2 | | |
| 122 | 5# CWT. 682 / 5017 | 5 | 104 | 150.84 | 6.5 | | | 575 | 867.25 | 8.7 | | 44 |
| 123 | 10# CWT. 72 / 2993 | 1 | 9 | 13.06 | 8.0 | | | 215 | 310.96 | 13.9 | | |
| 124 | 25# CWT. 95 / 5905 | | 7 | 9.41 | 13.6 | | | 337 | 486.52 | 17.5 | | |
| 125 | 50# CWT. 78 / 947 | | 3 | 5.07 | 26.0 | | | 59 | 84.89 | 16.1 | | |
| | TOTAL FLR. PKG. SM. | 6 | 126 | 182.72 | • | | | 1344 | 1977.54 | • | | 44 |
| •130 | FOREMAN - FLR. TRCKG. | 2 | 88 | 154.60 | • | | | 1048 | 1803.40 | • | | |
| 131 | FLOUR TRUCKERS | 6 | 244 | 336.53 | • | | 2 | 2573 | 3499.27 | • | 8 | 39 |
| 132 | FEED IN MEN | 1 | 44 | 60.24 | • | | | 610 | 832.34 | • | | 1 |
| 133 | CHECKERS | 2 | 86 | 125.31 | • | | | 1016 | 1484.16 | • | 56 | 55 |
| 134 | COOPERS | 4 | 173 | 248.57 | • | | 21 | 1923 | 2717.61 | • | 8 | 207 |
| 136 | CAR LOADERS | 7 | 424 | 563.64 | • | | | 5594 | 7407.90 | • | | 15 |
| 138 | BULK FLOUR LOADING | 1 | 32 | 45.34 | 59.0 | | | 298 | 415.79 | 81.7 | | |
| | WEEK / PERIOD | | | | | | | | | | | |
| 139 | LDG SMALL CWT 526 / 13754 | 2 | 82 | 120.33 | 6.4 | | | 1193 | 1702.11 | 11.5 | | 18 |
| | TOTAL FLOUR SHIPPING | 25 | 1173 | 1654.56 | 40.0 | | 27 | 14255 | 19862.52 | 40.2 | 72 | 335 |
| 141 | FEED PACKERS | 4 | 150 | 220.52 | 49.9 | | | 1583 | 2338.79 | 50.3 | | 28 |
| •150 | FOREMAN - FEED TRKG. | 1 | 44 | 77.30 | • | | | 546 | 939.20 | • | | |
| 151 | FEED TRUCKERS | 5 | 185 | 264.65 | • | | 13 | 2279 | 3212.62 | • | | 148 |
| ≈ | TOTAL SACKED FEED LDG | 6 | 229 | 341.95 | 32.7 | | 13 | 2825 | 4151.82 | 28.2 | | 148 |
| •160 | FOREMAN BLK FEED LDG | | | | • | | | | | • | | |
| 161 | BULK FEED LDG. - GEN. | 5 | 165 | 240.96 | • | | | 1764 | 2569.12 | • | 8 | 2 |
| | TOTAL BULK FEED LDG. | 5 | 165 | 240.96 | 98.5 | | | 1764 | 2569.12 | 98.8 | 8 | 2 |
| •170 | SACK DEPT. FOREMAN | 1 | 44 | 77.30 | • | | | 546 | 939.20 | • | | |
| 171 | ASST. HEAD SACKMAN | 1 | 40 | 58.80 | • | | | 527 | 774.36 | • | 16 | |
| 172 | SACKMEN | 1 | 40 | 56.90 | • | | | 449 | 633.99 | • | | |
| 173 | BAG MISCELLANEOUS | | | | • | | | 22 | 28.46 | • | | |
| | TOTAL SACK DEPT. | 3 | 124 | 192.90 | • | | | 1544 | 2376.01 | • | 16 | |
| •180 | WHSE. SUPT. & ASSTS. | 2 | 84 | 166.16 | • | | | 1042 | 2040.98 | • | | |
| 181 | SWEEPERS | 4 | 164 | 210.48 | • | | | 2069 | 2657.70 | • | | 1 |
| 183 | MECHANICS | 1 | 40 | 65.60 | • | | | 499 | 822.91 | • | 20 | 10 |
| 184 | OILERS | 2 | 85 | 122.05 | • | | 5 | 978 | 1384.18 | • | 4 | 62 |
| 186 | UNLOADING | | | | • | | | 40 | 55.44 | • | | |
| | TOTAL WAREHOUSE | 9 | 373 | 564.29 | • | | 5 | 4628 | 6961.21 | • | 24 | 73 |
| | TOTAL 100 - 186 | 108 | 4351 | 6402.82 | 12.0 | | 54 | 50952 | 74417.08 | 10.7 | 1389 | 928 |
| •200 | LABORATORY | 5 | 208 | 380.77 | • | | | 2340 | 4350.24 | • | | |
| 301 | ELEC. ASST. FOREMAN | 1 | 29 | 55.47 | • | | 1 | 448 | 865.69 | • | 27 | 28 |
| 302 | ELECTRICIANS | 3 | 100 | 174.76 | • | | | 1203 | 2101.94 | • | | 17 |
| | TOTAL POWER & STEAM | 4 | 129 | 230.23 | • | | 1 | 1651 | 2967.63 | • | 27 | 45 |
| •400 | MILL MGR. & OFF. ASST. | 2 | 84 | 204.23 | • | | | 1042 | 2367.55 | • | | |
| 401 | WATCHMEN | 3 | 128 | 170.32 | • | | 8 | 1704 | 2300.98 | • | | 88 |
| 402 | JANITORS - UTILITY | 4 | 152 | 194.96 | • | | | 1782 | 2270.13 | • | | |
| | TOTAL INDIRECT | 9 | 364 | 569.51 | • | | 8 | 4528 | 6938.66 | • | | 88 |
| •410 | MAINT. SUPT. & ASSTS. | 1 | 44 | 107.69 | • | | | 546 | 1335.36 | • | | |
| 411 | MILLWRIGHTS | 3 | 129 | 228.16 | • | | | 1462 | 2575.59 | • | 4 | 47 |
| 412 | SHEET METAL WORKERS | 3 | 126 | 203.74 | • | | | 1213 | 1988.34 | • | | 1 |
| 413 | MACHINISTS | | | | • | | | 358 | 610.76 | • | | 3 |
| 414 | PIPE FITTERS | | | | • | | | 281 | 475.28 | • | | 1 |
| 415 | PAINTERS | 1 | 32 | 50.88 | • | | | 443 | 687.55 | • | 16 | 3 |
| 416 | UTILITY | | | | • | | | | | • | | |
| 417 | REPAIRS - GEN. MAINT. | | | | • | | | 590 | 984.23 | • | 8 | 17 |
| | TOTAL MAINTENANCE | 8 | 331 | 590.47 | • | | | 4893 | 8657.11 | • | 28 | 72 |
| 421 | FUMIGATION - GENERAL | | | | • | | | 369 | 702.71 | • | | 170 |
| | TOTAL 100 - 421 | 134 | 5383 | 8173.80 | 9.7 | | 63 | 64733 | 98033.43 | 8.5 | 1444 | 1303 |
| | HOURLY EMP. TOTALS | | 4523 | 6514.23 | 11-5 | | | 54347 | 78336.93 | 10.1 | | |
| • | MONTHLY EMP. TOTALS | 20 | 860 | 1659.57 | 60.6 | | | 10386 | 19696.50 | 52.5 | | |
| 431 | VACATIONS - GENERAL | | 440 | 607.20 | • | | | 7720 | 11112.00 | • | | |
| 441 | HOLIDAYS - GENERAL | | | | • | | | 1080 | 1547.64 | • | | |
| 700 | "A" JOBS - CAP. ASSET | 2 | 84 | 141.85 | • | | | 749 | 1271.19 | • | | 19 |
| 800 | "R" JOBS - REPAIRS | | | | • | | | 134 | 207.16 | • | | |
| 901 | TRUCKING EXP. RETAIL | 1 | 50 | 72.84 | • | | | 964 | 1372.12 | • | | 20 |
| | GRAND TOTAL | 137 | 5957 | 8995.69 | 8.7 | | 63 | 75380 | 113543.54 | 7.2 | 1444 | 1342 |

| | | | | |
|---|---|---|---|---|
| HOURLY EMP. COST PER MAN HOUR | 1.440 | | 1.441 | |
| HOURLY EMP. COST PER CWT. | .125 | | .144 | |
| MONTHLY EMP. COST PER CWT. | .032 | | .036 | |

## STATISTICS

| | Week | Year | | Week | Year |
|---|---|---|---|---|---|
| A. GRAINGROUND - ACTUAL GROSS | 126334 BU. | 1312297 BU. | F. BULK LOADING - FEED | 16250 BU. | 171228 BU. |
| B. FLOUR PRODUCTS MFD - NET | 52116 CWT | 545096 CWT | G. BULK LOADING - FLOUR PROD. | 1889 CWT | 24343 CWT |
| C. FLOUR PACKED - 100 LB. & LARGER | 42215 CWT | 501494 CWT | H. SHIPPED FROM FLOOR STOCK | 3688 CWT | 56139 CWT |
| D. FLOUR PACKED - 50 LB. & SMALLER | 942 CWT | 15521 CWT | I. FED IN FROM FLOOR STOCK | 128 CWT | 215 CWT |
| E. FEED PACKED - IN BAGS | 7490 CWT | 79557 CWT | J. SHIPMENTS UNLOADED | 519 CWT | 5626 CWT |

**Fig. 11. Plant Labor Cost Weekly Report.**

670

**Depreciation.** The majority of milling companies use the straight-line composite depreciation method. However, individual cost and date of installation are important at time of disposition or replacement in order to gain the utmost from the depreciation reserve for tax purposes.

## Reports to management

**Period of reporting.** Reports to management are generally made on a monthly and fiscal-year-to-date basis. In the milling industry, the fiscal year generally ends in May or June because of harvesting.

### Financial reports.
1. Accounting period balance sheet.
   a. Accounts receivable summary—aged.
   b. Inventory summary by locations.
2. Accounting period profit and loss.
   a. Analysis of operating profit by mills.
   b. Analysis of operating profit by divisions and locations of the company (Bulk Flour—Family Flour—Feed—Grain Merchandising—Specialties—Elevators).
   c. Manufacturing expenses—by locations.
   d. Selling expense—by divisions and locations.
   e. Advertising expense—by divisions and locations.
   f. Administrative expense—by locations.
   g. Communication expense—by divisions and locations.
   h. Fixed charges—by locations.

### Operating reports.
*Statistical reports.* For each accounting period, the following reports are prepared:
1. Deliveries—by products—location from which made and by divisions.
2. Unfilled sales—by divisions—by locations.
3. Sales—cwts.—by divisions—by locations.

**Manufacturing control reports.** Six basic reports are prepared to keep top management informed of operating results:

1. *Production report.* This report of daily production with month-to-date figures (see Figure 9) shows management the over-all mill processing efficiency.

2. *Yield variation.* At the end of the accounting period, the calculation of yield variation (see Figure 8) explains to management in detail the reasons for loss or gain in production for the period and measures the results in dollars.

3. *Products—bushels and cwt. reconciliation.* This fiscal-year report is designed to account for all bushels of grain and all cwts. of products produced (see Figure 12).

PRODUCTION

JUNE 1, 19- TO MAY 31, 19-

| | PRODUCTS PRODUCED CWT. | MILL FEED PRODUCED CWT. | YIELD LBS./CWT. | THEO. YIELD BU/CWT. | GRAIN USED QUANTITY BU. | ACTUAL GROSS QUANTITY BU. | GRAIN USED YIELD BU/CWT. |
|---|---|---|---|---|---|---|---|
| FROM WHEAT GROUND (60 LBS. PER BU.) | | | | | | | |
| Regular flour and mill feed | 3,053,320.82 | 1,189,012.30 | 38.94 | 2.289 | 6,988,113 | 7,037,844 | 2.305 |
| Regular whole wheat | 40,297.00 | -- | -- | 1.670 | 67,296 | 68,345 | 1.696 |
| Malt and self-rising ingredients | 4,513.00 | -- | -- | 2.350 | 10,605 | -- | -- |
| Grind Adjustment-Weighover Gain*/Loss | -- | -- | -- | -- | -- | 28,677* | -- |
| TOTAL WHEAT PRODUCTS | 3,098,130.82 | 1,189,012.30 | | | 7,066,014 | 7,077,512 | |
| FROM KAFIR-MILO GROUND (56 LBS. PER BU.) | | | | | | | |
| Kafir-Milo grits and mill feed | 25,721.00 | 8,433.00 | 32.79 | 2.500 | 64,303 | 63,398 | 2.465 |
| TOTAL CWT. PRODUCTION | 3,123,851.82 | 1,197,445.30 | | | | | |

QUANTITY STATISTICS

JUNE 1, 19- TO MAY 31, 19-

| | FLOUR CWT. | RYE CWT. | MILL FEED CWT. | KAFIR-MILO GRITS CWT. |
|---|---|---|---|---|
| Inventory - opening | 25,775.20 | -- | 2,766.00 | 88.00 |
| Production | 3,098,130.82 | -- | 1,197,445.30 | 25,721.00 |
| Purchased - outside | 875.00 | 1.00 | 38.00 | -- |
| Purchased - inter-mill | 2,679.00 | -- | -- | -- |
| Fed-in | 4,246.70* | 4.00* | 4,359.70 | 109.00* |
| TOTAL | 3,123,213.32 | 3.00* | 1,204,609.00 | 25,700.00 |
| Delivered to trade | 3,013,928.32 | 1.00 | 1,200,158.00 | 25,700.00 |
| Delivered - inter-mill | 77,986.00 | -- | 550.00 | -- |
| Reconditioning losses and gains* | 21.55 | -- | -- | -- |
| Inventory losses and gains* | 873.11 | 4.00* | 37.00 | -- |
| Inventory - closing | 30,404.34 | -- | 3,864.00 | -- |
| TOTAL | 3,123,213.32 | 3.00* | 1,204,609.00 | 25,700.00 |

*Red.

**Fig. 12. Products—Bushels and Cwt. Reconciliation.**

4. *Grain handled and in store.* This can be a simple report by locations, showing by grains:

Bushels in store beginning of period ............................................ ——
Unloaded .................................................................... ——
Bought in store ............................................................. ——
(1) Total .................................................................... ——
Ground ...................................................................... ——
Loaded out .................................................................. ——
Sold in store ............................................................... ——
(2) Total .................................................................... ——
Net bushels in store—1 minus 2 ............................................... ——
Physical inventory .......................................................... ——
Difference .................................................................. ——

5. *Long and short position by grain and by location.* Figure 13 illustrates the report prepared daily to show the long and short wheat position by location. Similar reports are prepared for other grains. Figure 14 shows the long and short position for the period.

# Fig. 13. Daily Wheat Position.

DATE _____

| CASH WHEAT IN STORE — IN TRANSIT — TO ARRIVE | | | | | EQUIVALENT BUSHELS – UNFILLED FLOUR SALES | | | |
| --- | --- | --- | --- | --- | --- | --- | --- | --- |
| CASH WHEAT PREVIOUS REPORT | WHEAT BOUGHT OR SOLD TODAY | ACTUAL GROUND TODAY | O'FILLS ADJ. | TOTAL CASH WHEAT | UNFILLED PREVIOUS REPORT | SOLD (-PUR'ASE) TODAY | GROUND TODAY THEOR'CAL | CLOSING UNFILLED TODAY |
| 1,159,333 | 9,200 | | | 1,168,533 | 513,388 | 357,905 | | 871,293 |

## TODAY'S TRADES

| BOUGHT | | | SOLD | | |
| --- | --- | --- | --- | --- | --- |
| BUSHELS | FUTURE | PRICE | BUSHELS | FUTURE | PRICE |
| 150 | C Mch | 229 3/4 | | | |
| 25 | " | 229 1/2 | | | |
| 25 | " | 229 3/8 | | | |
| 25 | " | 229 1/2 | | | |
| 25 | " | 230 | | | |
| 50 | " | 229 5/8 | | | |
| 5 | N May | 241 1/2 | | | |
| 5 | " | 241 3/4 | | | |
| 5 | " | 241 7/8 | | | |
| 35 | " | 242 | | | |

### MILL – NET CASH WHEAT POSITION

| LONG | SHORT |
| --- | --- |
| 297,420 BU. | BU. |

### OPEN FUTURE TRADES

| | CHICAGO | | KANSAS CITY | | MINNEAPOLIS | | TOTAL | |
| --- | --- | --- | --- | --- | --- | --- | --- | --- |
| | LONG | SHORT | LONG | SHORT | LONG | SHORT | LONG | SHORT |
| MAY | 10 | | | | | 104 | | 94 |
| JULY | 20 | | | | | | 20 | |
| SEPTEMBER | | | | | | | | |
| DECEMBER | | | | | | | | |
| MARCH | | 225 | | | | | | 225 |
| NET FUTURES POSITION | | 195 | | | | 104 | | 299 |

### MILL – NET POSITION BUSHELS

1,760

673

| LOCATION | A BUSHELS | B BUSHELS | C BUSHELS | D BUSHELS | TOTAL BUSHELS | RYE E BUSHELS | KAFIR-MILO CWTS. | FEED OATS TONS |
|---|---|---|---|---|---|---|---|---|
| **LONG** | | | | | | | | |
| In store and in transit - October 31 Grain | (67,870) | 85,683 | 262,283 | 145,457 | 425,553 | 4,705 | 61.20 | 19.992 |
| Finished Products on grain basis | 101,227 | 121,264 | 183,059 | 45,555 | 451,105 | . . . . | . . . . | . . . . |
| Bought to arrive November 30 | 1,700 | 92,800 | - | - | 94,500 | . . . . | 11.80 | . . . . |
| Purchased during November - Grain | 466,217 | 223,100 | 86,884 | 8,646 | 784,847 | . . . . | . . . . | . . . . |
| Purchased during November - Finished Products | - | - | 18,436 | - | 18,436 | | | |
| Overfill - (Underfill) on purchases | 15,953 | 2,199 | - | - | 18,152 | | | |
| Transfers of Grain | - | (1,322) | - | - | (1,322) | 33 | | 30.650 |
| Adjustments - account weighup | 690 | 860 | - | (946) | 604 | | | .805 |
| Adjustments - account dockage | - | 2,873 | - | - | 2,873 | | | |
| **TOTAL - LONG** | 517,917 | 527,457 | 550,662 | 198,712 | 1,794,748 | 4,738 | 73.00 | 51.447 |
| **SHORT** | | | | | | | | |
| Unfilled sales October 31 - Grain | - | 3,221 | - | 2,000 | 5,221 | . . . . | | |
| Unfilled sales October 31 - Finished Products | 439,322 | 278,392 | 378,657 | 33,563 | 1,129,934 | . . . . | | |
| Sales during November Grain | 1,700 | 80,037 | - | 17,000 | 98,737 | | | |
| Sales during November Finished Products | 323,858 | 197,845 | 177,839 | 53,054 | 752,596 | | | |
| Overfill - (Underfill) on sales | - | (3,221) | (9,701) | - | 100 | | | (.003) |
| (Cancellation of sales) - grain | 8,219 | 1,191 | (999) | 291 | (3,221) | | | |
| Transfer of sales | 5,556 | (897) | - | (914) | - | | | |
| Shrink, transit loss and misc. adjustments | - | - | - | - | 2,746 | | | |
| **(TOTAL - SHORT)** | 778,755 | 556,568 | 545,796 | 104,994 | 1,986,113 | - | | (.003) |
| **Cash Grain Position - Long - (Short)** | (260,838) | (29,111) | 4,866 | 93,718 | (191,365) | 4,738 | 73.00 | 51.450 |
| Hedges - Long - (Short) | 331,000 | 36,000 | (10,000) | (90,000) | 267,000 | - | - | - |
| Net Position Long - (Short) | 70,162 | 6,889 | (5,134) | 3,718 | 75,635 | 4,738 | 73.00 | 51.450 |
| *Rye hedged in wheat - 4,422 bu. | | | | | | | | |
| **ANALYSIS OF CASH GRAIN POSITION** | | | | | | | | |
| Inventory - Grain | (216,792) | 33,822 | 107,698 | 79,763 | 4,491 | 4,738 | 73.00 | 51.450 |
| Finished Products | 71,318 | 89,257 | 137,633 | 38,663 | 336,871 | - | - | - |
| Bought to arrive | 203,200 | 47,400 | | | 250,600 | | | |
| | 57,726 | 170,479 | 245,331 | 118,426 | 591,962 | 4,738 | 73.00 | 51.450 |
| Less Unfilled sales - Finished Products | 318,564 | 199,590 | 240,465 | 24,708 | 783,327 | - | - | - |
| Cash Grain Position - Long - (Short) - November 30 | (260,838) | (29,111) | 4,866 | 93,718 | (191,365) | 4,738 | 73.00 | 51.450 |

Fig. 14. Long and Short Position by Location for the Period.

674

6. *Man-hour analysis.* This report measures plant efficiency and is an over-all cost control by departments. It can be relatively simple or detailed as best fits individual management requirements. Fundamentally it should show:

Employee cost per man-hour worked
Employee cost per cwt. produced
Cwts. produced per man-hour worked

The above factors can be maintained or expanded to show costs for current week, year to date, and comparative prior year. Figure 11, page 670, is an example of a very detailed man-hour report. A simpler form is shown in Figure 15.

PRODUCTION COST–______MILL Report No. 17

| DEPARTMENT | Current Week Ending | | | Year To Date | | Last Year To Date | |
|---|---|---|---|---|---|---|---|
| | Employees | Hours | Earnings | Hours | Earnings | Hours | Earnings |
| Milling | 17 | 918½ | 2285 64 | 13745½ | 31721 76 | 14626 | 33691 45 |
| Flour Packing (Large) | 10 | 518 | 1298 48 | 7036½ | 16171 23 | 8084½ | 17865 10 |
| Flour Packing (Small) | 12 | 568 | 1154 28 | 5608¾ | 10278 35 | 7544½ | 13431 39 |
| Wheat Unloading | 2 | 116 | 296 78 | 1742¼ | 3900 86 | 2302¼ | 5216 39 |
| Power (Maintenance) | 4 | 216 | 617 60 | 3179¼ | 3559 13 | 3368¼ | 9035 83 |
| Laboratory | 1 | 40 | 74 40 | 624 | 1109 28 | 633¾ | 1094 23 |
| Shipping & Warehouse | 22 | 1056½ | 2438 55 | 14804½ | 31491 93 | 17523 | 36050 59 |
| General Indirect | 9 | 421 | 1035 85 | 7838 | 18994 56 | 11699 | 30025 50 |
| Total Hourly Employees Working | 77 | 3854 | 9201 58 | 54578¾ | 122227 10 | 65781¼ | 146410 48 |
| Vacations | | 120 | 243 20 | 4560 | 9073 00 | 4200 | 7894 72 |
| Holidays | | – | – | 1770½ | 3504 17 | 1888 | 3659 12 |
| Total Hourly Payroll | | 3974 | 9444 78 | 60808¼ | 134804 27 | 71869¼ | 157964 32 |
| Total Cwt. Produced | | | 37.664 | | 551.960 | | 568.041 |
| Employees Cost Per Man Hour | | | 2.377 | | 2.213 | | 2.198 |
| Hourly Employees Cost Per Cwt. | | | .251 | | .244 | | .278 |
| Cwt. Produced Per Man Hour | | | 9.478 | | 9.062 | | 7.904 |
| STATISTICS | For Month of August | | | Year To Date 8/31/55 | | Last Year To Date 8/31/54 | |
| Plant Overhead Expense | $ 24,830.– | Per Cwt. | .175 | $ 76,878 | Per Cwt. .185 | $ 69,807. | Per Cwt. .159 |
| Direct Manufacturing Expense | $ 37,636.– | Per Cwt. | .265 | $ 108,590. | Per Cwt. .261 | $ 114,855. | Per Cwt. .262 |
| Total Manufacturing Expense | $ 62,466.– | Per Cwt. | .440 | $ 185,468. | Per Cwt. .446 | $ 184,662. | Per Cwt. .421 |
| Hours Mill Operated | | | 627 | | 1828½ | | 1856 |
| Total Cwts. Produced | | | 141,798 | | 415,398 | | 438,742 |

**Fig. 15. Simple Form of Man-Hour Analysis.**

**Sales efficiency reports.** To measure sales efficiency, it is necessary to know the cwts. of product sold, the potential of the territory, and the margin in relation to that received by other territories. A knowledge of the type of business served is necessary to evaluate the results properly. A simple report such as that shown in Figure 16 will serve as a starting point for analysis of salesmen's efficiency.

PROFIT AND LOSS STATEMENT

_Rabsy_ Division

Period June 1, 195-

_____ Salesman

_____ District

| | MONTH OF _April_ | | | CURRENT FISCAL YEAR TO DATE | | |
|---|---|---|---|---|---|---|
| | CWTS. | MARGIN | PER CWT. | CWTS. | MARGIN | PER CWT. |
| Unfilled Sales First of Month | 14,404 | $5,415.90 | $.376 | | | |
| PLUS: Current Month Bookings | 1,718 | 499.88 | .291 | | | |
| LESS: Unfilled Sales End of Month | 12,506 | 4,485.89 | .359 | | | |
| Deliveries | 3,616 | $1,429.89 | $.359 | 36,499 | $14,331.24 | $.393 |
| LESS: Salary and Expense | | 737.63 | .204 | | 8,124.06 | .223 |
|     General Selling, Sales Office and Administratioff | | | | | | |
|     Advertising | | | | | | |
| NET PROFIT | $ | $ | | $ | $ | |

**Fig. 16. Condensed Profit and Loss Statement to Measure Salesmen's Efficiency.**

## Special devices to reduce recordkeeping

**Tabulating equipment.** If the milling operation is large enough to maintain sufficient volume of daily work to keep the equipment busy, tabulating equipment is ideal. Selling for immediate to 120 days' delivery presents the constant problem of unfilled sales control. Punching a card at date of sale with all cost factors provides a means of perpetual control. Deliveries can be applied and daily balances, by grades, maintained. End-of-the-month or accounting-period calculations of standard cost of deliveries and unfilled sales is an easy job by tabulating, whereas it is a tremendous chore by manual calculation. Labor distribution as made on Figure 11 can be handled entirely by tabulating, as can all other statistical data. Volume must be the controlling factor, however, and a small milling organization having only one or two locations cannot often justify a tabulating installation.

Machine accounting, on the other hand, is probably as useful to the small miller as to the large miller in eliminating cumbersome ledgers and hand posting.

Machine accounting for control of outstanding warehouse receipts is practical and is used by a great many milling and grain firms.

# 24

# Food Canning and Freezing

by

**A. J. HOEFER**

Vice President, Libby, McNeill & Libby, Chicago

## Industry characteristics that affect the accounting system

**Nature of the business.** The canning and freezing industries cover a wide field of products and have many special problems. Although non-seasonal products do not involve significant or unusual accounting problems, the processing of seasonal products by canning or freezing does entail some problems and procedures that are unlike those of most other industries.

"Canning," as used in this text, refers to the process of preserving foods by heat in a can or glass jar; "freezing" refers to the preservation of food by freezing at sub-zero temperatures, whether packed in a tin can, carton, or other type of container. Both canners and freezers may use the tin can as a container.

The procedures described are those primarily suited to seasonal products because of their greater complexity; the adaptation of these procedures to nonseasonal products is fairly simple.

**Types of establishments.** The principal types of establishments are:

1. Single-plant, single-product companies
2. Multiple-plant, single-product companies
3. Single-plant, multiple-product companies
4. Multiple-plant, multiple-product companies

The use of more than one plant in a regional production area may be said to be one of the peculiarities of the seasonal processing industry. It results from the fact that highly perishable raw products can be transported only limited distances from the area of production to the processing plant; more than one plant is therefore required to support large-volume operations. Simple examples are canned cling peaches produced in California and canned peas produced in the Midwest, for each of which there are several multiple-plant companies operating in the respective areas.

The accounting for the several types of establishments is essentially the same, but in the case of a multiple-plant company that packs a particular product at more than one plant in a common producing area, it is frequently desirable to pool the costs and the income accounts of the several plants for that product, if sales are made out of the common pool rather than by individual plants. Although the use of pooled costs and income accounts is not necessary, it tends toward simplification and meets the situation realistically.

**Governmental control.** In order to protect the public health, various laws have been passed, the most important of which is the Federal Food, Drug and Cosmetic Act, adopted in 1938. This act superseded what was commonly known as the Wiley Act, passed by Congress on June 30, 1906. The present law applies to food products shipped in interstate commerce and prohibits adulteration and misbranding of foods; it also provides for definitions and standards of identity, quality, and fill of container. Administration of the act is handled by the United States Food and Drug Administration, and rules, regulations, and standards pertaining thereto are published in the *Federal Register* as issued.

Meats and meat products shipped in interstate commerce are governed by the Meat Inspection Law of 1907. This law provides, among other things, for inspection at the packing house and processing establishment by inspectors of the Meat Inspection Division of the Livestock Branch, Production and Marketing Administration, United States Department of Agriculture.

Plants processing certain sea foods or poultry products may voluntarily apply for Federal inspection and certification. The Food and Drug Administration has jurisdiction over specified sea foods, and the Production and Marketing Administration of the Department of Agriculture has jurisdiction over poultry products. In addition, the Production and Marketing Administration offers a grading service for any processor who desires it for determining and certifying the quality of canned fruits and vegetables.

States likewise have laws governing the handling and processing of food products. In addition, there exist both Federal and state authorities for certain "Marketing Orders" which may regulate the grading and, in some cases, the quantities of the raw products that may be harvested and used for canning. The Marketing Orders may authorize assessments against growers or processors, or both, for advertising purposes.

The fishing industry in United States waters is subject to regulations by the Fish and Wildlife Service of the United States Department of the Interior, and in international waters by certain international commissions.

The foregoing represents a thumbnail sketch of the most important areas of governmental control of the food industry. Except in war emergencies, there have been no governmental controls of prices, volume of production, or quantities, sizes or kind of containers or packaging materials used by the industry.

**Taxes and license fees.** In general, there are no taxes or license fees that are peculiar to this industry, other than those that are of a local nature and fees for inspection services relating to governmental controls described in the preceding paragraphs. Certain states, counties, and municipalities have sales and business tax laws that in some cases apply to food products and in others exempt them. In general, the taxes applying to this industry are the same as those applying to all industry within the area.

**General features.** *Competition.* The canning and freezing industries include many thousands of establishments and companies, both large and small. Sales competition is intense, and the industries have long been subject to fluctuating profit margins. Nonseasonal products, such as canned pork and beans, spaghetti, and many others, are customarily sold at narrow margins; margins on seasonal products, on the other hand, may fluctuate widely, depending upon the adequacy or inadequacy of supply. Although a short crop, occasioned by adverse weather, would normally permit higher selling prices, increases in price are restrained by selling prices of competing products, both processed and fresh. Furthermore, higher selling prices are usually offset in large measure, if not entirely, by higher costs arising from reduced production volume. A few companies, through research and successful advertising, have developed excellent consumer franchises for specialized products that are relatively unaffected by the normal competitive conditions in the industry.

*Seasonal influences.* The major part of canned and frozen food production consists of seasonal products, necessitating relatively large working capital and also large risk. Ordinarily, canners and freezers must contract with growers in the spring or earlier for seasonal vegetables that will not mature until summer or fall. At that time the processors must, in a relatively short harvest season, produce a supply large enough to last the ensuing twelve months. This high seasonality also limits plant utilization to a short period for many products, which results in high fixed investment per unit of production.

*Joint products, by-products.* In the case of many raw products, the finished products fall into various quality grades, each of which has a different selling price, although the raw product may have been bought at a uniform or average price. The various grades or varieties obtained from a ton of raw produce may therefore be described as "joint products" as distinguished from "by-products" which are obtained from residual waste.

By-products in the canning and freezing industries vary; in the citrus industry, by-products consist of cattle feed made from citrus peel, molasses made from juices pressed out of the peel, lemon oil extracted from lemon peels, and citric acid. Pineapple by-product yields vinegar, alcohol, citric acid, and sugar. Apricots yield apricot pits, from which oil is extracted. Fish residues are reduced to fertilizer. Pea vines and sweet corn cobs and husks are frequently fed to livestock as silage, but in some areas they are chopped up and ploughed into the soil to supply humus. For still other products, the residue is simply a worthless waste involving considerable expense to dispose of or destroy.

**Functional peculiarities.** *Buying and receiving.* This function has several variations and in turn consists of several functions. Seasonal vegetables are usually obtained by contracting with growers to plant a specified acreage, with the processor frequently furnishing the seed, doing the harvesting in order to insure harvesting when quality is best, and furnishing containers (field boxes) and transportation to plant.

Citrus fruits in some areas are purchased from co-operative associations and hauled in bulk loads to the processor's plant. Most other fruits are purchased just prior to harvest, are harvested by the grower, and delivered in field boxes supplied by the processor to the processor at a designated roadside point, processing plant, or receiving station.

Some processors who operate multiple plants in a general area maintain field receiving stations from which raw produce may be dispatched to any one of the several plants as needed. Peas must be "vined" or shelled, which is done by mechanical viners usually stationed in the growing area and operated by the processor at his expense.

Many processors render the service of spraying growers' fields against insects and other pests, and either charge growers for this service (resulting in a gain or loss from this operation) or absorb it themselves. All these subsidiary functions must be provided for in the organization and in the accounting of the processor.

*Production.* Generally, production problems are somewhat similar to production problems in any well-established industry, but they have the following distinguishing characteristics:

1. All supply requirements must be well provided for, because perishable raw produce cannot be held.

2. Work shifts fluctuate in varying degrees, owing to the effect of weather upon the maturity of the crops. With little exception, each day's receipts of raw produce must be processed that day.

3. Decisions as to the grades of product to be packed must be made immediately each day in the light of the quality of the raw produce received.

4. If bumper crops materialize which are beyond the capacity of the

plant to handle, quick and sound decisions must be made as to what to do with the excess. Frequently it is better to by-pass the excess rather than to risk continuing product deterioration by falling behind.

*Selling.* The majority of processors sell through established canned food and frozen food brokers who receive a brokerage or commission for their services. Some such processors sell direct to chain store organizations. Most such sales are made under the buyer's label. The larger multiple-plant processors who sell under their own labels or brands frequently maintain their own field sales forces operating out of branch sales offices, occasionally supplemented by brokers in restricted areas.

*Financing of customers.* Because of the processors' heavy investment in seasonal inventories, the industry does not lend itself to financing customers. From time to time, however, the better-financed members of the industry have granted customers extended payment terms in order to induce customers to stock up heavily, a practice that normally is not economically feasible because of the low margins and heavy working capital requirements in the industry. On the other hand, it is not uncommon for large buyers, who buy for their own label, to make advances to their processor suppliers against future production for which they have contracted.

**Financing peculiarities.** The large working capital requirements of the industry make it necessary to finance a substantial part of seasonal production through short-term bank borrowings. Usually, for the better-financed processors, this takes the form of unsecured promissory notes; however, for the majority of the industry, seasonal borrowings on promissory notes are secured by pledging inventories and placing them in the custody of a bonded field warehousing organization.

**Principal accounting problems.** Areas that present notable accounting differences from most other industries are:

1. The allocation of raw-product costs between several grades or kinds of product (joint products) packed therefrom.

2. Allocation of labor to "joint products" made from a single raw product.

3. Allocation of factory burden.

4. Treatment of postponed costs, such as the costs of labeling and casing, when finished product is stored unlabeled and uncased, to be later labeled with a buyer's label.

Each of these unique problems is discussed in subsequent sections.

## Functional organization

**Division into departments or activities.** A small organization is normally divided by functions as follows:

| | |
|---|---|
| Sales | Production |
| Procurement | Transportation |
| Farming, if any | Financial |
| Purchasing | Accounting |

In a larger enterprise, having multiple plants or divisions, the responsibility for administration of regional plants or divisions would customarily be delegated to a vice president, which would give rise to an organization structure approximately as shown in Figure 1.  The lines of authority indicated in the chart must of necessity vary to fit each individual organization.  The chart shows the controller as having staff authority over the accounting functions in the production divisions, but he may also have direct line authority.

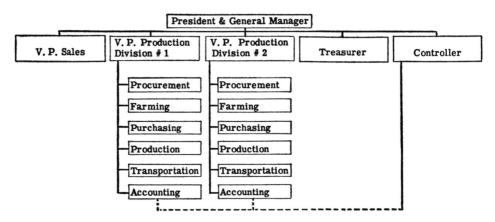

**Fig. 1. Organization Chart.**

## Principles and objectives of the system

**Principles to be applied in reflecting income, costs, and expenses.**  The obvious purpose of an accounting system is to provide management with accurate and detailed information with which to guide the business and to furnish essential reports to stockholders.  With respect to income, cost of sales, and expense accounts, this aim necessitates a segregation or analysis by products.  Segregation of income and expense in the accounts between sizes and grades of product is possible but hardly practical or necessary, as profit trends on individual items can be adequately determined by reference to the unit costs.

In reflecting the source of income, product sales in units and dollars, as well as deductions from sales (such as transportation costs, cash discounts, trade discounts, returned merchandise, and allowances for spoils) and net sales, should be posted to columnar sales analysis journals.  The bookkeeping may be done either manually or, if the scope of the operation warrants it, by bookkeeping machines or punch-card accounting machines. The end result should be the determination of gross and net income by individual products. Where there are several plants packing an identical product within a common geographical region, the sales and costs may, and probably should, be pooled; but where a particular product is packed in more than one geographical region, it would be preferable to segregate the sales by regions.

In accounting for costs, it is similarly essential that costs of raw product, labor, supplies, royalties, and all other direct expenses be allocated by product and also by plants, if more than one plant is involved. However, where there are several plants packing an identical product within a common geographical region, these costs may be combined or pooled. In that case, there must then be added to the direct costs described above a pro-rata share of plant overhead expense or burden, as described at page 696.

Expenses of a common nature, such as general expense, selling, broker-age, and advertising expenses, should be distributed pro rata to products on the basis of sales volume wherever no direct allocation is possible. However, if sales expense or brokerage is incurred in different proportions for different products, an actual distribution of such allocable expenses should be made in columnar analysis ledgers. Similarly, direct advertising of specific products should be allocated to the products advertised wher-ever possible. Where there is a common brand for several products, the advertising of a specific product under the common brand will undoubt-edly benefit all products sold under that brand. In this case, a certain pro-portion of the advertising cost may be apportioned to the several products involved, with the product directly advertised bearing the remainder. Since there is no certain mathematical formula for such apportionment, each company must use its own best judgment, in the light of the facts involved, to make the best possible determination.

Other expenses that merit careful study of their allocation are ware-housing and shipping and interest expense. The former may vary among the products as to cost per unit, because one product may require a longer warehousing period than another; therefore, this cost should be analyzed and distributed among products as accurately as possible. Similarly, in-terest expense will vary among products because of variations in capital employed in the several products and in the periods of time for which in-ventories must be carried. This expense should be allocated to products on the basis of the relative amount of capital employed.

**Specific objectives of the system.** The objectives of the system should be to produce a profit or loss statement for each product and supporting cost analyses showing computations of the unit costs of each item of the product line.

# Classification of accounts and books of account

## Balance sheet accounts.

| ASSETS | Debits from | Credits from |
|---|---|---|
| **Cash:** | | |
| Petty Cash .................... | Cash Book | |
| Bank Accounts ............... | Cash Collections Journal, Cash Book | Accounts Payable Distribution, Payroll Distribution, Raw Produce Distribution |
| Marketable Securities ........... | Accounts Payable Distribution | Cash Collections Journal |
| **Notes and Accounts Receivable:** | | |
| Customers' Notes ............. | Accounts Receivable Ledger | Do |
| Customers' Accounts .......... | Sales Journal | Do |
| Growers' Accounts ............ | Cash Book, Sales Journal | Raw Produce Distribution |
| Claims ...................... | Sales Journal or Journal Entry | Cash Collections Journal |
| Reserve for Bad Debts (Credit).. | Accounts Receivable | Journal Entries |
| **Inventories:** | | |
| Finished Product ............. | Inventory | |
| Transportation Paid on Finished Product ................... | Accounts Payable Distribution | Do |
| Casing and Labelling Reserve (Credit) ................... | Journal Entry | Do |
| Work in Process .............. | Inventory | |
| Raw Materials ................ | Do | |
| Supplies ..................... | Do | |
| Growing Crops ................ | Payroll, Accounts Payable Distribution, Journal Entries | Raw Produce Distribution |
| **Deferred Operating Expense:** | | |
| Factory Cost Ledger Control .... | *See Subsidiary Ledger (page 686)* | |
| Finished Pack Account (Credit).. | Journal Entry | Journal Entry |
| **Other Current Assets:** | | |
| Prepaid Insurance ............. | Accounts Payable Distribution | Do |
| Deposits ..................... | Do | Do |
| Investments .................. | Do | Cash Collections Journal |
| **Long-Term Advances:** | | |
| To Growers .................. | Cash Book | Raw Produce Distribution |
| Others ...................... | Do | Do |
| Plant and Equipment Control ..... | Accounts Payable Distribution, Payrolls, Journal Entries | Sales Journal, Journal Entries |

|  | *Debits from* | *Credits from* |
|---|---|---|
| Depreciation Reserve Control (credit) |  | Journal Entries |
| Construction in Progress .......... | Accounts Payable Distribution, Payrolls, Journal Entries | Plant and Equipment Ledger |
| Deferred Charges ............... | Accounts Payable Distribution, Journal Entries | Journal Entries |
| Other Assets .................... | Do | Journal Entries, Cash Collections Journal |

## LIABILITIES AND CAPITAL

| | | |
|---|---|---|
| **Notes Payable:** | | |
| Notes Payable, Banks .......... | Cash Book | Cash Book, Accounts Payable Distribution, or Journal Entry |
| Notes Payable, Others .......... | Do | Do |
| Drafts Payable ............... | Do | Do |
| **Accounts Payable:** | | |
| Trade ....................... | Do | Accounts Payable Distribution |
| Growers ..................... | Do | Raw Produce Distribution |
| Brokers ..................... | Do | Accounts Payable Distribution |
| Customers' Deposits .......... | Cash Collections Journal or Journal Entry | Cash Collections Journal |
| Officers and Employees ........ | Cash Book | Cash Collections Journal, Payrolls |
| **Taxes Payable:** | | |
| Federal Income Taxes .......... | Cash Book, Journal Entries | Journal Entries |
| Other Taxes ................... | Do | Do |
| **Accrued Liabilities:** | | |
| Salaries and Wages ............. | Cash Book | Payroll Distribution |
| Insurance .................... | Do | Accounts Payable Distribution or Journal Entry |
| Interest ...................... | Do | Do |
| Royalties .................... | Do | Accounts Payable Distribution |
| Others ....................... | Do | Do |
| Long-Term Debt ............... | Do | Cash Collections Journal |
| Reserves ..................... | Journal Entries | Journal Entries |
| **Capital Stock:** | | |
| Common ..................... | | Do |
| Preferred ................... | | Do |
| Capital Surplus ................ | Do | Do |
| Earned Surplus ............... | Do | Do |

## Income and expense accounts.

|  | *Debits from* | *Credits from* |
|---|---|---|
| Sales (credit) .................. | Sales Journal | Sales Journal |
| Transportation ................. | Accounts Payable Distribution | |
| Price Adjustments .............. | Sales Journal or Accounts Payable Distribution | |
| Trade Discounts ................ | Sales Journal | |
| Returned Goods ................ | Do | |
| Cash Discount .................. | Cash Collections Journal | |
| Cost of Goods Sold: | | |
|   Opening Inventory ............ | Inventory | |
|   Cost of Production ............ | Journal Entry (Pack Transfer account) | |
|   Outside Purchases ............ | Accounts Payable Distribution | |
|   Used in Remanufacture ........ | Journal Entry | |
|   Closing Inventory ............. | | Inventory |
| Warehouse and Shipping Expense... | Accounts Payable Distribution | |
| Brokerage Paid ................. | Do | |
| Selling Expense ................ | Do | |
| Advertising .................... | Do | |
| General and Administrative Expense | Payrolls | |
| Interest Expense ............... | Accounts Payable Distribution, Cash Collections Journal | |
| Other Income and Expense ....... | Journal Entry | Cash Collections Journal, Journal Entry |
| Income Taxes .................. | Do | |

All of the foregoing accounts are closed out to Earned Surplus by journal entries.

**Factory Cost Ledger accounts** (Subsidiary Ledger). A separate account must be kept for each product, for each of the prime cost accounts shown below. This procedure can be considerably simplified by the ingenious adaptation of columnar ledger sheets.

|  | *Debits from* | *Credits from* |
|---|---|---|
| Produce: | | |
|   Open Inventory .............. | Inventory | |
|   Purchases ................... | Raw Produce Distribution | |
|   Harvesting .................. | Accounts Payable Distribution, Payrolls | Sales Journal (Invoices to Growers) |
|   Sales ....................... | | Sales Journal |
|   Transportation .............. | Accounts Payable Distribution | |
|   Storage and Handling ......... | Accounts Payable Distribution, Payrolls | |

|  | *Debits from* | *Credits from* |
|---|---|---|
| Receiving Expense ............. | Accounts Payable Distribution, Payrolls | |
| Pea Viners Expense ............ | Do | |
| Buying Expense ............... | Do | |
| Seed and Plants Expense ....... | Journal Entry (for usage) | Sales Journal (Invoices to Growers) |
| Closing Inventory .............. | | Inventory |

Ingredient Supplies:

| | | |
|---|---|---|
| Sugar ........................ | } Accounts Payable Distribution, Inventory | |
| Vinegar ...................... | | Do |
| Salt .......................... | | |
| Others ....................... | | |

Package Supplies:

| | | |
|---|---|---|
| Cans ......................... | | |
| Glass Jars and Caps ........... | | |
| Cooperage ................... | | |
| Labels ....................... | } Accounts Payable Distribution, Inventory | |
| Imprinting Labels ............. | | Do |
| Cartons ...................... | | |
| Wraps ....................... | | |
| Fiber Cases .................. | | |
| Strapping and Wire Materials.... | | |

| | | |
|---|---|---|
| Direct Labor ................... | Payroll | |
| Casing and Label Labor ......... | Do | |
| Royalties ..................... | Accounts Payable Distribution | |

**Factory overhead accounts.** The following accounts are not segregated by products, except in totals as outlined at page 696.

|  | *Debits from* |
|---|---|

*Fixed Factory Overhead Expenses:*

Plant Administrative:

| | |
|---|---|
| Superintendent, Assistant Superintendent and General Foremen ......................... | Payroll |
| Employment and Industrial Relations .......... | Do |
| Clerical and Timekeepers ..................... | Do |
| Traveling .................................. | Accounts Payable Distribution |
| Stationery and Postage ...................... | Do |
| Telephone, Telegrams, Teletype ............... | Do |
| General Expense ............................ | Do |

Depreciation:

| | |
|---|---|
| Buildings .................................. | Journal Entry |
| Equipment and others ....................... | Do |
| Taxes—Real Estate .......................... | Accounts Payable Distribution |
| Insurance—Fire—Fixed Property ............... | Do |
| Rent—Building, Equipment, Etc. ............... | Do |
| Protection ................................. | Payroll |
| Laboratory ................................. | Do |

*Debits from*

Variable Factory Overhead Expenses.

| | |
|---|---|
| Indirect Labor: | |
| Departmental Foremen ...................... | Payroll |
| Plant Janitors ............................. | Do |
| Miscellaneous ............................. | Do |
| Payroll Expense: | |
| Social Security Taxes ....................... | Accounts Payable Distribution |
| Casualty Insurance ......................... | Do |
| Health and Welfare Cost .................... | Accounts Payable Distribution or Payroll |
| Pension Expense ........................... | Journal Entry |
| Group Insurance ........................... | Accounts Payable Distribution |
| Vacation, Holiday, and Disability Pay ........ | Payrolls |
| Repairs and Maintenance: | |
| Buildings ........................... ⎫ | ⎧ Payroll Distribution, Accounts |
| Equipment and Others .............. ⎬ | ⎨ Payable Distribution, |
| Changing Product Lines ............ ⎭ | ⎩ Journal Entries |
| Taxes: | |
| Personal Property | Accounts Payable Distribution |
| Other Taxes, Licenses, etc. .................... | Do |
| Insurance: | |
| Fire—Raw Stock and Supplies ................ | Do |
| Other ....................................... | Do |
| Heat, Light, Power: | |
| Gas, Oil, Coal, Steam ....................... | Do |
| Electric, Power, and Light ................... | Do |
| Water ....................................... | Do |
| Engineers, Firemen, Electricians .............. | Payroll |
| Operating Supplies: | |
| Mechanical ................................. | Accounts Payable Distribution |
| Sanitation and Others ....................... | Do |
| Sundry Operating Expense: | |
| Miscellaneous Auto and Truck Expense ........ | Accounts Payable Distribution, Journal Entries, Payrolls |
| First Aid Room ............................. | Accounts Payable Distribution, Payrolls |
| Sewage and Waste Disposal ................... | Do |
| Plant Spoils ................................ | Journal Entries |
| Plant Samples ............................... | Do |

**Books peculiar to the business.** The only basic book of account that is different from those ordinarily maintained in other industries is the Factory Cost Ledger, explained at page 698.

**Accounts peculiar to the business.** The following accounts, peculiar to the industry cost system, are explained at the pages indicated:

1. *Finished Pack Account* (see page 698).
2. *Factory Cost Ledger Account* (see page 698).
3. *Casing and Labelling Reserve Account* (see page 703).

## Peculiarities of procedures: sales-receivables cycle; purchases-payables cycle; cash receipts and disbursements

**Accounting for sales.**  This category involves:

Gross Sales
Deductions from Sales:
  Transportation absorbed
  Trade discounts
  Cash discounts
  Returned goods
  Allowances for trade spoils
Net Sales

Each of the above categories of sales and sales deductions should be posted to sales analysis journals which provide for product analysis—one for each category, unless the plant packs only a single product, in which event all categories may be posted to a single journal.  Simplified examples of the Gross Sales account and the Transportation account in the distribution journals are shown in Figures 2 and 3.

| | DISTRIBUTION JOURNAL | | | | | | | | | Account *Gross Sales* | |
| | | | | | | | | | | Month *January 19–* | |
| Invoice # | Product A | | Product B | | Product C | | Product D | | Product E | | Total | |
| | Cases | Amount | Cases | Amount | Cases | Amount | Cases | Amount | Cases | Amount | Cases | Amount |
| 100 | 30 | 150 00 | 10 | 42 00 | 80 | 240 00 | | | | | 120 | 387 00 |
| 101 | | | | | | | 200 | 390 00 | | | 200 | 390 00 |
| 102 | | | | | 50 | 150 00 | 100 | 195 00 | 50 | 190 00 | 200 | 535 00 |

Source of entry: sales invoices

**Fig. 2. Distribution Journal—Gross Sales Account.**

| | DISTRIBUTION JOURNAL | | | | | | | | | Account *Transportation* | |
| | | | | | | | | | | Month *January 19–* | |
| Source | Product A | | Product B | | Product C | | Product D | | Product E | | Total | |
| Vo. 1 | | | | | | | 30 00 | | | | | 30 00 |
| 2 | | | | | | | | | 43 10 | | | 43 10 |
| 3 | | | | | | | 19 10 | | 75 20 | | | 94 30 |

Source of entry; accounts payable vouchers or cash book

**Fig. 3. Distribution Journal—Transportation Account.**

It is not uncommon in the canning and freezing industries for certain products to be sold F.O.B. processing plant, while others are sold F.O.B. buyer's town, or F.O.B. designated basing points, thus necessitating the prepayment and absorption of transportation cost.  Obviously, if all sales are made F.O.B. processing plant, the accounts for handling freight charges become unnecessary.

Distribution sheets similar to that shown in Figure 3 should be maintained for each category of sales deductions.

Figure 4 is a simplified illustration of a distribution journal for a one-product operation.

In a large-volume operation, either bookkeeping machines or punch-card accounting may be utilized to provide the necessary distribution. If punch-card accounting is used, an excellent and valuable by-product—sales statistics by customers—will be provided for use in sales promotion.

**DISTRIBUTION JOURNAL**

Month _January 19—_

| Reference | Cases | Amount | Trans-portation | Trade Discount | Returned Goods | Trade Spoils |
|---|---|---|---|---|---|---|
| Invoice #100 | 280 | 840 00 | | 42 00 | | 2 10 |
| 100 | 50 | 150 00 | | 7 50 | | 38 |

Source of entry: sales invoices

**Fig. 4. Distribution Journal (One-Product Operation).**

**Billing and accounts receivable procedures.** Although billing and accounts receivable procedures in most cases are substantially identical in principle with other manufacturing businesses, the following peculiarities which frequently exist are worthy of note:

1. It is quite common to draw drafts on customers with documents attached. This practice involves a collection charge, which is chargeable to General Expense.

2. The accounts receivable may be sold to a factor for collection. This type of transaction involves a collection charge by the factor and an interest (or discount) charge.

3. If inventories are pledged to secure short-term or other indebtedness, a release of inventory from the custodian is required, and the proceeds of the draft are applied in whole or in part by the bank to the reduction of the indebtedness.

**Cash receipts procedures.** If customers are sold on open credit terms, cash receipts are handled in the ordinary manner by debiting the Cash or Bank Account and crediting the customer's account receivable. If drafts are drawn, the entry is the same, except that the collection charge deducted by the bank is charged to General Expense (sub-account, Collection Costs). If the draft is discounted at the bank, the discount is chargeable to interest expense. This is also the case when the accounts receivable are sold and the invoice is assigned to the factor. In the latter instances, assuming an invoice issued for $1,000.00 with cash discount of 1% for payment in ten days, collection charges of $\frac{1}{8}$%, and interest at 6% per annum, the following entry would result:

| | | | |
|---|---|---|---|
| Dr. | Bank Account | $987.77 | |
| Dr. | General Expense (Collection Costs) | 1.24 | |
| Dr. | Cash Discount | 10.00 | |
| Dr. | Interest Expense | .99 | |
| Cr. | Accounts Receivable | | $1,000.00 |

The recording of this and other entries affecting cash can be simplified by the use of a columnar cash collections journal.

**Purchase order and receiving procedures.** The receiving of ordinary supplies, such as containers, packaging and shipping materials, ingredients, and operating supplies presents no unusual problems, but there are some special problems involved in the buying and receiving of raw produce which necessitate the use of sound procedures and the maintenance of tight controls.

Raw produce is customarily purchased on a buying contract designed to meet competitive practices in each area. This contract usually establishes the number of acres or tons of produce to be grown, seed varieties to be used, cultural practices to be used, time and method of harvesting, grades of raw product to be delivered, price to be paid for each grade, and tolerances for produce that does not meet quality requirements. It is customary for processors to work closely with growers to schedule the time of harvesting and delivery. Upon delivery to the processing plant or to the processor's receiving station, a weight certificate is issued setting forth the number of boxes, crates, hampers, or bags (or other types of containers delivered), the gross weight, tare weight of vehicle, tare weight of containers, and net weight of produce. Grades are determined in most cases by sampling—in some cases by actual hand or mechanical grading—and the percentage of weight of each grade found to be present in the sample is then applied to the entire load. Because of the variability of loads of raw produce and its great effect upon production costs, close supervision over weights and grades of raw produce must be maintained. Since the raw produce must be processed quickly, opportunities to recheck or to locate and correct errors are limited. Periodic reconciliations (not less than daily) should be made between the number of containers of raw produce for which weight certificates are issued and the number of boxes run through the plant.

**Accounts payable procedures.** With the exception of raw produce, accounts payable procedures and purchase and expense distribution can follow ordinary procedures suitable for segregating expenses into the categories required.

Practices respecting the payment for raw produce vary widely, by areas and products. Some crops may be paid for on an individual-load basis, with the weight certificate already mentioned being a part of the check, separated by a perforation. Some crops may be paid for on a weekly basis or even at the end of the season—a practice which necessitates summarizing the deliveries (weight certificates) of each grower on a statement form that may be a detachable part of a check or separate from it (see Figure 5).

| Statement of deliveries by | | | | | Week ending 6/9/— |
|---|---|---|---|---|---|
| Weight Certificate | Boxes | Pounds No. 1 | Pounds No. 2 | Culls | Total |
| 3920 | 500 | 16,000 | 3,000 | 1,000 | 20,000 |
| 3987 | 385 | 13,010 | 1,820 | 390 | 15,220 |
| 4113 | 420 | 10,150 | 5,650 | 700 | 16,500 |
| TOTAL | 1,305 | 39,160 | 10,470 | 2,090 | 51,720 |
| Price per ton | | 60.00 | 30.00 | — | |
| Value | | 1,174.80 | 157.05 | | 1,331.85 |
| Less: Seed advances | | | | | 159.00 |
| Fertilizer advances | | | | | 210.00 |
| Cash advances | | | | | 100.00 |
| Net payment herewith | | | | | 862.85 |

**Fig. 5. Statement Accompanying Payment for Raw Produce.**

Payments made to all growers may be summarized from copies of each grower's statement into a grand total for the product, and a single summary entry made to the accounts for the produce paid for each day, or at the end of each week, or at the end of the season, depending upon when the checks are issued.

**Basis of allocation of distribution expense items.** Since the objective of the system is to provide profit and loss information by product line, distribution expenses should be allocated by product. This can be done by utilizing a distribution journal (see page 689) for multiple products wherever the kind of expense lends itself to direct allocation. Expenses to be allocated are:

1. General (including administrative) expense
2. Selling expense
3. Brokerage
4. Advertising
5. Warehousing and shipping
6. Interest expense

With the exception of brokerage, these expenses may not be directly allocable to products. The principles of allocation are outlined at page 683.

*Statistical records.* Obviously, the need for statistical records depends upon the size and scope of the business. In a business of limited size, a duplicate file of invoices, filed by customers, will serve as a substantial basis for all its statistical needs. From these statistics customer sales analysis can be prepared by product items sold; reference to the customers' accounts receivable will provide the total dollar billings. The method and extent of summarizing will obviously be determined by the number and complexity of transactions; if transactions are numerous, the use of machine accounting methods may prove practical.

Since most canner and freezer processors sell through brokers, the sales statistical records must also provide the sales volume sold by each broker. These data can also be abstracted from a customer invoice file. The file can be used to prepare a brokerage settlement statement for each broker involved. Preparation of this statement is facilitated somewhat if the customer's invoice file is divided according to brokers, since usually a particular broker will be responsible for a certain geographical area. This information can also be provided by machine accounting methods.

Since it is customary to sell against future packs of seasonal products, it is important that a record of stock and sales be maintained, although this record does not involve the accounting books. It can be maintained most informatively on a seasonal (crop-year) basis.

Figure 6 is a hypothetical report prepared prior to the commencement of production, incorporating (1) an estimate of the pack and (2) a summary of the future sales against the proposed pack. After the pack is finished, the actual pack figures would be used instead of the estimate, and subsequent changes in supply occasioned by warehouse spoilage or regrading from one grade to another (as from fancy to extra-standard or choice grade) would be reflected in the Regrades and Spoils column.

| | | | STOCK AND SALES REPORT | | Product: Spinach Date: March 15, 19— | |
| --- | --- | --- | --- | --- | --- | --- |
| *Item* | *Carryover 3/1/—* | *Estimated Pack* | *Regrades and Spoils* | *Total Stock* | *Sales* | *Unsold or Oversold* |
| 24/303 Fancy | 1,800 | 20,000 | | 21,800 | 20,000 | 1,800 |
| 24/2 " | — | | | | | |
| 24/2½ " | 500 | 10,000 | | 10,500 | 8,000 | 2,500 |
| 6/10 " | 100 | 5,000 | | 5,100 | 5,100 | — |
| TOTAL | 2,400 | 35,000 | | 37,400 | 33,100 | 4,400 |

Fig. 6. Stock and Sales Report.

## Production and cost system

**Estimated costs and actual costs.** As soon as production plans are made for any product, an estimated cost should be prepared. The form and the method for preparing either estimated or actual costs are substantially the same. Estimated costs, however, must be based upon:

1. Past historical experience.

2. An appraisal of the variations or improvements expected to occur in the forthcoming season.

3. Current costs and expected yields of raw produce, and current costs of supplies and labor.

4. An estimate of factory overhead or burden, and the rate at which it will have to be charged to each pack during the season to absorb fully the expense for the year.

In contrast to the foregoing, actual costs are an historical calculation based obviously on the actual costs incurred and yields obtained. The process can best be illustrated by reviewing the records and the methods to be used in calculating actual costs.

**Labor and materials controls.** The basis for this control is the Daily Product Cost and Yield Report. (See Figure 7.) This report sets forth the day's production by grades and sizes of product, the quantities of raw produce used, the *yield* of raw produce in terms of the percentage of prepared produce (after trimming and preparation) packed into the finished containers compared with the purchased weight, the ingredients and supplies used, and the labor costs. The daily reports may be summarized on a cumulative basis, and must be summarized at the end of each pack to provide the basis for a total cost for that pack.

Finished production, raw produce, and supplies used must be tallied each day and should be periodically reconciled with purchases and inventory.

From cost and yield reports, entries are made at the end of each month or may be made at the end of each seasonal pack to the Factory Cost Ledger, described at page 698.

A daily labor cost distribution should be made if possible. Time cards should provide space for distribution of the employee's time between products and product operations. (See Figure 11, page 705.)

Variations of this procedure are possible; for example, the departmental foreman may keep a record of hours worked by employees, by product operations, in a log or time book, which may serve as the basis for the labor distribution. In that event, a weekly time card may be used. This method makes for somewhat greater difficulty in balancing the labor distribution with the payroll, but if exercised judiciously, it can be sufficient for practical accuracy.

PRODUCT COST AND YIELD REPORT

Product ____CORN____

Date ____September 15, 19—____

## PRODUCTION

| Item | Actual Cases Packed | 24/303 Case Conversion Factor (See Note) | Equivalent Converted Cases | Cans Used | Fiber Cases Used |
|---|---|---|---|---|---|
| 48/8 oz. Fancy Cream Style | 1,429 | 1.00 | | 68,660 | 1,440 |
| 24/303 Fancy Cream Style | 3,510 | 1.00 | | 84,320 | 3,527 |
| 24/303 Extra Standard C.S. | 1,895 | 1.00 | | 45,511 | 1,905 |
| 48/8 oz. Fancy Whole Kernel | 1,605 | 1.00 | | 77,117 | 1,617 |
| 24/303 Fancy Whole Kernel | 6,543 | 1.00 | | 157,167 | 6,574 |
| 24/303 Extra Standard W.K. | — | | | | |
| 24/303 Standard Whole Kernel | 27 | 1.00 | | 650 | 28 |
| Total | 15,009 | | 15,009 | 433,425 | 15,091 |

## PRODUCE AND INGREDIENTS

| | Tons | Cost |
|---|---|---|
| Raw Produce Used.. | 333.38 | $8,304 |
| % #1 Grade .... | 96.5 | |
| #2 Grade .... | — | |
| Waste ........ | 3.5 | |
| Yield, Converted Cases Per Ton ... | 45.02 | |
| *Grade Yield:* | | |
| % Fancy ........ | 87.2 | |
| Extra Standard | 12.6 | |
| Standard ..... | .2 | |
| *Ingredients:* | *Pounds* | |
| Sugar ............ | 12,025 | |
| Salt ............ | 3,579 | |
| Corn Starch ..... | 1,025 | |

## LABOR COSTS

| | Amount | Per Converted Case |
|---|---|---|
| Receive ........ | $ 453 | .030 |
| Prepare ........ | 2,356 | .157 |
| Fill and Close... | 345 | .023 |
| Process ........ | 435 | .029 |
| Maintenance and Cleanup ...... | 750 | .050 |
| Case and Label.. | 660 | .044 |
| Pile ............ | 60 | .004 |
| Total ....... | $5,059 | .337 |

NOTE: Converted cases represents all cases converted to equivalent of 24/303 size (as 1.00) in the ratio of the relationship of cubic contents of the various can sizes. In the illustration, 48/8-oz. cans have the same cubic content per case as 24/303 (16-oz.) cans.

**Fig. 7. Daily Product Cost and Yield Report.**

The daily report illustrated in Figure 7 serves as a control of raw materials utilization, labor efficiency, and supply usage for the factory manager and other executive personnel. It also provides the cost accountant with the basic data to determine whether actual production costs are in line with the cost estimates and permits him to make revisions if necessary.

At the conclusion of the pack, a summary of the daily reports showing the season totals provides the necessary data for the construction of actual unit costs for the pack.

**Factory overhead (burden).** In a canning or freezing enterprise, much of the equipment and floor space are used for several products. It is therefore usually impractical to assign factory burden to different products at different specific rates. Moreover, the principle has long been recognized in these industries that factory burden should be absorbed by the products packed in proportion to their ability to bear. The simplest method, therefore, is to charge burden to product costs at a uniform percentage rate on the aggregate prime (direct) costs of production.

*Example:*

|  | Budgeted Production (Cases) | Prime Cost | Burden Assigned (Prime Cost × 15%) |
|---|---|---|---|
| Product A ...... | 286,000 | $ 569,545 | $ 85,780 |
| " B ...... | 500,000 | 1,054,347 | 158,153 |
| " C ...... | 350,000 | 887,000 | 133,000 |
| Total .......... | 1,136,000 | $2,510,892 | $376,933 |

Total factory burden = $376,933
($376,933 ÷ $2,510,892 = 15%)

The details of factory overhead show the dollar amount for each of the fixed and variable factory overhead expense accounts listed at pages 687 and 688.

For the purpose of simplicity, the above method of allocation of factory burden will be used in the ensuing examples and discussion. However, allocation of factory burden is by no means limited to this simple device. It would be quite proper to break down the factory burden into several groups of expense, if desired; for example:

*Group 1:* Plant supervision
Indirect labor
Janitor and cleanup
Casualty insurance
Vacation costs
Health and welfare costs
Pension costs

To be allocated among products (and sizes and grades of product) in proportion to direct labor costs.

*Group 2:* Fuel
Water
Power and light
Refrigeration
Firemen and engineers

To be allocated among products at a rate per case determined by experience tests, since it is known that certain products require more steam, refrigeration, or power than others.

*Group 3:* All other items of factory burden.
To be allocated among products in proportion to their prime costs.

Since weather and other conditions make it impossible to adhere to a pre-season budget, the rate of burden absorption must be revised from time to time in order that at the end of the year the full factory burden will have been absorbed.

**Work in process.** Because of the perishable nature of the raw products, work in process occurs only in specialized instances. It is, however, not uncommon for perishable raw produce to be canned or frozen for later use in remanufacture into mixed products; for example, peas and carrots, later combined into "peas and carrots," or corn and lima beans, later combined into succotash. In such cases, the original processed products (peas, carrots, lima beans, or corn) are treated as finished products when originally processed, and costs are calculated in the same manner as for any other finished product. When they are reused in manufacture, they are transferred from the inventory back into costs of production and start through another cycle of production. Since, however, in this second cycle they will not be required to undergo a complete preparation and processing operation, and since they will already have absorbed factory burden on their original prime cost, additional factory burden is included in the cost of the end product only to the extent that additional prime cost has been incurred.

A somewhat complex type of work in process occurs in the case of products that are first pickled or salted in brine, such as cucumbers for pickles, or cabbage for sauerkraut. These products reach the work-in-process state when they are salted in tanks, and all prime costs, plus a proper pro rata of factory burden, must be accumulated against them. Upon completion of cure, the accumulated aggregate costs, including the original cost of the raw product, are treated as the base product cost entering into the subsequent canning and processing operations. Here again, to avoid duplication, factory burden is added only on the additional prime cost incurred.

**Compilation of actual costs.** Because of the seasonal factors affecting most canning and freezing operations, it is usually impractical to close out production costs directly into Cost of Sales on any basis other than an annual basis. It is therefore expedient to accumulate all product manufacturing costs for the full operating year in a subsidiary ledger called the *Factory Cost Ledger,* and to credit to a contra account called the *Finished Pack account* all production that has been completed and charged to Cost of Sales. At the end of the year, the credits to the Finished Pack account must equal the costs and expenses accumulated in the factory cost ledger, and the one should then be closed out into the other.

**Factory cost ledger.**   This ledger is controlled by a control account in the general ledger bearing the same name, that is, Factory Cost Ledger, and contains the accounts described in the classification of accounts at page 686.   This ledger may be maintained on conventional ledger sheets if only a single plant is involved; but for a multiple-plant operation for which the accounting is done centrally, it is preferable to use columnar ledger sheets with a separate column for each plant.   In this ledger are accumulated all the product manufacturing costs, and it, together with the Daily Product Cost and Yield Report (Figure 7), provides the required information for the calculation of unit costs.

**Finished Pack account.**   This account may be maintained in the general ledger, but, since it is the contra account to the factory cost ledger, it can best be maintained in a separate section of that ledger.   Each month an entry is made debiting Cost of Sales and crediting the Finished Pack account for the factory cost value of production completed during the month, at the computed estimated costs.   When the pack of a particular product is finished, the entries made at estimated costs are adjusted to the final and actual costs.

**Calculation of unit costs.**   Periodically during the course of the pack of a product, the Daily Product Cost and Yield Report for the product is accumulated.   At the end of each month, the production totals shown thereon, multiplied by the unit costs, provide the basis for the entry described in the preceding paragraphs.   The utilization of supplies shown on the report furnishes the basis for the entry charging out the supplies used to the products on which used (Factory Cost Ledger).   At the end of the pack of each product, the Daily Product Cost and Yield Report also provides the necessary cumulative data from which actual unit costs are compiled.

*Apportionment of raw material costs among grades.*   Allocation of costs of raw materials and labor presents certain unique problems.   Raw produce purchased at a uniform price will usually pack out into several grades of finished product, and the cost of the raw product must be so apportioned that the more valuable grades of finished product bear a proportionately higher cost than the lower grades.

This apportionment requires the use of an allocation formula, the principle of which is that the relative value of produce of different finished grades must be in proportion to the selling prices of the respective finished products, less the direct costs of converting the raw product to the finished state.   However, such a formula based on the selling-price relationships of a single year may produce somewhat inequitable results if the price levels of that year should happen to be distorted from the normal relationship. It is therefore preferable to use the average of several years. The calculation of such produce-value relationships over a long period of years has given rise, in the cost accounting of many canners, to somewhat fixed differentials for each product, termed "grade differentials" or "relative value," which result in a simplified procedure. However, such fixed differentials must be tested from time to time to ascertain whether they remain representative of current trends. See example below.

Costs of ingredients such as sugar, salt, vinegar, and others represent no unusual problems. Comprehensive tests must be made to determine the quantity of each ingredient required per unit (case) of production; the actual usage of each must be allocated in proportion thereto, and any difference (excess or deficiency) should be carefully reconciled. This can in fact be done on a daily basis in order to provide effective operational cost control.

*Example:*

### COST OF RAW PRODUCE

| | |
|---|---:|
| Paid growers, 13,043,810 pounds | $143,481.91 |
| Buying cost | 9,842.30 |
| Net seed cost (difference between cost of seed and price charged growers) | 973.40 |
| Net harvesting expense (difference between cost of harvesting and price charged growers) | 1,664.80 |
| Transportation | 6,782.59 |
| Total | $162,745.00 |
| Equals per pound | .0125 |

### CALCULATION OF GRADE DIFFERENTIAL

| | Net Market Price Per Case | Less all Direct Costs (except Produce) | Difference in Market Value of Produce Per Case | Cases per Ton | Market Value of Produce Per Ton |
|---|---|---|---|---|---|
| 48/Buf. Fancy Cream-Style Corn | $4.15 | $1.80 | $2.35 | 44.33 | $104.17 |
| 24/303 Fancy Cream-Style Corn | 3.17 | 1.40 | 1.77 | 45.61 | 80.73 |
| 24/303 Extra Standard Cream-Style Corn | 2.43 | 1.40 | 1.03 | 45.61 | 46.98 |
| 48/Buf. Fancy Whole-Kernel Corn | 4.15 | 1.70 | 2.45 | 38.27 | 93.76 |
| 24/303 Fancy Whole-Kernel Corn | 3.17 | 1.30 | 1.87 | 38.27 | 71.56 |
| 24/303 Extra Standard Whole-Kernel Corn | 2.43 | 1.30 | 1.13 | 38.27 | 43.25 |
| 24/303 Standard Whole-Kernel Corn | 1.70 | 1.30 | .40 | 38.27 | 15.30 |

ALLOCATION OF RAW PRODUCE COST

| | | Grade Yield | | Market Value of Produce Per Ton | Grade Differ- ential (See Note) | Produce Cost Per Pound (See Note) |
|---|---|---|---|---|---|---|
| | | Tons | % | | | |
| *Fancy:* | | | | | | |
| 48/8 | Cream-Style Corn ...... | 564.000 | 8.65 | $104.17 | | |
| 24/303 | Cream-Style Corn ...... | 3,836.875 | 58.83 | 80.73 | | |
| 48/8 | Whole-Kernel Corn ..... | 130.650 | 2.00 | 93.76 | | |
| 24/303 | Whole-Kernel Corn ..... | 1,306.500 | 20.03 | 71.56 | | |
| | Weighted Average .... | 5,838.025 | 89.51 | $ 81.23 | 1.0472 | $.01309 |
| *Extra Standard:* | | | | | | |
| 24/303 | Cream-Style Corn ...... | 657.750 | 10.09 | 46.98 | | |
| 24/303 | Whole-Kernel Corn ..... | 13.065 | .20 | 43.25 | | |
| | Weighted Average .... | 670.815 | 10.29 | 46.91 | .6047 | .00756 |
| *Standard:* | | | | | | |
| 24/303 | Whole-Kernel Corn ..... | 13.065 | .20 | 15.30 | .1972 | .00246 |
| | | 6,521.905 | 100.00 | $ 77.57 | 1.0000 | $.01250 |

*Note:* The figures shown in the columns marked "See Note" are the relationships of the respective "market values of produce per ton" to $77.57, using $77.57 as 1.00 and $.01250, respectively.

*Allocation of labor costs.* Similarly, the allocation of direct labor expended on a product requires close analysis, which must be made on a departmental basis if it is to be accurate and effective. The analysis requires first the accumulation of basic test data.

*Example:*

ALLOCATION OF LABOR COSTS

CORN

| | Cream Style | | | Whole Kernel | | | |
|---|---|---|---|---|---|---|---|
| Labor Costs | *48/Buf.* | *24/303* | *Total* | *48/Buf.* | *24/303* | *Total* | *Grand Total* |
| Receiving .......... | $.029 | $.028 | $ 6,465 | $.023 | $.023 | $ 1,288 | $  7,753 |
| Preparation ........ | .179 | .174 | 40,145 | .164 | .164 | 9,184 | 49,329 |
| Canning (fill and close) | .034 | .014 | 3,720 | .046 | .022 | 1,352 | 5,072 |
| Cookroom ......... | .051 | .039 | 9,270 | .063 | .047 | 2,712 | 11,982 |
| Piling ............. | .002 | .002 | 460 | .002 | .002 | 112 | 572 |
| Mechanical ....... | .025 | .025 | 5,750 | .025 | .025 | 1,400 | 7,150 |
| Cleanup ........... | .030 | .028 | 6,490 | .027 | .027 | 1,512 | 8,002 |
| Case and label ..... | .050 | .040 | 9,450 | .050 | .040 | 2,290 | 11,740 |
| Total Per Case .. | $.400 | $.350 | $81,750 | $.40 | $.350 | $19,850 | $101,600 |
| Cases packed ....... | 25,000 | 205,000 | 230,000 | 5,000 | 51,000 | 56,000 | 286,000 |
| Total Labor ........ | $10,000 | $71,750 | $81,750 | $2,000 | $17,850 | $19,850 | $101,600 |

Receiving and preparation labor must be distributed to finished-product cost in proportion to the raw-product weight required to produce a finished case of each size can.

Filling and closing labor obviously has no relationship to the original raw-product weight, but must be allocated in proportion to the number of cans operated through the production lines. Labor cost per unit (case) on high-speed lines utilized for small containers will obviously be less than on slower-speed lines used on larger containers.

Processing (cooking or freezing), labeling, and casing require similar analysis.

If royalties are paid for the use of labor-saving machinery, they must be allocated in accordance with the royalty or usage charge. For allocation of factory burden, see page 696.

**The cost statement.** From the summary of the Daily Cost and Yield Reports for the pack, which must be reconciled with the Factory Cost Ledger (see page 698), the product cost statement is compiled in accordance with the rules previously outlined. This statement provides the foundation for the compilation of cost estimates for the following year (see page 694). It also provides the basis for the entry charging Cost of Sales and crediting the Finished Pack account (see page 698). Figure 8 shows

SUMMARY OF PRODUCTION COSTS

|  | CORN—<br>Total | PEAS—<br>Total | LIMA<br>BEANS—<br>Total | GRAND<br>TOTAL |
|---|---|---|---|---|
| Cases Packed .............. | 286,000 | 500,000 | 350,000 | 1,136,000 |
| Raw Product .............. | $ 162,745 | $ 499,347 | $ 530,000 | $1,192,092 |
| Ingredients .............. | 37,300 | 30,000 | 7,000 | 74,300 |
| Cans ..................... | 223,500 | 350,000 | 237,000 | 810,500 |
| Labels ................... | 15,800 | 30,000 | 22,000 | 67,800 |
| Case .................... | 28,600 | 45,000 | 29,000 | 102,600 |
| Labor, Direct ............. | 101,600 | 100,000 | 62,000 | 263,600 |
| Prime Cost .............. | 569,545 | 1,054,347 | 887,000 | 2,510,892 |
| Factory Overhead ......... | 85,780 | 158,153 | 133,000 | 376,933 |
| Factory Cost ............. | 655,325 | 1,212,500 | 1,020,000 | 2,887,825 |
| Warehouse and Shipping.... | 14,300 | 25,000 | 17,500 | 56,800 |
| Selling and Administrative.. | 85,627 | 148,750 | 119,000 | 353,377 |
| Interest ................. | 40,295 | 70,000 | 56,000 | 166,295 |
| Total Cost .............. | $ 795,547 | $1,456,250 | $1,212,500 | $3,464,297 |
| Selling Price .............. | $1,007,375 | $1,750,000 | $1,400,000 | $4,157,375 |
| Less: Transportation ....... | 71,500 | 60,625 | — | 132,125 |
| Cash Discount ....... | 20,300 | 35,000 | 28,000 | 83,300 |
| Trade Spoils ......... | 2,860 | 4,375 | 2,000 | 9,235 |
| Net .................... | $ 912,715 | $1,650,000 | $1,370,000 | $3,932,715 |
| Gross Margin .............. | $ 257,390 | $ 437,500 | $ 350,000 | $1,044,890 |
| Gross Margin % .......... | 25.5 | 25.0 | 25.0 | 25.1 |
| Net Profit—Before Taxes... | $ 117,168 | $ 193,750 | $ 157,500 | $ 468,418 |
| Net Profit % .............. | 11.6 | 11.1 | 11.2 | 11.3 |

**Fig. 8. Summary of Production Costs.**

# DETAILED UNIT COSTS AND RESULTS

| PRODUCT | Corn | | | | | | | |
|---|---|---|---|---|---|---|---|---|
| Size Packed | 48/Buf. | 24/303 | 24/303 | 48/Buf. | 24/303 | 24/303 | 24/303 | TOTAL |
| Grade | Fancy Cream Style | Fancy Cream Style | Extra Standard Cream Style | Fancy Whole Kernel | Fancy Whole Kernel | Extra Standard Whole Kernel | Standard Whole Kernel | |
| Cases Packed | 25,000 | 175,000 | 30,000 | 5,000 | 50,000 | 500 | 500 | 286,000 |
| Yield—cases per ton | 44.33 | 45.61 | 45.61 | 38.27 | 38.27 | 38.27 | 38.27 | 43.85 |
| Raw weight used—per case | 45.12 | 43.85 | 43.85 | 52.26 | 52.26 | 52.26 | 52.26 | 3,043.810 |
| Product cost—per pound | $ .01309 | $ .01309 | $ .00756 | $ .01309 | $ .01309 | $ .00756 | $ .00246 | $ .01250 |
| UNIT COSTS: | | | | | | | | |
| Raw Product | $ .59 | $ .57 | $ .33 | $ .69 | $ .69 | $ .40 | $ .13 | $162,745 |
| Ingredients | .15 | .15 | .15 | .05 | .05 | .05 | .05 | 37,300 |
| Cans | 1.05 | .75 | .75 | 1.05 | .75 | .75 | .75 | 223,500 |
| Labels | .10 | .05 | .05 | .10 | .05 | .05 | .05 | 15,800 |
| Case | .10 | .10 | .10 | .10 | .10 | .10 | .10 | 28,600 |
| Labor, Direct | .40 | .35 | .35 | .40 | .35 | .35 | .35 | 101,600 |
| Prime Cost | $ 2.39 | $ 1.97 | $ 1.73 | $ 2.39 | $ 1.99 | $ 1.70 | $ 1.43 | $539,545 |
| Factory Overhead, 15% | .36 | .30 | .26 | .36 | .30 | .26 | .21 | 35,780 |
| Factory Cost | $ 2.75 | $ 2.27 | $ 1.99 | $ 2.75 | $ 2.29 | $ 1.96 | $ 1.64 | $655,325 |
| Warehouse and Shipping | .05 | .05 | .05 | .05 | .05 | .05 | .05 | 14,300 |
| Selling, Advertising, and Administrative | .38 | .30 | .23 | .38 | .30 | .23 | .17 | 85,627 |
| Interest | .18 | .14 | .11 | .18 | .14 | .11 | .08 | 40,295 |
| TOTAL COST | $ 3.36 | $ 2.76 | $ 2.38 | $ 3.36 | $ 2.78 | $ 2.35 | $ 1.94 | $795,547 |
| Selling Price | $ 4.50 | $ 3.50 | $ 2.75 | $ 4.50 | $ 3.50 | $ 2.75 | $ 2.00 | $1,007,375 |
| LESS: Transportation | .25 | .25 | .25 | .25 | .25 | .25 | .25 | 71,500 |
| Cash Discount | .09 | .07 | .06 | .09 | .07 | .06 | .04 | 20,300 |
| Trade Spoils | .01 | .01 | .01 | .01 | .01 | .01 | .01 | 2,860 |
| Net | $ 4.15 | $ 3.17 | $ 2.43 | $ 4.15 | $ 3.17 | $ 2.43 | $ 1.70 | $ 912,715 |
| Gross Margin | $ 1.40 | $ .90 | $ .44 | $ 1.40 | $ .88 | $ .47 | $ .06 | $ 257,390 |
| Gross Margin % | 31.1 | 25.7 | 16.0 | 31.1 | 25.1 | 17.1 | 3.0 | 25.5 |
| Net Profit | $ .79 | $ .41 | $ .05 | $ .79 | $ .39 | $ .08 | $ .24 | $ -17,168 |
| Net Profit % | 17.5 | 11.7 | 1.8 | 17.5 | 11.1 | 2.9 | 12.0 | 11.6 |

a summary of production costs. Figure 9 illustrates how the detailed unit costs and results are compiled.

**Casing and labelling.** Many buyers of canned and frozen foods require that the product be labelled with their own labels. The buyers may either furnish the labels to the processor and receive a label allowance, or the processor may supply labels to the buyers' specifications. The processor may also have his own label or brands. The result of this variation in practice is that the finished product is frequently stored in the processor's warehouse unlabelled. This situation gives rise to the anomaly that the product is stored in the warehouse and yet is not finished until it is finally labelled and cased ready for shipment. If a special procedure were not employed to deal with this situation, it would be necessary to employ two sets of costs and inventory values: one for products not yet cased and labelled, and one for products completely finished.

A rather simple device to handle this situation with a single cost and inventory value is through the medium of a Casing and Labelling Reserve account, the operation of which is as follows:

1. All unit costs are computed on the basis of a fully cased and labelled product.

2. All allowances or payments made to buyers are charged to Costs of Label Supplies, just as if the processor purchased them entirely for his own use.

3. Similarly, all labor expended for casing and labelling is charged to the appropriate labor expense account in the factory cost ledger.

4. At the end of each accounting period, the Factory Cost Ledger account is debited, and the Casing and Labelling Reserve account is credited for the estimated cost of labelling and casing all product on inventory at that time which is not yet cased or labelled. The Casing and Labelling Reserve account appears on the balance sheet as a contra valuation account to the Inventory of Finished Goods.

**Pooled costs.** If more than one plant in a geographical area produces the same finished product, it may be desirable to "pool" the costs of the several plants packing that product, as the product will be sold interchangeably regardless of where it is packed. Pooling is accomplished by computing unit costs for each plant in the manner previously described, and then combining them into a composite weighted average.

**Inventory practices.** *Inventory records.* Conventional perpetual inventories should be maintained by whatever method best suits the size of the operation—inventory ledger form, visible index cards, accounting machines, or punch-card accounting. Entry sources are:

For production          —Daily Product Cost and Yield Report
For shipments                              —Sales invoices

For warehouse spoilage and regrading of stock from one grade to another, or other stock adjustments

—Stock adjustment report (Figure 10).

| STOCK ADJUSTMENT REPORT Date_____ | | | | |
|---|---|---|---|---|
| Item | Add | | Deduct | | Remarks |
| | Cases | Cans | Cases | Cans | |
| 24/2 Fancy Sugar Peas | | | 5 | 15 | Spoiled |
| 24/303 Extra Standard Sugar Peas | | | 100 | — | Regraded |
| 24/303 Standard Sugar Peas | 100 | — | | | " |

**Fig. 10. Stock Adjustment Report.**

*Inventory pricing.* Inventories are priced at the costs computed as described in the preceding paragraphs. If the same product is packed at more than one plant in a geographical area, and pooled costs are used, the inventory is priced at the pooled cost. If more than one season's pack of seasonal items is on hand at the same time, inventories should be priced on the basis of "first in, first out" unless the LIFO (last in, first out) method is used. (It is preferable not to average two years' inventory costs.) At the end of a fiscal year, if net market price (net selling price less direct cost to sell) is lower than cost, in the aggregate for any product, net market price should be substituted for cost.

For nonseasonal products packed throughout the year, unit costs should be computed each month instead of seasonally, and the same principles should be applied as for seasonal products.

*Importance of turnover.* The importance of turnover is accentuated in the seasonal processing industry because, at best, the turnover rate on products packed once a year is low and working capital requirements are high. It should therefore be a fundamental rule that inventories of a particular product should be sold before the next year's pack begins, and production programs should be such as to make this possible. The risks of loss on carryovers from one year to another are so great that a wise and prudent operator will carefully avoid this possibility.

## Time and payroll system

**Timekeeping and payrolls.** Aside from the variability of work shifts occasioned by the effects of weather on the availability of raw produce, timekeeping and payroll procedures present no problems. A simple and flexible system is, however, always preferable.

**Distribution of labor costs.**  Certain aspects of this subject were considered under the cost system (see page 694).

| Employee _____ |
|---|
| Clock # _____ |

|  | A. M. | IN _____ |
|---|---|---|
|  |  | OUT _____ |
|  | P. M. | IN _____ |
|  |  | OUT _____ |
|  | Overtime | IN _____ |
|  |  | OUT _____ |

|  | Total Hours | Rate | Amount |  |
|---|---|---|---|---|
| Straight time |  |  |  |  |
| 1 1/4   time |  |  |  |  |
| 1 1/2   time |  |  |  |  |
| Double  time |  |  |  |  |
| Total |  |  |  |  |

**PRODUCT**

|  | Hours | Amount |  |
|---|---|---|---|
|  |  |  |  |
| Receiving |  |  |  |
| Preparation |  |  |  |
| Filling |  |  |  |
| Casing & Labelling |  |  |  |
| Warehouse |  |  |  |
| Maintenance |  |  |  |
| Total |  |  |  |

Fig. 11. Time Card Showing Distribution of Employee's Time Between Products and Product Operations.

Variable work loads in canning and freezing operations frequently result in transfers of help between products or departments during the work week, thus necessitating considerable flexibility in labor distribution. The distribution is facilitated by the use of a time card or work card with space for the daily labor distribution. (See Figure 11.) It is usually unnecessary, and often impractical, to identify overtime pay with the particular operation on which it is performed. It is not only simpler, but usually more equitable, to allocate the employee's total earnings for the day, including overtime, to all the operations on which he may have worked. This practice, however, is a matter for discretion.

After the labor distribution has been made on the individual time cards, it may be recapped on a work sheet, or summarized directly from the time cards. It will usually be found that large numbers of employees will have worked on a single operation only; hence the cards can be sorted out by operations and then summarized directly by adding machine. Cards showing mixed distributions may be segregated and summarized on a work sheet.

The completed labor distribution is then ready for entry on the Daily Product Cost and Yield Report, and at the end of the week to the Factory Cost Ledger.

## Plant and equipment records

**Fixed assets.** Any accepted conventional method of maintaining plant and equipment records should be satisfactory in this industry. Experience has demonstrated that throughout most industries inaccuracies creep into plant and equipment records through the years and undermine their real significance. Yet, because of the relatively long lives of most fixed assets, a high degree of care and accuracy is called for to preserve the integrity of the record. Short seasonal operating periods in the canning and freezing industries and rapid changes in processes have historically produced frequent changes in equipment layouts. Unless such changes are promptly reflected in the plant and equipment records, they can soon become meaningless.

It is good practice to assign a serial number to each piece of equipment, to permanently affix the number to the physical item, and to enter the serial number in the property record as a permanent means of identification. To be of maximum benefit, the serial number should include the year of acquisition.

**Depreciation methods.** Depreciation may be computed on individual assets, on classes of assets, or on a composite basis, but if the latter method is used, the composite rate must be rechecked at regular annual intervals to make certain that it is appropriate. In general, the rates of depreciation recommended by the Internal Revenue Service for various types and classes of equipment should provide a fair basis, but these rates must be considered in the light of local conditions. Either straight-line or reducing-balance or sum-of-the-years'-digits methods may be used, as desired. Each of these methods has its own merit and the one should be selected that best serves the company's needs.

## Reports to management

**Financial reports.** *Income statement.* At the end of the accounting period, preferably monthly, an income (profit and loss) statement should be prepared, showing the sales, costs, and expenses for each product for the period and year to date, and the total for all products. If more than one plant is involved, a separate income statement may be made for each plant, or the common products packed in the several plants may be pooled. Illustrative income reports are shown in Figure 12 (showing source of entry) and 13 (showing a completed statement).

If the size of the business warrants it, a condensed income statement for all products and plants combined may also be made in the conventional form.

Other financial reports that are usually prepared are:

Condensed balance sheet, detailed balance sheet, or trial balance
Summary of cost of production (optional) (see pages 686–687)
Cost statements (see page 701)
Inventory of finished goods
Inventory of supplies

### General operating reports.

Production budget
Daily Cost and Yield Report (see Figure 7)
Stock Adjustment Report (see Figure 10)
Stock and Sales Report (see Figure 6)
Factory Overhead Statement (see page 696)

### Reports for production.

Production budget
Daily Cost and Yield Report
Stock Adjustment Report
Inventory of Finished Stock
Inventory of Supplies
Labor Distributions
Factory Overhead Statement

### Reports for purchasing.

Production budget
Inventory of supplies

Product_____                    _____19_____

| CASE CONTROL | Source of Entry |
|---|---|
| Total Net Volume—Cases ........ | |

Opening Inventory ...............
Production ......................
Outside Purchases ................
Closing Inventory ...............

Cost of Goods Sold—Cases .......

## INCOME STATEMENT

| Total Gross Volume $ | Sales Journal |
|---|---|

| | |
|---|---|
| Transportation ................... | Purchase and Expense Distribution |
| Price Adjustment ................ | Sales Journal and Purchase and Expense Distribution |
| Trade Discount .................. | Do |
| Returned Goods ................. | Do |
| Trade Spoils .................... | Do |
| Cash Discount ................... | Cash Collection Journal |

Total Deductions ..................

Net Volume .....................

| | |
|---|---|
| Opening Inventory ............... | Inventory Record |
| Production ..................... | Monthly Production Journal (Contra is Finished Pack Account) |
| Outside Purchases .............. | Purchase and Expense Distribution |
| Used in Remanufacture ......... | Journal Entry |
| Closing Inventory ............... | Inventory Record |

Cost of Goods Sold ..............

Gross Margin ...................

*Selling, Administrative, and Interest Expense:*

| | |
|---|---|
| Warehouse and Shipping ......... | Labor Distribution and Purchase and Expense Distribution |
| Brokerage ..................... | Expense Distribution |
| Selling Expense ................. | Payroll and Purchase and Expense Distribution |
| Advertising .................... | Purchase and Expense Distribution |
| General Administrative Expenses.. | Payroll and Expense Distribution |
| Interest ....................... | Purchase and Expense Distribution or Journal Entry |

Total Selling, Administrative, and Interest Expense

| | |
|---|---|
| Net Income from Operations ..... | |
| Other Income and Expense ...... | Journal Entry |

| | |
|---|---|
| Total Income Before Taxes ...... | |
| Income Taxes ................... | Journal Entry |

Net Income .....................

**Fig. 12. Income Statement (Showing Source of Entry).**

| CASE CONTROL | Corn | Peas | Lima Beans | Total |
|---|---|---|---|---|
| Total Net Volume—Cases ...... | 92,050 | 247,400 | 65,250 | 404,700 |
| Opening Inventory ............ | 18,050 | 37,400 | 25,250 | 80,700 |
| Production ................... | 286,000 | 500,000 | 350,000 | 1,136,000 |
| Outside Purchases ............. | 3,000 | | | 3,000 |
| Closing Inventory ............. | 215,000 | 290,000 | 310,000 | 815,000 |
| Cost of Goods Sold—Cases...... | 92,050 | 247,400 | 65,250 | 404,700 |

INCOME STATEMENT

| | Corn | Peas | Lima Beans | Total |
|---|---|---|---|---|
| Total Gross Volume $ | 320,100 | 844,300 | 256,080 | 1,420,480 |
| Transportation ................. | 21,240 | 26,390 | 159 | 47,789 |
| Price Adjustment ............. | | 3,910 | | 3,910 |
| Trade Discount ............... | | 9,800 | | 9,800 |
| Returned Goods .............. | | | | |
| Trade Spoils .................. | 900 | 2,380 | 1,030 | 4,310 |
| Cash Discount ................ | 6,402 | 16,886 | 5,112 | 28,400 |
| Total Deductions .............. | 28,542 | 59,366 | 6,301 | 94,209 |
| Net Volume ................... | 291,558 | 784,934 | 249,779 | 1,326,271 |
| Opening Inventory ............ | 43,200 | 97,400 | 76,300 | 216,900 |
| Production ................... | 655,325 | 1,212,500 | 1,020,000 | 2,887,825 |
| Outside Purchases ............. | 7,150 | | | 7,150 |
| Used in Remanufacture ........ | | | | |
| Closing Inventory ............. | 497,300 | 701,800 | 898,400 | 2,097,500 |
| Cost of Goods Sold ........... | 208,375 | 608,100 | 197,900 | 1,014,375 |
| Gross Margin ................. | 83,183 | 176,834 | 51,879 | 311,896 |
| Selling, Administrative, and Interest Expense: | | | | |
| Warehouse and Shipping ........ | 4,218 | 10,320 | 2,810 | 17,348 |
| Brokerage .................... | 11,203 | 29,550 | 8,962 | 49,715 |
| Selling Expense .............. | 4,801 | 12,665 | 3,840 | 21,306 |
| Advertising .................. | 6,402 | 16,886 | 5,112 | 28,400 |
| General Administrative Expense. | 4,801 | 12,665 | 3,840 | 21,306 |
| Interest ..................... | 12,804 | 33,772 | 9,630 | 56,206 |
| Total Selling, Administrative, and Interest Expense ............ | 44,229 | 115,858 | 34,194 | 194,281 |
| Net Income from Operations ... | 38,954 | 60,976 | 17,685 | 117,615 |
| Other Income and Expense ..... | | | | 3,150 |
| Total Income Before Taxes ..... | | | | 120,765 |
| Income Taxes ................. | | | | 62,798 |
| Net Income ................... | | | | 57,967 |

Fig. 13. Income Statement.

# 25

# Food Stores (Chain)

by

## F. D. SCOTT

Certified Public Accountant; Controller, Red Owl Stores, Inc.,
Minneapolis, Minnesota

## Industry characteristics that affect the accounting system

**Nature of the business.** The operation of a chain of retail food stores is a highly competitive business done on a cash basis and dependent upon high sales volume to compensate for a low profit margin. According to the latest industry figures available, net earnings after income taxes averaged a little better than one per cent of sales.

Rapid turnover of stocks in stores and warehouses is necessary not only to keep working capital requirements at a minimum but also to assure freshness of the merchandise to the consumer. Approximately 45 per cent of the volume in today's food store is in perishables—fresh fruit and produce, dairy products, and fresh meats. Careful handling, attractive display, refrigeration, and prepackaging are all measures taken to maintain the attractiveness of the product, to stimulate turnover, and to reduce waste and losses.

The chain food store plays an important role in the timely movement of the products from the field and processing plant to the consumer's table. Continued awareness of the factor of time in the distribution cycle is basic in this industry.

To meet the requirements mentioned, the system of multiple store locations served from a central warehouse or distributing point has been developed. The location and size of stores vary considerably, but generally the larger stores are located in or near the more heavily populated areas and the smaller stores in the smaller towns and communities. At present, the generally accepted classification of stores is as follows:

*Super-markets.* Complete self-service units having not less than 7,000 square feet of floor space and averaging not less than $500,000 in sales per annum. These qualifications are minimums, for it is not unusual to find stores with larger areas generating an annual sales volume of several millions of dollars.

*Self-service stores.* Self-service stores not meeting the requirements of the super-market.

*Conventional stores.* Small units where the customers are waited upon by the store personnel.

The general and staple lines of products handled in the stores are accumulated at a central warehouse for distribution. An average-size warehouse would be a single-story structure covering approximately 120,000 to 150,000 square feet and handling about 3,000 different items.

Most stores contract for local deliveries of dairy products, some fruits and produce, and local home-style bakery products. Some suppliers prefer to have their own men deliver and display their merchandise at the store level. Again, bulk commodities, such as flour, sugar, and salt, can sometimes be delivered direct to the stores from spot stocks in the area at a lesser cost than if delivered from a central warehouse. Carlots of potatoes, watermelons, and canning fruits many times can be diverted in route with deliveries made direct to stores, thus saving re-handling time and cost.

Many chains have gone into certain processing and manufacturing lines under their own private label for quality-control purposes and for cost reduction generally at the central warehouse locations. Some of these operations are:

1. Roasting private-label coffees.
2. Baking a line of commercial and home-style bakery products.
3. Prepackaging bulk commodities such as tea, candies, cookies, dried fruits, beans, and nuts.
4. Preparation of delicatessen items.
5. Cutting and boning carcass meats and packaging other meat products into retail sizes.
6. Manufacturing cellophane and polyethelene bags and containers.

The prepackaging of fresh meat and produce is becoming accepted more and more. At present, it is best done at the store level; consumer preferences can thus be observed and proper determination made of acceptable items.

Most chains own and operate their own fleet of transport carriers to service the stores in their respective areas. Truck operations are usually centered at the warehouse locations, including garages and repair and maintenance facilities. Flexibility in dispatching and scheduling deliveries to the stores and closer control over operations are obtained under this arrangement. Operating costs are generally less than common carrier rates.

**Governmental controls.** The industry is subject to the various Federal laws governing pure food requirements, proscribing discriminatory pricing methods, and enforcing fair labor practices. During periods of emergency, pricing and rationing regulations have been imposed by Federal authority. Some states have minimum markup laws and unfair trade practice regulations covering unfair competition within their boundaries.

**Taxes, licenses, fees.** Most states require food and tobacco licenses for each warehouse and store location. Local regulations vary, and in many localities special licenses are required for handling dairy products, soft drinks, and other products. Certain states require special licenses for handling oleomargarine and also tax the sale of the product. Cigarettes and tobacco are separately taxed in practically all states, and the distributor is required to purchase the necessary stamps in advance before sale and reimbursement by the purchaser.

Many states have adopted sales tax laws and impose upon the retailer the responsibility for the collection of the tax at the point of sale and subsequent remittance thereof to the state's treasury. Federal excise taxes apply to several product lines sold in the store, and these must be collected and remitted to the Treasurer of the United States. Each state has its own truck-licensing laws and regulations in respect to load weights and road restrictions. Attempts have been made from time to time by various states to impose special taxes on chain stores operating within their boundaries, but in general such laws have been removed from the statutes.

**General features.** Competition is generally furnished by good local independent dealers and by other chain operators within a given area. Since all competitors within given groups have access to practically the same sources of supply at comparable prices, the customer's acceptance of a particular store must be based upon factors other than price alone. Some of the factors recognized are the hours the store is open, parking facilities at the store location, well-stocked shelves and cases, clean and bright stores, meats properly trimmed, freshness of meats, fruits, and produce, courteous and friendly personnel, and sundry services, such as check cashing, paying of local utility bills, and "Kiddie Corrals" for the children.

During the year, activity is directed toward the promotion of products having a seasonal nature or having some appeal because of the season of the year. Some of these are:

Spring—seeds and garden supplies; housecleaning supplies.

Early summer—picnic foods, beverages, fresh garden fruits and vegetables.

Late summer—canning fruits and vegetables, and canning supplies.

Fall—canned foods for winter storage, and carcass meat cut for freezer storage.

Holidays—candies, cookies, fruits, nuts, fruit cakes, poultry, and party foods.

Winter—citrus fruits and juices, frozen fruits and vegetables. Replacement of canned goods and freezer stocks.

The search for new store locations is continuous, and decisions must be made with respect to the closing of stores or the investing of additional funds for remodeling and adding equipment to older stores. Surveys and studies of population trends, buying habits, and economic changes in the areas served are necessary before decisions in this respect can be made.

New products offered are appraised and investigated and their possible sales are tested in selected stores and areas before they are accepted for chain-wide stocks. The testing may be done with the co-operation of the manufacturer or producer.

Many companies submit their operating figures and statistics to their own associations for consolidation with other members' data and receive back the combined figures for comparison with their own operations.

**Functional peculiarities.** *Buying.* Responsibilities of the buying department generally include the procurement of the products and also the setting of the retail prices.

Factors considered in the procurement of the products include:

1. Areas in which the products are produced and the distances from shipping points to warehouse locations.

2. Number of brands and grades of the same product to be handled.

3. Quantities produced and packed during current seasons and their availability for future delivery.

4. Selection of products to be made available to all stores and those to be made available to a selected group only.

5. Extent to which packers will pack in acceptable case sizes so that repacking at the warehouses may be reduced to a minimum.

6. Probable impact of market changes on the buying habits of the consumer within the respective areas served by the stores.

7. Turnover of line numbers.

8. Balanced inventories with a minimum investment.

Factors considered in the setting of retail prices include:

1. Competition in the areas served by the stores.

2. Costs of the product up to the point of sale.

3. Desired markup on each line number.

4. Effect on over-all markup of variances that exist among products and among brands and grades of the same product.

5. Expected turnover at the store level.

6. Seasonal changes in the demand for certain kinds of products.

*Selling.* Selling policies are generally established at headquarters for the over-all promotional activities of the chain, including the following:

1. Title of the promotion, such as Birthday Sale, President's Month, Meat Round-up, and so on.

2. Beginning date and duration of the promotion.

3. Products to be offered as "specials."

4. Advertising to be used—newspaper, radio, television, handbills, and the like.

5. Prizes for customers, managers, and store personnel.

6. Store displays—banners, signs, and the like.

7. Sales quotas for each store.

The use of trading stamps has recently become a major factor in sales promotion. Under the plan, the customer is given stamps or tokens on the basis of his purchases, which are redeemable for premium merchandise in accordance with established catalogue values. Some states require redemption in cash, at the option of the customer. Stamp plans are generally contracted for with regularly organized trading stamp companies, although some food store operators own and operate their own stamp plan.

**Asset peculiarities.** The trend of the past few years has been away from the smaller "walk-in" type of store to the modern super-market located in the shopping center. Such shopping centers are generally located in the outlying areas of the cities and towns, away from the congested "downtown" areas. The use of the automobile has changed the shopping habits of many consumers, and such centers are built to afford ample and convenient parking facilities for the customer.

In order to handle the many frozen food products now available, and to lengthen and protect the freshness of other perishable products, the modern food store has been required to install various types of refrigerated display cases and coolers at a considerable investment. It is not unusual for the investment in a modern store's fixtures to amount to $100,000 or more for a given location. Some companies maintain a fixture-manufacturing division to supply most of their requirements for shelving, display racks, and cases, but procure the mechanical and refrigerated units from others.

The modern warehouse has been set up to handle a volume tonnage rapidly. Mechanical devices of all kinds are used to speed up the movement of the merchandise through the warehouse, such as towlines for selection purposes and power-driven lift and fork trucks for handling. Large refrigerated sections are also required to store and handle the perishable items.

The tractor and the trailer carrying from 20,000 to 30,000 pounds of mixed freight are used to move the products to the stores and point of sale promptly. Special refrigeration and heating attachments are necessary to protect the loads against temperature changes in all kinds of weather. The road and highway systems in the areas served also play an important part in this movement.

**Ownership peculiarities.** Expenditures for capital or fixed assets are generally restricted to fixtures and equipment, while the store and warehouse properties are leased. Construction of the property may be undertaken by the company, then sold upon completion and leased back to free the funds advanced during the construction period. Lease terms vary, but in the case of the larger units the terms may run from 15 to 25 years, with rentals based upon an amortization schedule covering the return of the investment to the lessor at the agreed-upon interest rate. Such leases are usually net, the taxes, insurance, maintenance and repair, and subsequent improvements to the property being assumed by the lessee.

**Financing peculiarities.** The industry is operated primarily upon the cash basis. Vendors' terms are generally seven to ten days or sight draft. Cash flow and commitments must be watched constantly and arrangements made for short-term bank financing to carry seasonal inventories, tax payments, construction advances, and the like. Working-capital requirements necessary to finance a given sales volume are not as extensive as is the case in other industries because of the necessity of turning inventories rapidly and because sales are primarily on a cash rather than a credit basis. A working capital ratio of 5 per cent of sales volume is considered more than adequate, provided inventories turn at least 12 times a year in the warehouses and better than 16 to 32 times a year in the stores. At times, long-term debenture financing may be used to maintain the working capital relation to sales or to replace working capital expended for fixtures, equipment, and improvements to leased premises.

Debenture financing was used rather extensively during the years of excess profits taxes, partly because of the resulting lower net cost of the money to the borrower. Loans of this nature may run from 20 to 25 years, with premium penalties for repayments in excess of those specified within the contract for the first 5 or 10 years. Additional equity financing in either convertible preferred or common stock may be necessary, depending upon the requirements set forth by the lenders of the debenture capital and the requirements of the borrower. In this connection, the formulas used in determining the relationship between debenture capital and equity capital include the rents on leased premises capitalized on a basis of about 8 per cent.

**Principal accounting problem.** Cash, inventories, fixtures, and equipment are physically spread throughout the area served by the respective companies in various amounts, depending upon whether the location is a warehouse point or a large or a small store. Each location, whether warehouse or store, is a separate accounting center, and the flow of information from these centers to the headquarters office depends upon the distances and the available means of communication. Some companies operate in small areas where the flow of information can be on a daily basis from each location. Others may serve larger areas with scattered locations, where the flow of information cannot possibly reach the headquarters office for several days. This time differential has an effect upon the processing of the accounting transactions and the rendering of operational reports for the various centers. A program of acceptable due dates for the flow of the information from the field to the office and the reports back to the field is essential.

## Functional organization

**Division into departments or activities.** The following is a representative departmental classification of the activities of the business, generally conducted under the direction and supervision of the various executives responsible therefor.

1. Retail operations or food store operations
2. Warehousing
3. Trucking and transportation
4. Manufacturing or other processing
5. Real estate and construction
6. Legal
7. Buying
8. Advertising
9. Financial
10. Corporate records
11. Controller's department

Accounting sections under the direction of the controller are established to accumulate the transactions for the departments indicated. In respect to accounting for retail operations, the transactions are accumulated by each store location. Other accounting sections generally coming under the controller's direction are:

Chief accountant
Tax accountant
Cash accounting
Store and warehouse inventory control
Fixture and equipment accounting
Payroll accounting
Accounts payable accounting
Tabulating division
General ledger accounting
Internal audit
Budgetary procedures
Service departments—filing, mailing, stenographic, print shop and stationery room, and the like.

An organization chart of a representative concern engaged in this business is shown in Figure 1. This company not only conducts its business through company-owned and -operated stores, but also serves a group of independently owned and operated stores under an agency franchise arrangement.

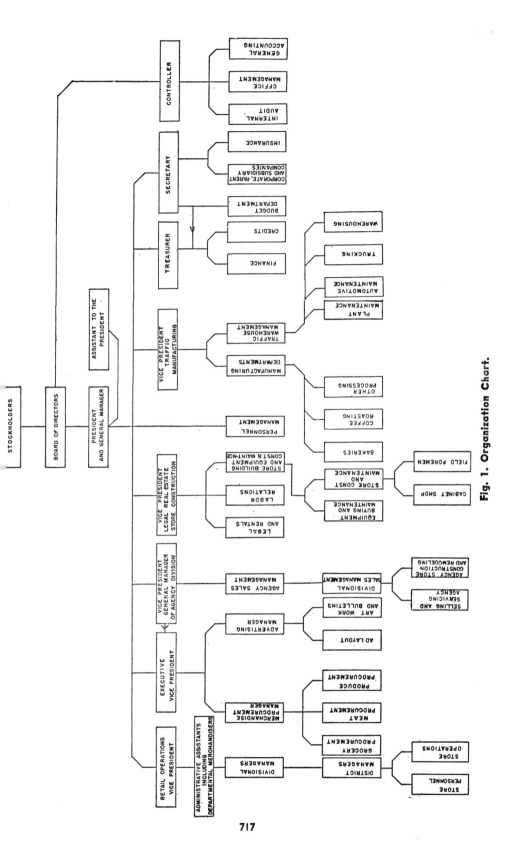

**Fig. 1. Organization Chart.**

717

A vice-president has been assigned the responsibility for directing the Agency Division. Direction and control of the budgetary procedures have been assigned to the secretary of the company, who reports to the treasurer in respect thereof. The controller is directly responsible to the board of directors.

## Objectives of the system

**Specific objectives of the system.** The principal objectives of the system are to establish effective control over cash, inventories, and store fixtures and equipment. To this end, current information in respect to cash receipts and disbursements, perpetual inventory records, property records, and an internal audit program are required. In this connection, the following procedures are generally adopted:

1. Transactions in the depository bank accounts are reported daily, indicating the previous day's balance, receipts and disbursements, and ending balances.

2. Store cash receipts are deposited intact daily in the local banks with advice thereof to the head office.

3. Funds are transferred to the head office depository and to disbursing accounts as required, usually by draft drawn against the local bank.

4. Weekly store reports are prepared and forwarded to the head office indicating:

   a. Cash receipts from sales and other sources.

   b. Deposit of receipts in local banks.

   c. Cash disbursements at store level for merchandise, salaries, store expenses, and the like.

   d. Merchandise receipts from warehouses, direct shipments, transfers between stores, and credit memos for merchandise adjustments.

   e. Markdowns and additional markups. (Dry groceries are reported at both retail and cost, as these inventories are controlled under the retail inventory method.)

5. Physical inventories are taken at least once each month of produce and meats in stores and warehouses, and are valued at cost.

6. Monthly computations are made of dry grocery book inventories at retail for each store, which are reduced to estimated cost by the percentage of markup. The general ledger control for store inventories is adjusted thereto. At least once each quarter, physical inventories of dry groceries at all stores are taken at retail and compared with the book figures, and differences are adjusted.

7. Monthly book inventories of dry grocery warehouse stocks by line number are prepared and valued at cost and the total reconciled with the corresponding general ledger control. Physical counts of these warehouse

stocks are made periodically covering selected line numbers or the entire warehouse stock. The quantities are compared with the book quantities and adjustments made, while the general ledger controls are adjusted for the value of the physical quantities.

8. Additions to store fixtures and equipment generally originate at the head office, while disposals and transfers are generally reported by the store or district manager as they occur. Physical inventories of fixtures and equipment are generally taken throughout the year for comparison with the book records.

9. An internal audit department is generally provided to make periodic cash audits and cash counts at the store level, as well as to take the periodic dry grocery inventories in the stores and warehouses and the periodic store fixture and equipment inventories. Meat and produce inventories may be taken by the store manager, but periodic counts of these items by others are usually provided for.

Punch-card accounting and tabulating equipment is generally used for billing the warehouse shipments at cost and retail to the stores and in preparing the book inventories of warehouse stocks and store fixtures and equipment. Accumulating the data for stores' operations is adaptable to punch-card accounting also, but other methods, such as the peg-board system, are generally used. In this manner, the entries for the general ledger controls can be accumulated directly from the store reports and the details can be posted directly to the subsidiary ledger accounts carried for each store's operations.

## Classification of accounts and books of account

### Balance sheet accounts.

| Assets | Debits from | Credits from |
|---|---|---|
| Cash in Banks and on Hand: | | |
| Depository Bank Accounts ...... | Cash Receipts Journal (supported by list of drafts drawn on store bank accounts and other general receipts) | Cash Disbursements Journal |
| Store Bank Accounts ........... | Summary of Store Reports | Cash Receipts Journal (for transfers to Depository Bank Accounts) |
| Change Funds ................. | Cash Disbursements Journal | Cash Receipts Journal |
| Due from Vendors, Claims, etc. ...... | Sundry Accounts and Claim Journal | Do |
| Merchandise Inventories: | | |
| Warehouses .................. | Voucher Record | Summary of Store Billings |

| Liabilities | Debits from | Credits from |
|---|---|---|
| Retail Outlets ............ | General Journal (setting up increase or decrease in beginning and ending inventories) | Summary of Store Billings |
| Prepaid Expenses ............... | Voucher Record (insurance, licenses, tax stamps, etc.) | General Journal (amounts absorbed) |
| Recoverable Construction Costs .... | Voucher Record | Cash Receipts Journal |
| Cash Surrender Value of Life Insurance ...................... | General Journal (setting up increase in annual values and adjustments) | Do |
| Property, Plant, and Equipment ... | Voucher Record | General Journal |
| Reserve for Depreciation ......... | General Journal | Do |
| Leasehold Improvements .......... | Voucher Record (for additions to leased premises) | General Journal (for amortization) |
| Deferred Charges and Other Assets. | Voucher Record, General Journal | General Journal |

| Liabilities | | |
|---|---|---|
| Notes Payable—Current .......... | Voucher Record | Cash Receipts Journal |
| Accounts Payable ............... | Cash Disbursements Journal | Voucher Register, Summary of Store Reports (for store purchases not paid at store level) |
| Accrued Expenses ............... | Do | General Journal (for local taxes, other accruals) |
| Provision for Federal and State Taxes on Income ............. | Do | General Journal |
| Long-Term Notes Payable ........ | Do | Cash Receipts Journal |
| Stockholders' Equity: | | |
|   Capital Stock ................. | Cash Disbursements Journal, General Journal | Cash Receipts Journal, General Journal |
|   Earnings Reinvested in Business.. | Cash Disbursements Journal (for cash dividends), General Journal (for stock dividends, losses—prior years' adjustments) | General Journal (for profits and prior years' adjustments) |

## Income and expense accounts.

| | | |
|---|---|---|
| Sales ......................... | | Summary of Store Reports, General Journal (for adjustments) |

|  | *Debits from* | *Credits from* |
|---|---|---|

**Cost of Sales:**

Merchandise .................. — Summary of Store Billings (for warehouse shipments), Summary of Store Reports (for purchases paid or incurred at store level), General Journal (for adjustments in inventories, etc.)

Warehousing .................. — Voucher Record, General Journal (for accruals and adjustments)

Transportation ............... — Voucher Record, General Journal (for accruals and adjustments)

Cash Discounts ............... — Cash Disbursements Record or Voucher Record

**Expenses:**

Store Expenses:

Salaries and Wages ...........  
Advertising ................  
Utilities (Heat, Telephone, Power, Water, etc.) ........  
Sundry .....................  
} These expenses are generally paid at the store level and are reported in the store's weekly reports. Postings to the general ledger controls come from the Summary of Store Reports.

Cartons, Wrappings, and Supplies — (Generally ordered from warehouse and postings come from the Summary of Store Billings)

Repairs and Maintenance ....... — (Generally paid from head office—postings from Voucher Record)

Fixed Charges:

Rent ......................  
Taxes .....................  
Licenses ..................  
Insurance .................  
Depreciation and Amortization.  
} Voucher Record, General Journal (for accruals and write-offs of prepaid items)

General and Administrative Expenses:  
Executive Salaries ..........  
Other Salaries and Wages .....  
Employer's Social Security Taxes ....................  
Traveling Expenses ........  
Supplies and Postage ........  
Utilities (Heat, Telephone, Power, Water, etc.) ........  
Memberships and Subscriptions  
} (Entries to these accounts generally come from the Voucher Record or from the General Journal entries for accruals, write-offs of prepaid items, and adjustments. This classification is generally set up for each administrative section of the operating and administrative departments recognized. (For a list of recognized departments, see page 716.)    Do

|  | *Debits from* | *Credits from* |
|---|---|---|
| Contributions .............. | | |
| Professional Services .......... | | |
| Sundry Expenses ............ | | |
| Pension Fund and Group Insurance .................. | | |
| Machine Rentals ............. | See note opposite General and Administrative Expenses, page 721. | |
| Repairs and Maintenance ..... | | |
| Fixed Charges: | | |
| Rent ..................... | | |
| Taxes ................... | | |
| Licenses ................. | | |
| Insurance ............... | | |
| Depreciation and Amortization | | |

| Miscellaneous Charges—Credits: | | |
|---|---|---|
| Interest Paid .................. | Voucher Record | |
| Interest Received .............. | | Cash Receipts Journal, Sundry Accounts, Claims Journal |
| Gain or Loss on the Disposal of Capital Assets ............. | General Journal | |
| Other Non-Recurring Items ..... | Do | |
| Provision for Taxes on Income .... | Do | |

**Other necessary records.** Subsidiary ledgers are kept for each store location covering each store's operations—sales and cost of sales by grocery, meat, and produce, and store expenses. Some companies further classify the expenses as between grocery, meat, and produce operations and prepare an over-all store report and separate departmental reports.

A book inventory at retail for each store's dry grocery stock is necessary for purposes of computing the cost under the retail inventory method and of comparing book inventories with the periodic physical inventories. A book record of these cost inventories, as well as of the physical inventories of meat and produce, is maintained in support of the corresponding general ledger control.

# Peculiarities of procedures: sales; cash receipts; merchandise receipts; retail price adjustments; purchases; cash disbursements

**Sales, cash receipts, merchandise receipts, and retail price adjustments.** The weekly store reports furnish the accounting information for store sales, disposition of the cash receipts, merchandise receipts, and retail price adjustments. Filled-in specimens of some of these reports are shown in Figures 2 through 12. It will be noted that provision has been made in these reports for the payment of local store expenditures by a draft drawn against the treasurer of the company and payable through a designated disbursing bank account. These drafts are included in the store's daily deposits, thus making it possible to deposit the day's receipts intact as indicated by the respective cash register readings.

The reports have been so designed that the various sections can be separated, audited, and processed through the various accounting sections simultaneously. The procedure pattern is as follows:

1. The Weekly Store Reports, Figure 2, are recapped for general ledger control entries, and sales are posted to the stores subsidiary ledger.

| BLANK STORES, INC.<br>Weekly Store Report | | STORE #62<br>Store Stamp | | |
|---|---|---|---|---|
| Manager's Signature _John Doe_ Week Ending _April 10, 19_ | | | | |
| **To account for:** | | Store Use | Office Use | |
| 1. Sales | | | | |
| Grocery............................................... | | 4699 23 | | |
| Meat................................................. | | 1428 89 | | |
| Produce............................................. | | 582 73 | | |
| *Over or (short) above depts. ....................... | | 1 37 | | |
| Coffee Bar.......................................... | | 362 73 | | |
| *Over or (short)................................... | | 2 12 | | |
| Donut Shop......................................... | | — | | |
| Other (describe)............... _Special Change Fund_ | | 300 00 | | |
| 2. Sales tax collected................................. | | 128 08 | | |
| 3. Eggs sold to dealers............................... | | 56 00 | | |
| 4. Other items (describe)............................. | | — | | |
| 5. Total receipts (Line 1 through 4) ................... | | 7561 15 | | |
| 6. Cash balance previous report....................... | | 310 00 | | |
| 7. Drafts drawn No. 14675 thru 14700 ................. | | 1588 94 | | |
| 8. Total (Line 5 through 7) ........................... | | 9460 09 | | |
| **Accounted for:** | | | | |
| 9. Merchandise purchases (Fig. 5) | | | | |
| Grocery  Cost.................. | | 693 05 | | |
| Retail............... | 791.19 | | | |
| Meat  Cost.................. | | | | |
| Produce  Cost.................. | | 65 50 | | |
| Retail............... | 82.50 | | | |
| Coffee Bar  Cost.................. | | 22 50 | | |
| Other  Cost.................. | | — | | |
| 10. Misc. (describe)............................ | | | | |
| 11. Other expense paid-outs (Fig. 6).............. | | 320 33 | | |
| 12. Gross salaries | | | | |
| Managers....................................... | 176.90 | | | |
| Clerks.......................................... | 366.81 | | | |
| Misc. .......................................... | | | | |
| 13. Total Gross Salaries........................... | 543.71 | | | |
| 14. Less salary deductions | | | | |
| Old Age Benefits .............................. | | | | |
| Withholding Tax................................ | 48.80 | | | |
| Group Insurance............................... | 23.55 | | | |
| Other Deductions.............................. | | | | |
| 15. Total Salary Deductions........................ | 72.35 | | | |
| 16. Net paid (Line 13 minus 15) ................... | | 471 36 | | |
| 17. Accounts Rec.-Coupons......... _Draft #14699_ ... | | 16 20 | | |
| 18. Sub-total (Line 9 through 17 - must equal line 7)... | | 1588 94 | | |
| 19. Cash deposited (Must equal line 5)............... | | 7561 15 | | |
| 20. Cash balance forward............................ | | 310 00 | | |
| 21. Total (Line 18 through 20)....................... | | 9460 09 | | |
| Note: Lines 8 and 21 must agree. | | | | |
| *Add overs and subtract shorts to get total receipts on line 5 | | | | |

**Fig. 2. Weekly Store Report.**

2. Bank deposits are posted from the All Checkers Combined Cash Summary, Figure 3, to the store bank accounts subsidiary ledger.

|  |  | SALES RECAP | | | | | | | Over or Short | Misc. Receipts (Describe) | Egg Sales | Deposits |
|---|---|---|---|---|---|---|---|---|---|---|---|---|
| Day | Reg # | Grocery | Meat | Produce | Coffee Bar | Other (Describe) | Sales Tax | TOTAL | | | | |
| | 1 | 269.21 | 72.16 | 20.83 | | | 6.28 | 368.48 | −.72 | | | 367.76 |
| | 2 | 179.13 | 51.20 | 15.02 | | | 4.20 | 249.55 | −.07 | | | 249.48 |
| M | 3 | | | | | | | | | | | |
| O | 4 | | | | | | | | | | | |
| N | 5 | | | | 63.02 | | .92 | 63.94 | +1.06 | | | 65.00 |
| | 6 | | | | | | | | | | | |
| | 7 | | | | | | | | | | | |
| TOTAL | | 448.34 | 123.36 | 35.85 | 63.02 | | 11.40 | 681.97 | + .27 | | | 682.24 |
| | 1 | 368.36 | 92.90 | 42.03 | | | 9.21 | 512.50 | +1.90 | | | 514.40 |
| T | 2 | 148.49 | 38.51 | 21.28 | | | 4.39 | 212.67 | −.15 | | | 212.52 |
| U | 3 | 51.71 | 28.19 | 15.03 | | | 1.59 | 96.52 | — | | | 96.52 |
| E | 4 | | | | | | | | | | | |
| S | 5 | | | | 55.57 | | .87 | 56.44 | +.94 | | | 57.38 |
| | 6 | | | | | | | | | | | |
| | 7 | | | | | | | | | | | |
| TOTAL | | 568.56 | 159.60 | 78.34 | 55.57 | | 16.06 | 878.13 | +2.69 | | | 880.82 |
| | 1 | 360.98 | 102.28 | 35.96 | | | 8.65 | 507.87 | +1.40 | | | 509.27 |
| | 2 | 251.12 | 75.19 | 30.81 | | | 6.49 | 363.61 | −.17 | | | 363.44 |
| W | 3 | | | | | | | | | | | |
| E | 4 | | | | | | | | | | | |
| D | 5 | | | | 65.70 | | .91 | 66.61 | −.31 | | | 66.30 |
| | 6 | | | | | | | | | | | |
| | 7 | | | | | | | | | | | |
| TOTAL | | 612.10 | 177.47 | 66.77 | 65.70 | | 16.05 | 938.09 | + .92 | | | 939.01 |
| | 1 | 308.32 | 62.38 | 40.28 | | | 8.04 | 419.02 | + .68 | | | 419.70 |
| T | 2 | 244.07 | 90.30 | 27.82 | | | 6.46 | 368.65 | +1.90 | | | 370.55 |
| H | 3 | 93.68 | 45.98 | 10.96 | | | 2.55 | 153.17 | — | | | 153.17 |
| U | 4 | | | | | | | | | | | |
| R | 5 | | | | 59.01 | | .52 | 59.53 | — | | | 59.53 |
| S | 6 | | | | | | | | | | | |
| | 7 | | | | | | | | | | | |
| TOTAL | | 646.07 | 198.66 | 79.06 | 59.01 | | 17.57 | 1000.37 | +2.58 | | | 1002.95 |
| | 1 | 370.71 | 93.22 | 65.70 | | | 9.77 | 539.40 | − .31 | | 56.00 | 595.09 |
| | 2 | 279.01 | 66.28 | 27.75 | | | 6.85 | 379.89 | −1.08 | | | 378.81 |
| F | 3 | | | | | | | | | | | |
| R | 4 | | | | | | | | | | | |
| I | 5 | | | | 63.09 | | .83 | 63.92 | + .43 | | | 64.35 |
| | 6 | | | | | | | | | | | |
| | 7 | | | | | | | | | | | |
| TOTAL | | 649.72 | 159.50 | 93.45 | 63.09 | | 17.45 | 983.21 | − .96 | | 56.00 | 1038.25 |
| | 1 | 761.01 | 257.09 | 99.32 | | | 20.39 | 1137.81 | − .60 | | | 1137.21 |
| | 2 | 508.13 | 177.34 | 69.31 | | | 14.77 | 769.55 | − .35 | | | 769.20 |
| S | 3 | 17.44 | 11.69 | 2.87 | | | .55 | 32.55 | — | | | 32.55 |
| A | 4 | 487.86 | 164.18 | 57.76 | | | 13.16 | 722.96 | −1.06 | | | 721.90 |
| T | 5 | | | | 56.34 | | .68 | 57.02 | — | | | 57.02 |
| | 6 | | | | | Special Change Fund | | | | 300.00 | | 300.00 |
| | 7 | | | | | | | | | | | |
| TOTAL | | 1774.44 | 610.30 | 229.26 | 56.34 | | 49.55 | 2719.89 | −2.01 | 300.00 | | 3017.88 |
| WEEKLY TOTALS | | 4699.23 | 1428.89 | 582.73 | 362.73 | | 128.08 | 7201.66 | +3.49 | 300.00 | 56.00 | 7561.15 |

STORE #62 — Store Stamp — Mgr's. Signature *John Doe* — BLANK STORES, INC. All Checkers Combined Cash Summary — Week Ending *April 10, 19—*

**Fig. 3. All Checkers Combined Cash Summary.**

3. List of drafts issued, Figure 4, is filed separately and drafts redeemed are checked off. The recap of open items at the end of the month supports the balance of the general ledger control.

4. The various paid-out reports (Figures 5, 6, and 7) (plus the following forms not reproduced here: petty cash vouchers for payments for merchandise and payments for expense items, and payroll envelopes) are posted to the stores subsidiary ledger purchase and expense accounts. Subsequently,

| | | | BLANK STORES, INC. | | STORE #62 | | | |
| | | LIST OF DRAFTS ISSUED AT STORES | | | Store Stamp | | | |

Mgr's. Signature _John Doe_        Week Ending _April 10, 19—_

| Draft Number | Amount | For Office Use Only | Draft Number | Amount | For Office Use Only | Draft Number | Amount | For Office Use Only |
|---|---|---|---|---|---|---|---|---|
| 14675 | 69 30 | | 14693 | 20 00 | | | | |
| 14676 | 4 44 | | 14694 | 389 42 | | | | |
| 14677 | 9 10 | | 14695 | 15 60 | | | | |
| 14678 | 6 80 | | 14696 | 42 50 | | | | |
| 14679 | 42 50 | | 14697 | 4 76 | | | | |
| 14680 | 12 14 | | 14698 | 22 50 | | | | |
| 14681 | 10 25 | | 14699 | 16 20 | | | | |
| 14682 | 65 00 | | 14700 | 471 36 | | | | |
| 14683 | 26 50 | | | | | | | |
| 14684 | 42 50 | | | | | | | |
| 14685 | 7 80 | | | | | | | |
| 14686 | 16 32 | | | | | | | |
| 14687 | 16 10 | | | | | | | |
| 14688 | 66 50 | | | | | | | |
| 14689 | 26 50 | | | | | | | |
| 14690 | 5 25 | | | | | | | |
| 14691 | 167 60 | | | | | | | |
| 14692 | 12 00 | | | | | | | |
| Total Drafts Used (Must agree with Line No. 7 on Figure #2) | | | | | | | 1588 94 | |

List all drafts used during the week in numerical order. All drafts must be accounted for. If a draft is voided mark this report accordingly and attach the voided draft to this report. Mail to office with weekly reports. It will not be necessary to retain a copy in the store.

Fig. 4. List of Drafts Issued at Stores.

| Draft Number | Date | Description | GROCERY Cost | GROCERY Retail | MEAT Cost | PRODUCE Cost | PRODUCE Retail | LUNCHEONETTE Cost |
|---|---|---|---|---|---|---|---|---|
| | | **BLANK STORES, INC** Weekly Merchandise Paid-Out Report | | | | | | STORE #62 |
| | | _John Doe_ Store Manager's Signature | | | Week Ending 4/10/– | | | Store Stamp |
| 14675 | 4/5 | Ice Cream | 69 30 | 83 35 | | | | |
| 14676 | 4/5 | Soft Drinks | 4 44 | 5 90 | | | | |
| 14677 | 4/5 | Bottle Refund | 1 40 | 1 40 | | | | |
| " | 4/5 | Soft Drinks | 7 20 | 8 65 | | | | |
| " | 4/5 | Produce Refund | | | | 50 | 50 | |
| | | | (82 34) | (99 30) | | (50) | (50) | |
| 14679 | 4/6 | Eggs | 42 50 | 42 50 | | | | |
| 14680 | 4/6 | Yeast | 12 14 | 15 34 | | | | |
| | | | (54 64) | (57 84) | | | | |
| 14682 | 4/7 | Potatoes | | | | 65 00 | 82 00 | |
| 14683 | 4/7 | Ice Cream | 26 50 | 32 70 | | | | |
| | | | (26 50) | (32 70) | | (65 00) | (82 00) | |
| 14684 | 4/8 | Eggs | 42 50 | 42 50 | | | | |
| 14685 | 4/8 | Bottle Refund | 1 20 | 1 20 | | | | |
| " | 4/8 | Soft Drinks | 6 60 | 8 70 | | | | |
| | | | (50 30) | (52 40) | | | | |
| 14689 | 4/9 | Ice Cream | 26 50 | 32 70 | | | | |
| 14690 | 4/9 | Soft Drinks | 4 80 | 6 10 | | | | |
| " | 4/9 | Bottle Refund | 45 | 45 | | | | |
| | | | (31 75) | (39 25) | | | | |
| 14694 | 4/10 | Milk, Cream + Butter | 389 42 | 451 60 | | | | |
| 14695 | 4/10 | Bottle Refund | 15 60 | 15 60 | | | | |
| 14696 | 4/10 | Eggs | 42 50 | 42 50 | | | | |
| 14698 | 4/10 | Bakery Goods | | | | | | 22 50 |
| | | | (447 52) | (509 70) | | | | (22 50) |
| | | **Total Purchases** | 693 05 | 791 19 | | 65 50 | 82 50 | 22 50 |

**Fig. 5. Weekly Merchandise Paid-Out Report.**

the Salary Statement, Figure 7, is posted to the individual employee's earnings and taxes-withheld records by the payroll section.

5. The cost value of merchandise receipts and adjustments, Figures 8, 9, 10, and 11, is recapped for general ledger control entries, and the details by store are posted to the stores subsidiary ledger purchase accounts.

6. The retail values on Figures 8 through 11 and retail price adjustments on Figure 11 are posted to statistical records by stores for purposes of inventory computations.

7. Invoices for direct shipments of merchandise not paid at the store level are forwarded to the accounts payable section for payment from the regular disbursing accounts.

For audit purposes, the All Checkers Combined Cash Summary, Figure 3, is supported in detail by the Checker's Daily Cash Reports, Figure 12. The Weekly Paid-Out Reports for merchandise and expenses are supported by petty cash vouchers. Signatures of parties to whom the disbursements are made are required in the absence of an invoice or other supporting data.

# BLANK STORES, INC.
## Weekly Expense Paid-Out Report

Week Ending _April 10, 19___

STORE #62

Store Stamp

_John Doe_
STORE/MANAGER'S SIGNATURE

| DRAFT NUMBER | DATE | DESCRIPTION | TOTAL EXPENSE | FREIGHT & DRAYAGE | PUBLICATION SPACE | RADIO TELEVISION | HEAT | LIGHT & POWER | WATER & ICE | TELEPHONE & TELEGRAPH | LAUNDRY | SUPPLIES | REFUSE DISPOSAL | REPAIRS & MAINT. | EXCHANGE | SUNDRY | CODE |
|---|---|---|---|---|---|---|---|---|---|---|---|---|---|---|---|---|---|
| | | | | 50 | 56 | 57 | 100 | 101 | 102 | 103 | 105 | 108 | 109 | 122 | 171 | | |
| 14678 | 4/5 | Freight - Sugar | 1 68 | 1 68 | | | | | | | | | | | | | |
| " | 4/5 | Laundry | 2 12 | | | | | | | | 2 12 | | | | | | |
| " | 4/5 | Postage | 3 00 | | | | | | | | | 3 00 | | | | | |
| | | | (6 80) | (1 68) | | | | | | | | (3 00) | | | | | |
| 14681 | 4/7 | Delivery expense | 1 25 | | | | | | | | | | | | | 1 25 | |
| " | 4/7 | Refuse disposal | 6 00 | | | | | | | | | | 6 00 | | | | |
| " | 4/7 | Repair meat grinder | 3 00 | | | | | | | | | | | 3 00 | | | |
| | | | (10 25) | | | | | | | | | | (6 00) | (3 00) | | (1 25) | |
| 14686 | 4/8 | Telephone | 16 32 | | | | | | | 16 32 | | | | | | | |
| 14687 | 4/8 | Bank exchange | 1 10 | | | | | | | | | | | | 1 10 | | |
| " | 4/8 | Recancelled stamp tax | 15 00 | | | | | | | | | | | | | 15 00 | |
| 14688 | 4/8 | Newspaper advertising | 66 50 | | 66 50 | | | | | | | | | | | | |
| | | | (98 92) | | (66 50) | | | | | (16 32) | | | | | (1 10) | (15 00) | |
| 14691 | 4/9 | Light power & water | 167 60 | | | | | 162 60 | 5 00 | | | | | | | | |
| 14692 | 4/9 | Radio advertising | 12 00 | | | 12 00 | | | | | | | | | | | |
| 14693 | 4/9 | Coal | 20 00 | | | | 20 00 | | | | | | | | | | |
| | | | (199 60) | | | (12 00) | (20 00) | (162 60) | (5 00) | | | | | | | | |
| 14697 | 4/10 | Express - bakery | 4 76 | 4 76 | | | | | | | | | | | | | |
| | | | (4 76) | (4 76) | | | | | | | | | | | | | |
| | | **Total Expense** | 320 33 | 6 44 | 66 50 | 12 00 | 20 00 | 162 60 | 5 00 | 16 32 | 2 12 | 3 00 | 6 00 | 3 00 | 1 10 | 16 25 | |
| | | ACCT NO. | | 50 | 56 | 57 | 100 | 101 | 102 | 103 | 105 | 108 | 109 | 122 | 171 | | |

For General Office Use Only

22    Managers Salaries _____

23    Other Store Salaries _____

**Fig. 6. Weekly Expense Paid-Out Report.**

BLANK STORES INC. SALARY STATEMENT    Store Stamp    **STORE #62**

REIMBURSED BY DRAFT NO. _14644_     Week Ending _April 10 19—_

| Social Security Number | Employee's Name (Manager please print and arrange alphabetically WITHOUT regard to department.) | No. Days Emp. | Basic Rate | GROCERY Hours Basic | Over Basic | Amount | MEAT Hours Basic | Over Basic | Amount | LUNCHEONETTE Hours Basic | Over Basic | Amount | Taxes Withheld | Group Ins. | Other | Net Amount Paid |
|---|---|---|---|---|---|---|---|---|---|---|---|---|---|---|---|---|
| | CLERK HIRE | | | | | | | | | | | | | | | |
| 310 45 4135 | Atkins, Geo. W | 6 | 52.50 | 45 | | 52 50 | | | | | | | 3 56 | 3 12 | | 45 82 |
| 483 41 7353 | Dorsen, Peter | 6 | 55.00 | | | | 47 | 7 | 67 81 | | | | 2 86 | 4 18 | | 60 77 |
| 893 01 4417 | Farrell, Robt F. | 6 | 50.00 | 45 | | 50 00 | | | | | | | 3 22 | | | 46 78 |
| 264 14 3669 | Gibbs, Minnie E. | 6 | 27.50 | | | | | | | 40 | | 27 50 | 3 38 | 3 95 | | 20 17 |
| 461 70 4529 | Hanson, Norma | 6 | 1.00 | 36 | | 36 00 | | | | | | | 2 10 | | | 33 90 |
| 113 04 4824 | Knight, Frank W. | 4 | .90 | 20 | | 18 00 | | | | | | | 2 38 | | | 15 62 |
| 242 10 482 | Lane, Maxine | 5 | 30.00 | | | | | | | 40 | | 30 00 | 4 10 | | | 25 90 |
| 507 41 1597 | Moore, Albert D. | 5 | .80 | | | | 20 | | 16 00 | | | | 1 24 | | | 14 76 |
| 721 42 6074 | O'Hara, Margaret | 5 | 1.00 | 34 | | 34 00 | | | | | | | 4 82 | | | 29 18 |
| 503 42 3049 | Olson, Myrtle | 6 | 35.00 | | | | | | | 40 | | 35 00 | 5 16 | | | 29 84 |
| | Total Clerks | | | 180 | — | 190 50 | 65 | 7 | 83 81 | 120 | — | 92 50 | | | | |
| | Total Clerks All Depts. (Item No. 12— FIG.2) | | | | | $366.81 | | | | | | | | | | |
| | Managers | | | | | | | | | | | | | | | |
| 641 02 9074 | Doe, John B. | 6 | | .59 | | 93 80 | | | | | | | 5 22 | 6 15 | | 82 43 |
| 273 81 9467 | Reed, Thomas A. | 6 | | | | | .59 | | 83 10 | | | | 10 76 | 6 15 | | 66 19 |
| | Total Managers | | | .59 | | 93 80 | .59 | | 83 10 | | | | | | | |
| | Total Managers All Depts. (Item No. 12— FIG.2) | | | | | $176.90 | | | | | | | | | | |
| **GRAND TOTAL** | | | 239 | | | 284 30 | 124 | 7 | 166 91 | 120 | — | 92 50 | 48 80 | 23 55 | | 471 36 |

_John B. Doe_
Grocery Manager

_Thomas A. Reed_
Meat Manager

FOR OFFICE USE ONLY

SALES TOTALS
Groc. & Prod. $
Meat $
Luncheonette $

Posting Proof

**Fig. 7. Salary Statement.**

The payroll envelope is a two-part form. The slip attached is signed by the employee and retained at the store level for inspection and audit by the Internal Audit Department. The envelope is retained by the employee for his records. Duplicate copies of the reports, except for the petty cash vouchers, as well as the cash register tapes, are kept at the store level. These tapes are periodically destroyed by the internal audit department after completion of cash audits made at the store level.

**Purchase and payment procedures.** The purchase order and receiving procedure for warehouse merchandise follows conventional lines. The routines provide for the preparation of basic accounting information in respect to description, quantities, and cost prices, including inbound freight and charges, at the time the purchase order is issued. Upon notification of physical receipt by the warehouse, the data can be quickly routed to the tabulating department and the stocks made available for order-filling and

BLANK STORES, INC.

Weekly Summary of Merchandise Received

STORE #62
GROC. DEPT.
Store Stamp

Manager *John Doe* Week Ending *April 10, 19—*

**SEC 1 - Direct Shipments of Merchandise**

| Line No. | Inv. Date | Cost | Retail | Office Use | Vendor |
|---|---|---|---|---|---|
| 1 | 4/5 | 18.97 | 24.09 | | A. Co |
| 2 | 4/6 | 72.89 | 92.57 | | B. Co |
| 3 | 4/6 | 35.00 | 44.50 | | C. Co |
| 4 | 4/7 | .94 | 1.20 | | AB. Co |
| 5 | 4/7 | 8.30 | 10.08 | | AB Co |
| 6 | 4/9 | 50.06 | 56.25 | | D Co |
| 7 | 4/9 | 331.44 | 387.40 | | BC. Co |
| 8 | | | | | |
| 9 | | | | | |
| 10 | | | | | |
| 11 | | | | | |
| 12 | | | | | |
| 13 | | | | | |
| 14 | | | | | |
| 15 | | | | | |
| 16 | | | | | |
| 17 | | | | | |
| 18 | | | | | |
| 19 | | | | | |
| 20 | | | | | |
| 21 | | | | | |
| 22 | | | | | |
| 23 | | | | | |
| 24 | | | | | |
| 25 | | | | | |
| 26 | | | | | |
| 27 | | | | | |
| 28 | | | | | |
| 29 | | | | | |
| 30 | | | | | |
| 31 | | | | | |
| 32 | | | | | |
| 33 | | | | | |
| 34 | | | | | |
| 35 | | | | | |
| 36 | | | | | |
| 37 | | | | | |
| 38 | | | | | |
| 39 | | | | | |
| 40 | | | | | |
| Office Use | | 517.60 | 616.09 | | |

**SEC. 2 - Bakery Shipments**

| Date Rec'd | Invoice Number | Cost | Retail | Bakery |
|---|---|---|---|---|
| 4/5 | 1401 | 20.14 | 26.30 | |
| 4/6 | 1520 | 16.10 | 21.26 | |
| 4/7 | 1630 | 22.82 | 30.14 | |
| 4/8 | 1782 | 18.30 | 24.52 | |
| 4/9 | 1840 | 28.90 | 37.62 | |
| 4/10 | 1901 | 40.05 | 57.89 | |
| Office Use | | 146.39 | 197.73 | |

**SEC. 3 - Transfers In-Merchandise Only**

| Form 10 No. | Cost | Retail | Store |
|---|---|---|---|
| 12634 | 19.36 | 21.48 | #51 |
| Office Use | 19.36 | 21.48 | |

**SEC. 4 - Warehouse Shipments**

| Date Rec'd | Invoice No. | Cost | Retail | Warehouse |
|---|---|---|---|---|
| 4/7 | 9830 | 34.10 | 42.60 | #2 |
| 4/7 | 9817 | 2249.84 | 2763.56 | #2 |
| Office Use | | 2283.94 | 2806.16 | |

**SEC. 5 - Meat & Provision Shipments**

| Date Rec'd | Invoice No. | Cost | Retail | Warehouse |
|---|---|---|---|---|
| Office Use | | | | |

**SEC. 6 - Credits & Transfers Out-Merchandise Only**

| Form 10 No. | Cost | Retail | Store or Vendor |
|---|---|---|---|
| 40948 | 17.76 | 22.20 | Store #50 |
| 40962 | 63.18 | 70.19 | Coffee Bar |
| Office Use | 80.94 | 92.39 | |

**Office Use**

| RECAP | ACCT. | COST | RETAIL |
|---|---|---|---|
| Direct Shipments | 2212 | 517.60 | 616.09 |
| Bakery Shipments | 731 | 146.31 | 197.73 |
| Transfers In | 734 | 19.36 | 21.48 |
| Warehouse Shipments | 730 | 2283.94 | 2806.16 |
| Meat & Provision Shipments | 732 | — | — |
| Cash Purchases -fig.5 | 736 | 693.05 | 791.19 |
| Total Merchandise Rec'd. | | 3660.26 | 4432.65 |
| Less: Credits and Transfers Out | | | |
| | 733 | | |
| Store Auditing | 734 | 80.94 | 92.39 |
| Traffic Dept. | 735 | | |
| Less: Eggs sold to Dealers fig. 2 | 736 | 56.00 | 56.00 |
| Net Merchandise Received | 701 | 3523.32 | 4284.26 |

**Fig. 8. Weekly Summary of Merchandise Received.**

| FORM 10 | | BLANK STORES, INC. Store Request for Credit | | | | | N⁰ 40948 | | |
|---|---|---|---|---|---|---|---|---|---|

**BLANK STORES, INC.**
**Store Request for Credit**

**N⁰ 40948**

TO _Store #50_

STORE STAMP

STORE #62
Grocery Dept.

ADDRESS_____  DATE _4/12/—_

| QUAN. | DESCRIPTION | UNIT | COST PER UNIT | COST EXTENSION | RETAIL PER UNIT | RETAIL EXTENSION |
|---|---|---|---|---|---|---|
| 3 Cases | Canned Goods | 1 | | 17 76 | | 22 20 |
| | | | | | | |
| | | | | | | |
| | LESS SALVAGE | | | | | |
| | TOTAL | | | 17 76 | | 22 20 |

| GIVE DETAILED EXPLANATION BELOW: | | LINE NO. | | FOR GENERAL OFFICE USE ONLY | | |
|---|---|---|---|---|---|---|
| INVOICE No. | DATE | | | DISTRIBUTION | COST | RETAIL |
| | | EXTENDED | DR. | | | |
| | Store Transfer | | DR. | | | |
| | | PRICED | DR. | | | |
| MANAGER'S SIGNATURE | John Doe | | CR. | | | |
| VENDOR'S REPRESENTATIVE | | O.K BY | CR. | | | |
| DRIVER | | | CR. | | | |

**Fig. 9. Store Request for Credit.**

---

**BLANK STORES, INC.**
**Report of Merchandise, Supplies and Services Received**      **N⁰**

| Quantity Received | DESCRIPTION | Unit | √ | Cost Per Unit | Cost Extension | Retail Per Unit | √ | Retail Extension |
|---|---|---|---|---|---|---|---|---|
| 5 Cases | Cookies | | | 35 00 | | .50 | | 44 50 |
| | | | | | | | | |

NO INVOICE RECEIVED FROM VENDOR.

| FREIGHT PREPAID | √ | | TOTAL | | 35 00 | | | 44 50 |
|---|---|---|---|---|---|---|---|---|
| FREIGHT COLLECT | | | | | | | | |

RECEIVED FROM
Name _"C" Company_
Address_____

DATE RECEIVED _4/6/—_

Store (Use Your Store Stamp)

STORE #62
GROC. DEPT.

| FOR GENERAL OFFICE USE ONLY | | | | SIGNATURE |
|---|---|---|---|---|
| Unit O. K. | Retail Price O. K. | Cost Extension O. K. | Retail Extension O. K. | |
| | | | | John Doe |
| | | | | Store Manager |

**Fig. 10. Report of Merchandise, Supplies, and Services Received.**

| | | | | | | | | | | | |
|---|---|---|---|---|---|---|---|---|---|---|---|
| BLANK STORES, INC. Report of Mark-Ups and Mark-Downs | | | | | | STORE #62 | | | | | |
| DATE *April 10, 19--* MGR.'S SIGNATURE *John Doe* | | | | | | Store Stamp | | | | | |

| | DESCRIPTION | Reg. Price | Sale Price | Diff. | On Hand Begin. | Rec'd | Stock at Close | Amt. Sold | MARK UP | MARK DOWN |
|---|---|---|---|---|---|---|---|---|---|---|
| **E G G S** | Eggs Sold Over Counter | | .05 | | 20 | 154 | 10 | 164 | 8.20 | |
| | Eggs Sold to Produce Dealers | | | | | | | | | |
| | Miscellaneous | | | | | | | | | |
| **FRUIT** | | | | | | | | | | |
| **B A K E R Y** | *Bread* | .21 | .17 | .04 | — | 320 | 12 | 308 | | 12.32 |
| | | | | | | | | | | |
| | | | | | | | | | | |
| **B U T T E R** | | | | | | | | | | |
| **C O O K I E S & C R A C K E R S** | | | | | | | | | | |
| **F L O U R** | | | | | | | | | | |
| **P A C K I N G O D P H A S E - P R O D** | | | | | | | | | | |
| **S U G A R** | | | | | | | | | | |
| **M I S C** | *Carton Cigarettes* | 2.40 | 2.35 | .05 | | | | 104 | | 5.20 |
| | *Damaged Mdse* | | | | | | | | | 3.19 |
| | *Case Sales* | | | | | | | | | 2.12 |
| | | | | | | | | | | |
| | | | | | | **TOTALS** | | | 8.20 | 22.83 |

**Fig. 11. Report of Markups and Markdowns.**

billing. A delay of a few hours in the flow of this information can create an out-of-stock position in the accounts and the "shorting" of orders even though the merchandise is in the warehouse at the time. Subsequent audit of the data processed by the tabulating department is made in the accounts payable department upon receipt of the vendor's invoice and the freight bills. Nominal differences are adjusted to over and short, and major differences are adjusted to the tabulating records and the general ledger controls.

Accounts payable and cash disbursement procedures are conventional.

| CHECKER'S DAILY CASH REPORT | | STORE #62 |
|---|---|---|
| | | Store Stamp |

REGISTER NO. _____    DATE _4/5/—_ CHECKER _η Hanson_

| | | |
|---|---|---|
| 1 | Currency | 3,3 7 00 |
| 2 | Coins | 32 76 |
| 3 | Checks | 48 00 |
| 4 | Total | 4 1 7 76 |
| 5 | Deduct change fund | 50 00 |
| 6 | Cash receipts | 3 6 7 76 |
| 7 | Register reading - today | 6 2 3 8 45 |
| 8 | Register reading - previous | 5 8 6 7 97 |
| 9 | Register receipts - today | 3 7 0 48 |
| 10 | Deduct total voids | 2 00 |
| 11 | Net register receipts | 3 6 8 48 |
| 12 | Over or (short) Diff. between #6 and #11 | (72) |

SALES RECAP

| | Grocery | Meat | Produce | Coffee Bar | Other (Describe) | Sales Tax | Total |
|---|---|---|---|---|---|---|---|
| Dept. sales | 2 71 21 | 72 16 | 20 83 | | | 6 28 | 3 70 48 |
| Deduct voids | 2 00 | — | | | | | 2 00 |
| Net sales | 2 69 21 | 72 16 | 20 83 | | | 6 28 | 3 68 48 |

**Fig. 12. Checker's Daily Cash Report.**

## Cost system

**Processing and manufacturing divisions.** The accounting requirements for the processing and manufacturing divisions of the company depend upon the extent to which such operations are carried on. Generally, a simplified cost procedure is all that is required to establish billing prices to the stores. An estimated price may be established for a given product and any over- or under-absorption of the costs adjusted to the stores' purchase accounts on the basis of shipments to them during the accounting period. Periodic test runs may be made or estimate cost sheets prepared from time to time to measure the reasonableness of the billing prices used.

Some companies place their processing and manufacturing divisions on a competitive basis with outside processors and require that the products be priced at the prices at which the stores could acquire their requirements from outside processors. Any profits or losses are absorbed by the respective divisions and are not redistributed to the stores. The efficiency of such operations is measured by the profits or losses sustained by these divisions and by whether the quality of the products produced is comparable with or better than that of competitive processors.

Inventory valuations of such products in the warehouses or in the stores are based upon the billing prices and are not adjusted for any over- or under-absorption of the manufacturing or processing costs developed during the accounting period.

**Allocation of expenses and other items.** Warehouse and transportation costs, cash discounts, and general and administrative expenses are generally allocated to the operations of each store. Average rates based upon tons handled, sales, or cost of sales may be practical and may give fairly accurate and satisfactory results of stores' operations in those instances where the stores are relatively uniform in size and the distances between stores and warehouses are nominal. However, where stores are of various sizes and several hundred miles apart, some other basis of allocation is required to measure more accurately the stores' operations. The following is an example of the bases that might be used in allocating certain costs.

*Warehouse costs.* Tonnage ordered by each store at rates reflecting differentials in time required to select and load orders of various weights.

*Transportation costs.* Tonnage delivered to each store at rates reflecting differentials in distances, time, and weights.

*Cash discounts.* Dollar value of warehouse shipments to each store.

*General and administrative expenses.* Time spent by supervisory personnel in stores—number of people supervised, warehouse shipments, or combinations of these factors.

Rates established must be periodically reviewed in order that any changes in the methods of operation, personnel, or size of order may be properly reflected.

## Payroll system peculiar to the business

**Place of payroll preparation.** Store payrolls are generally paid weekly and may be made up and paid in cash at the store level, or the payroll sheets may be sent to the head office, where checks are prepared and returned to the store for distribution. It is not unusual to find a combination of these procedures. The stores near to the head office may be paid by check and those farther away by cash at the store level. Distances and the time required to transfer payroll information and make the payments to the store people many times determine the procedure to be followed.

Warehouse, transportation, office, and other payrolls are generally prepared at the head office from time cards or time sheets submitted by the respective departments. Payments are generally made by check.

## Plant and equipment records—depreciation

**Property records.** Conventional property records are kept for each fixture and piece of equipment and are filed in location order by store, warehouse, garage, or office. Items of short life and nominal cost (not exceeding $10 or $15) are generally charged to expense at time of acquisition. Records of leased properties are also kept, supplying the usual identifying information, costs of the property being amortized, and the terms of the lease.

Depreciation is generally based upon useful life and written off on a straight-line basis providing one-half year's depreciation on new additions during the year and one-half year's depreciation on disposals and retirements during the year. Automotive and transportation equipment is sometimes written off on a mileage or ton-mile basis.

Improvements to leased premises are generally written off over the period called for in the lease, unless the useful life is less than the period of the lease.

Obsolescence is a factor that must be considered in establishing useful lives of store fixtures and equipment. Retirements or abandonments and their replacements in any store or group of stores may require an appraisal of like units in other stores and a reduction in their useful lives. Replacement programs may be established for completion within one or more years. They may be chain-wide or they may be for only a specific group of stores. The depreciation program should be sufficiently flexible to permit a realignment of rates whenever necessary.

## Reports to management

**Financial reports.** The generally accepted accounting cycle for the preparation of financial reports to management is by quarters covering 13 weeks each. The operating week begins Monday and ends Saturday, and, since most companies operate on a fiscal-year basis, the annual closing is at the close of business on the Saturday night nearest to the end of the last month of the fiscal year. This results in a 53-week year about every seventh year, and the odd week is picked up in the last quarter of that year.

Quarterly *balance sheets* are generally prepared in sufficient detail for management's purposes and in a form showing comparative figures for the same period for the previous year. Increases and decreases as between years are noted.

The *Statement of Operating Results and Earnings Reinvested in the Business* is generally shown for the year to date and for the current 13-week period then ended, indicating ratios to sales, both actual and budget, and budget variances. Supporting this statement are the detailed departmental expense accounts. If operating budgets are not used, the prior year's figures for the same periods, or the increases and decreases only as between the years, can be inserted.

The *Application of Funds Statement* can be prepared at the end of each quarter, if required, but an annual statement of this kind generally meets management's requirements.

Condensed statements are generally prepared at the end of each monthly period throughout the year, covering both the period and the year to date. These so-called "flash statements" are for trend purposes only and do not carry budget variances.

**General operating reports.** Reports on stores' operations are prepared and distributed to all levels of the supervisory staff, including the district managers. The division and district managers receive reports covering only the stores under their direction. These reports consist of:

1. *Weekly Comparative Sales Report* by stores, recapped by district, divisions, and in total.

2. *Weekly Clerk Hire and Man-Hour Report* by stores.

3. *Periodic Inventory Results* showing gross profits and percentages by stores.

4. *Statement of Physical Inventory Results, Grocery Department* and *Overstock Report* at time of count.

5. *Quarterly Store Operating Statements.* The recap of these statements reconciles the figures for the various stores with the respective totals indicated in the Statement of Operating Results and Earnings Reinvested in the Business for the quarter and the year to date down to the Net Operating Profit. On the store statement, this item is described as Net Store Income (Deficit).

**Reports for purchasing.** Each buyer maintains a separate record of the items he buys. This record is by line number and by warehouse location and indicates commitments made, quantities received and date, and the stock on hand at the end of each week. In addition, the following reports are prepared for the procurement department and management:

1. Daily lists of warehouse items that are out of stock.

2. Monthly list of items in warehouses 60 days or longer.

3. Monthly commodity analysis of warehouse shipments to stores by warehouse and by buyer, indicating the cost and retail value, the developed markup percentage, and the percentage of each commodity group to the total.

4. Monthly report of turnover developed for each warehouse and the overstock position, based upon comparison of book inventories with budgeted inventories for the period.

**Other reports to management.** Other basic reports to management consist of:

1. *Daily Cash Report* in respect to depository and disbursing bank accounts.

2. *Weekly Statistical Report* covering:
    a. Purchase commitments.
    b. Accounts payable and drafts drawn under letters of credit.

    c. Warehouse tonnages—inbound and outbound.

    d. Cash disbursements classified as to major expenditure.

    e. Cash received.

    3. Monthly production reports of manufacturing departments.

    4. Monthly reports on the *Capital Expenditure Budgets* and the *Repair and Replacement Budgets*.

Special analyses and projections are called for from time to time by the various executive departments covering specific operations assigned to them. Such reports, although essential to the respective departments, are not necessarily scheduled for continuous preparation. Policies in this connection will vary between companies. However, the continued preparation of a nonessential report can become a costly procedure.

## Special devices to reduce record-keeping costs

**Punch-card accounting.** Punch-card accounting and the use of electronic tabulating equipment have made it possible to save time in billing warehouse shipments to stores and effectively to control warehouse inventories. In this connection, the "pre-billing" method is in general use. Under this method, punched cards are prepared upon receipt of merchandise in the warehouse; these carry the item, description, line number, warehouse location number, unit retail price, unit cost price, and weight. Upon receipt of the store order, the proper cards are selected from the files, put through the machines, and a store invoice produced. These invoices are then routed to the warehouse for selection of the merchandise and its shipment to the store. Items ordered in excess of book inventories are listed daily for use of the procurement department. Items called for on the invoices but physically out of stock in the warehouse, owing to wrong selection or other warehouse errors, are reported by the warehouse and proper credits are issued for the adjustment. The accounting information at cost and retail is accumulated from the office copy of the invoice for use in crediting the warehouse inventory controls and charging the store's purchase accounts and the store's retail inventory controls.

The punched cards are numbered and book inventories can be computed at any time by subtracting the low number from the high number: the difference will represent quantities on hand, which can be costed from the cards and their values computed. Differences between high numbers represent receipts, while differences between low numbers represent shipments for any selected period.

Statistical information in respect to warehouse inbound and outbound tonnages is also available from the punched cards, and monthly runs of receipts and shipments are prepared from them.

Latest developments in electronic equipment make it possible to prepare and assemble automatically the data for invoice preparation and for computation of the book inventories (both in quantities and in value) at the end of any run. The "batch billing method" is the term applied to this procedure, but certain limitations have kept it from becoming as yet a practical application for all companies.

Punched-card and tabulating equipment afford fast and accurate means for preparing the property records and the depreciation accruals.

## Modification of system for small business

The data to be assembled and classified are basically the same for the small operation as for the larger operation. The major difference is in the volume. The accounting requirements of the smaller operation may be met by a small staff capable of keeping the daily volume of transactions up to date with a minimum of mechanical devices.

Budgetary procedures may not be used by the smaller operations. In lieu thereof, measurements of performance may be made against the results of the previous year for like periods.

Separate internal audit departments may not be necessary, provided the cash counts and audits, inventory-taking, and observations within the stores can be made part of the store supervisory staff's routine duties. Many larger companies require their store supervisory staff to do a certain amount of this work from time to time as part of their responsibility for good management of the stores under their direction.

# 26

# Funeral Directing

by

EUGENE F. FORAN

Business Counsellor, Eugene F. Foran and Associates,
Decatur, Illinois

---

## Characteristics that affect the accounting system

**Nature of the profession.** Funeral directing is a profession. Accountingwise, however, its position among professions is unique in that it furnishes burial goods and supplies in conjunction with its professional services. This dual role creates the necessity of accounting for professional services and expenses, and also for the use of inventories in accounting for supplies and burial goods.

The profession is regulated in each of the states through a licensing division of the state government. In addition, public health laws of the states place on the funeral director the responsibility of filing death certificates, an important vital statistics record. Public health and welfare laws of local, state, and Federal governments affect certain other phases of funeral directing.

The practice of funeral directing is built up by attaining the confidence of the community. This confidence is established through adherence to a strict code of ethics respected by funeral directors throughout the entire country. The extension of service to any income or social group is a characteristic fundamental to any profession. Therefore, an accurate, yet fair, method of determining fees and providing funeral service for *every income group* must be achieved.

The physical properties required in the practice of the profession follow the normal functions. The funeral home (mortuary) contains a funeral service room or formal chapel and rooms for visitation. For the care of deceased human bodies, there is a sanitary, well-ventilated operating room with facilities and equipment required by state law. This room will be found to compare in all these respects with a hospital operating room.

There are facilities for automotive equipment and also office, utility, and supply rooms. Throughout the establishment furnishings are provided suitable to the normal function of each section. A balanced selection of caskets, burial clothing, and burial vaults are displayed.

**Ownership peculiarities.** In any professional field there is a tendency to hand down the established practice from father to son (or daughter), and this characteristic is true in funeral directing. Others entering the practice as owners do so after an extended period of experience in funeral directing by (1) becoming a partner in an established practice, (2) establishing a new practice, or (3) acquiring an existing practice. The form of business organization in the profession is, for the most part, either individual proprietorship or partnership.

## Functional organization

**Division into activities.** Funeral service is divided into three general categories: (1) the preparation and care of the remains; (2) the use of the funeral home and related facilities; and (3) arranging for and directing the funeral service. The functions are twofold, that is, serving the living while caring for the dead. Accountingwise, however, there is no specific requirement for, or purpose served in, the departmentalization of the organization. In funeral homes handling a large volume of services, employees and assistants may be assigned to specific duties in the general categories mentioned.

Figure 1 shows the funeral service functions and their related cost components necessary for determination of funeral service fees.

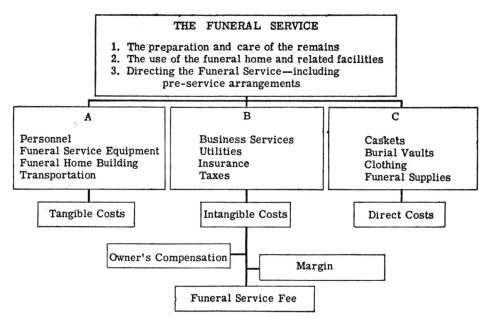

**Fig. 1. Funeral Service Functions and Related Cost Components.**

## Principles and objectives of the system

**Principle of the "income pattern."** The occasion of death and its frequency, measured only in mortality tables, is the factor initiating the development of the *income pattern.* The mortality frequency within each social or economic group, in a given community, is another element in the *income pattern.* In a given community there will be little variation in *this pattern* from year to year.

The system provides a record of funeral service fees. For each accounting period, individual funeral service fees are sorted by income categories, and a *pattern* emanates, reflecting the number of funeral services in each grouping, such as:

| Income Category | Unit Pattern |
|---|---|
| $200–$300 | 3 |
| 301– 400 | 5 |
| 401– 500 | 6 |
| 501– 600 | 4 |
| 601– 700 | 2 |

The use of the *income pattern,* together with the current mortality rate, provides the data by which normal projections may be obtained, and also a basis for allocating expenses and for determining fees. Total revenue, in itself, does not provide the data which the pattern of funeral service fees furnishes.

**Allocation of costs and expenses.** In funeral directing, as in all personal service professions, the method of distributing costs and expenses must reflect social as well as economic conditions. A substantial proportion of funeral services within a community are provided below the *average cost* per service. This situation is the result of meeting the professional requirement of furnishing services to every income or social group.

Payment for funeral services by governmental agencies and institutional groups seldom, if ever, covers the direct costs involved; therefore, no consideration is given in these cases to indirect costs. Infants' and children's funeral service fees have been traditionally nominal because of the economic factors usually present. These conditions eliminate the use of a straight *average cost* in the determination of funeral service fees.

The *average cost* computation is the first step in the allocation of costs and expenses in funeral directing. To this average cost are added the expenses and costs which are not recovered on the types of services mentioned in the preceding paragraph. This formula develops the cost to be used in the determination of funeral service fees. However, in serving all classes of society, a fair method of cost distribution is necessary. In funeral directing accounting, these costs are allocated, through the use of the *income pattern,* by applying costs and expenses in ratio to realization.

**Objectives of the system.** Any system used should readily disclose the information necessary for a clear understanding of income patterns, for allocating costs and expenses, and for determining fees. A fundamental objective of the system presented is to provide a guide for the practical distribution of costs and expenses in order that funeral fees may be determined through the application of sound accounting principles. This supplements the basic objectives of any accounting system, which are to provide management with (1) a chronological record of transactions, (2) a descriptive statement of conditions, (3) a tabulation of operational results, and (4) the data necessary for governmental reports.

## Classification of accounts and books of account

**Comment on the accounting system.** A fundamental requirement for any model accounting system is that it be rigid enough to form a guide from which individual applications can be patterned and yet be flexible enough to allow for individual deviations. The account classifications and the books of account described herein provide a framework for any system. The general provisions of this system have been accepted and are used more extensively than any other system of accounts for funeral directing.

**System requirements.** The system of accounts is basic and simple. In addition to the asset and liability accounts common to all businesses, an account is provided in which to record Advance Deposits on Contracts for Future Funeral Services, with a contra account showing Trust Funds for Advance Deposits on Contracts for Future Funeral Services. These accounts, while offsetting each other, should be shown on the balance sheet to disclose contingent liabilities and trust funds held. Income accounts are designed especially for the profession, and expense accounts are divided for convenience into general and automobile classifications. The costs of burial goods and supplies are determined by direct charges and credits to inventory and purchases accounts and the application of physical inventories of these items.

**The Accommodation Account.** In many areas, funeral directors advance monies, as an accommodation to the family being served, for the payment of cemetery charges, clergy and musicians' honorariums, telephone and telegraph tolls, transportation charges, and any other items of expense incidental to the funeral. The Accommodation Account is debited when payment is made by the funeral director; and this account is credited with a like amount when a charge is made to the funeral account. Any balance indicates an incomplete record of the transactions. One ledger account may be used; however, many prefer to use two ledger accounts, one for Cash Advances (debit) and the other Cash Advances Recovered (credit), the credit posting coming from the Funeral Service Charge record (see page 744).

**Statement form preferred in this system.** Funeral directing accounting requires only a combination journal and a funeral service charge (sales) journal. In a volume operation, a cash receipts record and a check record might be preferred in place of the combination journal. Therefore, instead

STATEMENT OF ASSETS, LIABILITIES, AND NET WORTH (CAPITAL)

ASSETS:

Cash .................................................................$ x
Bank ...................................................................... x
Accounts Receivable ....................................................: x
Inventories:

Caskets ....................................................$ x
Vaults ......................................... x
Clothing .......................................... x
Embalming Supplies ............................................ x
Funeral Supplies ............................................. x     x
Prepaid Expenses ..............................................^ x

Total Current Assets ......................................$ x

Trust Fund for Future Services ...............................$ x
Less, Contracts for Future Services ......................... x     x

| | Cost | Depreciation Allowed | Carrying Value |
|---|---|---|---|
| Property Accounts: | | | |
| Land ..............................$ | x | $    x | $    x |
| Buildings ......................... | x | x | x |
| Funeral Service Equipment ......... | x | x | x |
| Furnishings ....................... | x | x | x |
| Motor Equipment ................. | x | x | x |
| Total Cost and Depreciation ......$ | x | $    x | |

Net Carrying Value .............................................. x

TOTAL ASSETS ......................................$ x

LIABILITIES:

Accounts Payable .............................................$ x
Accrued Taxes (detailed) ..................................... x
Accrued Expenses ............................................. x

Total Current Liabilities ........................................$ x
Long-Term Indebtedness ...................................... x

TOTAL LIABILITIES ......................................$ x

NET WORTH (CAPITAL):

Owners' Equity (Capital) ....................................$ x
Net Gain for the Year ......................................... x
Total ..........................................$ x
Less: Owners' Withdrawals ................................... x

TOTAL NET WORTH ...................................... x

TOTAL LIABILITIES and NET WORTH ...................$ x

**Fig. 2. Balance Sheet.**

of presenting a list of accounts and their obvious posting source, we are presenting a suggested form for the balance sheet (Figure 2) and for the income and expense statement (Figure 3). Special attention is called to the presentation of income, costs, and expenses, because funeral service income consists of a combination of charges for professional and personal services, together with charges for burial goods. The determination of "gross margins" is completely omitted. Data showing "gross margins" or "gross profit" distort the facts and do not provide the reader proper information.

STATEMENT OF INCOME, COSTS, AND EXPENSES

INCOME:

Funeral Service Fees ..........................................................$ x
Burial Vault Sales .......................................................... x
Clothing Sales .......................................................... x
Other Service Fees .......................................................... x
Sundry Income .......................................................... x
Interest Income .......................................................... x

    TOTAL INCOME ........................................................$ x

COSTS and EXPENSES:

Burial Goods and Supplies ........................................$ x
Advertising ...................................................... x
Collection Costs ...................................................... x
Depreciation ...................................................... x
Dues and Subscriptions ...................................................... x
Employees—Salaries ...................................................... x
Funeral Service Expense ...................................................... x
Funeral Trip Expense ...................................................... x
Utilities ...................................................... x
Insurance Premiums ...................................................... x
Interest and Bank Service Charges ...................................................... x
Laundry and Cleaning ...................................................... x
Legal and Accounting Fees ...................................................... x
Office Expense and Licenses ...................................................... x
Repairs and Maintenance ...................................................... x
Services—Other Funeral Directors ...................................................... x
Taxes (detail) ...................................................... x
Telephone—Telegraph ...................................................... x
Travel ...................................................... x
Automobile Expense ...................................................... x
  Gasoline—Oil—Supplies ...................................................... x
  Auto Repairs ...................................................... x
  Auto Insurance ...................................................... x
  Auto License ...................................................... x
  Rental of Equipment ...................................................... x

    TOTAL FUNERAL COSTS and EXPENSES ............................. x

NET GAIN for PERIOD .........................................................$ x

Fig. 3. Statement of Income, Costs, and Expenses,

**Records peculiar to the system.** The division of Vital Statistics of the Department of Public Health in each of the states supplies death certificate forms. This record is completed and filed with the proper authorities, and in exchange the funeral director receives a burial permit, or a removal permit if disposition is to be at some other place. Statistical data required for the death certificate, together with information for the obituary, is retained by the funeral director. Usually these data are gathered on forms reflecting the custom of the community. Standard forms are available.

*Funeral service agreement.* A funeral service agreement is recommended. In addition to showing the funeral service fee, cash advances, and other items, the terms and manner of settlement should be stated and the persons responsible asked to authorize the service. These contracts are important when estates and other sources of settlement do not provide sufficient funds.

*The account receivable record* and all indexing should be in the name of the deceased. A chronological record as well as an alphabetical record is recommended. This is not a requirement for accounting, but it provides easy reference to each family group.

*Record of funeral charges and direct costs.* A record is maintained for entering funeral service charges and direct costs for each funeral. Figure 4 illustrates such a record. On this record funeral fees, vault sales, clothing sales, and cash advances (accommodations) are shown in separate classifications. Direct costs are listed for caskets, vaults, clothing, and cash advances. This record is the source for establishing the income pattern and it is also the source for posting (1) the general ledger income accounts,

| | DIRECT | COSTS | | | | | | |
|---|---|---|---|---|---|---|---|---|
| | Casket Cost | Vault Cost | Clothing Cost | Cash Advances | | | Total Direct Costs | |

(RIGHT SIDE)

| | | FUNERAL | SERVICES | Month of _____ 19_____ | | | | |
|---|---|---|---|---|---|---|---|---|
| Date | Name of Deceased | Acct. No. | Funeral Fee | Vault Sales | Clothing Sales | Cash Advances | | Total Charge |

(LEFT SIDE)

**Fig. 4. Record of Funeral Charges and Direct Costs.**

(2) charges to accounts receivable, and (3) inventory control accounts for caskets, vaults, and clothing.

*Cash, check, and invoice record.* In the average instance, a combination journal may be used to record cash receipts, bank deposits, checks issued, and invoices for merchandise purchased. The use of accounts payable is optional, because of the small number of transactions as compared with other types of businesses. There are no particular problems in connection with the use or form of these records. The handling of the payroll is by the ordinary method.

## Extension of credit; collections

**Responsibility for payment.** Death causes a change in legal status concerning liabilities of, and on behalf of, an individual. Contracts, verbal or otherwise, made by an individual during his lifetime are *his* liabilities; however, the funeral and interment expenses for a deceased person are not *his* liabilities but are liabilities of either (1) his estate, (2) persons legally responsible for them, or (3) those persons who may have assumed such responsibilities. Therefore, the extension of credit follows a different pattern in the funeral service profession from that followed elsewhere.

A Funeral Service Purchase Agreement is an important factor in collection procedure, as it contains authorization for the service and prescribes the manner in which payment is to be completed. An itemized statement is prepared and submitted, usually within ten days. The payment for funeral expenses is generally made in a single transaction. When necessary, however, provision is made for periodic payments.

When the collection of funeral expenses is to be made from the assets of the estate of a deceased person, a claim must be filed against the estate within the time provided by statute. Creditors' claims are ranked in preference according to state statutes; however, funeral expenses of the decedent against his estate are given a primary rating, subject to limitations as to amount of preference in some states. After filing, the claim is reviewed by the court, and after approval the administrator is authorized to make payment.

## Reports to management

**Frequency of reports.** The frequency of reports to management varies with the volume of services. Quarterly interim reports are usually sufficient when the number of services is 750 or less; when the volume of services is larger, management would be better informed through the use of monthly reports.

**Type of reports.** The report to management should include the following statements, together with the necessary supporting schedules:

1. Statement of Assets, Liabilities, and Net Worth (see Figure 2)
2. Statement of Income, Costs, and Expense (see Figure 3)
3. Statement of Source and Application of Funds
4. Statement Showing Income Pattern and Overhead Allocations

The manner of accumulating detailed information will vary with the style of recordkeeping preferred. The use of monthly summary and recapitulation sheets for income and expense classifications is recommended to eliminate multiple postings to the general ledger and to provide a chart of the monthly progress in the operating section of the accounting system.

# 27

# Furniture (Manufacturing)

by

## W. W. STEGMAN

Controller, Kroehler Mfg. Co., Naperville, Illinois.

---

## Industry characteristics that affect the accounting system

**Nature of the business.** Generally speaking, two classes of furniture are manufactured—office furniture and household furniture. Office furniture consists of desks, tables, chairs, and file cabinets. Household furniture includes upholstered living-room furniture; dining-room tables, chairs, buffets, cabinets, and so forth; kitchen tables, chairs, and stools; bedroom furniture; juvenile furniture; and outdoor furniture. These products may be constructed of wood, wrought iron, steel, upholstering materials, leather, and plastics. No one manufacturer attempts to produce all types of furniture. The line is usually limited to from one to five types of product.

Establishments vary in size from the one-man shop doing a bench-type production to the multi-plant organization that uses assembly-line methods and produces the raw material in its own lumber, spring, and cotton mills. As compared with most industries, in furniture manufacturing there are more small and fewer large organizations. The smaller manufacturers must limit their production to a bench-type operation. Also, many of the makers of expensive hand-made furniture maintain a bench-type operation in preference to an assembly-line setup.

Because of the large number of manufacturers of every type of furniture, competition in all lines is extremely keen, both in price and in quality of materials and workmanship.

With the exception of outdoor furniture, operations are not geared to special seasons. In most lines, there is an increase in orders during and immediately after each of the numerous shows for furniture dealers. However, with the present year-round demand for household furniture, this market-time bulge of former years is becoming less pronounced.

747

The nature of the industry practically limits its by products to the sale of waste, such as unusable lumber, sawdust, and scrap materials.

Research is a constant problem involving considerable expense to the industry. To meet competition, a manufacturer must bring out new designs periodically. Continuous experimenting and testing of finishes, padding, springs, frames, cover materials, hardware, tools, jigs, and the like, are necessary to produce the new designs.

**Functional peculiarities.** Competitive pricing of furniture adds to the importance of effective buying. A well-trained staff of procurement specialists is essential to profitable operations in the furniture industry. A close co-ordination of procurement, engineering, and sales is mandatory, especially in regard to fabrics and other cover materials. Buying too little or too much of a specific color and pattern of a particular grade of material can prove to be an expensive miscalculation. Purchasing records must be complete, current, and accurate in regard to qualities ordered, delivery dates, and prices.

Furniture markets are held in Chicago, New York, San Francisco, and at several other points two or three times during the year to permit manufacturers to display their new designs to furniture dealers. Most of the manufacturers have showrooms open to dealers throughout the year, in which they exhibit displays from the previous market. Many orders are received at the showrooms. Salesmen call on furniture dealers throughout the year in an effort to make sales. While out in their territory, salesmen are limited in their displays to sample swatches, pictures, color charts, wood-finish samples, and the like. Various arrangements for paying salesmen are made, ranging from salary plus travel expense to straight commission with no reimbursement for expenses.

Transportation of most types of furniture presents a considerable problem. Freight rates are high because of the bulk as compared with the weight of the product. Many factories operate their own trucking service, and in some cases free transportation is furnished to dealers within a defined radius of the factory, with a transportation charge being made for deliveries outside of that radius.

Generally speaking, furniture manufacturers do not make a practice of helping to finance their dealers. Most furniture is sold on a cash discount basis of 2%—30 days, net 60 days.

**Asset peculiarities.** Assets of a furniture manufacturer are comparable to those of other types of manufacturers, with the exception of inventories. A large inventory of raw materials is normal in plants processing their own lumber, owing to the time involved in preparing lumber for use. Finished goods inventories of upholstering plants are usually small, because much of the furniture is assembled on specific orders in regard to style and cover-material combinations.

**Principal accounting problem.** The determination of lumber costs appears to be the principal problem area, accountingwise, in the industry for all manufacturers using lumber in any way in the production of their furniture. Those manufacturers who buy green, rough-cut lumber and do all of the processing up to the point where the product is finished have the greatest problems.

The shrinkage from air or dry kiln, as well as the waste resulting from warping, splitting, rip, cut-off, and planing operations to bring the lumber to dimension-stock sizes, as well as the labor involved, must all be considered in arriving at the cost of full-dimension lumber. In proceeding from dimension lumber to the finished product, whether it be an upholstered sofa frame, a solid mahogany dresser, or a walnut veneer office desk, some waste always occurs in grading out unusable pieces of lumber or plywood owing to knots, warp, unsuitable graining, or the like.

Proper costing of lumber is most important, not only for the purpose of arriving at profitable sales prices for the finished product, but also for correct pricing of raw material, work-in-process, and finished goods inventories.

Ordinarily, lumber costs are calculated on the size of full-dimension stock of a specific part as it arrives at the machine operations. If lumber is purchased in dimension-stock sizes, its cost presents no problem. If, on the other hand, it has been processed through the yard, kiln, and mills of the manufacturer, all costs of the rough lumber and its processing should be reduced to the basis of dimension-stock footage or dimension-stock part, whichever best suits the accounting system.

## Functional organization

**Functional areas.** Whether the manufacturer is a five-man shop or a multi-plant organization with a large general office staff, the following functions must be performed:

*Engineering.* Designs must be developed or purchased, component parts determined, costs estimated, and method of production outlined.

*Industrial relations or personnel.* Qualified craftsmen and supervisors must be kept available to assemble the furniture.

*Purchasing.* Raw materials and supplies must be on hand in proper specifications and quantities.

*Building and equipment.* Adequate work space must be provided, with the necessary tools and equipment to produce the furniture.

*Production.* Production and materials must be controlled and the finished product packed and shipped to the dealer.

*Sales.* A staff of trained sales personnel must be maintained, their remuneration determined, terms of sale scheduled, and sufficient advertising and displays arranged in order to build sales volume.

*Accounting.* Adequate records must be maintained for tax purposes, reports to management, and the satisfaction of the owners of the business.

Figure 1 shows a flexible chart that can be used as the general office organization of a multi-plant concern, or as a single-plant operation with certain additions of manufacturing departments under the production division. The solid lines indicate the organizational chain of command, while the dotted lines show the functional tie-in of various accounting departments with other divisions and their departments.

**Tie-in of accounting departments with other divisions.** Cost Accounting obtains much of its data from Production Control, Material Control, and Engineering.

Accounts Receivable gets the customer invoices or shipping papers from the Packing and Shipping Department.

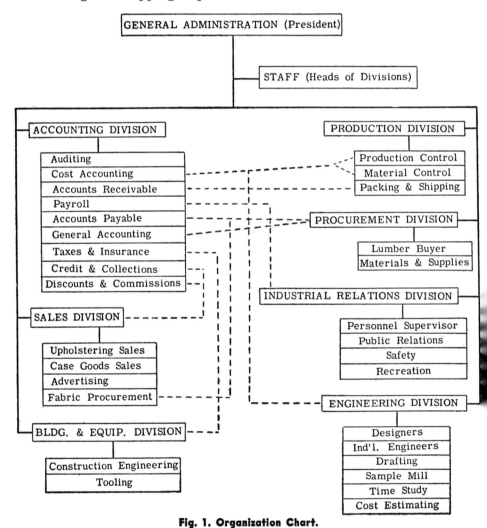

**Fig. 1. Organization Chart.**

Payroll must have names, rates, and time information from the personnel supervisor.

Accounts Payable must rely on the Procurement Division for the correctness of invoices from suppliers.

The General Accounting Department and the Tax and Insurance Department obtain all information required in connection with fixed assets from the Procurement Division and the Building and Equipment Division.

Credit and Collections furnishes the Sales Division with approvals or discontinuances of credit limitations on prospective as well as present customers.

Discounts and Commissions co-ordinates trade discount and sales commission rates with the Sales Division.

## Principles and objectives of the system

**Principles to be applied in reflecting income, costs, and expenses.** A certain amount of breakdown of sales by types of furniture is desirable for statistical use by the sales department and management. For example, the sales manager of an upholstering plant should have comparative sales-volume figures on dual-purpose sofas, hostess chairs, premium furniture, and regular-grade furniture. The sales manager for an office furniture manufacturer would likewise want to know the volume in wooden desks, wooden chairs, steel desks, steel chairs, file cabinets, and so forth. Such comparative information furnished promptly may lead to the investigation and correction of any difficulty causing a sudden decrease in the volume of a specific item.

A workable cost system is especially important in this industry. The continual change in designs, styles, and materials used makes it mandatory that accurate cost figures be available as a determining factor in the selling prices of new products. This cost-estimating may be done in either the accounting or the engineering department.

In addition to the cost-estimating operation, a standard cost system should be set up to control actual production costs, including direct labor and material, indirect labor, supplies, and factory burden. Costs should be broken down by products and further segregated by jobs, if desirable. All costs must be tied into and controlled by the various general ledger control accounts, including cost variance accounts. Standard costs for various parts and operations should be reviewed and tested periodically.

A departmentalization of the general administrative expenses, to achieve better control of general expenses, would yield a breakdown as indicated in the operating statement (Figure 8, page 771), namely: Administrative, Industrial Relations, Production, Accounting, General Procurement, Fabric Procurement, and Building and Equipment. Advertising and selling expenses are accumulated separately.

In order for an accounting system to function effectively, it must have a sound basis for the distribution of expenses. The job of determining whether expenses are to be classified as capital expenditures, production costs, manufacturing burden, administrative expense, or selling expense, and the proper breakdown within each group, is a function of trained personnel.

A voucher system of paying, recording, distributing, and accumulating expenses by account number in the voucher register appears to be the most satisfactory method of expense control. Under this system, postings of totals can be readily made at the end of each accounting period to the respective general ledger or expense ledger accounts.

**Specific objectives.** The following objectives are attained by the system described:

1. It furnishes adequate information and documentary evidence to meet the requirements of governmental bodies, management, and the owners.

2. It enables the sales division to plan its activities, by making available accurate cost estimates, information as to sales trends by types of furniture, reports on the ability of the factory to produce at a required volume, and reports on the availability of cash to finance the necessary inventories.

3. It provides information for production planning. Profitable production cannot be planned without up-to-date cost information on labor, material, factory burden, administrative expenses, and selling expenses. Intelligent planning for expansion or curtailment of either the production of styles of furniture or plant facilities is impossible without awareness of the effects accountingwise of such a move.

## Classification of accounts and books of account

### Balance sheet accounts.

| | | Debits from | Credits from |
|---|---|---|---|
| | ASSETS | | |
| | *Current Assets:* | | |
| 100 | Cash .................. | Cash Receipts | Cash Disbursements |
| 105 | Investments at Cost ...... | Voucher Register | Cash Receipts |
| 120 | Accounts and Notes Receivable ................. | Voucher Register, Sales Journal | General Journal, Cash Receipts |
| 125 | Allowance for Possible Losses ............... | General Journal | General Journal |
| | Inventories: | | |
| 130-01 | Raw Materials and Supplies ........... | Do | Do |
| 130-02 | Work in Process ....... | Do | Do |
| 130-03 | Finished Products ...... | Do | Do |

|  |  | Debits from | Credits from |
|---|---|---|---|
| *Fixed Assets:* | | | |
| 141 | Land ................... | Voucher Register, General Journal | Voucher Register, General Journal, Cash Receipts |
| 142 | Buildings .............. | Do | Do |
| 143 | Machinery and Equipment. | Do | Do |
| 152, 153 | Accumulated Allowance for Depreciation ......... | Voucher Register, Cash Receipts, General Journal | General Journal, Voucher Register |
| *Other Assets:* | | | |
| 190 | Deferred Charges ........ | Voucher Register | General Journal, Cash Receipts |
| 129 | Miscellaneous Receivables . | General Journal, Voucher Register | General Journal, Cash Receipts, Voucher Register |
| 191 | Cash-Surrender Value of Life Insurance on Officers | General Journal | General Journal |
| 192 | Goodwill ............... | General Journal, Voucher Register | Do |

## LIABILITIES

| | | | |
|---|---|---|---|
| *Current Liabilities:* | | | |
| 201 | Accounts Payable ........ | Cash Disbursements | Voucher Register, Cash Receipts |
| 202 | Short-Term Notes Payable. | Voucher Register | Cash Receipts |
| | Accruals: | | |
| 210 | Federal Income Taxes .. | Do | General Journal |
| 215 | Other Taxes ........... | Do | Do |
| 220 | Salaries, Wages, and Commissions ........ | Do | Do |
| | Capital Stock: | | |
| 250 | Preferred ............. | Stock Register | Stock Register |
| 251 | Common ............... | Do | Do |
| 252 | Earned Surplus .......... | General Journal | General Journal |

## Income and expense accounts.

| | | | |
|---|---|---|---|
| 300 | Sales .................. | General Journal, Voucher Register | Sales Journal, General Journal |
| 350 | Cash Discounts .......... | Cash Receipts, General Journal | General Journal |
| | Cost of Goods Sold ....... | Voucher Register, General Journal, Departmental Ledgers | Voucher Register, General Journal, Cash Receipts |

|  | Selling, Administrative, and General Expenses: |  |  |
|---|---|---|---|
| 7449 | Commissions ......... | Voucher Register, General Journal | General Journal |
| 7300 | Advertising .......... | Do | General Journal, Cash Receipts |
| 7400 | General Sales ......... | Do | Do |
| 7000 | General Administrative . | Do | Do |
|  | *Other Income:* |  |  |
| 905 | Profit from Sale of Investments and Equipment... | Do | Voucher Register, General Journal, Cash Receipts |
| 801 | Interest ................ | General Journal | Cash Receipts |
| 805 | Dividends .............. | Do | Do |
| 810 | Miscellaneous ........... | General Journal, Voucher Register | Do |
|  | *Other Charges:* |  |  |
| 901 | Interest ................ | Voucher Register | General Journal |
| 7599 | Federal Taxes .......... | Do | Do |

Sales and Cost of Goods Sold may be broken down by type or class of product on the statement of income. The manufacturing overhead statements reproduced at pages 772–776 show the detailed factory burden accounts.

If a standard cost system is used, Cost of Goods Sold would be shown at standard cost, and the following cost variances would be listed after Cost of Goods Sold:

Cost Variances:
    Price      —Material
    Quantity —Material
    Quantity —Waste
    General  —Labor
    General  —Factory Burden
    General  —Commercial Burden

**Expansion of chart of accounts.** A complete numerical chart of accounts would be lengthy and would not fit the needs of all furniture manufacturers. However, the following general outline, used with sub-numbers and plant numbers, is quite flexible and can form a basis for any requirement:

|  |  |
|---|---|
| 100–01 | Peoples National Bank |
| 100–02 | First State Bank |
| 105 | Investments |
| 120 | Receivables |
| 130 | Inventories |

| | |
|---|---|
| 140 | Fixed Assets |
| 150 | Depreciation Reserves |
| 190 | Other Assets |
| 200 | Payables |
| 250 | Capital Accounts |
| 1-300 | Sales, Plant No. 1 |
| 2-300 | Sales, Plant No. 2 |
| 1-350 | Cash Discounts, Plant No. 1 |
| 800 | Other Income |
| 900 | Other Charges |
| 1-4100 | Plant Engineering, Plant No. 1 (Last two digits of 01 to 49 indicate salaries or wages. 50 to 99 indicate expenses other than salaries and wages.) |
| 2-4200 | General Factory Expense, Plant No. 2 |
| 3-5100 | Mill No. 1, Plant No. 3 |
| 7000 | General Administrative Expenses |
| 7200 | General Accounting Expense |
| 7300 | General Advertising Expense |
| 7400 | General Selling Expense |

**Subsidiary ledgers.** The following are subsidiary ledgers with control accounts in the general ledger:

1. Accounts receivable ledger
2. Miscellaneous receivable ledger
3. Fixed assets ledger
4. Depreciation reserves ledger
5. Expense ledger
6. Commissions payable ledger
7. Annual physical inventory record
8. Dividends paid record
9. Payroll records

# Peculiarities of procedures: sales-receivables cycle; purchases-payables cycle; cash receipts and disbursements

**Accounting for sales.** Normally, the billing of sales is broken down as follows: first, between plants, where there is a multi-plant operation; second, between the general types of product, such as upholstered furniture, office furniture, bedroom furniture, and the like, where one operation produces more than one general type; third, between (1) quality groups, such as premium and regular furniture, (2) functional groups, such as chairs, tables, and buffets, and (3) construction-materials groups, such as wood and steel, leather and fabric covers, solid woods and veneers. No rule of thumb can be set up for the industry on sales breakdown. Each manufacturer must determine his requirements in this regard to coincide with his production and sales.

**Billing.** The billing department should be a part of or located convenient to the shipping department. The receipt of copies of freight bills, bills of lading, and other documentary evidence of delivery is a signal to the billing clerk that the order has been produced and delivered, and the time has arrived to prepare an invoice for the dealer. With shipping documents and price lists being used as a basis, invoices are typed in a sufficient number of copies to meet the needs of the customer, the accounts receivable department, any other department that uses invoice copies for sales analysis or distribution, and a file copy to which copies of shipping documents are attached. The copy of the invoice going to the accounts receivable department is used as a posting medium for making the charge to the proper dealer's account. The invoice copy is then filed in such a manner that it is readily available to the credit department for reference.

**Accounts receivable records.** Several methods of maintaining accounts receivable records are in use in the industry. Some manufacturers prefer to use the invoice copy as a part of their accounts receivable record. While the invoice remains unpaid, it is filed by dealer and by date in an open-account file. Upon payment, the invoice is removed from the open-account file, stamped with the date of payment, and similarly refiled in a paid-invoice file.

Other manufacturers whose volume warrants such an operation key-punch a card showing the pertinent information for each invoice and file the card by dealer and by date in an open-account file. When the invoice is paid, the punched card is removed, the date of payment is punched on it, and it is refiled for future reference and for the production of an account history by the use of tabulating machines.

A third group prefers to maintain a current, historical record by posting invoices and collections to a ledger account for each dealer.

As most furniture dealers pay by individual invoices, it is not a general practice in the industry to furnish dealers with monthly statements.

**Cash receipts procedure.** Cash receipts procedures vary to a certain extent among furniture manufacturers, depending on their size, number of plants, banking facilities, and type of accounts receivable system used. In a single-plant operation, it may be more practical for incoming checks to go directly to the accounts receivable department, where clerks use the checks as a medium for posting to the individual account, pulling the invoices from the open file, or withdrawing the key-punched cards which represent the invoices being paid. A cash receipts record of cash received, cash discounts allowed, and freight adjustments must be maintained on a daily basis so that it can be summarized and posted to the general ledger accounts in totals at the end of the month.

Some multi-plant organizations with widely separated plants find it more satisfactory to have dealers in the locality of a plant make their payments for invoices directly to a designated bank in that area, and thus eliminate several days' float during the time the checks would be in transit to the general office.

Under this system, the bank immediately deposits the checks to the manufacturer's account and mails a list of the payments to the general office, along with any vouchers, lists of invoices, and so forth, that it may have received. The accounts receivable department then uses the data received from the bank as posting media for crediting the dealer accounts and making entries in the cash receipts record.

**Purchase procedures.** Purchase-order and receiving procedure follows conventional practice.

Invoices are usually received in triplicate, two copies by the plant receiving department and one by the purchasing department. The purchasing department posts information from its copy to the Kardex card and files the invoice. The receiving department attaches its copies to each of the two purchase order copies, along with copies of receiving reports made on receipt of the material. The invoice, purchase order, and receiving report are checked for quantity, description, and price. One set is approved and sent to the accounts payable department for payment and the other set is filed.

Expense-distribution code numbers are entered on the purchase order by the purchasing department. Invoices for services, and the like, which are not supported by a purchase order, are approved and the distribution code number marked on the invoice by someone authorized to do so. After the accounts payable department has checked the distribution marked on the invoices, the extensions, and the prices, the invoices are ready for payment.

**Cash disbursement procedure.** With the exception of payrolls, the accounts payable department normally writes all checks. A three-copy, voucher-type check is desirable. The first copy is signed and sent to the payee; the second copy is stamped with a voucher number and filed alphabetically by payee's name; and the third copy is stamped with the same voucher number, attached to the invoice, receiving report, and purchase order, entered in the voucher register, and then filed in voucher-number order.

# Production and cost system [1]

**Developing cost estimates.** Estimated costs in the furniture industry are most important and should be calculated by either the engineers or the

[1] Acknowledgment is made to the National Association of Furniture Manufacturers for use of its *Cost Manual For Furniture Manufacturers* in preparing this section. Figures 2 through 7 are from the *N. A. F. M. Cost Manual.*

cost department immediately after a new design has been developed and a sample made. The results of the cost computation will be a determining factor in setting a profitable selling price on the design and in deciding on whether or not such a price will meet competition.

Forms similar to Figures 2 and 3 can be used as bills of material and cost sheets for this purpose. If production of the particular design is approved, the cost figures from the estimate may be used as standard costs for future production.

**Developing actual costs.** Ordinarily, a standard cost system with the cost ledgers definitely tying in with the financial ledgers is recommended for the furniture industry. Process costing might be preferable in a few instances where the manufacturer produces a continuous run of a few products, with little or no break in the production flow. The system can be set up on a job cost basis or a product cost basis, whichever best fits the requirements of the manufacturer.

**Material control.** Before production can be started on a particular design, it is necessary to check the bill of material against the inventory to determine which, if any, of the component parts are on hand. The procurement department must be advised to obtain from outside sources parts and hardware that are not to be produced within the plant. Drawings, specifications, and engineering samples of parts should accompany a copy of the production order to the several production departments so that sufficient parts will be produced to assemble the number of finished units called for by the production order. A procedure of issuing mill tickets is quite often used for this purpose. For example, if 300 units are being produced requiring 300 part #6051 top rails, a mill ticket calling for 300 #6051's will be prepared and sent to the mill. When these parts are completed, the mill ticket will be attached to the stack of parts for identification.

**Labor costs.** The distribution of direct labor wages to the various job numbers must be most accurate, and the total direct labor charged to all jobs for the period must tie in with the total wages of the direct labor departments or sections. Accuracy is essential, since factory overhead is generally distributed by departments on the basis of direct labor dollars.

The total accumulation of direct labor costs by jobs can be handled by either of two methods. The actual cost in dollars may be entered on an accumulation sheet, or actual minutes can be accumulated, as shown in Figures 4 (case goods) and 5 (upholstering), whichever method best suits the accounting system. If minutes rather than dollars are accumulated, it will be necessary to compute the average cost per 100 minutes for each direct labor department in order to have the rates available for further computations.

## COST SHEET

| Amount | Name | Date | Item No. |
|--------|------|------|----------|

### LABOR

| Department | Minutes | Rate per C | Amount |
|------------|---------|------------|--------|
| Machine Labor | | | |
| Cabinet Labor | | | |
| Trim Labor | | | |
| Packing Labor | | | |
| Total | | | |
| % Labor Waste | | | |
| Total Machine, Cabinet, Trim & Packing Labor | | | |
| Finishing Labor | | | |
| Upholstering Labor | | | |
| Total | | | |
| % Labor Waste | | | |
| Total Finishing & Upholstering Labor | | | |
| Total Direct Labor per 100 units | | | |
| % Direct Labor, Factory Burden | | | |

### LUMBER, PLYWOOD & SQUARES

| | | |
|---|---|---|
| Lumber | | |
| Squares | | |
| Crating | | |
| Plywood | | |
| Total | | |
| % Manufacturing Waste | | |
| Total Lumber Cost | | |

### MATERIALS

| | | |
|---|---|---|
| Hardware | | |
| Glue, Nails, Paper, Tape, Sandpaper, etc. | | |
| Cartons, Pads, etc. | | |
| Total | | |
| % Manufacturing Waste | | |
| Total Assembling & Packing Materials Cost | | |
| Finishing Materials | | |
| Upholstering Materials | | |
| Total | | |
| % Manufacturing Waste | | |
| Total Finishing & Upholstering Materials Cost | | |
| Total Manufacturing Materials Cost | | |

| | |
|---|---|
| | Total Factory Cost |
| Figured by | % Administrating & Selling Burden |
| | Total Cost |

*Courtesy, National Association of Furniture Manufacturers, Inc.*

**Fig. 2. Cost Sheet (Page 1).**

LUMBER, PLYWOOD & SQUARES

Amount _____    Item No. _____

| No. per 100 Units | Name of Part | Rough Size | | | Description | Finished Size | | | Net ft. per 100 Units | Percent of Waste | Gross ft. per 100 Units | Cost per M.Feet | Cost per 100 Units | Extension |
|---|---|---|---|---|---|---|---|---|---|---|---|---|---|---|
| | | L | W | T | | L | W | T | | | | | | |

Fig. 2. Cost Sheet (Page 2).

*Courtesy, National Association of Furniture Manufacturers, Inc.*

HARDWARE

| Part | Manufacturer | Description | Cat.No. | Amt.Reg. | Price | Unit of Price | Cost per 100 Units |
|------|--------------|-------------|---------|----------|-------|---------------|--------------------|
|  |  |  |  |  |  |  |  |
|  |  |  |  |  |  |  |  |
|  |  |  |  |  |  |  |  |
|  |  |  |  |  |  |  |  |
|  |  |  |  |  |  |  |  |
|  |  |  |  |  |  |  |  |
|  |  |  |  |  |  |  |  |
|  |  |  |  |  |  |  |  |
|  |  |  |  |  |  |  |  |
|  |  |  |  |  |  |  |  |
|  |  |  |  |  |  |  |  |
|  |  |  | Total |  |  |  |  |

CARTONS

| Manufacturer | Description | Amt.Reg. | Price | Unit of Price | Cost per 100 Units |
|--------------|-------------|----------|-------|---------------|--------------------|
|  |  |  |  |  |  |
|  |  | Total |  |  |  |

FINISH MATERIAL

| Manufacturer | Kind of Material | Number | Amt.Reg. | Price | Unit of Price | Cost per 100 Units |
|--------------|------------------|--------|----------|-------|---------------|--------------------|
|  |  |  |  |  |  |  |
|  |  |  |  |  |  |  |
|  |  |  |  |  |  |  |
|  |  |  |  |  |  |  |
|  |  |  |  |  |  |  |
|  |  |  |  |  |  |  |
|  |  |  |  |  |  |  |
|  |  |  |  |  |  |  |
|  |  |  |  |  |  |  |
|  |  |  | Total |  |  |  |

*Courtesy, National Association of Furniture Manufacturers, Inc.*

**Fig. 2. Cost Sheet (Page 3).**

COST SHEET
(Upholstered Furniture)

Amount      Name                    Date     Item No.

| | Minutes | Rate Per C | Direct Labor & Material | Factory Burden % | Factory Burden Amount | Total Cost |
|---|---|---|---|---|---|---|
| **Cover Cost per Yard** | | | | | | |
| **COVER COSTS** | | | | | | |
| **FRAME COSTS:** | | | | | | |
| Material | | | | | | |
| Direct Labor: | | | | | | |
| Mill Departments | | | | | | |
| Finishing Departments | | | | | | |
| Assembly Department | | | | | | |
| Total | | | | | | |
| % Material Waste | | | | | | |
| % Labor Waste | | | | | | |
| **TOTAL FRAME COST** | | | | | | |
| **UPHOLSTERING COSTS:** | | | | | | |
| Material | | | | | | |
| Direct Labor: | | | | | | |
| Cutting and Sewing Department | | | | | | |
| Springing Department | | | | | | |
| Upholstering Department | | | | | | |
| Moulding Department | | | | | | |
| Cushion Department | | | | | | |
| Total | | | | | | |
| % Material Waste | | | | | | |
| % Labor Waste | | | | | | |
| **TOTAL UPHOLSTERING COST** | | | | | | |
| **PACKING AND SHIPPING COSTS:** | | | | | | |
| Material | | | | | | |
| Direct Labor | | | | | | |
| Total | | | | | | |
| % Material Waste | | | | | | |
| % Labor Waste | | | | | | |
| **TOTAL PACKING AND SHIPPING COST** | | | | | | |
| TOTAL COST EXCLUSIVE OF COVER | | | | | | |
| TOTAL FACTORY COST INCLUDING COVER | | | | | | |
| % Administrating and Selling Burden | | | | | | |
| Total Cost | | | | | | |

Figured by

*Courtesy, National Association of Furniture Manufacturers, Inc.*

**Fig. 3. Cost Sheet for Upholstered Furniture (Page 1).**

Note: Page 2 of Fig. 3 consists of ten ruled columns.

## UPHOLSTERING MATERIAL

| Part | Manufacturer | Description | Cat. No. | Amt. Req. | Price | Unit of Price | Cost per 100 Units |
|------|--------------|-------------|----------|-----------|-------|---------------|--------------------|
| | | Spring, Coil | | | | | |
| | | Spring, Coil | | | | | |
| | | Spring, Coil | | | | | |
| | | Spring, Bars | | | | | |
| | | Spring, Bars | | | | | |
| | | Spring, Cushions | | | | | |
| | | | | | | | |
| | | Burlap | | | | | |
| | | | | | | | |
| | | Buttons | | | | | |
| | | Washers | | | | | |
| | | Cambric | | | | | |
| | | Cardboard | | | | | |
| | | Cardboard Strips | | | | | |
| | | Cotton | | | | | |
| | | | | | | | |
| | | Rubber | | | | | |
| | | | | | | | |
| | | Denim | | | | | |
| | | | | | | | |
| | | Ribbon | | | | | |
| | | Labels | | | | | |
| | | | | | | | |
| | | Hairflex | | | | | |
| | | Silatex | | | | | |
| | | | | | | | |
| | | Cord# | | | | | |
| | | Cord# | | | | | |
| | | Cord# | | | | | |
| | | Tacks | | | | | |
| | | Twine | | | | | |
| | | Thread | | | | | |
| | | Staples | | | | | |
| | | | | | | | |
| | | Edging | | | | | |
| | | Fringe | | | | | |
| | | | | | | | |
| | | Total | | | | | |

## PACKING MATERIAL

| Part | Manufacturer | Description | Amt. Req. | Price | Unit of Price | Cost per 100 Units |
|------|--------------|-------------|-----------|-------|---------------|--------------------|
| | | | | | | |
| | | | | | | |
| | | | | | | |
| | | | | | | |
| | | | | | | |
| | | | | | | |
| | | Total | | | | |

*Courtesy, National Association of Furniture Manufacturers, Inv.*

**Fig. 3. Cost Sheet for Upholstered Furniture (Page 3).**

**FRAME MATERIAL**

Lumber & Hardware

Item No. _____

Amount _____

| No. per 100 Units | Name of Part | Rough Size | | | Description | Finished Size | | | Net ft. per 100 Units | Percent of Waste | Gross ft. per 100 Units | Cost per M ft. | Cost per 100 Units | Extension |
|---|---|---|---|---|---|---|---|---|---|---|---|---|---|---|
| | | L | W | T | | L | W | T | | | | | | |
| | | | | | | | | | | | | | | |
| | | | | | | | | | | | | | | |
| | | | | | | | | | | | | | | |
| | | | | | | | | | | | | | | |
| | | | | | | | | | | | | | | |
| | | | | | | | | | | | | | | |
| | | | | | | | | | | | | | | |
| | | | | | | | | | | | | | | |
| | | | | | | | | | | | | | | |
| | | | | | | | | | | | | | | |
| | | | | | | | | | | | | | | |
| | | | | | | | | | | | | | | |
| | | | | | | | | | | | | | | |
| | | | | | | | | | | | | | | |
| | | | | | | | | | | | | | | |
| | | | | | | | | | | | | | | |
| | | | | | | | | | | | | | | |
| | | | | | | | | | | | | | | |
| | | | | | | | | | | | | | | |

*Courtesy, National Association of Furniture Manufacturers, Inc.*

ACCUMULATIVE RECORD OF ACTUAL MINUTES
EXPENDED ON EACH JOB.

CASE GOODS

Month Ending: 1/31/5—

| Job. No. | Item | Slash | Machine | Cabinet | Finishing | Rubbing | Pack. | Total |
|---|---|---|---|---|---|---|---|---|
| 1 | # | 5000 | 18,000 | 7,000 | — | — | — | 30,000 ✓ |
| 2 | | 4,000 | 14,000 | - | — | - | - | 18,000 |
| 3 | | 1,000 | 2,000 | - | — | — | - | 3,000 |
| 4 | | — | - | - | 1,000 | 500 | 500 | 2,000 |
| | | | | | | | | |
| | | | | | | | | |
| | | | | | | | | |
| | | | | | | | | |
| | | | | | | | | |
| | | | | | | | | |
| | | | | | | | | |

*Courtesy, National Association of Furniture Manufacturers, Inc.*

**Fig. 4. Accumulated Record of Actual Minutes Expended on Each Case Goods Job.**

## ACCUMULATIVE RECORD OF ACTUAL MINUTES EXPENDED ON EACH JOB

UPHOLSTERING

Month Ending:

| Job No. | 1 | 2 | 3 | 4 | 5 | 6 | 7 | 8 |
|---|---|---|---|---|---|---|---|---|
| Item | | | | | | | | |
| Department: | | | | | | | | |
| Mill #1 | | | | | | | | |
| Mill #2 | | | | | | | | |
| Mill #4 | | | | | | | | |
| Finishing | | | | | | | | |
| Frame Assembly | | | | | | | | |
| Cut & Sew | | | | | | | | |
| Spring | | | | | | | | |
| Upholstering | | | | | | | | |
| Moulding | | | | | | | | |
| Cushion | | | | | | | | |
| Pack & Ship | | | | | | | | |
| Totals | | | | | | | | |

*Courtesy, National Association of Furniture Manufacturers, Inc.*

**Fig. 5. Accumulated Record of Actual Minutes Expended on Each Upholstery Job.**

**Burden control.** Many of the burden costs are of a variable nature, such as repairs and maintenance, tools, jigs, miscellaneous factory supplies, repairs to defective and damaged merchandise, and so on. In order to arrive at an equitable burden percentage rate to be applied to direct labor for the year, it is necessary that these variable costs be estimated with a fair degree of accuracy.

Fixed costs, such as indirect labor, rent, light, water, depreciation, taxes, insurance, and so on, are much more predictable and can be estimated quite accurately by past experience and by taking into consideration any changes in building, equipment, and personnel for the previous years.

Centers of burden or departments should be clearly defined in order that burden rates can be computed and applied to direct labor in a logical manner. If no departmentalization of centers of burden is employed, a blanket rate would have to be used, which would result in an overcharge to some direct labor functions and undercharges to others, unless all products are uniform in character and processing. For example, building maintenance, repairs, depreciation, and taxes would be much greater for the mill operation than for the operation of the lumber yard. If a blanket rate is used, yard costs would be out of line, giving a false impression.

Considerable thought should be given to the bases used in the distribution of burden, in order to establish burden rates by departments. Rent, heat, light, real estate taxes, and building depreciation should be distributed to each department or burden center on the basis of area occupied. The total expense of service departments such as personnel, medical, payroll, and cafeteria should be distributed to all other departments that they serve on a basis of personnel count. Expense of other non-productive departments such as material control, production control, and plant engineering must be distributed to productive departments in some logical manner to be determined by the particular circumstances of the plant. General factory expenses will probably be distributed to operating departments on the basis of estimated direct labor hours or dollars. After each production department has received its distributed share of the expense of all of the nonproductive departments, its total expense is computed and then divided by the estimated total direct labor dollars to arrive at its respective factory burden rate for the year.

Administrative and selling expenses (including all general office expenses) are usually estimated for the year and distributed to production costs on a basis of total factory costs. This expense is usually referred to as "commercial burden."

**Work-in-process costs.** Such costs must be determined periodically and at the end of the year for inventory and cost-of-sales purposes. To accomplish this under the standard cost system, it is necessary to maintain stand-

| JOB INVENTORY SHEET |
| CASE GOODS |

DATE ENTERED: *1/2/5-*    JOB NO.: *1*    QUANTITY: *100*    ITEM: *#8001 Chest*

| LUMBER | | | | | | LABOR | | | | |
|---|---|---|---|---|---|---|---|---|---|---|
| AT STANDARD: | | | $1,268.00 | | | AT STANDARD: | | | | $885.00 |
| Kind | Month | Footage | Per M Cost | Total | To Date | Month | Minutes | Rate | Total | To Date |
| 4/4 Maple | Jan. | 3840 | 140.00 | | | Jan. | 30,000 | 1.905 | | |
| 5/4 Maple | | 29 | 163.00 | | | Feb. | 15,000 | 1.894 | | 855.60 |
| 8/4 Maple | | 255 | 179.00 | 587.97 | | | | | | |
| Oak | | 2618 | 87.00 | | | | | | | |
| 4/4 Maple | Feb. | 2000 | 141.00 | | | | | | | |
| 5/4 Maple | | 482 | 173.00 | | | | | | | |
| Soft maple | | 602 | 98.00 | 652.15 | 1240.12 | | | | | |
| | | | | | | | | | | |
| | | | | | | | | | | |
| | | | | | | | | | | |
| Total Actual Cost | | | | $1240.12 | | Total Actual Cost | | | | $855.60 |
| Profit/Loss on Cutting | | | | 27.88 | | Profit/Loss on Cutting | | | | 29.40 |
| Profit/Loss Per Item | | | | $.2788 | | Profit/Loss Per Item | | | | $.294 |

SHIPMENTS:

| Month | Quantity | Variance on Lumber | Variance on Labor |
|---|---|---|---|
| Feb. | 60 | $16.73 | $17.64 |
| March | 30 | 8.36 | 8.82 |
| April | 10 | 2.79 | 2.94 |
| | | | |
| Proof | 100 | $27.88 | $29.40 |

*Courtesy, National Association of Furniture Manufacturers, Inc.*

**Fig. 6. Job Inventory Sheet (Case Goods).**

ard cost sheets similar to the job inventory sheets shown in Figures 6 and 7. Labor and material costs are posted to these sheets and the total cost to date is calculated at the end of each month. The sum of the total costs from all job inventory sheets on which the job has not been completed is the total work-in-process inventory as of that particular date, after the applicable burden has been added.

The explanation of the accumulation of direct labor costs (page 758) and Figures 4 and 5 tell how direct labor time and costs are accumulated by

JOB INVENTORY SHEET
UPHOLSTERING

DATE ENTERED:          JOB NO. :          QUANTITY:          ITEM:

| LUMBER | | | | | | PADDING | | | | | |
| AT STANDARD | | | | | | AT STANDARD | | | | | |
| Kind | Mo. | Foot-age | Cost | Total | To Date | Kind | Mo. | Amount | Cost | Total | To Date |
|---|---|---|---|---|---|---|---|---|---|---|---|
| | | | | | | | | | | | |
| | | | | | | | | | | | |
| | | | | | | | | | | | |
| | | | | | | | | | | | |
| | | | | | | | | | | | |
| | | | | | | | | | | | |
| | | | | | | | | | | | |
| | | | | | | | | | | | |
| | | | | | | | | | | | |
| | | | | | | | | | | | |
| | | | | | | | | | | | |
| | | | | | | | | | | | |
| Total Actual Cost | | | | | | Total Actual Cost | | | | | |
| Profit/Loss on Cutting | | | | | | Profit/Loss on Cutting | | | | | |
| Profit/Loss Per Item | | | | | | Profit/Loss Per Item | | | | | |

| LININGS | | | | | | SPRINGS & STRIP STEEL | | | | | |
| AT STANDARD | | | | | | AT STANDARD | | | | | |
| Kind | Mo. | Yard-age | Cost | Total | To Date | Kind | Mo. | Amount | Cost | Total | To Date |
|---|---|---|---|---|---|---|---|---|---|---|---|
| | | | | | | | | | | | |
| | | | | | | | | | | | |
| | | | | | | | | | | | |
| | | | | | | | | | | | |
| | | | | | | | | | | | |
| | | | | | | | | | | | |
| | | | | | | | | | | | |
| | | | | | | | | | | | |
| Total Actual Cost | | | | | | Total Actual Cost | | | | | |
| Profit/Loss on Cutting | | | | | | Profit/Loss on Cutting | | | | | |
| Profit/Loss Per Item | | | | | | Profit/Loss Per Item | | | | | |

*Courtesy, National Association of Furniture Manufacturers, Inc.*

**Fig. 7. Job Inventory Sheet (Upholstering) (Page 1).**

jobs for posting in totals to the job inventory sheets. It may be desirable to set up accumulation sheets for some or all of the direct materials used in production so that material costs may be accurately allocated to specific jobs.

## JOB INVENTORY SHEET
### UPHOLSTERING

#### COVER

| Number | Mo. | Yard-age | Cost | Total | To Date | STAN-DARD | Profit/Loss Cutting | Profit/Loss Per Item | Shipments Mo. | Shipments Quan. | Shipments Variance |
|--------|-----|----------|------|-------|---------|-----------|--------|----------|-----|-------|----------|
|        |     |          |      |       |         |           |        |          |     |       |          |
|        |     |          |      |       |         |           |        |          |     |       |          |
|        |     |          |      |       |         |           |        |          |     |       |          |
|        |     |          |      |       |         |           |        |          |     |       |          |
|        |     |          |      |       |         |           |        |          |     |       |          |
|        |     |          |      |       |         |           |        |          |     |       |          |
|        |     |          |      |       |         |           |        |          |     |       |          |
|        |     |   Totals |      |       |         |           |        |          |     |       |          |

#### LABOR

| | AT STANDARD | | | |
|---|---|---|---|---|
| Month | Minutes | Rate | Total | To Date |
| | | | | |
| | | | | |
| | | | | |
| Total Actual Cost | | | | |
| Profit/Loss on Cutting | | | | |
| Profit/Loss Per Item | | | | |

#### SHIPMENTS

| Month | Quantity | Variances Lumber | Padding | Linings | Springs, etc. | Labor |
|-------|----------|--------|---------|---------|---------------|-------|
| | | | | | | |
| | | | | | | |
| | | | | | | |
| | | | | | | |
| | | | | | | |
| | | | | | | |
| | | | | | | |

**Fig. 7. Job Inventory Sheet (Upholstering) (Page 2).**

**Variances from standard costs.** The method of using job inventory sheets not only furnishes information for work-in-process costs, but also furnishes a basis for the monthly entries for variances from standard cost. In addition, it is an analysis of costs for the particular job or cutting for production control purposes.

**Analyzing costs.** The profit or loss both per cutting and per item are computed on the job inventory sheets in order to point up variations between actual and standard cost on the particular job. More definite information can be obtained by further analyzing accumulation records, invoices, payroll distribution, and time cards in order to pinpoint the cause of unusual fluctuation in costs. Machinery breakdowns, defective materials, inexperienced help, and inadequate patterns must be taken into consideration in such an analysis. The relationship between the set-up time required and the size of the job is an additional factor that must be considered in controlling production and costs.

**Inventory practices peculiar to the business.** Lumber probably presents the greatest inventory problem throughout the industry, especially for those manufacturers who buy green, rough lumber and process it through their own yards, kilns, and dimension mills.

Yard and kiln labor may be treated as direct labor, indirect labor, or an additional cost of the lumber. The most practical and most commonly used method is that of allocating this labor to the cost of the lumber. In this manner, lumber arriving at the dimension mill has a definite cost per foot, just as cured lumber purchased from an outside source would have.

Waste and shrinkage in the yard and kiln also add to the difficulty of pricing lumber for inventory and cost purposes. As this loss varies considerably between lots of lumber, average percentages should be determined by kinds of wood and applied to the cured lumber.

Physical inventories should be taken at regular intervals in the yard and kiln.

During the past several years of rising prices, the last-in, first-out (LIFO) method of inventory pricing has been most commonly used throughout the industry. It is the method generally considered to reflect income more clearly. Some manufacturers continue to use first-in, first-out (FIFO) or weighted averages in pricing their inventories.

A standard cost system facilitates the pricing of work-in-process and finished goods inventories by the accumulation of direct material, direct labor, and burden costs on the specific jobs and products.

Inventory control against loss and shrinkage can be effectively handled with the aid of a standard cost system. Job inventory sheets will immediately point up discrepancies in material costs that can be traced back to the inventory records and the cause of excess usage can thus be determined. The job cost system simplifies the maintenance of inventory records and furnishes a means of following materials from the inventory through production to the finished product.

## Reports to management

### Financial reports.
1. Report of bank balances .................... Daily
2. Balance sheet ........................... Monthly
3. Profit and loss statement .................. Monthly
4. Budget report ...........................Monthly

5. Annual audit report ...................... Yearly
6. Annual report to stockholders .............. Yearly

## General operating reports.

1. Operating statement ....................... Monthly
2. Manufacturing overhead statement .......... Monthly

| | OPERATING STATEMENT (Exclusive of Cost of Materials and Inventory Variations) | | | | Exhibit _____ | | | |
|---|---|---|---|---|---|---|---|---|
| | CURRENT PERIOD | | | | TOTAL TO DATE | | | |
| | | % TO SALES | | % TO SALES | | % TO SALES | | % TO SALES |
| NET SALES | | | | | | | | |
| DIRECT LABOR | | | | | | | | |
| Interplant transfer | | | | | | | | |
| Net direct labor | | | | | | | | |
| OVERHEAD: | | | | | | | | |
| Indirect labor | | | | | | | | |
| Expenses | | | | | | | | |
| Apportioned charges | | | | | | | | |
| Total | | | | | | | | |
| Interplant transfer | | | | | | | | |
| Net overhead | | | | | | | | |
| Ratio to net direct labor | | | | | | | | |
| Unabsorbed overhead | | | | | | | | |
| TRUCKING DEPARTMENT | | | | | | | | |
| Unabsorbed overhead | | | | | | | | |
| GENERAL EXPENSES: | | | | | | | | |
| Administrative | | | | | | | | |
| Industrial relations | | | | | | | | |
| Production | | | | | | | | |
| Accounting | | | | | | | | |
| General procurement | | | | | | | | |
| Fabric procurement | | | | | | | | |
| Building & equipment | | | | | | | | |
| Total administrative | | | | | | | | |
| Advertising | | | | | | | | |
| Selling | | | | | | | | |
| Total general expenses | | | | | | | | |
| COMMISSIONS | | | | | | | | |
| Total operating cost (Exclusive of cost of materials and inventory variation) | | | | | | | | |
| Net sales minus specially priced items Ratio of general expenses to above | | | | | | | | |

Fig. 8. Operating Statement (Exclusive of Cost of Materials and Inventory Variations).

These two operating reports are generally referred to in the industry as "burden" statements.

The operating statement (Figure 8) is supported by exhibits covering General Administrative Expense, General Accounting Expense, General Engineering Expense, and General Sales Expense and a manufacturing overhead statement of the dimension lumber mill (illustrated in Figure 9 below).

| | MANUFACTURING OVERHEAD STATEMENT | Schedule | | | | | | | | |
|---|---|---|---|---|---|---|---|---|---|---|
| Line No. | | CURRENT PERIOD | | | | | TOTAL TO DATE | | | |
| 1 | DIRECT LABOR | | | | | | | | | |
| 2 | INDIRECT LABOR | | | | | | | | | |
| 3 | Supervisory | | | | | | | | | |
| 4 | Leadman | | | | | | | | | |
| 5 | Sweeper | | | | | | | | | |
| 6 | Overtime—direct labor | | | | | | | | | |
| 7 | —indirect labor | | | | | | | | | |
| 8 | Common labor—job mover | | | | | | | | | |
| 9 | Maintenance—machinery | | | | | | | | | |
| 10 | —buildings | | | | | | | | | |
| 11 | Lumber grader—sorter operations | | | | | | | | | |
| 12 | Dimension grader | | | | | | | | | |
| 13 | Transfer car operator—bundler | | | | | | | | | |
| 14 | Lumber stacker—loader | | | | | | | | | |
| 15 | Dry kiln operator | | | | | | | | | |
| 16 | Truckers | | | | | | | | | |
| 17 | Inspection | | | | | | | | | |
| 18 | Miscellaneous | | | | | | | | | |
| 19 | Total indirect labor | | | | | | | | | |
| 20 | Ratio to direct labor | | | | | | | | | |
| 21 | EXPENSE: | | | | | | | | | |
| 22 | Maintenance—machinery | | | | | | | | | |
| 23 | —buildings | | | | | | | | | |
| 24 | Operating supplies | | | | | | | | | |
| 25 | Miscellaneous | | | | | | | | | |
| 26 | Total expense | | | | | | | | | |
| 27 | Total departmental expense | | | | | | | | | |
| 28 | Ratio to direct labor | | | | | | | | | |
| 29 | Apportioned charges (Sched. 6) | | | | | | | | | |
| 30 | Total manufacturing overhead | | | | | | | | | |
| 31 | Ratio to direct labor | | | | | | | | | |
| 32 | Total manufacturing cost (exclusive of materials) | | | | | | | | | |
| 33 | Cost per M ft. lumber produced | | | | | | | | | |

**Fig. 9. Manufacturing Overhead Statement—Dimension Lumber Mill.**

The manufacturing overhead statement is illustrated in Figures 10, 11, and 12. The form shown in Figure 10 is used for the following departments: Mill No. 1, Mill No. 2, frame assembly, finishing, upholstering, cutting, sewing, cushion, packing, and shipping.

Fig. 10. Manufacturing Overhead Statement—Total Operating Department.

| No. | Item | PLANT #1 | PLANT #2 | PLANT #3 |
|---|---|---|---|---|
| 1 | DIRECT LABOR | | | |
| 2 | Ratio to net sales | | | |
| 3 | INDIRECT LABOR: | | | |
| 4 | Supervisory | | | |
| 5 | Leadman | | | |
| 6 | Janitor | | | |
| 7 | Extra operations | | | |
| 8 | Instruction | | | |
| 9 | Apprentice | | | |
| 10 | Differential & Utility | | | |
| 11 | Overtime direct labor | | | |
| 12 | Overtime indirect labor | | | |
| 13 | Make sand belts | | | |
| 14 | Material handler | | | |
| 15 | Maintenance—machinery | | | |
| 16 | —buildings | | | |
| 17 | Stockkeeper—checker | | | |
| 18 | Inspection—regulate | | | |
| 19 | Repair | | | |
| 20 | Dispatcher-assistant-stockkeeper | | | |
| 21 | Dispatch helper-job handler | | | |
| 22 | Accumulate—match | | | |
| 23 | Clean | | | |
| 24 | Unload—load—salvage stock | | | |
| 25 | Miscellaneous | | | |
| 26 | Waiting time | | | |
| 27 | Total indirect labor | | | |
| 28 | Ratio to direct labor | | | |
| 29 | EXPENSES: | | | |
| 30 | Maintenance—machinery | | | |
| 31 | —buildings | | | |
| 32 | Operating supplies | | | |
| 33 | Miscellaneous | | | |
| 34 | Total expenses | | | |
| 35 | Total departmental expense | | | |
| 36 | Ratio to direct labor | | | |
| 37 | APPORTIONED CHARGES: | | | |
| 38 | Total overhead | | | |
| 39 | Ratio to direct labor | | | |
| 40 | Ratio to net sales | | | |
| 41 | Cost allowance | | | |
| 42 | Cost rate | | | |
| 43 | Unabsorbed overhead | | | |

**Fig. 10. Manufacturing Overhead Statement—Total Operating Department.**

The same form is used for the departments mentioned at page 772.

773

## MANUFACTURING OVERHEAD STATEMENT — UPHOLSTERING PLANTS

| Line No. | | TOTAL | Line No. | PLANT #1 | Line No. | PLANT #2 | Line No. | PLANT #3 | Line No. |
|---|---|---|---|---|---|---|---|---|---|
| 1 | INDIRECT LABOR: | | 1 | | 1 | | 1 | | 1 |
| 2 | Supervisory | | 2 | | 2 | | 2 | | 2 |
| 3 | Supervisory assistants | | 3 | | 3 | | 3 | | 3 |
| 4 | Janitor | | 4 | | 4 | | 4 | | 4 |
| 5 | Cooks and helpers | | 5 | | 5 | | 5 | | 5 |
| 6 | Overtime premium | | 6 | | 6 | | 6 | | 6 |
| 7 | Maintenance—machinery | | 7 | | 7 | | 7 | | 7 |
| 8 | —buildings | | 8 | | 8 | | 8 | | 8 |
| 9 | Receiving and stockroom | | 9 | | 9 | | 9 | | 9 |
| 10 | Chief inspector | | 10 | | 10 | | 10 | | 10 |
| 11 | Elevator operators | | 11 | | 11 | | 11 | | 11 |
| 12 | Watchman | | 12 | | 12 | | 12 | | 12 |
| 13 | Repair department | | 13 | | 13 | | 13 | | 13 |
| 14 | Moving depts. and equipment | | 14 | | 14 | | 14 | | 14 |
| 15 | Interfactory shipments | | 15 | | 15 | | 15 | | 15 |
| 16 | Inventory labor | | 16 | | 16 | | 16 | | 16 |
| 17 | Salvaging stock | | 17 | | 17 | | 17 | | 17 |
| 18 | Vacation and holiday pay | | 18 | | 18 | | 18 | | 18 |
| 19 | Christmas bonus | | 19 | | 19 | | 19 | | 19 |
| 20 | Mat'l. handler | | 20 | | 20 | | 20 | | 20 |
| 21 | Miscellaneous | | 21 | | 21 | | 21 | | 21 |
| 22 | First aid & medical | | 22 | | 22 | | 22 | | 22 |
| 23 | Dispatch & helper | | 23 | | 23 | | 23 | | 23 |
| 24 | Total indirect labor | | 24 | | 24 | | 24 | | 24 |
| 25 | Ratio to direct labor | | 25 | | 25 | | 25 | | 25 |
| 26 | EXPENSES: | | 26 | | 26 | | 26 | | 26 |
| 27 | Moving depts. and equipment | | 27 | | 27 | | 27 | | 27 |
| 28 | Maintenance—machinery | | 28 | | 28 | | 28 | | 28 |
| 29 | —buildings | | 29 | | 29 | | 29 | | 29 |
| 30 | Cafeteria and dining room | | 30 | | 30 | | 30 | | 30 |
| 31 | Repair department | | 31 | | 31 | | 31 | | 31 |
| 32 | Interfactory handling | | 32 | | 32 | | 32 | | 32 |
| 33 | Employees welfare | | 33 | | 33 | | 33 | | 33 |
| 34 | Traveling | | 34 | | 34 | | 34 | | 34 |
| 35 | Operating supplies | | 35 | | 35 | | 35 | | 35 |
| 36 | Rent & storage | | 36 | | 36 | | 36 | | 36 |
| 37 | Interfactory freight | | 37 | | 37 | | 37 | | 37 |
| 38 | Miscellaneous | | 38 | | 38 | | 38 | | 38 |
| 39 | Salary Charge | | 39 | | 39 | | 39 | | 39 |
| 40 | Expense Charge | | 40 | | 40 | | 40 | | 40 |
| 41 | Total expense | | 41 | | 41 | | 41 | | 41 |
| 42 | Total general factory expense | | 42 | | 42 | | 42 | | 42 |
| 43 | Ratio to direct labor | | 43 | | 43 | | 43 | | 43 |
| 44 | Ratio to net sales | | 44 | | 44 | | 44 | | 44 |

MANUFACTURING OVERHEAD STATEMENT — UPHOLSTERING PLANTS

Schedule

| Line No. | | TOTAL | Line No. | PLANT #1 | Line No. | PLANT #2 | Line No. | PLANT #3 | Line No. |
|---|---|---|---|---|---|---|---|---|---|
| 1 | INDIRECT LABOR: | | 1 | | 1 | | 1 | | 1 |
| 2 | Supervisory | | 2 | | 2 | | 2 | | 2 |
| 3 | Supervisory assistant | | 3 | | 3 | | 3 | | 3 |
| 4 | Senior clerk | | 4 | | 4 | | 4 | | 4 |
| 5 | Intermediate clerk | | 5 | | 5 | | 5 | | 5 |
| 6 | Junior clerk | | 6 | | 6 | | 6 | | 6 |
| 7 | Secretaries and stenographers | | 7 | | 7 | | 7 | | 7 |
| 8 | Machine operator | | 8 | | 8 | | 8 | | 8 |
| 9 | Typists | | 9 | | 9 | | 9 | | 9 |
| 10 | Overtime | | 10 | | 10 | | 10 | | 10 |
| 11 | | | 11 | | 11 | | 11 | | 11 |
| 12 | Miscellaneous | | 12 | | 12 | | 12 | | 12 |
| 13 | | | 13 | | 13 | | 13 | | 13 |
| 14 | Total indirect labor | | 14 | | 14 | | 14 | | 14 |
| 15 | EXPENSES: | | 15 | | 15 | | 15 | | 15 |
| 16 | Traveling | | 16 | | 16 | | 16 | | 16 |
| 17 | Operating supplies | | 17 | | 17 | | 17 | | 17 |
| 18 | Telephone & telegraph | | 18 | | 18 | | 18 | | 18 |
| 19 | Postage | | 19 | | 19 | | 19 | | 19 |
| 20 | Stationery & office supplies | | 20 | | 20 | | 20 | | 20 |
| 21 | Tabulating | | 21 | | 21 | | 21 | | 21 |
| 22 | Memberships & publications | | 22 | | 22 | | 22 | | 22 |
| 23 | | | 23 | | 23 | | 23 | | 23 |
| 24 | | | 24 | | 24 | | 24 | | 24 |
| 25 | Miscellaneous | | 25 | | 25 | | 25 | | 25 |
| 26 | Total expense | | 26 | | 26 | | 26 | | 26 |
| 27 | Total departmental expense | | 27 | | 27 | | 27 | | 27 |

Fig. 12. Manufacturing Overhead Statement—Production Control Department, Plant Engineering Department, Industrial Relations Department, Payroll Department, Material Control Department.

775

MANUFACTURING OVERHEAD STATEMENT - UPHOLSTERING PLANTS

| Line No. | | TOTAL | Line No. | PLANT #1 | Line No. | PLANT #2 | Line No. | PLANT #3 | Line No. |
|---|---|---|---|---|---|---|---|---|---|
| 1 | APPORTIONED CHARGES: | | 1 | | 1 | | 1 | | 1 |
| 2 | Fire insurance | | 2 | | 2 | | 2 | | 2 |
| 3 | Compensation insurance | | 3 | | 3 | | 3 | | 3 |
| 4 | Depreciation | | 4 | | 4 | | 4 | | 4 |
| 5 | Taxes - property | | 5 | | 5 | | 5 | | 5 |
| 6 | -social security | | 6 | | 6 | | 6 | | 6 |
| 7 | General engineering expense | | 7 | | 7 | | 7 | | 7 |
| 8 | U.I.U. pension expense | | 8 | | 8 | | 8 | | 8 |
| 9 | | | 9 | | 9 | | 9 | | 9 |
| 10 | Total | | 10 | | 10 | | 10 | | 10 |
| 11 | Plant engineering expense | | 11 | | 11 | | 11 | | 11 |
| 12 | General factory expense | | 12 | | 12 | | 12 | | 12 |
| 13 | Production control expense | | 13 | | 13 | | 13 | | 13 |
| 14 | Power, heat & light expense | | 14 | | 14 | | 14 | | 14 |
| 15 | Industrial relations expense | | 15 | | 15 | | 15 | | 15 |
| 16 | Payroll expense | | 16 | | 16 | | 16 | | 16 |
| 17 | Material control expense | | 17 | | 17 | | 17 | | 17 |
| 18 | | | 18 | | 18 | | 18 | | 18 |
| 19 | Total apportioned charges | | 19 | | 19 | | 19 | | 19 |
| 20 | Ratio to direct labor | | 20 | | 20 | | 20 | | 20 |
| 21 | Ratio to net sales | | 21 | | 21 | | 21 | | 21 |

Fig. 13. Manufacturing Overhead Statement—Apportioned Charges.

It will be noticed that Apportioned Charges are distributed to the various plants as item 37 of the Manufacturing Overhead Statement—Total Operating Department (Figure 10). A separate exhibit (Figure 13) shows the items included in Apportioned Charges and how the total that appears as item 37 is obtained.

### Reports for measuring sales efficiency.

Comparative statement of orders received ................. Weekly

Comparative statement of net sales ..................... Monthly

Sales analysis by customer ............................. Monthly

Sales analysis by sales territory ........................ Monthly

Comparative salesmen's commission analysis ............. Monthly

### Reports for production.

Production report ....................................... Weekly

Lumber production and waste report ..................... Weekly

Lumber inventory report ................................ Weekly

### Report for purchasing.

Material usage and requirements report ................ Bi-Weekly

# Index